Impact

Embark on a transformative journey into the world of user research with *Impact* by Nikki Anderson. In the realm of product creation, understanding your users is the cornerstone of building life-changing products. This comprehensive guide is your key to establishing a robust user research practice within your organization, ensuring that decisions are rooted in empathy, understanding, and a deep connection with your audience.

Impact goes beyond the surface of having a great idea; it delves into the intricacies of creating competent, passionate, and skillful teams. Nikki Anderson, drawing from her wealth of experience, provides invaluable insights into setting up a research practice that becomes an indispensable resource for your colleagues. This book is not just a guide; it's a thought partner, offering a step-by-step approach to navigate the complexities of establishing a research practice, making it accessible even for those new to the field.

Nikki Anderson, founder of User Research Strategist, helps user researchers become strategic decision-makers through her Substack, podcast, and speaking engagements. Known for transparency and actionable insights, she's shaping the future of research while chasing waves and geeking out over Pokémon.

Impact
A Complete Guide to Creating a User Research Practice at Your Organization

Nikki Anderson

CRC Press
Taylor & Francis Group
Boca Raton London New York

CRC Press is an imprint of the
Taylor & Francis Group, an **informa** business

Designed cover image: Shutterstock

First edition published 2026
by CRC Press
2385 NW Executive Center Drive, Suite 320, Boca Raton FL 33431

and by CRC Press
4 Park Square, Milton Park, Abingdon, Oxon, OX14 4RN

CRC Press is an imprint of Taylor & Francis Group, LLC

© 2026 Nikki Anderson

Reasonable efforts have been made to publish reliable data and information, but the author and publisher cannot assume responsibility for the validity of all materials or the consequences of their use. The authors and publishers have attempted to trace the copyright holders of all material reproduced in this publication and apologize to copyright holders if permission to publish in this form has not been obtained. If any copyright material has not been acknowledged please write and let us know so we may rectify in any future reprint.

Except as permitted under U.S. Copyright Law, no part of this book may be reprinted, reproduced, transmitted, or utilized in any form by any electronic, mechanical, or other means, now known or hereafter invented, including photocopying, microfilming, and recording, or in any information storage or retrieval system, without written permission from the publishers.

For permission to photocopy or use material electronically from this work, access www.copyright.com or contact the Copyright Clearance Center, Inc. (CCC), 222 Rosewood Drive, Danvers, MA 01923, 978-750-8400. For works that are not available on CCC please contact mpkbookspermissions@tandf.co.uk

Trademark Notice: Product or corporate names may be trademarks or registered trademarks and are used only for identification and explanation without intent to infringe.

ISBN: 978-1-041-04648-6 (hbk)
ISBN: 978-1-041-04642-4 (pbk)
ISBN: 978-1-003-62927-6 (ebk)

DOI: 10.1201/9781003629276

Typeset in Times
by KnowledgeWorks Global Ltd.

Contents

Acknowledgments ix
About the Author xi
Introduction xiii

PART ONE What Is a Research Practice? — 1

1 What Is a Research Practice? — 3
2 Why Is a Research Practice Important? — 5
3 Connecting Research to Business — 6

PART TWO Reflect on the Current State — 49

4 Viewing Stakeholders as Users — 51
5 Assess the Current User Research Maturity — 60

PART THREE Set Up Operations and a Framework — 65

6 Set Up Core Research Operations — 67
7 Create a Research Framework — 142

PART FOUR Define Your Playbook — 151

8 Introduction to the Five Phases — 153
9 Phase One: Problem Discovery — 155
10 Phase Two: Problem Definition — 162
11 Phase Three: Solution Design and Refinement — 168

| 12 | Phase Four: Testing and Execution | 173 |
| 13 | Phase Five: Maintain and Iterate | 179 |

PART FIVE Methodology Breakdown 183

14	Problem Discovery Methods	185
15	Problem Definition Methods	218
16	Solution Design and Refinement Methods	232
17	Testing and Execution Methods	258
18	Monitor and Iterate Methods	277
19	Bonus: Uncommon Methods	327

PART SIX Analysis and Synthesis Breakdown 331

20	Demystifying the Synthesis Process	333
21	Running Synthesis Sessions	337
22	An Analysis and Synthesis Process for Generative Research	346
23	Writing Insights and Recommendations	356

PART SEVEN Creating Effective and Realistic Deliverables and Outcomes 379

24	Writing Reports	381
25	Using the Pyramid Principle	390
26	Session Summaries	407
27	Research Newsletters	413
28	Personas	417

29 Ecosystem Maps	**434**
30 UX Scorecard	**438**

PART EIGHT   Activating Your User Research   **443**

31 Bring Your Insights to Life	**445**

PART NINE   Juggling It All   **479**

32 Using AI as a Thought Partner	**481**
33 Democratizing User Research	**493**
34 Time Management	**540**
35 Navigating Burnout	**543**

PART TEN   Test and Iterate   **547**

36 Feedback and Iteration	**549**
Index	553

Acknowledgments

Writing a book is an exhilarating and, at times, overwhelming experience. After writing articles for such a long time, and quite a few fiction novels, I thought about how writing a user research book might feel. At first, there was a lot of hesitancy. What can I say and compile that I, and a thousand others, haven't yet said? What can I create that can actually help people in their day-to-day jobs doing user research?

And it's for that very same reason that writing a book is not a solo activity. It takes a village of people to keep you going, to motivate you when things get difficult or confusing, to remind you that what you have to say matters.

I want to say a big THANK YOU to all the people who stood in my corner and cheered me on. Here are all the people without whom this book would not exist:

To my parents, Bill and Sue, for your support in believing in me when I made this wild career jump, from day one.

Thank you immensely to my wonderful beta readers who read the entire manuscript in its rough form and provided me with amazingly insightful and helpful feedback: Chris Andrews, Annie Evans, Greta, Ambrase, and Luiz Almeida. This book would not be where it is now without your thoughts!

Thank you to everyone in the user research community sharing their takes and thoughts on user research. I'm truly standing on the shoulders of giants and get so inspired by so many people, such as Indi Young, Barry O'Reilly, Jim Kalbach, Steve Portigal, Janelle Ward, Amy Santee, Holly Cole, Emma Boulton, and Dave Hora.

Thank you to John Labriola for being the most wonderful manager I could have ever asked for. You believed in me when I couldn't and I wouldn't be where I am without your support and guidance.

A huge thank you to all my clients, mentees, and members: working with you has taught me so much and I learn something new from each of you every single day.

Even if this book just impacts one person, I will be over the moon. Thank you so much for reading.

About the Author

Blogger, podcaster, and founder of User Research Strategist, Nikki Anderson is passionate about transforming user researchers into strategic, impactful professionals who drive meaningful business decisions. Through her weekly Substack, she equips researchers with tools, insights, and frameworks to elevate their craft and influence organizational outcomes.

Originally from Boston and now rooted in Jersey, Nikki founded User Research Strategist to help researchers move beyond tactical execution and embrace their role as strategic business partners. Her mission is clear: there's no one-size-fits-all approach to research, but with the right mindset and resources, researchers can create real business impact while embracing creativity and confidence.

A prolific writer, Nikki has authored over 250 user research articles, featured on platforms like dscout and Dovetail, that explore the full spectrum of user research—from crafting strategic research plans to managing career transitions. Her podcast, Dear Nikki, with over 10,500 plays, is a favorite in the research community, addressing hard-hitting topics like burnout, failure, and building influence in the workplace.

As a speaker at more than 100 conferences, including UXInsight, UXRConf, UX360, and ResearchOps, Nikki is known for her transparency, vulnerability, and actionable advice. Her work consistently garners praise as "the most vulnerable, transparent, and impactful talk/article/webinar I've experienced all year."

When not helping researchers redefine their careers, Nikki can often be found chasing waves along the Jersey shore, nerding out over Pokémon (Charmander holds a special place in her heart), and coaxing her veggies to grow with questionable serenades.

Introduction

User research is a special topic in any organization. It can help us turn a start-up or commonplace organization into a company that can positively impact and change the lives of humans.

Creation of life-changing products, their scale, and their users' satisfaction all start with deep understanding. By discovering and empathizing with users' pain points, needs, goals, and motivations, we can mitigate the risks we take in the decisions we make toward building amazing and profitable products. Doing this means setting up the team for success by establishing a research practice that colleagues can rely on to get the critical information they need to make better decisions, and to understand who users are and why they use (or don't use!) a certain product or service.

That's why I wrote *Impact*. My goal is to provide you with a comprehensive guide for setting up a research practice within your organization. I aim to help you think through every step you need, to leap over obstacles that get in the way, to empower you to make your best decisions, and to guide you in creating a unique process for your situation and circumstance. While this book is geared toward user researchers at digital product/tech organizations, it can also be used by anyone who is "in charge of" user research at a company—from the beginner who hasn't done much user research, to the seasoned user researcher who wants to try new approaches. If you are someone trying to integrate user research into your organization, I am hoping this book will become your go-to resource for creating an impactful user research practice.

I have not only seen but encountered many obstacles up close and personal during the course of my own time as a user researcher. I now coach user researchers across the globe and work as a freelance researcher, and I have seen firsthand how organizations of all kinds are dealing with the obstacles they encounter when it comes to research. In this book, I share real-life examples of my experience. I share how you can start a research practice at your organization, and help research reach its full potential.

Before we dig into the book, I would like to explain how it is organized and how to best use it.

HOW THIS BOOK IS ORGANIZED

It is really important to note that what a research practice looks like can vary greatly from organization to organization. Research practices are only good in their current context, organization, and environment. That's why it is so important for you to take the content of this book and interpret it into your own unique environment. And to revise your practice as our field evolves and changes.

I organized the content of this book in a particular order. Here's how to use the content in each of these parts:

Part One includes an overarching definition of a user research practice, and why it is important for you to set one up at your organization.

Part Two focuses on defining the current state you are in, in terms of your current role on the team, your practice, the user research maturity in your organization, and your mindset. As I mentioned, it is important for you to take the content of this book and apply it to your context, so knowing where you are now and what you are operating in will help optimize the lessons in this book.

Part Three includes everything you need to set the foundation for a successful research practice. It offers guidance on operations to make your practice efficient and effective. These are all the things I do when I start working at an organization.

Part Four dives deeper into each phase of the user research process, from problem discovery all the way to monitoring and iteration of a product/service/feature. This part gives you the basis for creating your own user research playbook, so that you feel comfortable and confident with whatever problem comes your way. There may be some slight overlap in information so, as not to be repetitive, you will see references for deep dives on particular methodologies, deliverables, and activation ideas. This is so that you can focus in this part on building your actual process rather than the intricacies of different methods, which are covered in later parts.

Part Five focuses on the different methodologies that are mentioned in Part Four and deep dives into these methods. This part should be used as a reference point, especially when approaching a method you are unfamiliar or uncomfortable with. Let this be a basic guide for you. I will include further resources on each method to continue your learning even further.

Part Six talks through approaches to analysis and synthesis, helping you to navigate topics like tags/codes, setting up synthesis, and when to synthesize.

Part Seven is similar to Part Five but goes in-depth on the different deliverables and outcomes that we covered throughout the user research process. Similarly, it is a guide to these deliverables and outcomes, and I will reference other materials for further learning.

Part Eight includes one of the most crucial parts of your user research practice, which is activating the insights from your studies. You can use this as a guide for understanding the different ways you can take your insights from the problem space to solution land, and positively impact teams' decision-making.

Part Nine focuses on juggling these different topics, including thinking through democratization, time management, and burnout.

Part Ten includes the importance of getting feedback from others and treating this practice as an iterative, living concept.

Introduction xv

YOUR PERSONAL GUIDE

This isn't a "read-once, from-front-to-back" kind of book for most readers. It is a guide for you to create and continue evolving your research practice. It is a reference for you to keep at the side of your desk for when you encounter any doubt, or want to mix up your approach to a project.

If you are newer to user research and haven't yet set up a practice, then I recommend that you use this book as your personal guide. I would recommend going through the book step by step and doing the action items for that particular part. Just like Rome wasn't built in a day, a user research practice doesn't have to be either. As you encounter different obstacles or new methods, refer back to the table of contents and flip to the appropriate chapters.

If you are someone who has more extensive experience and user research knowledge, and is comfortable with setting up a practice, then skimming through the key concepts in this book might spark some new ideas for approaches different to what you are using now. *Impact* focuses on the three cornerstones of usability: building and establishing a research practice that is effective, efficient, and satisfactory. It is about you becoming more confident in bringing user research to an impactful space in your current role.

I wrote this book with the assumption that you have the ability to influence your organization. I do understand that sometimes this is really difficult to do and things may be pre-established. If this is the case, I recommend that you try a few new things from this book, continue to gather feedback, and iterate on your practice.

I truly hope that *Impact* helps you create a research practice that impacts your organization in making confident decisions and creating products that deliver real value to humans.

You can find all the templates referenced in this book here: https://www.userresearchstrategist.com/

PART ONE

What Is a Research Practice?

What Is a Research Practice?

You've decided to embark on this wonderful journey of creating a user research practice at your organization—hooray! But wait, where are you supposed to start?

There aren't many organizations with a standardized user research practice in place. Maybe there is a little thought about who users are, a few surveys being run, and usability tests conducted, but nothing formalized.

WHY IS THIS THE CASE?

If you've been like most of us, me included, and hopped on Google when you first tried to establish a research process, the results might have been as they were for me—absolutely overwhelming, dizzying, and nonsensical. There was some advice out there, but nothing that went through a cohesive process of setting up research for success through an established practice.

When there aren't many examples to follow, sometimes the formalization of processes can get pushed to the wayside. The "we'll do it later" phrase can appear, and later becomes later, and later, and later. To no one's fault! Setting up a research practice takes time and energy. But it's also important to know that what you are doing makes sense, and it's aligned with what you need.

So, the first question we are going to tackle is: what is a user research practice?

A user research practice is an effective, efficient, and satisfactory set of research processes that help teams make better decisions to build products that provide value for customers. A user research practice sets a clear and straightforward precedent for how research is conducted at an organization and impacts the product development process.

Your user research practice can include anything under the sun that helps you define a structured, straightforward, and clear playbook about user research in your organization.

You might have noticed that I used the three cornerstones of usability—efficiency, effectiveness, and satisfaction—to describe a user research practice. The reason I use these terms is because I want you to start thinking about your research process through the lens of a researcher mindset. It's easy for us to want to set up our first user research project and talk to users as soon as possible. In fact, it's exactly what I did for years before realizing that I was trying to operate on a shaky foundation. Once I switched to creating a more formal process, everything became easier:

- We had operating procedures for how to recruit, instead of scrambling for every project.
- There was a set of questions for intake instead of disjointed Slack messages.
- We had a clear and transparent prioritization process to help stakeholders understand what we were focused on and why.
- With question-gathering workshops, I created a clear research roadmap and backlog, which helped me do the most impactful research for my teams and company.
- I no longer worried about questions coming my way with a confident understanding of my research process and approach.

By approaching your user research practice with a research mindset, you will be able to think like your practice is a product and your colleagues are your users. What does it mean to approach creating this practice with a user research mindset?

- Question your assumptions, whether that be about a project, a user, or your stakeholders.
- Triangulate the resources you are using to set up your practice (that includes this book!).
- Be critical of your assumptions and biases.
- Talk to your colleagues to get honest and continuous feedback.
- Be open to iterating and changing your process when it makes sense.

With this in mind, you will create a practice that is usable and eventually, hopefully, enabling research to be impactful and influential in your organization.

Why Is a Research Practice Important?

2

Making user research a formalized practice enables us to move more quickly, and really highlights the efficiency of user research in an organization. Have you ever been told that you need to do research faster? That people would do it if it didn't take so long? That people don't come to you because there is no time?

You certainly aren't alone. The thing is, research does take longer than other parts of the product development process. Which is why it is so critical for you to create a standardized practice at your organization. A user research practice enables you to move more quickly and streamline the parts of user research that usually aren't fun or fulfilling (hello, recruitment!).

Not only that, but with a practice in place, you are better setting up the organization for success in the future. By setting up a user research practice, you:

- enable your teammates to do their most impactful work;
- help teams make better decisions that deliver value and motivate them;
- encourage the organization to see the value of research;
- excite your colleagues about solving problems in interesting and innovative ways;
- demonstrate the need for additional researchers;
- attract other user researchers to your organization.

On top of all of that, creating a research practice is a phenomenal way to level up your career. As a researcher, creating a user research practice is a highly valued skill at any organization. Even if you are joining a company that has something established, you could bring a very unique and new perspective based on your previous experiences.

So, whenever you can, try to make the wonderful process of user research easier for yourself and your team by creating a research practice that brings user research to the forefront of your organization.

Connecting Research to Business

3

Tying the impact of research to business metrics can be challenging. For many researchers, the struggle lies in bridging the gap between qualitative insights and tangible business outcomes. How does a one-on-one interview influence revenue? How can usability testing tie back to retention?

I grappled with these questions for much of my career. At one point, I avoided them altogether, believing that metrics belonged to product managers, marketing, or leadership. But reality caught up with me when I found myself in an organization where no one—except the person who hired me—believed in user research. To prove my worth, I needed to show the concrete impact of research on the company's success.

This chapter is designed to help you do the same: make research indispensable by clearly tying it to business outcomes.

ALIGNING UXR GOALS WITH COMPANY OKRs

Understanding OKRs

OKRs (objectives and key results) are a goal-setting framework that helps teams set ambitious yet achievable goals and measure progress. They consist of:

- Objectives (O): What you want to achieve. These should be clear, ambitious, and inspiring.
- Key results (KR): How you will measure progress toward the objective. They should be specific, measurable, and time-bound.

The purpose of OKRs is to help align individual and team efforts with broader organizational goals, ensuring that everyone is working toward a common vision.

User research often operates in the background, influencing decisions indirectly. OKRs can help by:

- Prioritizing what matters most and avoiding spreading efforts too thin
- Making it easier to communicate the value of research to stakeholders
- Aligning with and contributing to business goals, even if company goals are vague
- Providing a clear framework for tracking progress and iterating on research efforts

STEP-BY-STEP PROCESS TO WRITING EFFECTIVE OKRs

Writing impactful OKRs as a user researcher involves a structured approach. Below is a detailed step-by-step breakdown to guide you through the process.

Step 1: Identify Your Broad Goal

The first step in writing effective OKRs as a user researcher is to identify a broad goal—a high-level focus area that you want to improve, influence, or achieve. This might seem simple at first, but it requires thoughtful consideration and alignment with your role, team priorities, and the broader company vision.

Before you start brainstorming, it's crucial to understand where your research work fits into the larger picture. Research doesn't happen in isolation; it impacts multiple areas of the business.

Ask yourself these questions:

- How does my research contribute to product development, marketing, sales, or customer support?
- What are the biggest challenges my team faces that research could help solve?
- Are there recurring themes or pain points that stakeholders frequently mention?
- How is user feedback currently influencing decisions (or not influencing them)?
- What does success look like for my team, and how can research contribute to it?

Key focus areas

Research can support various aspects of the business. Consider focusing your broad goals in one of these categories:

1. Product impact:
    a. How can research support better product decisions?
    b. What areas of the user experience need improvement?
    c. Where are users struggling the most?

2. Stakeholder engagement:
   a. How can I make research insights more actionable for teams?
   b. Are stakeholders engaging with research in meaningful ways?
   c. How can I educate the organization about the value of research?
3. Process improvement:
   a. Are our research processes efficient and scalable?
   b. Do we have standardized ways to document and share findings?
   c. Are we duplicating efforts or working in silos?
4. Personal growth:
   a. What skills do I want to develop as a researcher?
   b. How can I become more effective in my role?
   c. Are there methodologies I need to learn to enhance my work?

Gathering input

Creating research goals shouldn't happen in a vacuum. You should gather insights from multiple sources to inform your goals and ensure they align with business needs.

Who to talk to:

5. Product managers:
   a. What are their biggest challenges when it comes to user insights?
   b. Are they satisfied with the current level of research support?
6. Designers:
   a. Do they have enough data to make design decisions?
   b. What research findings have been most useful to them?
7. Engineers:
   a. How can research better support product development?
   b. Are there areas where research could reduce risk in decision-making?
8. Customer support and success teams:
   a. What common user pain points are they seeing?
   b. Are there gaps in knowledge that research could help address?
9. Marketing teams:
   a. What are the key messages being communicated to customers?
   b. How can research help validate marketing efforts?

In addition to stakeholder conversations, leverage data to identify research opportunities. Look at:

- Analyze customer complaints, reviews, and survey responses
- Identify where users are dropping off or struggling through product analytics
- Look for recurring themes that haven't been fully addressed in past research
- Consider what competitors are doing and how user needs are evolving

Brainstorming goals

Once you've gathered insights from stakeholders and data, it's time to start brainstorming broad goals. Here are some techniques to help generate ideas:

Technique 1: Pain point mapping
1. Write down major challenges your team or users are facing (e.g., "Users find it difficult to navigate our app").
2. Identify areas where research could provide solutions (e.g., "Conduct usability testing to identify friction points").
3. Translate those into broad goals (e.g., "Improve the usability of our core features to reduce user frustration").

Example output:

- Pain point: "Users struggle with checkout."
- Research focus: "Conduct usability tests to improve conversion rates."
- Broad goal: "Enhance the checkout experience to reduce cart abandonment."

Technique 2: Reverse engineering success
Think about what a successful outcome would look like and work backward to identify what research can do to contribute to that success.

Ask yourself:

1. If our product team achieved their goals, how would research have played a role?
2. If the company's revenue increased, how could research insights have contributed?

Example:

- Success = Faster product development cycles.
- Research contribution = More efficient stakeholder alignment with research findings.
- Broad Goal: "Improve research communication to accelerate product development."

Technique 3: The "So that" method
A great way to ensure your goals have a clear purpose is to keep asking "so that" after every goal you write down. This helps tie your research activities to a larger impact.

Example

- Goal: "Improve usability testing."
  - So That → "Users have a smoother onboarding experience."
  - So That → "New users activate more quickly."
- Final Broad Goal: "Enhance onboarding usability to increase user activation."

Technique 4: Stakeholder alignment sessions
Organize short brainstorming sessions with key stakeholders (product, design, marketing) and ask:

- What's the one thing research could do to help you make better decisions?

- If you had unlimited research support, what would you prioritize?
- Where do you feel uncertain about our users?

These conversations often uncover valuable focus areas you might not have considered.

Prioritizing your broad goals

By now, you'll probably have a list of potential goals. It's time to prioritize them based on:

1. Impact versus effort: Choose goals that will have the most meaningful impact with reasonable effort.
2. Alignment with company priorities: Even if goals aren't clear, align with universal business goals like growth, retention, or customer satisfaction.
3. Feasibility: Ensure you have the resources and stakeholder buy-in to achieve these goals.

Examples of well-defined goals
To inspire you, here are some solid broad goals based on different areas of focus:

Product-focused goals:

- "Improve the usability of the onboarding process to reduce churn."
- "Identify key usability barriers in the core product features."
- "Ensure accessibility compliance across all major features."

Stakeholder engagement goals:

- "Increase collaboration between UX research and cross-functional teams."
- "Develop a research storytelling framework to improve stakeholder buy-in."
- "Create a system for delivering digestible insights to leadership."

Operational efficiency goals:

- "Standardize research processes to improve efficiency and scalability."
- "Create a research repository for better knowledge sharing across teams."
- "Implement research planning frameworks to improve stakeholder engagement."

Personal development goals:

- "Improve public speaking skills to present research findings more effectively."
- "Gain proficiency in survey design to support quantitative research needs."
- "Learn advanced synthesis techniques to provide deeper insights."

By following these steps, you'll be well-equipped to brainstorm and define broad goals that are impactful, achievable, and aligned with your role as a user researcher.

Once you have these broad goals, you can move to the next step of refining them into actionable objectives and key results.

Step 2: Turning a Broad Goal into a Clear Objective

Once you've identified your broad goal, the next step is to refine it into a clear, actionable objective that serves as the foundation of your OKRs. A well-crafted objective should inspire action and clearly articulate what you're trying to achieve without being too vague or too task-oriented.

Why objectives matter?

Objectives give direction to your efforts and align them with a larger purpose. They should:

- Provide clarity by answering the question "What are we trying to achieve?"
- Ensure focus by keeping your efforts aligned with your role and business needs
- Motivate action by creating a sense of purpose and progress

Characteristics of a strong objective

A good objective should be:

Actionable

- It should drive meaningful activity and inspire progress
  - Bad example: "make research better"
  - Good example: "improve how research insights are shared to increase their influence on decision-making"

Impact-driven

- Your objective should focus on the why behind the goal, not just what you want to do
  - Bad example: "conduct usability tests"
  - Good example: "enhance the onboarding experience so that new users activate faster"

Specific but not restrictive

- Keep it broad enough to allow flexibility in execution but focused enough to guide your work
  - Bad example: "improve usability"
  - Good example: "identify and address usability barriers to improve product adoption"

Formula to create a strong objective

A simple and effective way to structure your objective is:

[Action] so that [desired impact]

This formula helps you tie the goal to a tangible outcome and ensures the objective connects to business priorities.

Examples:

- Improve user onboarding so that new customers can achieve their goals faster
- Increase research visibility so that more teams incorporate insights into their decision-making
- Streamline research processes so that studies are completed faster and with higher quality

Refining your broad goal into an objective

To transform your broad goal into a well-structured objective, follow these steps:

Identify the root problem
- Why is this goal important?
- What challenges does it address?
- How will achieving it make a difference?

Define the desired impact
- Think about the larger effect of achieving this goal
- Who benefits from it, and how?
- What positive changes will it bring?

Align with stakeholders
- Ensure your objective aligns with team or business needs
- Check if it contributes to product, customer, or operational goals

Make it inspiring but achievable
- Your objective should be motivating without being overwhelming
- It should challenge you but still be realistic within the given timeframe

Example of refining a broad goal

Broad goal: Improve the effectiveness of research reports

Step 1: Identify the root problem
- Stakeholders struggle to understand findings and apply them to their work
- Reports are too long and not actionable

Step 2: Define the desired impact
- Make insights more digestible so that teams can make informed decisions faster

Step 3: Align with stakeholders
- Product teams need concise and relevant findings to prioritize their work

Final objective: Improve research reporting so that stakeholders can easily apply insights to decision-making

Common mistakes to avoid

1. Making it too vague
    a. Avoid objectives like "do better research" or "help the team"
    b. Be specific about what you want to achieve
2. Focusing too much on tasks
    a. Objectives should describe the outcome, not just the actions you'll take
    b. Instead of "run five user interviews," focus on what you hope to achieve through them
3. Not considering the bigger picture
    a. Always connect your objective to a larger business or user need
    b. Think about how your research efforts will contribute to the company's success

EXAMPLES OF WELL-WRITTEN OBJECTIVES

Product-focused objectives

- Enhance feature usability so that customers can achieve their goals with less effort
- Improve the checkout experience so that cart abandonment rates decrease
- Strengthen accessibility compliance so that more users can engage with the product

Stakeholder engagement objectives

- Increase stakeholder participation so that research findings influence more product decisions
- Improve collaboration with marketing so that campaigns are better aligned with user needs
- Enhance research visibility so that insights are incorporated earlier in the design process

Operational efficiency objectives

- Standardize research processes so that projects are completed more efficiently
- Build a research repository so that teams can easily access and use past insights
- Improve cross-functional communication so that research handoffs are smoother

Personal development objectives
- Improve facilitation skills so that workshops are more engaging and productive
- Gain expertise in mixed-method research so that insights are more comprehensive
- Develop storytelling skills so that research presentations are more compelling

Step 3: Defining Measurable Key Results

Once you have a clear objective, the next step is to define key results that measure progress and indicate whether you are achieving your objective. Writing effective key results is crucial because they provide a clear way to track success, help prioritize efforts, and ensure alignment with business goals. Without strong key results, your objectives can become vague aspirations rather than actionable targets.

Key results define how you will measure success in achieving your objective. They break down the objective into tangible, measurable, and trackable outcomes that demonstrate progress.

Key characteristics of effective key results

1. Specific: clearly define what success looks like without ambiguity
2. Measurable: use metrics, numbers, or milestones to track progress
3. Achievable: they should stretch you but remain realistic
4. Relevant: they should directly contribute to the objective
5. Time-bound: include a deadline or timeframe to create urgency

Key results formula

A simple way to structure key results is to use the formula:

Achieve [specific outcome] by [metric or milestone] within [timeframe]

Example:
- Increase stakeholder engagement with research reports from 50% to 80% by the end of Q2
- Conduct ten usability tests to identify and address three critical friction points by Q3

How to brainstorm key results that align with your objective

Thinking through key results requires a structured approach. Follow these steps to create meaningful key results that align with your objective.

Break the objective into measurable parts

Look at your objective and ask:

- What are the key actions that contribute to this goal?
- What metrics or indicators will tell me if I am making progress?
- How will I know if I have succeeded?

Example objective: improve research reporting so that stakeholders can easily apply insights to decision-making

Breakdown:

1. Stakeholder engagement with reports (measurable through feedback, meeting attendance)
2. Actionable insights included in reports (measurable through stakeholder implementation)
3. Report clarity and accessibility (measurable through qualitative feedback and revisions)

Potential key results:

- Increase stakeholder satisfaction with research reports from 60% to 85%
- Ensure 75% of reports result in at least one product change
- Reduce report length by 30% without losing key insights by Q3

Identify relevant metrics

To create measurable key results, identify quantifiable data points that can track progress. Common categories of metrics for UXR include:

1. Engagement metrics
   a. Number of stakeholders attending research presentations
   b. Number of teams using research insights in their work
   c. Increase in the number of research requests from product teams
2. Performance metrics
   a. Reduction in usability issues identified post-launch
   b. Increase in feature adoption rates after research recommendations
   c. Reduction in time spent conducting research due to improved processes
3. Quality metrics
   a. Stakeholder satisfaction scores (collected via post-research surveys)
   b. Reduction in repetitive research requests by standardizing documentation
   c. Increase in usability test completion rates
4. Operational metrics
   a. Reduction in the time taken to complete a research project
   b. Increase in the number of research studies conducted per quarter
   c. Percentage of research insights that lead to actionable changes

Think in terms of outputs versus outcomes

When writing key results, it is important to differentiate between outputs and outcomes. Outputs measure the completion of tasks, while outcomes measure the actual impact of those tasks. For example:

- Output-based key result: conduct five user interviews by the end of the quarter
- Outcome-based key result: reduce user drop-off rate by 15% based on insights from user interviews

Focusing on outcomes ensures that your key results reflect meaningful progress rather than just activity.

Set ambitious but realistic targets

Key results should push you beyond your comfort zone but still be achievable within the timeframe. Consider past performance and available resources when setting targets. Ask yourself:

- What would be a stretch goal without being unrealistic?
- What constraints might limit progress?
- What resources are available to achieve these goals?

For example:

If the team conducted three usability tests last quarter, an ambitious but realistic key result might be to complete five usability tests this quarter.

Ensure alignment with stakeholders

Your key results should align with the needs and expectations of stakeholders, ensuring that they see value in the research efforts. Discuss your key results with product managers, designers, and other relevant teams to gain alignment and buy-in.

Questions to ask stakeholders:

- What research outcomes would be most valuable to your work?
- How do you measure success in your area, and how can research support it?
- What would make you feel that research is having a meaningful impact?

Prioritize the most impactful key results

Not all potential key results will have equal impact. Prioritize those that will drive the most meaningful change and are within your control. Consider:

- Which key results align most closely with business objectives?

- Which are easiest to measure accurately?
- Which provides the most value to stakeholders?

Examples of strong key results

Product-focused key results
Objective: enhance feature usability so that customers can achieve their goals with less effort

- Increase task completion rates from 70% to 90% within the next quarter
- Conduct ten usability tests to identify the top three usability issues
- Reduce support tickets related to usability by 20%

Stakeholder engagement key results
Objective: increase stakeholder participation so that research findings influence more product decisions

- Achieve 80% attendance in research readouts by the end of the quarter
- Ensure that three research reports directly influence product roadmap decisions
- Collect stakeholder feedback with an 85% satisfaction rating

Operational efficiency key results
Objective: standardize research processes so that projects are completed more efficiently

- Implement a research repository with 100% of the team onboarded by Q2
- Reduce research turnaround time from six weeks to four weeks
- Increase the number of completed research projects per quarter by 25%

Personal development key results
Objective: improve facilitation skills so that workshops are more engaging and productive

- Co-facilitate three workshops with senior researchers for mentorship
- Receive positive feedback from at least 80% of workshop participants
- Complete one professional facilitation training course

Step 4: Evaluating and Refining OKRs

Once you have defined your objectives and key results, the next step is to evaluate them to ensure they are clear, achievable, and aligned with your role, team, and organization. Proper evaluation helps ensure your OKRs are focused on meaningful outcomes rather than vague aspirations or overly ambitious goals. Without careful evaluation, OKRs can become ineffective and fail to provide the direction and impact they are meant to achieve.

Evaluating your OKRs is crucial for a few reasons:

- It helps identify whether your key results are truly measurable and achievable
- It ensures alignment with company, team, and personal goals
- It prevents setting unrealistic or unfocused goals that can lead to frustration
- It allows you to make adjustments before implementation, saving time and effort
- It provides clarity for yourself and your stakeholders on what success looks like

Key principles of evaluating OKRs

When evaluating your OKRs, keep the following principles in mind to ensure they are meaningful and effective:

Clarity

- Are the objective and key results easy to understand?
- Can someone outside your team quickly grasp what you are trying to achieve?
- Are the key results free from ambiguity?

Alignment

- Do your OKRs align with broader team or organizational goals?
- Do they contribute to business impact, such as improving product adoption or customer satisfaction?
- Are stakeholders supportive and involved in the outcomes?

Measurability

- Do the key results have clear metrics to track progress?
- Can you measure progress objectively without subjective interpretation?
- Are there systems in place to gather the required data?

Achievability

- Are the key results challenging yet realistic?
- Do you have the necessary resources to achieve them?
- Have you considered potential blockers or constraints?

Impact

- Will achieving these OKRs lead to meaningful improvements?
- Do the key results focus on outcomes rather than just outputs?
- Are they solving a real problem that impacts the user experience or business success?

How to evaluate your OKRs

Apply the SMART criteria
To ensure your OKRs are well-structured, evaluate each of them using the SMART criteria (specific, measurable, achievable, relevant, time-bound).

Example of a poorly structured key result
Improve research participation

When evaluated against SMART:

- Specific: participation in what activities?
- Measurable: what percentage increase or number of stakeholders?
- Achievable: is it realistic within the given timeframe?
- Relevant: does it contribute to business goals?
- Time-bound: by when should this be achieved?

Improved key result after evaluation
Increase stakeholder participation in research planning meetings from 40% to 70% by the end of Q2

Conduct a stakeholder review

Schedule a meeting with key stakeholders—such as product managers, designers, and leadership—to review your OKRs and get their input. Questions to ask during stakeholder reviews:

- Do these objectives align with your team's goals?
- How would achieving these key results support your work?
- Do you have concerns about feasibility or relevance?
- Are there other areas where research could provide more value?

Test for clarity with peers

Run your OKRs by a peer or mentor who is not directly involved in your work. Ask them to:

- Restate the objective in their own words to ensure it is clear
- Identify if the key results make sense and are easy to follow
- Suggest areas for simplification or greater focus

If they struggle to understand your OKRs, it's a sign they may need to be reworked for clarity.

Check for balance between ambition and reality

While OKRs should stretch your capabilities, they should not be so ambitious that they become unattainable. Consider the balance between ambition and feasibility by asking:

- Are these key results achievable within the given timeframe?
- Are they too conservative and lacking challenge?
- Do they push the team in a productive way without causing burnout?

Example of balancing ambition and reality
- Overly ambitious: "double stakeholder engagement in research by the end of Q1"
- More balanced: "increase stakeholder engagement by 25% over the next two quarters"

Align with available resources

Evaluate whether you have the necessary resources—time, budget, personnel, and tools—to achieve your key results.

If your OKRs require significant resources beyond your control, consider adjusting them or seeking additional support from leadership.

Example resource-related questions:

- Do I have the tools and platforms needed to track my key results?
- Are there enough people available to support the research efforts?
- Will budget constraints limit the execution of these OKRs?

Create a tracking plan

Having clear OKRs is not enough; you need a plan to track progress regularly. Decide:

- How often will you check progress (weekly, bi-weekly, monthly)?
- What tools will you use to track metrics (spreadsheets, dashboards, project management tools)?
- Who will be responsible for monitoring progress?

Example of tracking plan
Check progress on key result 1 every two weeks using stakeholder survey results, and review the findings in our monthly team meeting

Score your OKRs using a confidence scale

Before finalizing your OKRs, score each key result on a scale of 1 to 10 based on:

1. Your confidence in achieving it
2. The clarity of how to achieve it
3. The availability of resources

If your confidence score is below 7, consider refining that key result to make it more realistic.

Common mistakes to avoid

1. Setting too many key results
   a. Having too many key results can dilute focus and make tracking difficult
   b. Focus on 2–4 key results per objective to ensure meaningful progress
2. Focusing only on output, not outcomes
   a. Avoid key results that measure only actions ("run 10 interviews")
   b. Instead, focus on the impact of those actions ("reduce onboarding confusion based on interview insights")
3. Ignoring qualitative measures
   a. While numbers are important, qualitative feedback can provide rich insights into progress
   b. Include qualitative measures such as stakeholder satisfaction or usability improvements
4. Not revisiting OKRs regularly
   a. OKRs should be living documents that are reviewed and adjusted regularly
   b. Set aside time each month to assess progress and make any necessary changes

Examples of well-evaluated OKRs
Product-focused OKRs   Objective: improve onboarding usability so that new users activate faster

- Increase completion rate of the onboarding flow from 65% to 80%
- Reduce the average onboarding time from ten minutes to seven minutes
- Conduct usability testing with 15 users to identify top friction points

Stakeholder engagement OKRs   Objective: increase stakeholder participation in research efforts so that decisions are more user-driven

- Host three cross-functional workshops with an attendance rate of 90%
- Collect qualitative feedback from 80% of stakeholders on research impact
- Develop a research insights dashboard with 100% adoption by the product team

COMMON OKR SCENARIOS

Writing OKRs as a user researcher can be challenging, especially when organizational goals are unclear, when working in a specific industry such as B2B or B2C, or when supporting teams outside of product development. In each of these scenarios, it's important to tailor your objectives and key results to focus on what you can control and how your research can create meaningful impact.

> **Scenario 1: When company goals are unclear**
>
> When your company's goals are unclear or not well communicated, it can feel overwhelming to set meaningful OKRs as a user researcher. Without clear direction, it's easy to feel disconnected from broader business objectives, leaving you unsure of how to align your work effectively. However, even in the absence of well-defined goals, you can still create impactful OKRs by focusing on areas that universally contribute to business success, product improvement, and operational efficiency.

Focus on Business Fundamentals

When company goals are unclear, aligning your OKRs with fundamental business priorities can provide a strong foundation. These priorities often remain consistent across industries and include:

- Acquisition—Helping attract new users/customers through better user experiences or messaging.
- Activation—Ensuring users successfully engage with the product and realize its value.
- Retention—Keeping existing users engaged by addressing pain points and improving satisfaction.
- Revenue—Supporting business growth through pricing optimization, upsell opportunities, or customer insights.
- Customer satisfaction—Improving product experience to increase loyalty and advocacy.

Example OKRs Based on Business Fundamentals

Objective: Improve the onboarding experience so that new users activate successfully.

- Conduct usability testing with 10 new users to identify onboarding friction points.
- Reduce drop-off rates in the onboarding flow from 40% to 25% by Q3.
- Increase onboarding completion rates from 60% to 75%.

Objective: Increase research visibility so that more teams leverage insights for decision-making.

- Conduct three research readouts across departments by the end of the quarter.
- Develop a standardized insights-sharing process to be used by at least five teams.
- Increase stakeholder engagement with research reports by 50%.

Align with Team-Level Priorities

Even if company-wide goals are unclear, each department within the organization likely has its own priorities. Your job is to align your research efforts with these priorities to ensure your work remains relevant and valuable.

How to Identify Team-Level Priorities

- Product team—Are they focusing on feature adoption, usability improvements, or innovation?
- Marketing team—Do they need insights to improve messaging and conversion rates?
- Customer support team—Are they looking to reduce ticket volume by addressing recurring user pain points?

Questions to Ask to Uncover Team Priorities

1. What are your biggest challenges in understanding user needs right now?
2. Are there any recurring user pain points that you need better insights on?
3. How do you currently use research, and what would make it more valuable?
4. What metrics are most important to your team's success?
5. Are there any upcoming initiatives where research could provide support?

Once you gather insights from different teams, tailor your OKRs to address their most pressing needs.

Example OKRs Based on Team-Level Alignment

Objective: Provide actionable insights to product teams so that feature improvements are better informed.

- Conduct three in-depth user research studies focused on priority features.
- Increase the number of research-backed design iterations from two to five per quarter.
- Achieve a 90% satisfaction rating from product managers on research relevance.

Objective: Support marketing efforts so that campaign messaging resonates better with target audiences.

- Conduct five user interviews to test marketing messaging effectiveness.
- Develop two persona updates based on recent research findings.
- Improve ad click-through rates by 20% based on research-driven insights.

Leverage Past Research Insights

Even if current goals are unclear, past research findings can provide a roadmap for impactful OKRs. Look at previous reports, studies, and stakeholder feedback to identify recurring themes or unresolved challenges that still need attention.

Ways to Leverage Past Insights

- Identify patterns across past studies that indicate ongoing user challenges.
- Look for research gaps where further investigation could provide deeper insights.
- Revisit recommendations that were never fully implemented and measure their current relevance.
- Analyze stakeholder feedback on past research reports to determine areas for improvement.

Example OKRs Based on Past Research

Objective: Address recurring usability issues so that user frustration is reduced.

- Identify the top five recurring usability complaints from past research.
- Conduct follow-up usability testing to validate and prioritize these issues.
- Develop a roadmap with design and engineering to address three key usability pain points by the end of the quarter.

Work on Research Operational Improvements

If product or business goals remain too vague to work with, focus on improving the efficiency and impact of your research practice. Internal goals related to research processes, stakeholder engagement, and knowledge sharing can provide a valuable foundation for your OKRs.

Key areas for operational OKRs

1. Efficiency—Streamlining processes to complete research faster and with greater consistency.
2. Documentation—Creating centralized repositories to make past insights easier to access.
3. Stakeholder engagement—Improving how research is shared and communicated across teams.

Example OKRs for Operational Improvements

Objective: Improve research efficiency so that insights are delivered faster and with greater consistency.

- Reduce the average research project timeline from six weeks to four weeks.
- Implement standardized research templates used in 100% of projects.
- Train 100% of the team on the new research workflow by Q3.

Objective: Increase accessibility of research insights so that stakeholders can easily apply findings.

- Develop a research repository with at least 20 reports uploaded by the end of the quarter.
- Ensure that 80% of product teams use the repository for decision-making.
- Improve stakeholder satisfaction with research access from 60% to 85%.

Focus on Personal Growth and Development

In the absence of clear company goals, focusing on personal development within your research practice can be highly beneficial. Strengthening your skills and capabilities contributes to long-term success and prepares you for more strategic contributions when business goals become clearer.

Key areas for personal growth OKRs

1. Expanding knowledge of new research methodologies.
2. Improving research communication and storytelling.
3. Enhancing facilitation skills for workshops and stakeholder meetings.

Example personal development OKRs

Objective: Improve my facilitation skills so that research workshops are more engaging and productive.

- Co-facilitate at least three workshops with senior researchers by the end of the quarter.
- Receive feedback from 90% of participants on workshop effectiveness.
- Complete one professional facilitation training course by Q2.

Objective: Expand my skills in quantitative research so that insights are more data-driven.

- Complete an online course on quantitative research methods by the end of the quarter.

- Conduct two mixed-method studies combining qualitative and quantitative data.
- Present findings to stakeholders with improved data visualization techniques.

The key is to focus on what you can control and to create OKRs that provide measurable value regardless of external uncertainties. By applying these strategies, you can confidently move forward with OKRs that ensure your research efforts remain impactful, even in an environment where strategic direction is uncertain.

Scenario 2: Writing OKRs for B2B versus B2C research

User research in B2B and B2C environments presents unique challenges and requires tailored OKRs to address different user behaviors, expectations, and decision-making processes. It's essential to tailor OKRs to the specific needs of B2B and B2C environments, ensuring that objectives align with business goals and that key results measure progress effectively.

KEY METRICS TO TRACK FOR B2B VERSUS B2C RESEARCH OKRs

For B2B:

- Adoption rates across different departments within a client organization
- Time-to-value metrics (how quickly the client can see results)
- Stakeholder engagement in research initiatives
- Customer satisfaction scores from key business users
- Long-term retention and renewal rates

For B2C:

- User retention rates over different time periods (30, 60, 90 days)
- Conversion rates (sign-ups, purchases, subscriptions)
- User satisfaction scores and sentiment analysis
- Session duration and feature adoption rates
- Drop-off rates in critical user flows

HOW TO APPROACH B2B RESEARCH OKRs

B2B user research often focuses on understanding the workflows, challenges, and pain points of businesses that use your product. The goal is to help these organizations achieve their objectives more efficiently and provide value across different stakeholders in the business.

COMMON B2B RESEARCH CHALLENGES

- Dealing with multiple decision-makers, from executives to end-users
- Addressing complex product integrations and feature customizations
- Longer feedback cycles due to extended procurement processes
- Focusing on long-term relationships rather than short-term engagement

KEY FOCUS AREAS FOR B2B OKRs

1. Improving product adoption across different teams in client organizations
2. Reducing friction in onboarding and training processes

3. Enhancing product usability for specific industries or workflows
4. Strengthening stakeholder relationships through research-backed insights
5. Providing data-driven recommendations to influence enterprise clients' long-term strategy

HOW TO CREATE B2B RESEARCH OKRs
1. Engage with different stakeholders—Collaborate with account managers, customer success teams, and IT departments to understand business needs.
2. Focus on usability and efficiency—B2B users prioritize tools that improve their efficiency, so research should aim to identify bottlenecks and friction points.
3. Leverage long-term tracking metrics—Customer retention, feature adoption, and training success are critical in B2B environments.

EXAMPLE B2B OKRs

Objective: Improve the usability of enterprise features so that customers achieve their business goals more efficiently.

- Conduct 15 usability tests across three enterprise clients to identify common pain points.
- Implement five usability improvements that reduce task completion time by 20%.
- Increase product NPS among enterprise users from 65 to 80 by the end of Q3.

Objective: Enhance the onboarding experience so that enterprise clients adopt the product more quickly.

- Create an onboarding research framework tailored to three key industries.
- Reduce onboarding time from eight weeks to six weeks by streamlining workflows.
- Increase training completion rates from 50% to 75% by the end of the quarter.

Objective: Strengthen cross-functional collaboration with client success teams so that research insights directly address enterprise challenges.

- Conduct quarterly alignment meetings with customer success teams to identify top client pain points.
- Develop a research insights report that leads to at least three process improvements.
- Achieve 80% adoption of research-backed recommendations by enterprise clients.

HOW TO APPROACH B2C RESEARCH OKRs
B2C user research focuses on understanding individual customer needs, behaviors, and motivations to drive product engagement and satisfaction. Unlike B2B, where

research often focuses on optimizing workflows and enterprise-wide solutions, B2C research emphasizes accessibility, convenience, and emotional connection.

COMMON B2C RESEARCH CHALLENGES
- High volume of users with diverse needs and preferences
- Short attention spans and lower tolerance for complexity
- Competitive landscape with rapidly evolving consumer trends
- Fast feedback loops through user reviews and social media

KEY FOCUS AREAS FOR B2C OKRs
1. Improving user experience and satisfaction to increase retention
2. Identifying pain points in key user journeys (checkout, onboarding, engagement)
3. Optimizing conversion rates by enhancing usability and reducing friction
4. Enhancing personalization to better meet user expectations
5. Reducing drop-off rates and increasing feature adoption

HOW TO CREATE B2C RESEARCH OKRs
1. Gather direct user feedback—Use surveys, app reviews, and usability testing to understand customer needs.
2. Focus on emotional drivers—B2C users are more influenced by branding, aesthetics, and convenience.
3. Utilize rapid testing cycles—Implement continuous discovery to validate assumptions quickly and iterate.

EXAMPLE B2C OKRs

Objective: Improve the checkout experience so that customers complete purchases with fewer frustrations.

- Conduct ten usability tests on the checkout flow to identify the top three friction points.
- Reduce cart abandonment rate from 45% to 30% within the next quarter.
- Increase mobile checkout satisfaction scores from 3.5 to 4.5.

Objective: Enhance the personalization of the app so that users feel more engaged and return more often.

- Develop and test three new personalization features based on user feedback.
- Increase feature adoption rates from 20% to 40%.
- Improve user retention rates by 15% by offering personalized recommendations.

Objective: Optimize onboarding so that new users can understand product value faster.

- Conduct interviews with 50 new users to identify gaps in the onboarding process.

- Improve onboarding completion rates from 60% to 80% by streamlining key steps.
- Achieve an onboarding satisfaction score of 85% based on post-onboarding surveys.

Scenario 3: Writing OKRs for non-product teams (marketing, customer support)

User researchers are often embedded in or work closely with non-product teams, such as marketing and customer support, which have their own unique challenges and goals. Unlike product teams, where research typically focuses on usability and feature optimization, non-product teams require research to support business functions like brand messaging, customer engagement, churn reduction, and support efficiency.

In these settings, writing effective OKRs requires a deep understanding of how research can directly impact customer acquisition, retention, and satisfaction, rather than just product functionality.

Both marketing and customer support teams rely on user research to:

- Understand customer needs, behaviors, and motivations to shape communication and support strategies.
- Improve customer experience by identifying pain points in messaging, service interactions, and touchpoints.
- Evaluate campaign effectiveness and ensure marketing initiatives resonate with the target audience.
- Optimize support processes to reduce ticket volumes and enhance self-service options.

CHALLENGES OF CONDUCTING RESEARCH FOR NON-PRODUCT TEAMS

1. Indirect connection to product success: Research efforts might not always tie directly to feature changes but can impact brand perception, customer loyalty, and advocacy.
2. Different stakeholder expectations: Marketing and customer support teams might prioritize short-term gains, while research focuses on long-term insights.
3. Varied data sources: Non-product teams often rely on sources like NPS scores, customer feedback surveys, and support tickets, which may require different research approaches.
4. Balancing qualitative and quantitative insights: Understanding emotional and behavioral aspects of customers requires a mix of quantitative metrics (conversion rates) and qualitative insights (sentiment analysis).

How to Write OKRs for Marketing Teams

Marketing teams focus on acquiring and retaining customers by developing messaging, campaigns, and strategies that resonate with target audiences. Research can provide valuable insights to guide content creation, branding, targeting, and channel selection.

Where research can support marketing teams

1. User personas and segmentation
   a. Developing accurate personas based on research insights to guide campaign strategies.
   b. Identifying key demographic and psychographic traits that influence purchase decisions.
2. Message evaluation and positioning
   a. Ensuring brand messaging resonates with different customer segments.
   b. Testing different value propositions to understand what drives conversion.
3. Campaign effectiveness
   a. Evaluating how well marketing campaigns are performing and where adjustments are needed.
   b. Measuring engagement and understanding barriers to adoption.
4. Brand perception and awareness
   a. Conducting research to understand how customers perceive the brand.
   b. Gathering insights to inform rebranding efforts or market positioning.

Create OKRs for marketing teams

1. Collaborate with marketing stakeholders: Identify their goals related to customer acquisition and engagement.
2. Analyze existing marketing data: Use customer surveys, campaign analytics, and website behavior to find gaps in understanding.
3. Prioritize actionable insights: Focus on research that can directly impact messaging, targeting, and conversion optimization.

Example Marketing OKRs

Objective: Provide actionable insights to marketing so that campaigns better resonate with the target audience.

- Conduct ten customer interviews to validate campaign messaging before launch.
- Develop three updated personas based on recent research findings by the end of Q2.
- Increase email engagement rates by 20% after implementing research-driven messaging adjustments.

Objective: Improve the effectiveness of marketing content so that it aligns with customer needs and behaviors.

- Analyze 50 customer feedback survey responses to identify content gaps.
- Conduct five usability tests on the marketing website to improve navigation and content accessibility.
- Increase content engagement (time spent on page) by 25% within three months.

How to Write OKRs for Customer Support Teams

Customer support teams are responsible for resolving user issues, improving satisfaction, and ensuring retention. Research can help these teams by uncovering pain points, improving self-service solutions, and enhancing the overall support experience.

Where Research Can Support Customer Support Teams
1. Reducing support ticket volume
   a. Identifying recurring issues that can be addressed proactively through better documentation or product changes.
   b. Improving self-service resources like FAQs and chatbots based on user behavior and feedback.
2. Enhancing customer satisfaction
   a. Understanding what factors contribute to dissatisfaction and frustration.
   b. Identifying opportunities to enhance empathy and personalization in support interactions.
3. Improving support workflows
   a. Evaluating the effectiveness of current support processes.
   b. Providing insights on how agents can better assist customers.
4. Proactive support initiatives
   a. Conducting research to anticipate customer needs and improve the overall support strategy.

Create OKRs for Customer Support Teams
1. Analyze support data: Review common support issues, ticket trends, and customer feedback to identify recurring problems.
2. Engage with support managers: Understand their pain points in delivering fast and efficient support.
3. Identify opportunities for self-service: Research ways to empower customers to resolve issues independently.

Example Customer Support OKRs

Objective: Reduce support ticket volume so that customers can resolve common issues more independently.

- Conduct 15 usability tests on the help center to identify navigation issues.
- Reduce support tickets related to onboarding by 25% within the next two quarters.
- Improve chatbot resolution accuracy from 60% to 85% based on research findings.

Objective: Enhance the customer support experience so that users feel more satisfied with their interactions.

- Analyze 100 customer support calls to identify communication challenges.
- Conduct eight user interviews to understand common frustrations with the current support process.
- Increase CSAT (customer satisfaction score) from 75% to 90% by the end of Q3.

Remember, OKRs aren't just about tracking numbers, they're about making your research more strategic, measurable, and impactful. And the more you refine your OKRs, the easier it'll be to advocate for your work and drive meaningful change in your organization.

MAPPING RESEARCH OUTCOMES TO BUSINESS METRICS

Tying the impact of research on metrics can be challenging. I struggled with it for a large part of my career. How did I take a 1×1 interview and show how it impacted our revenue? Often, it felt like a lofty goal that I would never accomplish, and for a while, I left it to the wayside. Metrics were for other roles, not user research.

While that attitude served me for a little, there was a bumpier road ahead that I couldn't see. After a round of layoffs and struggling to find a new role, I finally accepted a job offer.

However, I quickly realized how much of an uphill battle my role would be because no one, besides the person who hired me, believed in user research. I didn't know people could self-select into believing or not believing in a literal craft, but here we were. I was terrified of losing another job and being unable to pay rent, so I tried to embrace the challenge.

The number one question I continuously got bombarded with was, "What is the impact of user research?"

I had the jaws of a fish as I opened and closed my mouth, unable to create a concrete answer. Eventually, I defaulted to the only things I knew to say:

"We understand our customers better so we can make customer-centric decisions"

"If we understand people's needs or pain points, we create relevant products for them."

"We can reduce time guessing or basing ideas off assumptions that might fail."

Although I had witnessed user research do many amazing things, I couldn't fully articulate the impact in a way my colleagues understood or cared about. This plagued me. I constantly felt defeated and unvalued because I didn't know how to tie something like qualitative research back to what people cared about: money.

And for a long time, I "stood my ground," which really meant that I was hugely antagonistic and stubborn when it came to incorporating business into user research. I used to say that I, as a user researcher, was not there for the business and didn't care about the business. I was there for the user. And usually, in my mind, the business and the user were pitted against each other as villain and victim.

By creating a mindset and environment where it was me + users versus the business, I was stuck in the middle of a complete mess. I lacked trust with my colleagues, got into fights (literally, I yelled at people), and spun on the hamster wheel of trying to prove the value of user research without business.

Fast forward a few months to when I sat in a performance review. My interviews, usability testing, and synthesizing skills were spot-on. I was good, if not great, at conducting user research. But I had a huge glaring gap in skills like stakeholder management, tying research to the business, and workshop facilitation.

I was super bummed about that performance review and, unfortunately, didn't have much guidance on how to make it better. Was I going to lose my job over it? Likely not. However, I quickly saw there was no way I was going to advance in my career if I didn't figure something out. And I knew exactly what I needed to work on.

Formulating a Plan

It took me a few weeks to do some research and formulate a plan for how I was going to tackle this issue.

The first thing I did was research "business." It was tough because it was such a broad area and scope. I wasn't super familiar with how businesses operate, what goals they had, or what metrics were important to them, so it took a lot of Googling and some embarrassing question-asking.

I learned how important revenue was to a company—it shouldn't have been such an "ah-ha" moment, but in my need to be so user-centric, I lost complete vision of the holistic picture.

A company (usually) needs to make money to create a product/service. Customers want a product/service that helps them achieve their goals or alleviate a pain point. When they find that experience, they give the company money.

A product/service aligned with customers' needs = more money for a company.

User research could help determine the experiences, needs, and pain points of users to increase the amount of money a company was making.

Finally, I started to wrap my head around this concept, but I still wasn't sure how to apply it because that sounded like one of the fishy and vague answers I gave about user research impact. I wanted something more concrete.

Stakeholder Interviews

I was in the green with some of my stakeholders and definitely not a fan favorite with others (remember those fights I spoke about?), so this part was very challenging for me at first. But I knew I needed to talk to my stakeholders to learn more about their goals and the business. Without this, how was I going to draw concrete ties between user research and impact?

Biting my tongue, I bought a lot of "I'm sorry, please talk to me" lunches and coffees. I started the conversation by sharing that I was sorry about any disagreements made and sharing why I had acted in that way. Then I spoke about what and how I was trying to change. Most of my stakeholders were super kind and understanding, and they also apologized back. For a few, we were never really able to repair the relationship, but, hey, 80/20 rule, right?

As I spoke to these stakeholders, I learned about goals and started to see patterns and trends evolve in what they were talking about. There was a lot of concern or goals around the same terminology. With this, I went back to Google to further investigate.

Uncovering the Pirate Metrics

Through my research, I stumbled on something called the pirate metrics, named aptly for the acronym AARRR.

This model, coined by Dave McClure in 2007, highlights the five most critical metrics for businesses to track for success. Not only did these make sense to me based on my desk research, but they were also commonly referred to in my stakeholder interviews.

I wanted to understand how to concretely tie user research to these hugely important metrics. With that, I would no longer feel as much like a fish out of water. Instead, I could start to answer the questions about my impact more confidently and know that I was helping the business and users.

Tying User Research to the Metrics

Off I went on this adventure that would change my career forever. I dedicated as much time as possible to understanding these pirate metrics and figuring out how I could tie user research projects to each of them.

This is everything I learned and still practice to this day for each of the pirate metrics. I'll be using a specific example from a travel company I used to work for.

Acquisition—How People Find and Are Introduced to Your Product/Service

Acquisition is all about getting new customers into your product/service so that they, essentially, know it exists. There are many ways a company can do this, such as:

- SEO
- Marketing (including email and social media)
- Sales
- Paid advertising

When I was working at the travel company, acquisition was hugely important to us because we didn't have complete market share and, instead, shared the space with quite a few competitors. Getting customers without a ridiculously high customer acquisition cost (CAC) was incredibly important to our revenue.

We struggled a lot with finding new customers because of the sheer amount of competition out there and also because of the trust (or lack thereof) that comes with using a third-party ticketing product.

However, I knew how important it was to think about helping improve our acquisition, so I met with the acquisition product manager and we brainstormed the most important metrics within the acquisition space:

- Increasing traffic to our main page
- Reducing bounce rate from our main page (without any clicks)
- Increasing time spent on page
- Understanding the breakdown of where our traffic is coming from

These are all relatively high-level, top-of-funnel (TOFU) metrics and, to me, they seemed quite broad and generic, but it was the best we could do. (PS—these things all take time to learn and I'm still learning more about metrics/business, so always take the time to experiment).

With that, I started to identify some research projects I could do to help these TOFU metrics (I love calling something in product Tofu). With that, I came up with the following projects:

Content testing through a highlighter test. The reason I decided on a highlighter test was because it is a great method to help determine value proposition and what information is necessary to help users achieve their goals. It can also reduce the amount of text on a page to focus on what is essential to the user. During this test, I copied and pasted the text from our homepage into a Google Doc and I asked them to use three colors:

- Green = text that was helpful to them
- Orange = text that was confusing
- Red = text that was unnecessary

After they highlighted, we went through the content, and I asked them follow-up questions on why they highlighted certain things in the specific colors, how they might reword confusing content, and also if there was content missing that might be helpful.

We then went on to test A/B versions of copy and content to see what was most effective. This was to help reduce bounce rate and increase time spent on the page.

Five-second tests. Once we updated our copy, I wanted to use five-second tests to understand what message we were communicating to our users. Could people understand we were a ticketing platform? Did they understand what we were able to give them or what needs we were trying to meet? We used this to continue to refine our message and clarify how we could help users achieve their goals from the moment they laid eyes on our platform. This was also to reduce bounce rate and increase time spent on the page.

Closed word choice survey. Finally, we wanted to understand the types of words people associated with us, namely around the "trust family," since trust was a huge object of concern with us being a third-party ticket platform. I set up a survey with several images of our website and sent it out to participants, asking them to select all the words they would use to describe our platform. I used words like:

- Empowering
- Approachable

- Disconnected
- Friendly
- Irrelevant
- Patronizing
- Untrustworthy
- Trustworthy
- Skeptical
- Easy
- Relevant
- Simple

I also followed up with some open-ended questions, such as "please describe why you chose those words" to try to get further insight. We ended up having to contact some respondents to get a better insight into why they chose certain words through quick interviews. This was also to reduce bounce rate.

Lastly, I did some work with the four forces diagram in Jobs to be Done. This looks at why people stay with or switch between products when it comes to their habits, anxieties, pushes, and pulls. I conducted about 15 interviews with non-users of competitors to understand a bit about why they used several different competitors and why they switched between them. It was super interesting to learn about people's anxieties and habits when it came to travel, and this helped us with creating some great messaging to help foster trust and make people look at us as a reliable platform. This helped a lot with reducing bounce rate.

Activation—How People Begin to Use Your Product/Service

It's all good if people find you, but that first interaction is key. After running my business for almost two years full-time now, I know how important it is to activate users and get them to take that first step with you.

- There are many ways to activate users, and it hugely depends on your product/service/organization, but when you think about activation, think about the primary conversion metrics that determine the success of certain channels and campaigns, rather than high-level or micro-conversions. This could look like a funnel:
- Someone comes to your website
- They see a value in your work
- They try a free trial or book a demo or sign up for a newsletter

Activation is the beginning of your relationship with the customer. Before this, they're anonymously researching your business and competitors before they take any specific action that allows you to begin directly engaging with them.

When it came to the travel company I was working at, we actually didn't have too many activation channels besides "booking a ticket," which is a conversion, but there were many steps prior to that conversion. So, I sat down with the product manager and we thought through some activation metrics:

- Increase number of newsletter signups
- Increase number of trip searches
- Increase first-time ticket purchases

This was tough for me to apply user research on because I wasn't sure exactly how to impact activation without going into full-blown conversion rate mode. I also wanted to test some of the other metrics outside of purchasing a first ticket, like just searching or signing up for our newsletter. So I came up with a few project ideas to try to help more with these metrics:

Walk-the-store interviews. I spoke to about 15 users who hadn't yet purchased with us to understand how they felt when they landed on our page and when they were searching for a trip. In this interview, they shared their screen and took me through their reactions and perceptions of what they said and what they were doing. It was very much qualitative and gave us some great feedback on confusing elements and components, as well as some glaring mistakes in the experience. This was to help searching for a trip.

1×1 interviews with first-time purchasers. I then wanted to dive into the first-time purchasing experience with users, so I screened for people who had recently purchased their first ticket with us. The reason behind this (and me not doing a usability test at this phase) was to understand the qualitative side of their experience. How had it been for them? What had been confusing? What had been missing? Another 15 people walked us step-by-step through their first experience, which gave rise to even more pain points and improvements we could make in the experience. This study hugely helped with increasing people who purchased their first ticket since we could streamline the experience for them.

I struggled quite a lot with newsletter sign-ups and ended up continuously surveying our audience to understand why they signed up for our newsletter. I knew it would be tough to understand why people didn't, so I decided to instead tap on what we had and could easily find out. Through understanding why people signed up and the value they got from it, we were better able to articulate that in our content. We also had an unsubscribe survey to understand why people unsubscribed from us to get improvements from that side. There were fewer responses to the unsubscribe survey, but we were still able to take some actions from it. This hugely helped with increasing newsletter sign-ups.

Retention—How People Come Back to and Continue to Use Your Product/Service

Ah, the bread and butter. We get people, but nothing is better than keeping people (as serial killer-ish as that sounds). Retention is king/queen/royalty because when people purchase multiple times from you, their value to you as an organization skyrockets.

There are many ways to measure retention, like:
- Customer lifetime value
- Churn rate
- Returning to your website
- Opening emails repeatedly
- Checking your product repeatedly in a given timeframe

Now, I'm just going to say it: churn is a tricky subject, which I will cover in its own full article because churn research gives me the heebie-jeebies.

Retention was another big hitter for us since our CAC was so high. We were getting customers, but we weren't retaining them, which was not helping grow our revenue. So we really focused on the following metrics:

- Increasing repeat order rate and customer lifetime value
- Increasing repeat searches
- Increasing the number of accounts made

Retention Research Is the Most Fun for Me, so I Really Leaned into These Projects and Ran

1×1 generative research interviews. Retention is all about creating a product that helps people achieve their goals more effectively and efficiently than competitors while alleviating any pain points to achieve the goal. To me, generative research interviews are a slam dunk in getting that information. I took these interviews away from the product and into the complexities of planning a trip from end-to-end, including their needs, goals, and pain points.

This study led to some key understandings of what our customers needed and led to an understanding of where we were failing to meet those needs and alleviate those pain points. We were able to pivot and change the product in ways to better align with users through things like easier price comparison, eco-friendliness of trips, and sharing trips with friends. This led to an increasing repeat order rate and customer lifetime value.

Usability testing (quantitative and qualitative). I first started with some qualitative usability testing, going through the process of booking a trip and asking people about their experience as they went through it. On its own, this study led to huge learnings on how we could improve the experience of our product through clunky filters, inability to link to trips, no favoriting, etc. Once the qualitative side was done and we made improvements, I went on to benchmark the current experience using task-based usability tests and measuring time on task and task success, as well as the Single Ease Questionnaire and System Usability Scale to gather more data on usability and satisfaction. We saw people struggle with basic tasks and were able to make critical fixes that helped increase the usability of our platform, which directly contributed to increasing repeat searches as well as increasing repeat order rate and customer lifetime value.

Accounts were really difficult to understand because, well, to be honest, we didn't really have any value in our accounts. You didn't need one for anything other than storing your data to use more easily again (e.g., storing credit card information). I deprioritized this and, unfortunately, wasn't able to get to it before I left the company. If I could have, I would have probably run some surveys to understand the current value of the account (if there was one) and also maybe running interviews with people using competitor accounts to understand the value they were getting from those.

Referral—How People Share Your Product/Service with Others (Positive and Negative Sentiments)

Referral is all about people spreading the word about your product/service with other people—either with a positive or negative sentiment. Referrals can be great because, if positive, they can almost feel like free customers. Referral metrics can look like this:

- Engaging with referral campaigns or emails
- Using a referral bonus or program within your program/service
- Leaving reviews

When we sat down to talk about referrals, we had some metrics we wanted to start tracking and thinking about:

- Increasing sign-ups through a bonus referral program (that we hadn't yet created)
- Increasing our review rating
- Increasing shared trips

Referrals were a very interesting area for me and one that I wish I had invested more time into, but we had a lot of other priorities at the time. I didn't have the bandwidth to dive in and learn how to conduct referral-related research as much as I wanted. However, I was able to sneak in some research when it came to referrals:

Data triangulation. We had quite a few reviews on our apps, and I decided it might be interesting (and fun, in a sadistic way) to go through these reviews and sort the data. I did this in a very manual way, combing through the qualitative reviews and creating a Miro board with categories and tags. I wish I had a photo for you, but I didn't manage to snag one, but the categories consisted of:

- Pain points/problems people were coming up against and complaining about
- Feature requests which I needed to dig into more deeply in future research because they were quite shallow
- Positives of what we were doing well that we could use more of

Within these major categories, I found patterns and trends and used the amount of reviews/mentions to help me weigh them for prioritization. For instance, a huge pain point people encountered in our system was a delayed email confirmation that ended up freaking people out that they had bought a ticket from a bad third-party app. We were able to fix this relatively quickly and easily. This project directly impacts our metric of increasing our review rating.

1×1 interviews and concept testing. Since one of our main metrics was about a referral program we hadn't yet created, I had to start from scratch on this project, which was quite exciting. I held about 15 1×1 interviews about referral programs where I asked really broad questions on people's previous experiences with referral programs both inside and outside of the travel sphere (previous experiences with products, even if they are outside of your industry, are much more reliable than asking future-based questions). We were able to understand some key pain points and the needs of our customers. With this, we built a concept of a referral program, which I then used to run a concept test with 12 more people. We evolved the concept with this feedback and eventually shipped the feature, which we then were able to finally apply our metric to increasing sign-ups through referrals.

Usability testing. We had heard from previous research done in one of our retention projects that sharing trips easily with others was an important feature for our users. We thought that increasing trip shares (especially with people that didn't have the app or an account) would be an interesting metric to track because it may boost people's motivation to use us. We conducted a usability test on the sharing trips functionality and then monitored its usage. We found, interestingly, that when users shared trips with others, they also shared their referral code, which helped us increase sharing trips and sign-ups through referrals simultaneously.

Revenue—How People Are Generative Revenue (against Costs) for Your Product/Service

Now, all of the above stack up into and impact revenue. If you aren't getting new customers and retaining them, likely you aren't making money. Revenue can be broken down into so many different ways, such as:

- Revenue that exceeds CAC
- Monthly recurring revenue
- Minimum revenue
- Breakeven revenue

There was no one project that I could attribute to in terms of revenue, but rather it was the accumulation of the multiple projects I did with this new intention of directly impacting business as much as I could.

Because I was able to impact the metrics we determined above, I could indirectly link my work back to any revenue shifts that we saw in the business.

ESTIMATING POTENTIAL IMPROVEMENTS ON PRODUCT METRICS

I've received quite a lot of questions on the topic of estimating potential product improvements based on insights. I talk a lot about how important it is to report insights in terms of outcomes like:

> Fixing the navigation could reduce drop-off rates by 20%, which would boost conversions by 15%.
>
> We need to redesign the onboarding flow to reduce friction, starting with a simpler first step. This will lead to a 10% increase in user retention.

Seems simple? Just put some interesting numbers in there, and huzzah, we have buy-in. But, honestly, I didn't start my career doing this, and it took me years to understand how to put numbers to my findings and insights.

However, when I started doing this, the change was transformative. People paid attention, listened, didn't zone out during reports, and even prioritized my work. Stakeholders need to understand the value of your insights. It's not enough to report findings; you need to show how implementing your recommendations will drive measurable outcomes.

By learning to estimate improvements, you become not just a researcher but a strategic partner in product development.

But how do we really do that? Especially if we are more geared toward words rather than numbers. Here is my step-by-step process for estimating improvements and relating numbers back to my research.

Step 1: Define the Target Metric

The first step is to identify the specific product metric your recommendation will impact. This ensures your research aligns with measurable outcomes.

How to define the metric:

1. Understand business goals: Meet with stakeholders to identify the metrics they prioritize. Common examples include:
   a. Conversion rates: Percentage of users who complete a desired action (e.g., sign-ups, purchases).
   b. Retention rates: The proportion of users returning over a defined period.
   c. Drop-off rates: Percentage of users abandoning a flow (e.g., onboarding).
   d. Engagement metrics: Time spent, number of sessions, or feature usage.
2. Align metrics with insights: Choose a metric directly related to the problem uncovered in your research. For example, if users abandon onboarding, focus on the onboarding completion rate.

3. Document the target metric: Write down the specific metric so you stay aligned during the estimation process. For example:
   a. Finding: Users drop off at Step 3 of onboarding due to a confusing form
   b. Metric: Onboarding completion rate

Step 2: Gather Baseline Data

To estimate an improvement, you need a clear understanding of the current state of the metric—this is your baseline.

How to collect baseline data:

- Access analytics: Use tools like Google Analytics, Mixpanel, or Amplitude to gather current metrics. If you don't have access, collaborate with your product or data teams and ask them how they measure analytics.
- Record key data points:
  - Current value: What is the current metric value? For example, a 60% onboarding completion rate.
  - Affected population: How many users does this metric represent? For example, 10,000 users go through onboarding monthly.
  - Segments: Are there specific groups (mobile users, international users) with different behaviors?
- Visualize the data: Create a chart or table summarizing baseline data for easy reference.

Step 3: Craft a Hypothesis

A hypothesis links your research insights to a measurable improvement. It includes three elements:

- The problem: What is causing the issue?
- The solution: What are you proposing to solve it?
- The expected outcome: What measurable improvement will result?

How to write a hypothesis:

1. Identify the problem. Use your research findings to articulate the issue:
   a. What's happening? Users drop off at Step 3 of onboarding.
   b. Why is it happening? The form has too many fields, causing friction.
2. Propose a solution. Define a specific, actionable recommendation tied to the problem. For example: Reduce the form fields from ten to five to simplify onboarding.

3. Estimate the improvement. This is the most challenging part for many researchers. Follow these steps:
   a. Use past data: If similar changes were made previously, analyze their impact. For example: Simplifying a checkout process in the past improved conversion rates by 8%.
   b. Leverage industry benchmarks: Research typical improvements for similar changes. For example: UX benchmarks show that reducing form fields can improve completion rates by 5%–15%. You can use the following places to research this information:
      i. Nielsen Norman Group (NNG)
      ii. Baymard Institute
      iii. Forrester Research:
      iv. Gartner
      v. Open Data Institute
      vi. Kaggle Datasets
      vii. ACM Digital Library
4. Analyze the room for improvement. Look at the size of the problem. If 40% of users drop off at Step 3, aim to reduce drop-offs by 10%–20%. Be conservative: Use a cautious estimate for initial predictions (e.g., 5%–10%).

Example hypothesis

Reducing form fields will reduce drop-offs by 10%–15%, increasing onboarding completion rates from 60% to 65%–70%

Step 4: Model the Potential Impact

Once you have a hypothesis, calculate the impact of your proposed change on the metric. This involves applying the improvement percentage to the baseline data.

How to calculate the impact:

- Identify the affected population.
- Determine the number of users impacted by the metric:
  - 10,000 users go through onboarding monthly
- Apply the improvement percentage. Use the formula:
  - Improved Metric = Baseline Metric * (1 + Improvement Percentage)

Example:

Baseline completion rate = 60%
Improvement estimate = 10%
60% * (1 + 0.10) = 66%

Quantify the Results

Calculate the number of additional users completing the flow: Additional Users = Total Users * Improvement Percentage
   Example:

10,000 users × 10% = 1,000 additional completions.

Translate into Business Value

If possible, calculate the financial or business impact. If each completion generates $20 in revenue:

1,000 * 20 = $20,000 additional monthly revenue

Step 5: Evaluate Your Hypothesis

Evaluating your estimate ensures your recommendation is grounded in reality. Use these methods to refine your predictions. You can do this through:

- Usability testing: Test your proposed changes with a small group of users in a controlled environment to observe how they interact with the new design or feature.
    - Create a prototype or mockup of the proposed solution.
    - Ask users to complete tasks using the new design and measure success rates, time on task, or satisfaction.
    - Compare results to the baseline behavior observed with the current design.
- Wizard of Oz testing: Simulate the new experience without building the full solution. The user interacts with what appears to be a functional system, but parts are manually operated behind the scenes.
    - Set up a partially functional prototype where manual effort substitutes for backend functionality.
    - Observe how users engage with the simulated change and gather feedback on their behavior and satisfaction.
- Split funnel analysis: Instead of comparing users in two distinct groups (as in A/B testing), analyze different stages of the user journey to identify where the proposed change would have the most significant impact.
    - Break down the user journey into smaller steps (e.g., Step 1: Account creation, Step 2: Onboarding completion).
    - Identify where drop-offs occur and use the data to test small changes in targeted areas of the funnel.

- Scenario modeling: Model the potential impact of your proposed solution by simulating changes in metrics based on user behavior patterns and historical data.
  - Use historical data to model "what if" scenarios for the change. For example: "If 20% of users who currently drop off at Step 3 continue instead, how would completion rates change?"
  - Compare modeled results to real-world observations after implementation.

Step 6: Communicate the Findings

Presenting your estimates clearly and persuasively is key to gaining stakeholder buy-in.

Start with the problem: "40% of users drop off during onboarding due to a complex form."

Propose the solution: "Reducing the form fields from 10 to 5 will simplify the process."

Share the estimated impact: "This could increase the onboarding completion rate from 60% to 66%, adding 1,000 new users per month and $20,000 in monthly revenue."

Impact Estimation Template

1. Step 1: Define the problem
   a. What's the issue? Example: 40% of users drop off at Step 3 of onboarding due to a complex form.
   b. What's the impact? Example: This results in a 60% onboarding completion rate and a loss of potential revenue.
2. Step 2: Proposed solution
   a. What's the change you're recommending? Example: Simplify Step 3 by reducing form fields from 10 to 5.
   b. Why does this solve the problem? Example: User feedback indicates that long forms are a primary pain point.
3. Step 3: Target metric
   a. What metric does this impact? Example: Onboarding completion rate.
4. Step 4: Baseline data.
   a. Current metric value: Example: 60% completion rate.
   b. Affected population: Example: 10,000 users start onboarding each month.
5. Step 5: Hypothesis
   a. Expected improvement range. Example: Reducing form fields will increase completion rates by 10%–15%.
   b. Data source/benchmarks for the estimate. Example: Historical data shows similar changes improved completion rates by 12%. Example: UX industry benchmarks indicate a range of 5%–15% for form simplification.

6. Step 6: Modeled impact
   a. New metric value: Example: 66%–69% completion rate (10%–15% improvement on 60%).
   b. Additional users completing onboarding: Example: 1,000–1,500 additional users monthly.
   c. Business impact: Example: If each completed onboarding generates $20 in revenue, this adds $20,000–$30,000 per month.
7. Step 7: Evaluation plan
   a. How will you evaluate the hypothesis?
      i. Example: Conduct usability testing with a prototype.
      ii. Example: Run a cohort analysis to track behavior over time.
8. Step 8: Next steps
   a. Develop a simplified prototype for testing.
      i. Evaluate the hypothesis.
      ii. Share results and adjust the estimate as needed.

Estimating potential improvements transforms your research from observation to actionable strategy. It allows you to connect user needs with business goals, ensuring your insights drive measurable change. By presenting clear, data-backed outcomes, you build trust with stakeholders and increase the likelihood of implementation. This practice not only amplifies the impact of your work but also positions you as a strategic partner in product development. Over time, this approach strengthens your credibility and helps you deliver meaningful results for both users and the business.

Try It!

Through this experience, the entire trajectory of my career shifted in such a positive way. I started thinking about projects not just with the user's goals in mind but also with the business too. It hugely accelerated my career to tie these knots together and show the value of user research through this lens, which stakeholders greatly appreciated.

I recommend starting with one of these letters/topics and going to a trusted colleague to talk through metrics and potential user research projects that could impact the metrics. This is hugely a brainstorming session at first, especially if you are new to metrics + UXR, so a trusted colleague who is open to talking through potential ideas and experimenting is key.

If you don't have any colleagues open to this discussion, try to brainstorm on your own (this is something I did for a while before I found trusted colleagues) and talk to other peers or join a community—you can check out my user research membership—to get feedback and ideas.

But, the first thing is to start with one of the letters and go from there in trying—you might not get it right the first time (I certainly didn't), but it is a great skill to practice and hone over time!

The most important part of creating a research process is to make it your own and contextualize it to your current experience. The time I see research practices fail is when someone tries to adopt a practice from another company, as if it will fit into a different environment. In my first role as a user researcher, I worked at a small business-to-business start-up. I spent hours Googling how to set up a research practice and, in the end, took IDEO's design research process. This was the most ideal formalized process I'd seen, and I wanted to make it work.

Unfortunately, copying and pasting IDEO's research framework into the small business-to-business company I worked at was truly a mess. The context of my organization was completely different. We had five users total and moved at breakneck speed, so we couldn't always sit for observation sessions before creating something to test. The process broke down, and I quickly realized that I couldn't simply overlay an idealized process over any environment. I had to take into consideration the constraints and nuances of my current context to create a practice that truly worked for my teams.

By shaping the research practice to the needs of your teams and organization, you are setting yourself and your research up for ample success. In this section, we will go through several exercises of reflecting on your current environment and then use that information to create a strategy and subsequent practice that is relevant to your organization.

PART TWO

Reflect on the Current State

4 Viewing Stakeholders as Users

If you had told me that one day I would enjoy stakeholder management, I would have laughed. Tears would have streamed down my face. I hated stakeholder management with every bone in my body. Why? Because I wasn't good at it and I fear what I'm not good at. With this reaction, I got angry and frustrated, often feeling helpless in my relationships with stakeholders. They just "didn't get it."

A lot of people who conduct user research have felt this way. You beg people to do the research, to get included in meetings, to see a roadmap or some sort of planning, to get wind of a feature release more than a few days before it's scheduled, to not base things off gut assumptions or shower ideas, to listen to what users said, especially if it goes against assumptions or hypotheses, and to see the importance and value in user research.

This begging game can take a toll on your mental health and emotional well-being. It can be exhausting for your role to be comprised of begging people to take you seriously. To not have your work valued or understood. It was a place I visited far too often, that made me consider being an interior designer, or a bookshop owner (still in the running, to be honest), a dog walker, or literally anything else besides a user researcher. I took it so personally that it nearly ruined my career—I got into a screaming match with a stakeholder in front of some very important people.

However, if you're wondering how to get stakeholders involved in your research process or care about your research, all is not lost. You are not alone, and there is something you can do.

It took me years before I had this shift in my mindset, like a key unlocking a hidden mystery that was in front of my face the whole time. The advice sounds simple, but I needed to hear it and repeat it to myself:

Stakeholders are our users.

Viewing my stakeholders as users changed many things for me, as it forced me to adjust the way I worked and interacted with them. We constantly tell our teams to focus on our users. Whenever they aren't sure about something, we tell them to ask users. Whenever they want to make decisions, we beg them to keep users in mind. We ask them to empathize with users. Yet, do we do this with stakeholders?

At various times in my career, I was upset and frustrated with my stakeholders. They wouldn't engage in research, or they didn't care about learning the correct way to engage with user research. I would try to get them to stop coming to me with a method in mind, and encourage them to come to me with questions. But repeatedly, they wanted to "do user testing to validate designs." When, in reality, they needed to test a concept.

I would spend hours on reports or deliverables, and no one seemed to care. At one point, when I was working with a low budget, I created my own repository from scratch. I got a few developer friends to help make it perfect. My stakeholders could not ignore research now because I had set them up for success. They didn't use the repository.

I spun in circles until I realized what I was doing. I created reports, personas, repositories, and even research projects, but these outcomes were mine. I made them based on the rules and best practices I had learned over the years. Years of Googling how to create a journey map, reading articles and books, and taking courses had culminated in me learning specific techniques. But, in a given moment, I couldn't tell you why certain information was the best to put in a persona, just that it was.

And that was the key for me. I'd committed the acts we begged teams not to do. I had ignored my users. I didn't think about their needs, goals, pain points, or motivations. Instead, I thought about what I was taught to do. And I made so many assumptions about what was the right way of doing things.

But our stakeholders are our users, and it is crucial to think about them in this way. If we don't, we risk missing the mark on our deliverables, and potentially our entire process. It's the equivalent of asking a designer to create something without any user feedback. And that has to change.

HOW TO SHIFT YOUR MINDSET

Shifting your mindset into thinking of your stakeholders as users, and your research as their product, takes time and effort, but it is well worth it. You will be able to take a step back from research, to truly understand your stakeholders, and to create studies that they will naturally care about. Here's how you can start working like this.

Empathize with Stakeholders

The first step is to begin with empathizing with your stakeholders, similar to how you might empathize with users. Often, stakeholders are left out of a researcher's process. You ask yourself, "How should I structure this report?" or "What information should I include in this deliverable?" Stakeholders are using those reports, deliverables, and all other research products, but they are rarely consulted.

If you don't understand your stakeholders, how do you create an experience for them that aligns with their needs and goals and alleviates their pain points? The best way to start is to put your research hat on and step into your role as a user researcher, looking internally at your teams and stakeholders. And what better way to empathize with your stakeholders, than to conduct a one-on-one interview with them, similar to how you might with a user.

Set up 60-minute one-on-one sessions with each stakeholder you want to learn more about. When you do this, explain that you want to understand more about their role, goals, and previous experience with user research. And then, go forth and research! Keep an open mind during these sessions, make sure to not get defensive if they don't find user research compelling, and truly look at them through a lens of curiosity.

Stakeholder Interviews

Whenever you go into any session, it is important to have a clear goal, outcomes, and a script. Of course, goals vary depending on what information you need from stakeholders, but some common goals for these stakeholder interviews are:

- understanding stakeholder needs when it comes to user research (as well as their learning needs and how they digest information);
- identifying the pain points they have in their team, as well as with user research;
- discovering the goals they have for themselves and their teams;
- uncovering their previous experiences (and anxieties) with user research;
- understanding their mental model about user research and how they currently interact with user research and deliverables.

And some outcomes include:

- having a better understanding of what stakeholders are working on so that I can best align my work to support them (and show them the value of user research);
- understanding their pain points about user research so that I can ensure the projects I pitch help ease those pain points and anxieties;
- creating and sharing a user research process that makes sense to me as well as to my stakeholders so that we are aligned and reduce any barriers to entry;
- empathizing with them in understanding how they interact with user research to make it the best possible experience.

Whenever you reach out to stakeholders to book this session, you can share this short blurb for context:

> I would love to take this hour to understand more about your role, your goals for yourself and team, as well as your previous experience with user research and your current experience with our research process. Think of this as a user interview, except this time you are the user!

Conduct the Interviews

There is something slightly easier about user interviews because, theoretically, you are likely never going to see the participant again. Or, at least for the most part, you aren't working with them day-to-day (unless you are conducting a lot of internal/organizational research). With stakeholder interviews, it can be tricky because sometimes they won't want to share information that hurts your feelings. So, you have to do your best to remain as objective as possible and remind them of this. Your introduction can call this out and reassure them that you are really there to learn and improve with their feedback and can't do it without their honest thoughts!

Below is an example of a script you can use to guide your stakeholder interviews.

> I'd love to chat today about your current goals for yourself and team, as well as any needs you have for user research that come to your mind. Additionally, I want to hear about any pain points you have with user research, based on your previous experience as well as our current process and approach. I know this might be tough to share, but I really appreciate your honest feedback because that is the only way we can improve and make this as seamless an experience for you as possible! My outcome is to truly understand your experiences and thoughts, so please feel free to share – you won't hurt my feelings.

In terms of the interview questions, you can be a bit more leading in your questions and even ask some future-based questions than you might in a formal user interview. However, whenever you can, try to follow open-ended question techniques! I organize my questions via my goals, so my script could look something like:

Goals, needs, and pain point questions

- What are your main goals day-to-day? For this quarter? Beyond?
- What would you like to achieve yourself?
- What are some metrics/OKRs that you would like to improve? Why?
- What would the ideal outcome be by the end of this quarter? The end of the year?
- What areas are you struggling with when it comes to achieving these goals?
- What are some of your ideas to achieve these goals/OKRs/metrics?
- What are generally some areas in the process that you struggle with? How would you improve this?

Previous experience with UX research questions

- If I asked you to define user research for me, how would you explain it?
- Have you ever worked with a user researcher before? If yes, tell me about the experience.
- How do you feel about user research?
- Tell me what happened the last time you did user research.
- Tell me about a time when research went poorly. What happened? How would you improve it?

- What are the most significant barriers you feel to conducting or including user research?
- How could we improve our relationship?
- How could you imagine user research helping you with (the goals, needs, and pain points mentioned above)?

Analyze the Interviews

Just like with any other user research project, analyzing the information makes it actionable! You can create an affinity diagram (you can use it as a jumping-off point) for each stakeholder, categorizing each space with goals, needs, pain points, previous experiences, and process feedback.

As an example, I'm working with a product manager on the retention team at a meal kit subscription company. The first thing I do is my stakeholder interview and affinity diagram:

You can then identify any themes across stakeholders to highlight things like:

- where I can make improvements in the user research process;
- pain points that stakeholders are having that I can address;
- research needs or goals that span different teams, which could become holistic and impactful research projects.

This is the first step in beginning to work with and align better with your stakeholders. And it leads perfectly into the next step. Please, try not to skip these interviews, as they give us the context we need to be successful!

Whether you have been at your organization for a week, six months, or two years, it is never too late to conduct stakeholder interviews and go through this process!

Align Your Work with Stakeholders' Needs and Goals

Now that you have all this information from stakeholders, you can get to work in aligning with them so that you are doing your most impactful and valuable work. Here are the steps to use the information you found to better collaborate with your stakeholders.

Form Potential Research Ideas Based on Your Affinity Diagram

Now that you have all this amazing data, it's time to take some ideas and make them concrete. Through this affinity diagram, there is information on stakeholders' needs and goals for their teams. The most impactful research you can do (and the easiest way to show value to teams) is if you conduct research that immediately and positively impacts stakeholders' needs and goals.

Let's take a look at the earlier example:

From this information, my stakeholder needs to understand:
1. Why people are canceling their boxes.
2. What pain points or unmet needs are coming up.
3. How to alleviate those unmet needs or pain points.
4. What is missing or confusing about the experience.

This gives me some potential ideas for user research that I can jot down. If you want, at this step, to go one step further, you can already start to prioritize the potential project ideas. Whenever you prioritize, you can use an impact and effort matrix, which looks at how much impact the research project would have on the team/organization and how much effort the end-to-end project would take.

Additionally, you can look across stakeholders to identify similar themes/patterns in needs to think through some potential cross-functional research that would positively impact multiple teams!

Brainstorm Ways to Address Stakeholders' Pain Points or Anxieties

Before running straight into a research plan, it's essential to look into what their pain points or anxieties surrounding research are. If you tackle these up front, you are more likely to ease stakeholders' minds and get buy-in for your research. I always say that transparency and empathy are key, so addressing pain points head-on is super-effective.

Going back to the example:

To address these anxieties, I would:
1. Ensure the goals of the research address the business problem and metrics.
2. Make sure we are getting information that can help make decisions to move the metrics further.
3. Use a mixed-methods approach to help with small sample size anxiety.
4. Find an approach that delivers value quickly (even if it's only part of the study).

Understand Stakeholders' Overarching Needs and Learning Style to Choose a Deliverable

Now on to the next step, which looks at diving a bit deeper into a particular project. At this stage, you can float a potential research idea that stakeholders mentioned and that you think would be a really impactful project. If you did your prioritization exercise above, then you can use the most prioritized projects to get a bit more information. If you haven't already prioritized your ideas, now is a great time to do so.

Once you pick 1–2 projects, you need to get a slightly deeper understanding of what type of information the stakeholder needs, and the decisions they are trying to make. For this step, you can simply send them the following prompt to fill out:

> I need (information needed) to answer (questions they have) by (x timeline) in order to make (the decisions they need to make).

If you want to do this in a more interview-style format, you can use the following questions:

- What type of information do you need at the end of the project?
- What decisions do you want to be able to make?
- What are the top three questions you need answered?
- In which ways do you best digest information?
- How could you imagine seeing these results?

Let's look at a quick example of answers to these questions and potential outcomes:

> This information will really help you with going deeper into the goals of a project, the timeline, and the type of deliverable that might be best.
> Once you have this information, it is time to look at ways you can improve the current research process, and include those in the research plan that you will pitch to your stakeholder.

Brainstorm Ways to Improve the Current Process

Based on the feedback you've already gathered, you might be ready to create a research project plan to pitch to your stakeholder. However, before you do that, I recommend brainstorming ideas and ways to improve the current process. Refer back to the interview you did with your stakeholder to understand the feedback they gave you on the current research process. Some improvements might include:

- including an intake form to get research requests easily in one place and reduce meetings;
- creating transparency by having a clear prioritization process;
- reducing barriers by including a sign-up sheet for each project;
- making sure to include research plans in your project as an easy way to pitch your research plan (or roadmap) based on their goals and needs.

Once you have all the above information, it's time to share a research plan or a roadmap based on the goals and needs you identified. This research plan or roadmap can be for an individual stakeholder, as well as a group of stakeholders, if you've identified cross-functional research projects.

Let's look at an example from the project above:

Research Plan
Goals:
- understand the top reasons people cancel their box after the discount period;
- uncover the decision-making process of box cancelation after the discount period;
- identify the major pain points with the box before cancelation during the discount period.

Success metrics: Fewer cancelations after the discount period & more boxes/customer.
Methods: Survey + 1×1 interviews.
Recruitment:
- Survey: 150 people who recently canceled after a discount period ended + 150 who are currently in the discount period.
- 1×1 interviews: 15 people who recently canceled after the discount period.

Deliverable: Report with visuals + recommendations to make changes based on pain points & needs.
Next steps: Ideation workshop to solutionize the pain points.
Outcome: Prototypes and ideas to test with users.
Timeline: 4–5 weeks (survey results ready in 1.5 weeks).

This research plan addresses:

- slow research anxiety by including a quantitative component that gets us some quick intermediate insights;
- small sample size worry by including a survey;
- directly impact business and team goals through the goals and ideation session to immediately create solutions;
- the way people digest the research by including a few different types of visualization in the report.

Taking the information you learned and using that to curate your research plan will get you much more buy-in from stakeholders because you will have addressed their anxieties as well as highlighted the direct impact research can have on their goals and needs!

Instead of a research plan, you can put together a roadmap of various projects, which I will touch on later in this book.

How to Work with Stakeholders that "Don't Care"

You usually get into user research because you love talking to people, trying to understand them, bringing data together, and sharing information with others. However, it isn't everyone's cup of tea. People who do research are specialists, and not every stakeholder will love your specialty. The best you can do is show them how you can help support them. Because even if they don't love user research, they can appreciate it.

It took me up to eight months to shift some relationships with stakeholders. It can take three to six months to change these relationships and gain trust. Keep at it and be consistent—building trust can take a lot of time!

If your stakeholders still don't care or won't talk to you, here are some things you can do to be effective in your role WHILE building your case studies:

- Do product-team agnostic research. These types of projects are those you can do without needing to get buy-in or concrete information from the team. They include studies on big topics such as personas or journey maps. You don't necessarily need to talk to your teams about these projects, and they can still be impactful to the entire organization.
- Look into data analytics, past research, or customer support to identify research projects. Specifically, look into areas of the product that aren't performing well, such as places where you see a high drop-off or bounce rate. Or pull through tickets with pain points and find patterns among them. These pieces of data can help you understand where you could research more to deeply understand potential problems and pain points.
- Work with any champions you can. Even if it means not working across multiple departments or doing the organizational research that you want, starting with people that care about your work is helpful. I've had to start small, with one or two teams, and build "case studies" within the organization before other teams became interested in how I could help them.
- Do user research for other departments. There are so many departments that can benefit from user research, such as marketing. If you are struggling to work with your product teams, reach out to other colleagues you could support through your research skills, and use that as a jumping-off point to prove the value.

And, once you have the space to apply and interview at other companies, do so!! You deserve to be valued!

5 Assess the Current User Research Maturity

Thinking about and assessing the quality and effectiveness of user research at your current company is critical. Starting from where you are is one way to set yourself up for the most success as possible. Knowing the current maturity level of your organization will help you make effective decisions on what practices or processes might work for your current context, rather than trying everything at once and feeling as though it has all failed (been there, done that).

Rather than trying something that wouldn't work in the context of your organization, you are meeting people where they are. You are taking advantage of this knowledge by making smart decisions and bringing in relevant processes, rather than trying the "square peg, round hole" approach.

It can also feel overwhelming when trying to understand where to start when it comes to building a research practice. Assessing the current user research maturity at your organization can help you prioritize what you will work on first, setting the foundation for a successful practice.

Let's dive in!

What Is User Experience Maturity?

The concept of User Experience maturity essentially gauges how proficient your organization is in handling UX and user research practices. It's a valuable exercise to assess both the broader UX maturity and the specific level of user research maturity. I highly recommend evaluating both aspects. Fortunately, some dedicated researchers have delved into this space and created valuable resources for you to leverage.

UX maturity models serve as a roadmap to comprehend the role of user research within a company. They help identify whether user research is non-existent, merely a tool to validate design choices, a means to unearth new insights, a method for innovation, or a combination of these factors. Such models offer a structured framework, enabling you to ascertain your current position on the user research maturity scale and the steps required to progress.

In general, the more user research mature a company is, the smoother the integration of user research into its organizational processes becomes. So, what benefits can evaluating user research maturity bring to your organization? Here are several compelling reasons:

- Greater Understanding of User Research Buy-In: Assessing your position within a UXR maturity model provides insight into how much support and recognition user research currently enjoys within your organization.
- Actionable Insights: It offers specific action items for user researchers to steer the company toward a more user-centric approach.
- Improved Buy-In: By understanding your organization's maturity level, you can tailor your approach to user research in a way that's most suitable and effective for your specific context.
- Clarity: It answers important questions like, "Am I on the right track?" or "What should I do next?"
- Direction: It shows you what you can impact right away to feel a tangible benefit.

When I initially assessed UXR maturity in my organization, it compelled me to pause and reflect. While I had ambitions for advanced generative research on complex topics, I had to ask whether we were ready for that. What foundational steps were necessary? Rather than rushing ahead impatiently, I carefully considered the groundwork required to ensure our organization's future success. This exercise can be enlightening and immensely helpful in determining the most suitable starting point for your particular circumstances.

1. Now, let's explore how to evaluate user research maturity. UX maturity models typically feature five or six different levels, depending on the resource. Here are the most commonly encountered stages of UX research maturity:
    1. Absence/Unawareness of UX Research: The organization is unaware of user research and its value. There's a lack of processes and engagement in user research.
    2. UX Research Awareness: Ad Hoc Research: The organization is aware of user research but misunderstands its purpose. It's often employed to validate changes or purely for cosmetic enhancements. Ad hoc research requests typically arise late in the development pipeline.
    3. Adoption of UX Research into Projects: User research enters projects earlier than in the previous stage and starts becoming an integral part of the development cycle (e.g., agile).
    4. Maturing UX Research into an Organizational Focus: User research becomes embedded in the organizational process. Teams and stakeholders embrace it and conduct research when necessary.
    5. Integrated UX Research Across Strategy: User research transcends minor aesthetic changes; it informs product strategy and other strategies across the organization (e.g., marketing, account management, etc.).

6. Complete UX Research Culture: Every User Researcher's Dream: The entire company prioritizes research and is driven by a profound need to understand users. UX is an intrinsic part of the organization's thought processes at all levels.

CASE STUDY: USER RESEARCH MATURITY MODEL AT fromAtoB

For this organization, we were between a laggard and early user research maturity, which is certainly where I didn't want us to be since user research was extremely limited in its potential for influence.

With this map, I listed all the obstacles we were facing when it came to our low level of research maturity and then divided the hurdles and opportunity areas into three areas: operational, organizational, and strategic.

Operational hurdles
Goal: Improve day-to-day user research

- no external testing;
- small budget;
- long recruitment process;
- no easy GDPR consent tools;
- few tools for scheduling, recruitment, synthesis;
- no concept of UX data tracking.

Organizational hurdles
Goal: Ingrain user research into the organization

- little understanding of user research;
- UX (and user research) siloed from the organization;
- little leadership buy-in (e.g., takes too long, costs too much);
- no shared concepts and understanding of users (e.g., personas, journey maps).

Strategic hurdles
Goal: Move from tactical user research to influencing product strategy

- no discovery research;
- no prioritization from senior leadership.

I decided on the following steps to advance the user research maturity at the organization:

1. Move in the direction of discovery research. I ran generative research studies regularly, but there was a lot more work I needed to do in terms of education and how to work alongside our squads with this discovery research.

2. Get a larger budget. Without a larger budget, I had very little leeway in terms of tools to help with recruitment, consent, and tracking data. I set to figuring out how to price out exactly what I needed and gave my manager two options to work with.
3. Start beta and pilot programs as soon as we have new concepts applicable to these types of methodologies.
4. Diversify our methodologies to more easily collect data (e.g., include unmoderated testing to speed up feedback-gathering).
5. Increase our data collection and analytics game regarding user research metrics (such as time on task and task success).
6. Create outputs that foster shared understanding throughout the team, such as personas, user journeys, user scenarios, and comic storyboards.
7. Integrate research throughout all the different departments (e.g., marketing, customer support).
8. Create more frameworks and processes across user research, especially in our agile development.

I immediately got to work on these specific action items and kept the hurdles in the back of my mind.

Although I already had an idea that this was necessary to level up user research, it was undoubtedly helpful to map out where we currently were on a pre-defined model, where I could easily see the next steps. Especially in times of confusion or when you hit the "what do I fix next" wall, UXR maturity models are a crucial partner for getting you clarity and inciting action.

PART THREE

Set Up Operations and a Framework

Set Up Core Research Operations

6

Research operations can take a lot of your time, so much so that there is a role dedicated to setting up and maintaining these operations. Now, typically, people who are conducting user research have to set up these operations on their own. You might not have a ResearchOps person available in your organization to help you with this.

If you do, I highly recommend working closely with that individual so you can learn ResearchOps from an expert. If you don't, it's time to dig in and set up your core research operations. And, even if you don't have an expert on your side, I promise you can do it! It's great practice to learn how to set up research operations from scratch. It will give you the foundation necessary for you to succeed and excel as a user researcher and give you the space to do more of what you love: actual research.

If you set this up from the get-go, or whenever you start reading this book, it will make your role a lot easier. You are paving the way for yourself, others at your organization, as well as future hires, to be successful.

RESEARCH PLANS

In my first role as a user researcher, I had little concept of planning. My colleagues and I would talk about research that needed to be done, and I would go and do it. At the time, I didn't have the capacity to question why we were doing specific projects, asking certain questions, or what the outcomes were supposed to be.

My main downfall was perfectionism. I wanted to appear like I was good at my job and that I knew everything. We have to survey our users to determine what about our app was unintuitive? Sure thing! We have to do discovery research to verify our assumptions? Can do!

I didn't know how to structure a goal—trust me, searching for user research goals and examples of them ten years ago led to absolutely nothing. The Interwebs was not my friend back then. I didn't know what to question, let alone how to respond to my stakeholders when they had questions. What did this lead to?

- Lack of clarity on what I was trying to research (either too broad or narrow in scope), which made it a nightmare to figure out appropriate methodologies and which questions to ask.
- Mismatched expectations on what colleagues got as outcomes of the research project.
- Inability to focus during the research because I was unsure about what topics I needed to cover or what I could skip.
- Little alignment on why we were doing the research project and what would make it successful in the end.

What this list leads to is one word: disappointment. I don't know about you, but to me nothing is worse than disappointing my team. And I've also found that with disappointment comes skepticism. If research isn't bringing value, do we need to do it? What's the point? That's the last thing I wanted. So, I vowed to do better and, over time, built a research plan that I now use as a starting point (yes, still, to this day!) for my research projects.

WHAT IS A USER RESEARCH PLAN?

A user research plan is a document that lists the different parts of the research project, including why the research is happening and the research outcomes. They give you and the team an amazing overview of the research project, and remind people exactly what the project is about, which greatly helps with scope.

The best part of a research plan is aligning people into a shared understanding so that everyone's expectations are properly set up. Expectations are key when it comes to user research. If a stakeholder is expecting that they will get a journey map out of a research project and we come to them with a written report, it won't be the best of times. Or, if a stakeholder expects deep insights and we conduct a survey, there will be a huge mismatch in the outcome.

A research plan is a forcing function (in the best sense possible) to get everyone's thoughts and expectations of a research project out on paper, giving you, the researcher, clarity on how to best navigate the project for the necessary outcomes.

WHY ARE USER RESEARCH PLANS SO IMPORTANT?

When it comes to documentation or doing things that are slightly more work, I say they are important for two main reasons:

1. Aligning people within the organization.
2. A great document to reference in your case studies.

For a while, the documentation didn't feel like enough of a reason to me, but when I got laid off, had the rug pulled out from me, and was scrambling to understand two years of work, research plans were a lifesaver.

Research plans allow you to articulate your thought process and are a great first draft for a case study. They enable you to go back and review what you did, the impact you had, and remember with more detail the projects you completed. As I said, this is hugely important for job seeking. So, if documentation and alignment aren't enough, do it for your future self!

Outside of that, we've already spoken a bit about why research plans are so important, but just to reiterate, they are necessary alignment documentation that properly manages expectations.

When I started to use research plans in my projects, it was like night and day. I felt so much more confident in my decision-making and my thought process. Since I had information from my stakeholders, I could make much more informed decisions. I had so much more direction to create solid research goals, choose a methodology, and write questions that got the relevant information. Not only that, but my stakeholders, overall, were so much more satisfied with my research. Because we took the time to align on the expectations and outcomes of the research, I got them the information they needed to make the decisions they were originally stuck on.

Among those, research plans are critical to the success of a project because they:

- give you and the team focus on the research project and keep the research on track when scope creep occurs;
- serve as a fantastic point of reference for future research projects (and for new people coming into the organization);
- help ensure you aren't doing the same research projects repeatedly;
- provide you with the information you need to do the most effective and efficient research you can for the team;
- allow everyone to give their thoughts on the research project to invite collaboration;
- they can give you some great case studies.

WHEN TO USE RESEARCH PLANS

Research plans are a fantastic way to start any research project. I truly use them still, to this day, to plan out research, whether that's in a full-time role or as a contractor. In the most recent project I've run, I started right from a research plan.

I highly recommend starting every user research project with a research plan. This means I open up a new research plan document whenever someone comes to me with a research idea through:

- email
- Slack

- coming to my desk
- a post-it note
- a meeting follow-up
- a proactive research project comes to my head
- a next step after a research project emerges.

HOW TO PUT A RESEARCH PLAN TOGETHER

Now that we've talked about the amazingness of a research plan, how do you put one together? Here are the components I include in each of my research plans:

- the background of the research project, including relevant business key performance indicators and potential impact
- the internal stakeholders involved
- hypotheses and assumptions you and the team have
- a research statement and goals
- success criteria of the project
- the methodology
- user experience metrics, if applicable
- participants and the recruitment process
- deliverables and next steps from the project
- an approximate timeline of the project
- a discussion guide/usability task script
- resources, such as links to any other documentation.

Let's dive into each of these sections to get a clear understanding of what they mean and why they are important.

PROJECT BACKGROUND

In this section, you are talking about how the project came to be and why it is an important project to tackle at this moment. I like to talk about it from both the business and the user's point of view, because both are extremely important for user research. We need to be aligned with the business and the user. When you talk through the importance of the project, address how it could help users, such as uncovering their unmet needs or pain points, as well as what could be impacted on the team, product, and organizational level.

INTERNAL STAKEHOLDERS INVOLVED

For this part, you list who is involved in the project. If you want to go a step further, you could apply the RACI model to this section, which I really like to do. RACI stands for:

- Responsible: who is directly responsible for successfully completing a project task;
- Accountable: the person with final authority over the successful completion of the specific task or deliverable;
- Consulted: someone with unique insights the team will consult;
- Informed: someone who isn't directly involved, but you should keep up to speed with the progress.

This model is super because it is very clear what role each person plays and what they can expect regarding the effort they need to put in for the research project. If you are having a hard time establishing these roles, I recommend playing some delegation poker.

HYPOTHESES AND ASSUMPTIONS

This area is all for the hypotheses and assumptions you, the team, and the wider organization have about this particular project.

- Hypotheses are ideas or concepts we are unsure about that we're looking to understand better.
- Assumptions are ideas or concepts we believe are true.

I like to highlight these separately because they are hugely different from each other—when it comes down to it, assumptions can be dangerous because they are things we believe are true, whereas we are typically more open to hypotheses.

Writing these down is a great moment to challenge stakeholders' thoughts and a wonderful information-gathering moment for researchers. Being aware of people's hypotheses and assumptions can help you navigate research to better understand and evaluate them. Remember, in user research, we never validate assumptions or hypotheses because we can't operate on large enough sample sizes. Instead, we are exploring and evaluating these hypotheses and assumptions.

RESEARCH STATEMENT AND GOALS

This section gets into the actual research information and what we are trying to understand and achieve. A research statement is what we are trying to learn about users at a high level. Here is a model you can use:

> We want to better understand how users [think about/make decisions on/interact with] [subject of research/product] in order to [create/improve] [product/website/app/service].

This statement gives one or two sentences that describe what the overarching project is about. It is important to solidify this statement because it helps you to create your research goals.

Now, when it comes down to it, I believe the most important thing in a research project is research goals. If you decide to take only one thing from this article, take the goals! Research goals directly relate to your research statement in the sense that they are the more in-depth areas we want to explore in our research statement that will help us answer what we are trying to learn. Our research goals should address what we want to learn and how we are going to study the research statement.

These goals are the things we want to be able to gather information about by the end of the study. They aren't posed as questions, but we want to be able to "answer" them in the sense of getting enough data to feel comfortable making decisions. Below are some models you can use for creating research goals.

Common generative research goals:

- Discover people's current processes/decision-making about [research subject] and how they feel about the overall experience.
- Learn about people's current pain points, frustrations, and barriers about [current process/current tools] and how they would improve it.
- Understand what [research subject] means to people (how they define it) and why it is important to them.

Common evaluative research goals:

- Evaluate how people are using a [product/website/app/service].
- Evaluate how people are currently interacting with a [product/website/app/service].
- Uncover the current tools people are using to [achieve goal] and their experience with those tools. Uncover how they would improve those tools.

6 • Set Up Core Research Operations   73

These definitely aren't all the goals you could have, but they can give you a structure and a jumping-off point for writing your research goals. If you're having a hard time coming up with goals, you can ask yourself these questions:

- What do we want to learn about [research topic]?
- What type of experiences do we want to learn about?
- What information do we want at the end of the study?
- What decisions are we trying to make by the end of the study and what can help us make those decisions more confidently?

I recommend, for each study, having no more than three goals. I've found that going over three goals increases the scope and makes it hard to get in-depth information on each goal.

SUCCESS CRITERIA

For a while, I didn't include success criteria in my research plans because I wasn't always sure how to apply them to user research. However, they are extremely important to consider because they help you determine the success of the project. This success criterion doesn't have to do with things like UX metrics (e.g., task success) or the product necessarily, but rather looks at how you would deem the project as a success by the end.

Ideally, your success criteria should be measurable and should relate back to your research goals. A great question to ask is, "What would determine this research project a success in the end?"

The answer could be one of the following:

- Identified and clearly articulated the top five pain points.
- Discovered the top three most frustrating moments of users.
- Held three ideation workshops.

For this part, really think about what would make you and your team sit at the end of a project and say, "That was a success."

METHODOLOGY

Your methodology (or methodologies) should enable you to get the information for your research statement and goals in the most effective and efficient way. You can also speak here about different phases of research. For example, you might start with one method and follow up with another in a different phase. This helps the team understand how you are going to get the necessary information from users.

UX METRICS

If you are conducting a quantitative study, such as a quantitative usability test, tree testing, or first-click test, you will have metrics you are trying to track. In this section, list out the metrics you will track for the study, such as:

- time on task
- task success
- number of errors
- SEQ (Single Ease Questionnaire)/UMUX (Usability Metric for User Experience).

PARTICIPANTS AND RECRUITMENT

Once you understand the information you need from your study, it's time to write about the people you need to gather that information from. Recruiting the right participants makes or breaks a research study. Using a screener survey is one of the best ways to ensure you are intentionally getting the right participants, who can give you the exact information you need to accomplish your study's goals.

- For this process, the first step is brainstorming the criteria your participants must have to answer your study goals. You can do this by asking yourself a few different questions:
- What are the questions your users have to answer to get you meaningful information?
- What gaps in knowledge do you have that you need your participants to fill in?
- What behaviors do you need to understand more?
- What habits are you trying to target?
- What are the goals the user is trying to accomplish?

You can answer these questions directly in the research plan and then link out to a separate screener survey. In this section, I also recommend writing through your actual recruitment process, including:

- how many people you will recruit (don't forget to overrecruit, just in case!);
- how you will recruit them, and what tools you will use;

- will the sessions be remote or in-person;
- how long each session will be;
- any participant demographics;
- incentive amounts;
- a link to the screener survey.

DELIVERABLES/OUTCOMES AND NEXT STEPS

In this part of the plan, talk through the deliverables or outcomes you expect from the research. Sometimes, it is easier for stakeholders to start with what they want from the research and to reverse-engineer from here. So, there have been times when I started the research plan from this section.

However, it is important in this section to talk about why that particular deliverable or outcome makes sense for the project. So, try not just to list deliverables, but rather also explain why that deliverable was chosen.

Since a research plan is a continuously evolving document, I always return to it to add the next steps. I usually do this after the research, but if you have an inkling that you might need to follow up with some other research, it's good to put that in ahead of time. You can also talk through workshops you will run after the research is complete.

APPROXIMATE TIMELINE

Everyone cares about time and how long something will take, so I always put in approximate timelines as soon as I can to help ensure expectations are aligned. The last thing I want is for a stakeholder to come to me, expecting the research to be done, when we still have two weeks. In the timeline, I include each part of the research process, such as:

- planning and scoping;
- recruitment;
- conducting research;
- analyzing and synthesizing;
- report-building;
- share-outs;
- workshops.

I always tend to add 1–2 weeks of buffer time, just in case. I'd much rather deliver something early than late.

DISCUSSION GUIDE/TASK SCRIPT

This section is optional in the sense that you can have it in a separate document. I like to keep it together because it's easier to track and get feedback on one longer document. For this, you are writing down your discussion guide, task script, or whatever form of questions you are going to ask the participant.

RESOURCES

In this section, you are keeping track of all the different resources relevant to the project, which can be anything like:

- intake document
- screener survey
- raw data (e.g., videos, notes)
- synthesis board
- report
- other relevant studies or previous research that's been done.

This is especially helpful for people who might not have been directly involved in the project, or new people joining the organization who want to get more information.

BRINGING IT TOGETHER

As you can see, there is a lot of information in a research plan, which is why those one-sentence research requests wouldn't do and why an intake process can make your life so much easier. When I started, it took me hours (days, really) to put together a research plan because it was new, and I was still learning. With practice (and time), I can now put one together more quickly. Sometimes it can be tempting to skip the plan, but I recommend sticking to it, not only for the team but for yourself!

HOW TO INVOLVE OTHERS IN THE PROCESS

There are two ways to complete a research plan: on your own or with stakeholders. I filled out a lot of research plans independently when I was just beginning at certain organizations or when I didn't have that much stakeholder buy-in. It's the less ideal version, but it is a realistic one. Sometimes people won't be interested in your research plans, and that's okay. Remember, you aren't only documenting this important information for others but also for yourself.

If you are able to include stakeholders in the process, yay! There are a few ways you can go about doing this:

1. Filling out the research plan alone to the best of your ability (ideally based on an intake document) and then sending it to them to get asynchronous comments.
2. Inviting them to a meeting to review it and talk through feedback.
3. Filling out the research plan together in a meeting and then asking for comments/feedback after people have let the information sink in.

Any of these are fine. The third one takes more time, but it does allow for more educational moments, and I've tended to use this approach when first introducing research plans into an organization so that stakeholders understand them better. Over time, I even got to the point where stakeholders were able to fill out their own research plans for simple projects and send them to me to review—it was awesome!

Examples

Generative Research Plan Example

Project Background

The search team was approached by senior management, who wants navigational search to be made a priority in the Merchant Portal. There isn't much understanding of what users think of search functionality, how they would use it, or the level of impact search would bring to the user's experience. We want to delve deeper to uncover how implementing navigational search would impact the business and users. Business objectives include:

- increased time spent on the platform;
- increased retention (we know search is a major pain point).

Internal Stakeholders

- Responsible: Nikki—UX Researcher, Richard—UX Designer, Heather—Product Manager.
- Accountable: Nikki, UX Researcher
- Consulted: Heather—Product Manager, Karen—Dir. of Product, Curtis—Engineer
- Informed: Karen—Dir. of Product, Trevor—CPO

HYPOTHESES AND ASSUMPTIONS

Hypotheses

Search will help users navigate through the Merchant Portal and help them get through their tasks and goals more effectively and efficiently.

Our Assumptions Included

1. search is the most important thing to focus on right now;
2. users need a search functionality to properly navigate the Merchant Portal.

Research Statement and Goals

Research statement: We want to understand better how users currently find content through the Merchant Portal in order to understand how to improve the experience for them (through a search functionality or otherwise).

Goals

- discover how users currently search through content within the Merchant Portal;
- uncover users' pain points when it comes to finding content within the Merchant Portal;
- identify how users think about search and their unmet needs when it comes to finding content within the Merchant Portal.

Success Criteria

This project will be successful if we are able to:

- Identify and clearly articulate the top three pain points of users when it comes to finding content within the Merchant Portal.
- Uncover and clearly articulate the top three unmet needs when it comes to finding content within the Merchant Portal.

- Have enough information to help us create 2–3 designs to test with users in follow-up research.
- Run an ideation workshop to create design ideas.

Methodology

- 1×1 interviews to uncover the current experience of users with finding content on the platform. Within this conversation, we might have them share their screen to give us additional context. This open-ended methodology allows us to dig into their current process, pain points, and unmet needs without leading them down a particular solution path.
- A survey to help us prioritize the top three pain points and unmet needs of a wider population so that we know which to focus on first, and we can then put the others in the backlog.

PARTICIPANTS AND THE RECRUITMENT PROCESS

Participants

12–15 participants with the following criteria:

- current users of the platform;
- small businesses only (first focus, could do others later).

Recruitment

- Reach out to account managers to get introductions to potential participants (link to recruitment email).
- Using HotJar/recruitment tool asking users to sign up for a session.
- Sending out a link to sign up in the upcoming marketing email.
- Link to the screener survey.

Session Logistics

- 90-minute sessions.
- Remote (via Zoom).
- Incentive amount: $100.

DELIVERABLES AND NEXT STEPS

Deliverables

- Research summaries for each participant.
- Report on the qualitative insights.
- A visual representation of the top three pain points and top three unmet needs with any necessary contextual data.

Next Steps

- ideation workshop—scheduled for [APPROX DATE];
- follow-up concept or usability testing with ideas on [APPROX DATE];
- if need be, dig deeper into subsequent important pain points and unmet needs in future projects.

Approximate Timeline

- Planning and scoping—3 days.
- Recruitment—2 weeks.
- Conducting (in conjunction with recruitment)—2 weeks.
- Analysis and synthesis—2 weeks.
- Sharing—1 week.
- Workshops—2 days.

Total time: Approximately seven weeks.

Discussion Guide

These are just sample questions, not the exact discussion guide I used for this particular project.

Goal one: Discover how users currently search through content within the Merchant Portal

- Walk me through your step-by-step experience the last time you searched for content within the Merchant Portal.
- Describe how the experience made you feel.
- Explain what you mean by [subjective word].

Goal two: Uncover users' pain points when it comes to finding content within the Merchant Portal

- Describe the last frustrating experience you encountered while finding content within the Merchant Portal.
- What exactly about [experience] made it frustrating?
- Walk me through what you did to fix the problem.
- Talk me through another common frustration you have while finding content within the Merchant Portal.
- Describe the process you went through to fix the problem.
- Explain how the experience made you feel.

Goal three: Identify how users think about search and their unmet needs when it comes to finding content within the Merchant Portal

- Talk me through what's missing from the experience of finding content within the Merchant Portal.
- Explain why that is important to you.
- Describe another tool you use to find content and walk me through the differences between that tool and the Merchant Portal.

Resources

- intake document;
- screener survey;
- raw data (e.g., videos, notes);
- synthesis board;
- report.

EVALUATIVE RESEARCH PLAN EXAMPLE

Background of the Research Project

We have heard, from previous research, the importance of sustainability and eco-friendly choices when it comes to our users picking how they will travel to certain destinations. We've conducted research on how users think about this during their travel process and when selecting travel. With this, we have designed two prototypes to test with users to understand how they align with users' mental models and expectations. From the business side, we are hoping to impact:

- additional marketing tools and brand positioning through eco or sustainable travel;

- increase brand loyalty and usage of our platform by X%;
- increase repeat purchase rate by X%;
- increase customer lifetime value by X%.

Internal Stakeholders

- Responsible: Nikki—UX Researcher, Alex—UX Designer, Fraser—Product Manager.
- Accountable: Nikki, UX Researcher.
- Consulted: Marjorie—Product Manager, Jim—Dir. of Product, Hannah—Engineer.
- Informed: Ray—Dir. of Product, Douglas—CPO.

HYPOTHESES AND ASSUMPTIONS

Hypotheses

- Users value sustainability as a factor in their travel choices.
- Users are willing to take the time to look for more sustainable travel options.

Assumptions

- Users have different levels of understanding and awareness regarding sustainable travel.

Research Statement and Goals

Research statement: We want to understand better how users interact with sustainable choices within our platform to create an experience that aligns with their needs and mental models.

Research Goals

- Evaluate how participants interact with the sustainability prototype.
- Uncover any pain points or confusion participants encounter when interacting with the prototype.
- Uncover other current tools participants use to understand their sustainability when choosing travel options.

Success Criteria

- Clearly identifying any problems with the prototype and prioritize the top three to fix before the feature goes live.
- A clear workflow of how people interact with the prototype.
- Understanding the top three tools participants use to currently meet their needs.
- An ideation workshop that addresses any gaps or problems with the experience.

Methodology

A qualitative usability test to properly evaluate the prototype and understand how people are interacting with and reacting to the prototype, as well as assessing any problems or confusion with the prototype. We will share the prototype with the users in the Zoom chat, and they will share their screens and interact with the prototype.

PARTICIPANTS AND RECRUITMENT

Participants

7 participants with the following criteria:

- Current users of the platform.
- Have used sustainability tools in the past three months to help pick travel options.
- Located in the US.

Recruitment

- Using HotJar pop-up to get people to sign up.
- Sending out a link to sign up in the upcoming marketing email.
- Sending a link to our current panel.
- Link to the screener survey.

Session Logistics

- 60-minute sessions.
- Remote (via Zoom).
- Incentive amount: $50.

DELIVERABLES AND NEXT STEPS

Deliverables

- Research summaries for each participant.
- Report that includes:
  - annotations of the prototype highlighting the main issues;
  - a workflow of how participants interacted with the prototype;
  - deep-dive into the top 2–3 tools participants currently use to make sustainability choices.

Next Steps

- ideation workshop—scheduled for [APPROX DATE];
- if needed, follow-up concept or usability testing with ideas on [APPROX DATE];
- potential follow-up research with those who are less familiar with sustainability.

Approximate Timeline

- Planning and scoping—3 days.
- Recruitment—1 week.
- Conducting (in conjunction with recruitment)—1 week.
- Analysis and synthesis—1 week.
- Sharing—2 days.
- Workshops—1 day.

Total time: Approximately four weeks.

USABILITY TASK SCRIPT

These are just sample questions, not the exact usability task script I used for this particular project:

- Describe your first impression when you look at this screen.
- Explain what you see.
  - Eventually, prompt them if they miss the sustainability tag.
- Talk me through what you think of the sustainability tag.

- Using the last time you searched for a trip, walk me through, step-by-step, that experience while using this prototype.
  - Describe what is missing from this experience.
  - Talk me through the most confusing part of this experience.
- Tell me about another tool you use to pick sustainable travel (screen share if possible).
  - Walk me through how you use it.

Resources

- intake document;
- prototype;
- raw data (notes, videos);
- synthesis board;
- report.

Practice Makes Perfect

Research plans take time to get used to and perfect, but they are well worth the effort! My recommendation is to take your time when planning your next project and use a research plan (even if it takes a little longer). As you practice, you will naturally become faster at this process! It's a great way to think about your research projects, and I promise, it will make them that much more enjoyable and successful!

CASE STUDY: JTBD RESEARCH PLAN AND INTERVIEW GUIDE

Background

Creating a holistic approach to research will enable us to find gaps and opportunities within our product and help us generate new ideas and work together on solving the user's pain points. Jobs to be Done (JTBD) focuses on understanding why our customers hire us (our product) in order to reach their goal. By speaking to our users about their jobs, we can better understand what made them choose our product, what they are trying to achieve, and how they use our product to progress. This also shows us gaps in where our product is failing to help our users move forward toward their goals.

Goals

- Discover and understand how users are currently interacting with the fromAtoB platform through their end-to-end journey.
- Identify users' pain points within the fromAtoB platform, as well as any hacks they currently use or bugs they encounter.
- Uncover opportunities for further innovation and improvement.

Business Objectives

- Obtain a better understanding of how our product is currently being used, and if the most important tasks are easily achievable.
- Increase retention and acquisition through increased CLV.
- Decrease customer support outreach by creating a more effective, efficient, and satisfactory experience for customers.
- Increase revenue through increased conversion rates, due to a better overall purchasing experience.

PERSONAS

To Be Determined

Methodology

- one-on-one 60-minute research sessions;
- mix of in-person and remote via Zoom video conference (hope to achieve 50/50 split);
- JTBD-focused.

Participants

- 12–18 sessions per quarter;
- both users and non-users of the fromAtoB platform, including users of competitors;
- have traveled (and bought tickets) 3+ times from any platform in the past 6 months;
- English-speaking;
- mix of male and female (50/50 split);
- B2C focus.

INTERVIEW GUIDE

Hi there, I'm Nikki, a user experience researcher at fromAtoB. First off, thank you so much for being willing to participate in this session. We really value your feedback and use what we learn from you within our product team to help us make customer-focused decisions.

For the next 60 minutes, we are going to be talking through how you use the fromAtoB platform. The best way to think about this is that we are filming a documentary, so we want all the details on when you first started thinking about planning a trip and when you made the decision and experiencing it for the first time. I will first ask some broad questions, and then ask others that get into the more specific details of your experience. How does that sound?

Remember, this isn't a test or an interview, and I want this to be more of a conversation. There are no right or wrong answers; we are mostly interested in your opinion and honest feedback. Feel free to stop this session at any time if you need to take a break or feel uncomfortable.

Do you mind if I record this session? It is for notetaking purposes and will only be used internally; all of your answers will be kept confidential. Do you have any questions before we begin? Let's get started!

Journey:

This isn't necessarily just about the fromAtoB platform; we want to understand the surrounding environment and context too.

- Tell me about the last time you used fromAtoB?
  - Where were you?
  - When was it? Weekend, weekday?
  - Around what time?
  - Was there anyone else with you?
  - Were you using anything else at the time? Other websites or apps?
  - Were you doing anything else at the same time? Watching TV, online shopping?
  - What were you looking for? What were you trying to accomplish?
- Describe what made you actually think about booking the trip.
- Talk me through what made you want to take a trip.
  - Walk me through what made you want to plan a trip.
  - Describe the thoughts in your mind.
  - Explain what prompted you to think about a trip.
- How many times did you visit fromAtoB before you bought tickets?
  - If you ended up not buying from fromAtoB, why? Where did you buy instead?
- Tell me about when you first tried to find websites or apps like this?
- Tell me about how you looked for something to solve this problem.
  - Describe the kinds of solutions you tried.
  - Explain your experience with them.
  - Do you still use them? Why/why not?

- Walk me through why you first decided to use fromAtoB?
  - When did you hear about us? How did you find us?

Emotions—process:

- I would love to talk about the last time you took a trip in order to understand the end-to-end process. Talk me through the planning process, starting right from when you thought about planning a trip.
  - Describe how you felt during this planning?
- Walk me through the actual searching and purchasing process.
  - How did you feel during this?
- Now, you bought the tickets; tell me about the actual travel.
  - Describe anything that happened during that time that impacted your planning or travel back?
  - Describe how you felt during the travel part of the trip?
- Tell me about why you travel.
  - Explain what motivates you to travel.

Wrap-up:

Thank you so much for participating today; we really appreciate your time. This session was extremely helpful for us. Again, all of your answers will be kept completely confidential. Since this session was so valuable, would it be okay for me to contact you again, in the future, to participate in another research session? Do you have any other questions for me? Thank you again!

CASE STUDY: RESEARCH PLAN FOR USABILITY TESTING

Background

We are looking to further understand how customers think about what swapping and upgrading ingredients means. This research will help uncover users' thoughts and perceptions on swapping/upgrading. This will allow us to iterate on the current version of prototypes to ensure we are aligned with users' expectations or show us how to pivot to meet those needs.

Business Objective

Understand how customers think of swapping different ingredients in order to optimize the amount of choices and flexibility we provide in the menu with the intention of increasing retention and overall customer satisfaction.

Research Goals

1. Determine what swapping, upgrading, and menu flexibility mean to the classic customers.
2. Illustrate the perceptions users have behind swapping or upgrading ingredients.
3. Evaluate how usable the swapping/upgrading prototype flow is.

KEY STAKEHOLDERS

Nikki

Methodology and Sample

- one-on-one 60-minute usability tests in the office and remote;
- main person responsible for grocery shopping;
- classic 3 × 2 subscribers;
- n=10 interviews;
- in-person or remote on prototype.

INTERVIEW GUIDE

Introduction (2 minutes):

> Hi there. Thank you so much for participating. At [Company], we really value our user's feedback and do everything we can to incorporate your thoughts into our products, which is why we asked you to come in today. I'm Nikki, the user experience researcher at the company.

For this 45-minute session, I will first be asking you some general questions and then having you complete a set of tasks on our mobile app or mobile browser. As we go through the different tasks, it would be great if you could work through them as you would if you were at home and talk out loud during the process. This helps us understanding what you are thinking during the tasks! Also, this is a prototype, so not all things will work, and if something isn't working, please explain what you would have expected. After that, we are going to do a brief exercise to help us further understand how you think about these concepts.

No one who is listening designed this, so we promise your feedback won't hurt our feelings! We appreciate honesty.

You can stop this session at any time if you feel uncomfortable. All of your answers will be confidential and anonymous, and there are no wrong answers. I know that was a lot of information and I will remind you during the session.

Before we begin, do you mind if I record this session? Again, it will be completely confidential and just used internally for our developers and designers to watch.

DO YOU HAVE ANY QUESTIONS BEFORE WE START?

Prototype guide—upgrading protein (20 minutes):

I'm going to have you complete a few tasks now—remember there is no wrong answer and please talk out loud while we are completing the tasks!

My Menu > Select Meals

- When you land on this screen, what do you think? What does it mean to you?
- Is there anything confusing or missing?
- How would you select your meals for the week?
- What do you think of the "upgrade" tag? What does it mean to you?
- If you clicked it, what would you expect would happen?
- What are your thoughts on the price?

Edit Menu

- What does this screen mean to you?
- Which recipes are selected?
- Imagine you didn't want the first meal on the list; what would you do?
- What would you expect to happen when you click that?

Edit Menu > Upgrade

- What do you think of this screen?
- You want to choose the "Minute Steak Fajitas"; what would you do?
- What would you expect to happen if you clicked there? What does the "upgrade" tag mean to you?
- If you clicked "upgrade," what would you expect would happen?
- What would your meal be?
- What would the amount of money you were being charged be?

Edit Menu > Save

- What do you think of that interaction?
- What would you change? What is confusing/missing?
- You want to change the upgrade and go back to a regular meal; what would you do?
- What would you do next?
- What would you expect to have happen?

Pop-up > Accept

- What do you think of this screen?
- Is it confusing? Is anything missing?
- What would you change/improve?
- What is the final price? Does that make sense?
- How would you go back?
- What would you do next?
- What would you expect to have happen?

Alert Screen > "Keep Meals"

- What does this screen mean to you? What do you think?
- What is confusing or missing?
- What would you change or improve?
- What do you think of the compensation?
- What would you expect to have happen once you clicked "Keep Meals?"
- Where would the "select again" button take you?
- You click "Keep Meals"; what do you expect would happen?

My Menu and Success Bar

- What does this screen mean to you?
- What is confusing? What is missing?
- What did you think of that entire experience?
- What happens now?
- How would you change the menu again?
- If you did, what would happen?
- How does this experience feel compared to our current menu?

Prototype guide—swapping protein (20 minutes):

I'm going to have you complete a few tasks now—remember there is no wrong answer and please talk out loud while we are completing the tasks!

My Menu > Select Meals

- When you land on this screen, what do you think? What does it mean to you?
- Is there anything confusing or missing?
- How would you select your meals for the week?
- What do you think of the "swap it" tag? What does it mean to you?
  - If you clicked it, what would you expect would happen?
  - What are your thoughts on the price?

Edit Menu

- What does this screen mean to you?
- Which recipes are selected?
- Imagine you didn't want the first meal on the list, what would you do?
- What would you expect to happen when you click that?

Edit Menu > Swap

- What do you think of this screen?
- Imagine you wanted to choose the "Pan Seared Chicken," what would you do?
- What would you expect to happen if you clicked there?
- Do you notice anything different on this card?
- What does the "swap it" label mean to you?
- If you clicked "swap," what would you expect would happen?
- What would your meal be?
- What would the amount of money you were being charged be?

Edit Menu > Save

- Could you talk about why this isn't an additional cost? How does that make you feel? [PROBE INTO PROTEIN QUALITY]
- What do you think of that interaction?
- What would you change? What is confusing/missing?
- You want to go back to a regular meal, what would you do?
- What would you do next?
- What would you expect to have happen?

Pop-up > Accept

- What do you think of this screen?
- Is it confusing? Is anything missing?
- What would you change/improve?
- How would you go back? Why would you go back?

Alert Screen > "Keep Meals"

- What does this screen mean to you? What do you think?
- What is confusing or missing?
- What would you change or improve?
- What would you do next here?
- What would you expect to have happen once you clicked "Keep Meals?"
- Where would the "select again" button take you?
- How do you feel about this screen?
- Imagine you clicked "Keep Meals," what do you expect would happen?

My Menu and Success Bar

- What does this screen mean to you?
- What is confusing? What is missing?
- What did you think of that entire experience?
- What happens now?
- How would you change the menu again?
- If you did, what would happen?
- How does this experience feel compared to our current menu?

General follow-up questions for prototype (3–5 minutes):

1. What was missing from this experience?
2. What didn't make sense or felt confusing?
3. What were you expecting that did not happen?
4. What was the most frustrating part of the process?
5. What are some points that would improve this process?
6. What was your favorite part of the experience?

Wrap-up (1 minute):
Thank you so much for participating today, we really appreciate it and this session was extremely helpful for us. We use this feedback within our product team to make decisions on how to improve our products and to prioritize our product roadmap. Again, all of your answers will be completely confidential and anonymous. If possible,

would it be okay to contact you again in the future to complete another research session in the future?

EXAMPLE RESEARCH PLAN FOR BENCHMARKING

Background

Conducting a benchmarking study allows us to test how fromAtoB web and app are progressing over time, through our different iterations and changes. This can validate or disprove our hypotheses, and can also ensure we are moving in the right direction within our product. With benchmarking metrics, we will have, both, quantitative and qualitative data to aid us in making data-driven and customer-centric decisions. In addition, benchmarking enables us to understand where we fall compared to competitors or industry standards.

Hypotheses

- By testing the current desktop version with these metrics, we will be able to see where the problems and pain points lie.
- With a baseline of metrics, we will be able to track whether UX changes we make actually improve the experience for users.

Research Goals

- Understand how our product (web & app) is progressing over time, through iterations.
- Identify the overall experience/satisfaction of fromAtoB (web and app).
- Evaluate the difficulty or ease of completing the most important tasks on the web and app.
- Create a baseline for us to then compare future iterations and changes to.

Business Objectives

- Obtain a better understanding of how our product is currently being used, and if the most important tasks are easily achievable.
- Increase retention and acquisition, through increased CLV.
- Decrease customer support outreach by creating a more effective, efficient and satisfactory experience for customers.

Methodology

- one-to-one 45 minute benchmarking tests;
- in-person and remote testing;
- website;
- frequency: quarterly or biannually;
- tool: Zoom, lookback.io.

Top User Goals

- book a ticket to a destination;
- compare ticket and trip solutions;
- check booked trip information;
- access and use ticket during travel;
- share the trip with others (co-planning);
- get relevant updates before, during and after travel.

Metrics

- time on task;
- binary task success (fail or pass);
- number of errors;
- SEQ (single ease questionnaire);
- SUS.

Participants

- 20 participants;
- current users, leisure travel;
- male/female split (to understand if there are gender differences);
- language: English;
- user location: Germany.

Anticipated Timeline (Total): 4 Weeks

- Recruiting: 5 days.
- Running tests: 2 weeks.
- Analysis: 3–5 days.

INTERVIEW GUIDE

Hi there, I'm Nikki, a user experience researcher at fromAtoB. First off, thank you so much for being willing to participate in this session. We really value your feedback and use what we learn from you within our product team to help us make customer-focused decisions.

For the next 60 minutes, I am going to be asking you a few questions about our website, and then ask you to perform several tasks. We are going to be looking at two different scenarios. First we will complete the task and then, right after, we will discuss your thoughts on it. Remember, this isn't a test, more of an observation, so there are no right or wrong answers. Feel free to stop this session at any time if you need to.

Do you mind if I record this session? It is for notetaking purposes and will only be used internally, all of your answers will be kept confidential. Do you have any questions before we being?

Task script:

Great, let's get started with the first scenario. Remember, there is no wrong way to do this-we are mostly interested in your process and approach!

TRAIN

- Imagine you were going on a vacation from Berlin to Munich from March 14th to March 17th. Go to fromAtoB.de and search for that criteria.
    - Overall on a scale of 1–7, 1 being very easy to complete and 7 being very difficult to complete, how did you feel about this task?
- Imagine you had to take the train, what would you do?
    - Overall on a scale of 1–7, 1 being very easy to complete and 7 being very difficult to complete, how did you feel about this task?
- You need to make sure to leave around 18:00 on Friday, find these relevant results?
    - Overall on a scale of 1–7, 1 being very easy to complete and 7 being very difficult to complete, how did you feel about this task?
- Additionally, you have a budget of 200 EURs for the total trip, find relevant results?
    - Overall on a scale of 1–7, 1 being very easy to complete and 7 being very difficult to complete, how did you feel about this task?
- Imagine you were coming back Sunday afternoon, how would you find a trip with similar criteria (train and under 200 EUROs total) for the way back?
    - Overall on a scale of 1–7, 1 being very easy to complete and 7 being very difficult to complete, how did you feel about this task?

- (overview page) You're going to be tired on the way there, so you would like to upgrade one of your tickets to first class. How would you do this?
  - Overall on a scale of 1–7, 1 being very easy to complete and 7 being very difficult to complete, how did you feel about this task?
- Since you have a lot of work to do, you would prefer to sit by the window and with a table. How would you do this?
  - Overall on a scale of 1–7, 1 being very easy to complete and 7 being very difficult to complete, how did you feel about this task?
- Pay with a credit card
  - Overall on a scale of 1–7, 1 being very easy to complete and 7 being very difficult to complete, how did you feel about this task?
- How would you confirm and book?
  - Overall on a scale of 1–7, 1 being very easy to complete and 7 being very difficult to complete, how did you feel about this task?
- How would you gauge whether or not a trip was successfully booked?
  - Overall on a scale of 1–7, 1 being very easy to complete and 7 being very difficult to complete, how did you feel about this task?

Great! We are done with the tasks for right now, I just have a few more questions for you in this scenario:

- If you needed to cancel this ticket, or change it, after purchasing, how might you do that?
- Imagine you had a problem with your ticket, how might you contact us?
- Imagine you needed the ticket during travel, what might you do to access it?
- How might you share this trip with other people (friends, family)?

Finally, we just have a quick survey for you to fill out, just with your thoughts on the overall experience. We would really appreciate your honesty and all answers will be kept confidential!

Wrap-up:

Thank you so much for participating today, we really appreciate your time. This session was extremely helpful for us. Again, all of your answers will be kept completely confidential. Since this session was so valuable, would it be okay for me to contact you again, in the future, to participate in another research session? Do you have any other questions for me? Thank you again!

RECRUITMENT

There is so much value in talking to users, but we have to make sure they are the right ones. For example, I finally secured some budget for a generative research project on how people plan travel. I got 15 participants signed up quickly, who had used our platform recently, and I was super excited.

The first person came to the interview, and I hunkered down ready for 90 minutes of mind-blowing insights. I asked them, "I'd love to hear exactly how you planned your last trip, starting all the way from the beginning." The person looked at me and said, "I didn't plan it. My partner did." My stomach sank. I ended the interview early because there was not much to talk about. But that had to be a fluke, right? No. Out of the next four participants, only one had planned the trip. In my excitement, I had rushed through recruitment and not been intentional about the people I needed to speak to, and which criteria I needed them to have.

By setting up operations for recruitment from the start, you're making your life easier when you do have to recruit quickly. In this chapter, we will explore the key ways you can set up your recruitment process for success.

SEGMENTATION

User segmentation plays a pivotal role in user research, yet it often proves to be a challenging endeavor. Effectively dividing your user base into distinct segments constitutes the foundational step toward impactful recruitment, and it's a step I've occasionally overlooked or skipped due to its complexity. I always advocate for commencing your research journey with segmentation whenever possible because it significantly simplifies your task.

Segmentation can manifest in various forms, and its definition can vary depending on who you consult. In the realm of product and UX, I define segmentation as the process of taking a large group of individuals and partitioning them into smaller subgroups or segments based on shared characteristics.

WAYS TO SEGMENT YOUR AUDIENCE

Primary Demographics

Traditionally, researchers have focused on fundamental customer demographics, including age, gender, education, income, employment status, occupation, race, location, marital status, family, and homeownership. While these details hold interest in certain contexts, they should not serve as the sole basis for segmentation. Such data alone fail to provide deep insights into your audience's thoughts, needs, and challenges, which are critical for genuine improvement and innovation.

Behaviors/Usage

Moving beyond primary demographics, examining what people do offers a deeper understanding. Identifying patterns in behaviors and usage can reveal areas for enhancement or new creations, depending on whether your product caters to these behaviors. Consider investigating:

- habits
- hobbies
- daily tasks
- routines
- goals and aspirations
- product/feature usage frequency
- support interactions
- customer longevity
- perceived usability and satisfaction.

Interaction

Understanding how people interact with your product or service takes you a step closer to comprehending your customers and forming meaningful segments. Analyze interaction patterns through data analytics, exploring trends in:

- entry points to your product
- user flows (success paths versus error scenarios)
- drop-off points
- click-through rates.

Feelings

The feelings context delves into why people engage in specific activities or use particular products. It helps to answer the deeper question of "why." When pursuing feeling-based segmentation, consider factors such as:

- motivations
- goals
- values
- personality traits
- lifestyle choices.

Environmental Context

The environmental context examines where users are and who else might be involved in their activities. This theme gains significance when dealing with diverse roles operating within a shared ecosystem that requires separation into distinct segments. For environmental segmentation, contemplate:

- collaborators in tasks
- in-person versus online interactions
- in-office versus remote settings
- home-based versus mobile activities
- multi-tasking versus single-tasking behaviors
- desktop versus mobile device usage.

Timing

Timing holds great relevance, especially if your audience follows specific seasonal or event-driven patterns. Investigate when people make particular choices or engage with your product:

- seasonal trends
- holiday influences
- time of day preferences
- day of the week dynamics (weekdays versus weekends)
- regularly scheduled routines (e.g., appointments)
- major life events (e.g., birthdays, weddings).

With the myriad ways to segment your audience, you may feel overwhelmed by the sheer volume of data available. Rest assured, you don't need to employ every piece of information to segment your customers, as that would result in an unmanageable number of segments, rendering recruitment impractical.

Instead, two primary approaches can guide your segmentation efforts:

1. Profit:
    Start by focusing on revenue-generating customers, as they form the lifeblood of your business. Segment customers based on their revenue contributions, then delve into understanding their behaviors, motivations, and sentiments. This approach can unearth unmet needs or pain points that have the potential to significantly enhance your product.
2. Study Goals:
    Segmentation becomes more contextual and tailored to your organization's objectives when guided by your study goals. Whenever contemplating segmentation, consider the specific goals you aim to achieve with your study, and utilize this information to determine the data you need. Here are a few real-world examples of how I've applied segmentation in the past, driven by study goals:

Personas:
: For a company seeking to create personas, I initially felt overwhelmed by the diversity of clients and users. To narrow the scope, I consulted account managers and reviewed data on revenue generation. This led me to focus on recruiting social media managers from large US-based companies, as they were the most frequent users and significant revenue drivers.

GenZ:
: In another project focused on fashion trends, market research and analysis of user age ranges revealed that GenZ had the most interest in and potential revenue impact for our platform.

Location:
: In the food delivery space, identifying locations and order frequency as profit-driving factors allowed us to target specific areas and investigate reasons behind lower order frequency, ultimately improving customer retention.

There are many ways to potentially segment your users to ensure you are getting the best users for your project. Once you have an idea of segmentation, you can dive into creating a screener survey, which will help you find those amazing participants that can give you all the information you need to successfully answer your research goals.

SCREENER SURVEYS

Screener surveys are indispensable tools for launching research projects effectively. These concise surveys serve the critical purpose of qualifying participants, ensuring you select the best-suited individuals to provide the insights you need. The strategic use of screener surveys offers numerous advantages, including:

- Targeting Relevance: Screener surveys enable you to identify and engage with participants who possess the specific characteristics, habits, and behaviors essential for a comprehensive understanding of your research objectives.
- Sample Size Control: By segmenting participants into different categories, you can precisely control your sample size. This precision empowers you to create meaningful deliverables that drive actionable outcomes, avoiding the pitfalls of overly large or inadequate sample groups.
- Maximizing Return on Impact: Investing time and resources in recruiting the right participants through screener surveys ensures that your research efforts yield the highest return on investment. This approach minimizes the risk of wasting valuable time and money on participants who do not align with your research goals.

- Participant Fatigue Mitigation: Avoid overwhelming your participant pool by constantly soliciting their involvement. Screener surveys allow you to engage only those users who meet the criteria for your specific research, preventing participant fatigue.

Creating an exceptional screener survey requires a systematic approach. Here are the steps to guide you in crafting an effective one.

1. Define Ideal Participant Criteria

Begin by outlining the criteria that define your ideal research participants. Consider the questions you need to ask to achieve your research goals and the specific information you require. Ask yourself:

- What are the overarching goals of your research?
- What questions must participants answer to provide meaningful insights?
- Where are the gaps in your knowledge that participants need to fill?
- What behaviors and habits are pertinent to your study?
- What objectives are participants trying to accomplish?

2. Formulate Questions

Once you've brainstormed the necessary criteria, create at least one question for each criterion. Aim to keep the screener survey concise, ideally comprising five to ten questions, to minimize participant drop-off rates.

3. Craft Well-Written Questions

Take the time to write clear and precise survey questions, as this is crucial for attracting high-quality participants. Common mistakes to avoid include:

- Vague criteria: Ensure criteria leave no room for interpretation.
    - Vague criteria: People who have wanted to move recently.
    - Precise criteria: People who have visited 3+ apartments in the past 60 days.
- Future-based questions: Focus on past behavior whenever possible.
    - Future-based question: Will you look at apartments in the next 60 days?
    - Past-based question: Have you looked at 3+ apartments in the past 60 days?
- Leading questions: Avoid questions that steer participants toward specific responses.

- Leading question: Do you prefer listings with photos?
- Non-leading question: How do you feel when apartment listings don't have any photos available online?
• Inaccurate multiple-choice options: Prevent overlapping or ambiguous choices.
    - "How many people currently work at your company?"
        - 1–10
        - 100–150
        - 150–200
        - 200–250
        - 250–300
        - Over 300
    - "How many people currently work at your company?"
        - 1–100
        - 101–150
        - 151–200
        - 201–250
        - 251–300
        - Over 300
• Double-barreled questions: Keep each question focused on a single topic.
    - Double-barreled question: "How do you feel about the information and/or functionality on this website?"
    - Two separate questions: "How do you feel about the functionality of this website?" AND "How do you feel about the information on this website?"

4. Organize Questions Logically

Arrange your questions in a logical order that starts with broad qualifying information and progressively narrows down to specific details. This prevents participants from being screened out after investing considerable time in the survey.

5. Diversify Question Types

Blend closed- and open-ended questions to elicit a comprehensive understanding of participants. A balanced mix, such as a 60/40 ratio of closed to open-ended questions, enhances your ability to select the most suitable individuals.

6. Include Open Text Field and N/A Options

Ensure that participants have the option to express "Not Applicable" or "I Don't Know" when necessary. Also, incorporate an "Other" category accompanied by an open text field, permitting participants to offer responses in their own words.

7. Conduct a Dry Run

Before deploying the screener survey, conduct a dry run with colleagues to gauge its clarity, simplicity, and effectiveness. This step is vital in identifying and rectifying any issues before sending the survey to potential participants.

Screener surveys are vital instruments for precision in research recruitment. By following these steps and meticulously crafting your screener survey, you can confidently select the right participants for your research, ensuring that your efforts yield valuable insights and actionable outcomes.

EXAMPLE OF A SCREENER SURVEY

We own a plant shop in Brooklyn, New York, selling groups of exotic plants. We have been posting our plants on social media, and people from around the United States are contacting us and asking if we have an online shop.

We want to consider this option but are still determining what people want or expect. We want to conduct user research to:

- Understand how people currently purchase plants online and what their end-to-end experience is like.
- Uncover the pain points and frustrations people encounter when buying plants online.
- Identify other plant stores they have purchased from and what the experience was like with those stores.
- Evaluate how they interact with our online plant store prototype.

While also looking at the goals, I would then ask myself:

- What gaps in knowledge do you have that you need your participants to fill in?
- We need to understand how people currently purchase plants online, so we need participants who have recently gone through that particular experience.
- Why would people purchase plants online versus going into a store?
- What behaviors do you need to understand more?

We need to understand the end-to-end experience of how people have purchased a plant online, from searching to unboxing. I would create a screener survey with this information to ensure I target the right people:

1. Where are you currently located?
    - Type in (screen out anything within 50 miles of Brooklyn)

2. How often have you visited an online plant store in the past three months?
   - I haven't visited any in the past three months (screen out)
   - 1–3 times
   - 4–6 times
   - Over 6 times
   - Other (open text field)
3. How many plants have you purchased online in the past three months?
   - I haven't purchased any plants online in the past three months (screen out)
   - 1–3 plants (screen out)
   - 4–6 plants
   - Over 6 plants
   - Other (open text field)
4. How often have you bought plants in-store in the past three months?
   - I haven't purchased any plants in-store in the past three months (screen out)
   - 1–3 plants
   - 4–6 plants
   - Over 6 plants (screen out)
   - Other (open text field)
5. From which store did you most recently purchase a plant online?
   - (Short open text)
6. Describe your most recent experience purchasing a plant online.
   - (Long open text)

WAYS TO RECRUIT

Recruiting participants for your research project is a multifaceted task, influenced by factors like your timeline, target audience, and budget constraints. To help you navigate this landscape effectively, here's a comprehensive overview of common recruitment methods, along with creative approaches to incentivize participants without breaking the bank.

Common Recruitment Methods

- Agency: Collaborating with a specialized recruitment agency is a go-to option for many research endeavors. Agencies have the expertise and networks to locate participants matching your criteria efficiently.
- Recruitment tool: Utilizing online recruitment tools or platforms can be a cost-effective solution, especially for smaller-scale studies. These tools often provide access to diverse participant pools.

- Cold Emailing: Reaching out directly to potential participants via email is a direct and personal approach. Craft a compelling message to pique their interest and encourage participation.
- Through Your Team: Leverage your existing resources, such as account managers or marketing teams, to tap into their networks. They may have direct access to individuals relevant to your research.
- Intercept: Intercepting users on your website or app is a proactive method. You can engage visitors with a quick survey or prompt them to participate in your research.
- Social Media: Platforms like Facebook groups, Reddit, LinkedIn, and Slack communities are rich sources of potential participants. Engage with these online communities to identify and recruit individuals interested in your study.
- Events: Hosting or participating in industry events, webinars, or conferences can help you connect with potential participants. These events provide a platform to engage and recruit attendees.
- Social Ads: Running targeted social media advertising campaigns can help you reach a specific demographic or audience. Craft compelling ad creatives to attract potential participants.
- Snowball Effect: Harness the power of your existing participants by asking them to recommend others who fit your criteria. This method can create a network effect that expands your participant pool.

Incentives on a Budget

While incentives can boost participation rates, not everyone has a large budget to offer substantial rewards. Here are creative ways to incentivize participants without significant financial commitments:

- Raffle for a Prize: Offer participants a chance to win a valuable prize, such as a gift card or a popular gadget, by entering them into a raffle. This approach can generate excitement and engagement.
- Sending Swag: Send branded merchandise or swag items, like T-shirts or stickers, to participants as a token of appreciation. This not only incentivizes participation but also promotes your brand.
- Early Access to Features: If you're researching a product or software, provide participants with exclusive early access to new features or updates. This can be a compelling incentive for tech-savvy individuals.
- Discount Codes: Offer participants discount codes or coupons for your products or services. This not only incentivizes participation but also encourages future engagement with your brand.
- Product Upgrades: Upgrade participants to a premium version of your product or service for a limited period. This demonstrates the added value of your offering and encourages continued usage.

- Extended Trial Offers: Extend the trial period of your product or service for participants. This gives them more time to explore and provide valuable feedback.
- Feedback on Roadmap: Engage participants by involving them in discussions about your product roadmap. Their input can influence future developments, making them feel invested in your brand's success.
- Donation to Charities: Instead of offering personal incentives, pledge to make a donation to a charitable cause on behalf of participants. This not only motivates participants but also promotes a sense of social responsibility.

The key to successful participant recruitment lies in flexibility and creativity. Experiment with different recruitment methods and incentives until you discover the ideal combination that aligns with your budget and resonates with your target audience. Personally, I've found a combination of intercepting users on our platform, leveraging the snowball effect through participant recommendations, and sweetening the deal with raffles or discount codes/product upgrades to be highly effective.

SAMPLE SIZE AND STATISTICAL SIGNIFICANCE

The question of statistical significance and qualitative user research plagues so many people. Getting constantly questioned about your sample sizes can be exhausting. However, we don't need to worry! Statistical significance and qualitative user research don't need to be lumped together. Let's dive into how you can deal with these types of questions!

GET COMFORTABLE WITH WHAT STATISTICAL SIGNIFICANCE MEANS

When it comes to statistical significance, you generally start with a null hypothesis, which means you assume there is NO relation, effect, or difference between the two things we measure. So, for instance, if you were doing a study investigating the relationship between drinking sparkling water and being able to run fast, you would start the study assuming there was no relation between the two.

You then conduct your research using a p-value to determine if the data is statistically significant. The p-value tells you how often you would expect to see a test statistic as extreme or more extreme than the one calculated by your statistical test if the null hypothesis of that test was true. If a p-value is less than 5%, you have reached statistical significance and can reject the null hypothesis.

If you investigated the relationship between drinking sparkling water and running faster, and your p-value was .05 or below, you would reject the null hypothesis. This means you would reject that there is no relationship between drinking sparkling water and running faster. You have observed, instead, that there is a relationship between the two.

Statistical significance can tell you whether or not the null hypothesis is supported. Significance testing assumes the null is true. Therefore, P-values only provide information against the null hypothesis and are not in favor of it.

Statistical significance cannot tell you:

- if any alternative hypotheses are true;
- the effect size of a result;
- the importance of a result;
- why the null hypothesis is not supported, or why your alternative hypothesis might be true.

THE RELATIONSHIP BETWEEN STATISTICAL SIGNIFICANCE AND QUALITATIVE DATA

Quantitative research is statistical because it has numbers attached to it. With quantitative research, you see averages or percentages. Quantitative methods allow you to measure variables and test specific hypotheses, while qualitative methods enable us to explore concepts and experiences in depth.

QUALITATIVE RESEARCH USES NON-STATISTICAL METHODS

When it comes to determining and using statistical significance, it simply does not make sense in qualitative research. Qualitative research, as it exists, is a non-statistical approach. With qualitative research, you do not try to measure certain variables, nor do you try to test specific hypotheses. Never in my life have I used qualitative research to determine whether or not a null hypothesis is supported.

One of the other reasons that qualitative research is not statistical is that you are not trying to generalize or widen our scope of understanding. Instead, you are trying to understand what is taking place on a deep level.

With qualitative research, you are in the first phases of your study. You aren't looking to understand if your findings represent a broader population because you don't have findings yet. You have to go deep before you go wide, or you will miss crucial insights that you can later test at large.

Theoretical saturation means you no longer learn anything new during your research sessions and aren't making new connections during analysis. When it comes to qualitative data, this is the type of "significance" you are looking for. If necessary, you can always follow up with quantitative data using a mixed methods approach.

FORMATIVE VERSUS SUMMATIVE TESTING

Whenever dealing with usability testing, you typically use the formative versus summative approach. Usability testing can be tricky because it can involve quantitative-looking data, but it is still a relatively qualitative approach with a smaller sample size.

Formative evaluations zero in on uncovering issues within a design or experience and why/how those issues occur for participants. Usability testing is a fantastic example of a formative approach. You test the design and experience with usability testing to understand problems and help inform the product development process.

With this iterative approach, you might test and iterate on the design several times until the team feels they are on the right path. You conduct formative testing in the earlier stages of the product development process.

With formative testing, you are:

- uncovering the issues that occur;
- understanding why those issues are occurring;
- understanding how those issues are occurring.

During formative evaluations, you are NOT looking at how many people encounter an issue. Therefore, statistical significance is irrelevant in qualitative usability testing (formative approach).

Summative testing, also known as quantitative testing, answers those questions that stakeholders are asking. Summative testing looks at how many people are impacted by an issue and how much impact an issue has. With a summative approach, you use a larger sample size.

However, I would still argue that summative testing and statistical significance are not 100% related. This is because, as we remember, statistical significance is looking at whether or not the null hypothesis is supported. Instead, effect size is more important within summative testing, which leads me to my last approach to the statistical significance question.

EFFECT SIZE

Effect size tells you how meaningful the relationship between variables or the difference between groups is. It indicates the practical significance of a research outcome. A large effect size means that a research finding has practical significance, while a small effect size indicates limited practical applications.

While statistical significance tells you whether there is an effect between variables, effect size can tell you how large of a difference there is (or isn't). Effect size is the most helpful answer when stakeholders ask about statistical significance, comparing two or more product variations (such as comparative usability testing).

With a limited sample size (which comes with any qualitative-based user research), you won't be able to detect small differences between variables. Still, you will be able to see larger differences, which is what matters most and creates actionable recommendations for the teams.

ASK THESE QUESTIONS TO UNDERSTAND STAKEHOLDERS' FEARS

Stakeholders usually ask questions due to fears and anxieties. These questions might help you understand what they are really concerned about so you can better address their direct questions.

- "What are you worried about with the results?"
- "What concerns you about the sample size?"
- "What are some reasons you feel we need more people?"
- "What kind of information are you looking for when asking about the sample size?"

Instead of looking for whether or not the null hypothesis is supported, stakeholders are concerned that a small sample size is not representative of the given population or doesn't tell them how many people are impacted by our findings. By uncovering these deeper concerns, we can readily address the problem: effect sizes.

IDEAS ON WHAT TO SAY TO THE STATISTICAL SIGNIFICANCE QUESTION

Whenever faced with the ongoing debate of statistical significance and qualitative data, you can say:

> "Statistical significance, when it comes to research, was initially aimed at being able to replicate our studies an infinite number of times with the same results, and being able to publish knowledge that is representative of people. We are not trying to do either of those things. We are studying what is currently happening with the population of our users (which I segmented in X or Y ways to achieve as much generalizability as possible).

Testing with so few people will never get us statistical significance. But remember: we are not trying to prove that the world is operating in a certain way. We are trying to understand the pain points or issues our users are experiencing so we can improve our product. These issues are generally straightforward and do not need proof of statistical significance. The findings are based on the struggles of people representative of our users.

If you watched five people hit a pothole and get a flat tire, how many more would you need to watch before you identified it as a problem?"

AND TAKE A DEEP BREATH!

Creating an Intake Process

User research requests can flood in from various channels, such as emails, Slack messages, or casual in-person discussions. Implementing a formalized research intake process within your organization can be a game-changer, benefiting both you and your colleagues through:

- Efficiency and Reduced Meetings: Imagine a scenario where you no longer need to chase down stakeholders for essential project details or engage in back-and-forth meetings to grasp the context of a research request. A formalized intake process consolidates all necessary information on a single page, reducing interruptions and time spent in context meetings.
- Enhanced Meeting Efficiency: When you enter project kick-off meetings armed with comprehensive information gathered through the intake process, you avoid starting from scratch. This leads to more efficient discussions with stakeholders, focusing on logistics rather than basic project comprehension.
- Improved Prioritization: The intake document allows you to better prioritize user research requests by clearly assessing their impact. It becomes a visual tool to gauge the significance of each project within the broader context of your organization's goals.
- Stakeholder Education: By guiding stakeholders through the intake document, you educate them about the critical components of shaping a research project. Over time, this passive education process empowers them to think strategically about user research.

I've spent a lot of time creating and iterating on an intake document that had the most ideal questions to gather context and make research requests more efficient. You can see the intake document that I use below—steal whatever makes sense for your organization, and always feel free to leave behind anything that doesn't make sense for your context.

EXAMPLE INTAKE DOCUMENT

Purpose of this document: Filling out this sheet is the first step in getting answers to your research questions. We will use this information to understand and align with your request, maintaining a high quality of our research output.

THERE ARE 15 QUESTIONS TOTAL; EXPECTED TIME: 20–30 MINUTES

Please note:

- This step does not guarantee that research will happen but rather helps us decide on priority, feasibility, approach, and timeline.
- Summarizing rather than just pasting links shows us you've thought about your research needs and that your project is clear for our researchers, who may be unfamiliar with your topic. Though some ambiguity is fine, you should be able to fill in this document completely.
- If you have questions about this document, please reach out to the researcher in contact.

Project Name:
Requesting Team & Contributors:
Date:
Background

1. What led you to request research support now?
2. For example, we completed desk research and found we need more information on the X concept.
3. What phase of your project are you in? Is it discovering new information, testing a concept or an idea, or something else?
    The Big Picture
4. Please talk about the impact this particular research will have on this particular team.
5. If applicable, please explain how this research will impact other teams and the overarching organization.
    Deep-dive into Your Research Need
6. What level of support do you anticipate needing for this project?
7. For example, we offer support on recruitment, interview guide writing, interview guide review, interview moderation, and analysis. Please indicate all

6 • Set Up Core Research Operations   113

you believe you would need help with. If you have someone on your team experienced with user research, ask them what level they are comfortable with running the study.
8. What are your questions for the research project?
9. For example, we want to understand how customers think of the X concept, uncover how users interact with the prototype, and discover pain points on a current flow.
10. What groups of customers do you want to learn about?
11. For example, age range, gender, users versus non-users, country, language, and any special criteria (e.g., needs to have bought X in the past Y months)
12. What customer problem/need are you trying to solve? If you have any documentation, like an Epic or Design Brief, summarize and link it here.
13. For example, we are testing an idea that helps customers achieve X or Y goal. Please include any documents here.
14. How do you know this is a customer problem or a customer need?
15. For example, here are some quotes from other research that highlights the problem or analytics that show negative behaviors.
16. What would you do with the insights from this research? Is there someone (e.g., designer, developers) "ready" to act on the insights generated from this research?
17. For example, we would like to know if our concept is going in the right direction or what changes we need to make with a prototype.
18. By when do you need insights in your hands (i.e., analysis of the research is completed) to move forward?
19. For example, we need insights by X date because that is when Y is happening.
20. Is there any other information you think is important and useful as we begin to discuss your project?
21. For example, we also found this competitor research that is super relevant. Please include any links to the information here.
Looking Back
22. How have you acted on previously completed research that backs up the solution you've designed (User Research, Market Research, Business Intelligence, on-site data, A/B testing, Analytics, customer care, NPS)?
23. For example, we have done discovery research or A/B testing that shows X, Y, and Z.
24. What important and unanswered questions do you still have after evaluating past research that you want to address in this current research?
25. For example, although we have done quantitative research in the past, we are still unsure about why customers are behaving in certain ways.
26. Please include any links to solutions (e.g., prototypes) you have considered.
27. For example, we have used previous research from other research sessions to create this prototype. Please link to any prototypes here.

28. Please fill out the following statement:
    a. I need (information you need) to answer (questions you have) by (your timeline) in order to make (the decisions you need to make).

By implementing a formalized intake process like this, you lay a strong foundation for your user research practice. This structured approach will pay dividends in the long run, aiding in prioritization, roadmap development, and stakeholder education, ultimately contributing to more impactful user research outcomes.

QUESTION GATHERING

One of the most effective ways to identify and spotlight impactful questions across your organization, leading to strategic research, is through a question-gathering workshop.

A question-gathering workshop serves as a powerful tool to comprehend and align with stakeholders on a broader scale. It's a platform to discover the significant questions that various teams have in mind and to identify how these questions interconnect throughout the product or service.

To conduct a question-gathering workshop, invite relevant stakeholders from various departments, such as:

- Product managers
- Designers
- Sales
- Marketing
- Customer support
- Account management
- Developers
- Potentially even C-suite executives.

During this collaborative workshop, you collect all the questions these stakeholders pose, categorize them into themes, and prioritize them.

This is a long list of people! You would have a workshop filled with 20 people if we took two from each department. That's a lot when it comes to asking individuals' questions and opinions. Whenever you have this many people to invite, I recommend conducting two workshops and trying not to have more than 10 participants per workshop. Additionally, think about the relationships across departments. For example, if product and account management don't get along well, separate them into different workshops.

I recommend thinking about who you need in your workshop to answer the most significant questions across your organization.

PLAN THE WORKSHOP

1. Introduce the Workshop

Start by introducing the workshop goals and outcomes. This gives people a positive mindset of understanding what we are doing today, why they're here, and what we'll accomplish by the end of the session. In this session, discuss what you expect from them as participants.

2. Do an Icebreaker

Similar to research interviews, start with a warm-up. This can be in the form of an icebreaker, a fun activity for participants before diving in. My favorite is "The Aliens Have Landed," where you imagine aliens have landed and are interested in learning what your organization does, but you can only communicate through emojis.

3. Brainstorm Questions

During this three-part stage, everyone brainstorms big questions about users. If workshop participants are struggling with this, you can prompt them by asking, "What are the gaps in our knowledge?" or "What would you need to know about users to make better decisions?"

a. Question sharing

This is the section that takes the most time in the workshop, and where you have to be careful with the number of participants. Each person reads up to two questions they have to the group, and the group discusses the question.

b. Question coaching

Sometimes stakeholders can write leading or unclear questions. If that's the case, you can come in and help them reframe the question in an unbiased way. For example, one of my stakeholders wrote, "How often are our users pulling analytics data from our platform for presentations?"

This particular question is a bit leading and narrow, so instead, I coached the stakeholder to ask a more open-ended question and get at what he wanted to understand, "In what situations are users pulling analytic data?"

c. Question grouping

While participants are sharing questions, start to group similar questions together into clusters, as these will become themes of questions that can impact multiple teams.

4. Prioritize

The next step is prioritizing the questions and mapping them on an impact and effort matrix. You can prioritize through dot voting so each participant has a certain number of votes on the most impactful research projects for the organization.

Once you get an idea of the topic projects, you can plot them on a matrix to understand the estimated effort the project will take. This effort includes how much effort the research study portion of the project will be because it's essential you take on only a few high-effort projects at a time.

5. Address Next Steps and Wrap Up

In this part of the workshop, take the time to address any questions and assign action items. One of those items for you will be to create or update your research roadmap based on the exercise. You will also meet with the relevant teams to develop a research plan and kick off the projects.

AFTER THE WORKSHOP

After the workshop, it's time to dive into the initiatives you've uncovered. Create or update your research roadmap based on the questions and priorities identified. Seek feedback from stakeholders about the workshop to continually improve your facilitation skills and the workshop itself.

By taking a proactive approach through question-gathering workshops, you'll ensure your research efforts align with strategic organizational goals. This structured approach helps you identify high-impact research projects, maintain an efficient research practice, and foster collaboration across departments. Don't hesitate to gather feedback and iterate on your workshop process to keep it effective and valuable.

PRIORITIZING RESEARCH PROJECTS

Ensuring your research efforts are both relevant and impactful is essential for your career growth. Repeatedly conducting the same usability tests can lead to stagnation and frustration. A well-structured project prioritization process can lead to several positive outcomes.

- Diverse Project Portfolio: Prioritization enables you to work on a more diverse set of research projects, broadening your skill set and experiences.

- High-Impact Research: By focusing on prioritized projects, you ensure that your work has a meaningful impact on your organization, enhancing both your credibility and your case studies.
- Transparency: Prioritization brings transparency to your team and colleagues, helping them understand why certain projects take precedence over others.
- Objective Assessment: A structured prioritization process allows for an objective evaluation of projects across the organization, reducing bias and subjective decision-making.
- Implementing a project prioritization process streamlines your research intake, eliminating the need to constantly decide which project to tackle next or manage an overwhelming workload.

A SIMPLE PROJECT PRIORITIZATION PROCESS

Your project prioritization process doesn't need to be overly complex. When a research request comes in, you can swiftly assess its priority by asking a series of questions and applying an objective prioritization measure. Here are the key questions to consider when determining the priority of an incoming research project.

1. Team or Company Priority:
   - Is this project aligned with the team's or company's current priorities and strategy?
   - Where does this topic fall within the team's backlog or roadmap?
   - If you can't find this information, reach out to the product manager or product lead for guidance.
2. Impact Assessment:
   - What impact will the research have?
   - How many teams or departments can benefit from the insights?
   - Prioritize projects that offer cross-functional value by helping multiple teams simultaneously.
3. Research Question Clarity:
   - Does the research question make sense?
   - Is the scope too broad or too business-oriented?
   - Ensure that the research question is clear, relevant, and conducive to meaningful investigation. Work with the team to refine vague or unsuitable questions.
4. Previous Research:
   - Has similar research been conducted before?
   - If yes, has the team reviewed it, and do they want to explore new angles or gather updated data?

- Examine existing research to avoid redundancy. Usability tests from a few years ago may warrant repetition, but generative research often remains relevant.
5. Qualitative Research Suitability:
    - Does this project require qualitative user research?
    - Does it align with the capabilities of qualitative research to provide valuable insights?
    - Ensure that the research approach matches the objectives. For topics like brand perception or large-scale behavioral data, other research methods may be more appropriate.
6. Project Feasibility:
    - Is the project set up for success?
    - Is the design team available to implement changes based on research findings?
    - Does the team have the time and capacity to incorporate research outcomes into their sprint cycles?
    - Confirm that the project is viable and that the team is prepared to act on the insights promptly. Projects that cannot be implemented within a reasonable timeframe may need to be postponed.
7. Level of Researcher Support:
    - What level of support does the team need for this project?
    - Can the team participate actively in research sessions and contribute to analysis and reporting?
    - Evaluate the team's capacity and willingness to collaborate. Projects with lower priority can be pushed through if the team can provide substantial support.
    - Example of levels of support:
    - Full support indicates that you are doing everything to run the research project, from script development to recruitment and analysis and report-writing. The team needs to be present in the interviews and analysis for this to be effective.
    - Medium support means that you are conducting around 50% of the interviews, reviewing the documents (such as the interview guide), and helping with 50% of the synthesis sessions. At medium support, encourage the team to write the report and invite you to double-check it to make sure they interpreted the insights correctly.
    - Minimum support implies that you are doing very little active work. At this level, you can recruit and review the interview guides, but are not conducting any of the interviews or synthesis sessions. I always recommend taking a look at the report, however, to ensure it is sound. You should reserve this level of support only for teams with a high degree of experience in user research.
8. Evaluating Design Decisions:
    - Is the research request focused on validating design decisions?
    - Clarify the role of research. Research is not meant to validate predetermined ideas but to generate insights and inform decisions.

9. Researcher Capacity:
   - Do you have the capacity to take on this project in a timely manner?
   - Consider your current workload and capacity. Maintain a research roadmap and backlog to manage your time effectively.

By systematically addressing these questions, you can grade the priority of different projects. provides a structured and objective approach to project prioritization, ensuring that you allocate your time and resources wisely and focus on research initiatives that align with organizational goals and deliver meaningful value.

RESEARCH QUESTION PRIORITIZATION

Question prioritization goes one step further in the process and looks at the actual questions you receive in a project that you intend to move forward with. Stakeholders might come to you with a research request full of questions. Some of these questions might not be answerable by research, some might be downright leading, or there may be way too many to answer in one particular project.

Question prioritization allows you to dig deeper into the project you are working on to help create the best project possible with your stakeholders. When you have a clear question prioritization process, it becomes easier to manage big projects and to explain to stakeholders what questions make sense for an impactful outcome.

Your first step in question prioritization is to ensure the questions being asked are ideal for research and make sense. To do that, you can make a list of questions that aren't ideal. Here are some I have come across.

- Shallow questions that start with the words:
  - Do...
  - What...
  - Can...
  - Which...
  - Are...
- Questions with product/tech jargon.
- Future-based questions.
- Questions that already had the answer in them (leading questions).
- Positive questions.

Once you identify the problematic questions at your organization, your next step is to try to find patterns and trends in combating and rewriting them. Using the problematic questions from above, here is what I came up with:

- shallow questions → Story-based questions;
- questions with product/tech jargon → Basic questions;

- future-based questions → Past-based questions;
- leading questions → Neutral questions;
- positive questions → Negative questions.

SHALLOW QUESTIONS

Shallow questions are the most common problematic questions because they are the easiest to write. They usually require a one-word answer and contain absolutely no depth.

The problem with shallow questions is, if you are going to ask them, ask them in a survey. Don't ask them in a qualitative interview. Qualitative interviews are all about getting rich data and stories. Asking someone a yes/no question does not get you a story. It gets you a yes or a no.

Shallow questions all lead us to shallow information, where qualitative user research just doesn't shine. If you want to know which feature is most frustrating to users, you shouldn't waste your time doing qualitative interviews! You should run a survey, and then you can answer that question with a larger sample size.

If you are going to do qualitative user research, do it for the right questions. It's a waste of everyone's time, money, energy, and effort to ask shallow questions in interviews.

Your questions should get users to open up with a specific story, so, ideally, your questions should prompt that information from them. For story-based data, you can use the TEDW framework.

- T = "Tell me about…" or "Talk me through…"
- E = "Explain…"
- D = "Describe…"
- W = "Walk me through…"

Let's rewrite some shallow questions to story-based questions:

- What's a problem that our product has helped you solve recently? → Tell me about the last time you had a problem and used our product to fix it.
- Are there any features that you don't use in our product? If so, why? → Describe a feature you don't use in our product. Explain why you don't use X feature.
- Which feature helps you solve problems the most? → Describe a time when our product helped you solve a problem.
- Can you use our product well? → Walk me through how you use our product step by step.

- What's something you've learned from using our product? → Explain something you've learned through using our product.
- Are you satisfied with our product? → Describe how you feel about our product.
- What tools are most important to help you accomplish your key responsibilities? → Walk me through a tool you use to help you achieve X goal.
- Does our product fit into your workflow? → Talk me through how our product impacts your workflow.
- What are some alternatives to our product you've used or considered? → Describe another similar product you've used.

Each of these new questions now prompts much more of a story-based answer, which is the superpower of qualitative research.

QUESTIONS WITH PRODUCT/TECH JARGON

Your users aren't usually in our field. They don't think about things like success metrics and "jobs" that products do. If I were to ask you your success metrics for using Instagram, what would you tell me? Well, maybe you could come up with an answer since we work in the field, but it would be a weird thing to get asked, right? What about if I asked you how successful Instagram's marketing campaigns were?

Whenever you ask jargon questions, you risk getting unreliable data. Someone might just answer without really understanding what they are saying. You also open up a gap between you and your users when it comes to rapport. You go from being conversational to having a business meeting.

There's no need to use fancy terms or words. Use easy-to-understand language that ensures everyone is on the same page, making it easy for your participants to understand you to ensure you're getting more reliable data.

Let's rewrite some jargon questions.

- How do you measure success with our product? → Explain the number one reason you use our product.
- If you could ask us to develop any feature, what would it be? → Describe something that's currently missing from our product. (Follow-up: tell me about a situation where that could have helped you.)
- What is the job that our product does for you? → Explain how this product impacts you.
- What additional functionality would you like our product to have? → Talk me through a time when you weren't able to achieve X goal using our product.

FUTURE-BASED QUESTIONS

Humans are terrible at predicting the future. We can't predict what we are going to do tomorrow with any reliability or validity. We can say what we wish and hope might happen, but we can't say for sure what will happen. And we can't predict what we may pay for. Most future-based questions are on either purchasing or usage behavior.

Instead, the best thing you can do is ask about the past, as it is the best predictor of future behavior. If someone has used something in the past, they are more likely to use it again. If a user has behaved a certain way in the past, they are more likely to do it again. If a user has bought something in the past, they are more likely to buy it again.

For this, you are going to travel back to the past for everything, even innovation! Because innovation comes from helping what people have done in the past in a new way. Users have been figuring out how to do things forever, so you can always ask about past behavior.

If you don't discover what users did in the past and their past processes, you stifle your ability to understand and work toward innovation. There's always a past to dig into. Let's see how to rewrite these kinds of questions.

- If you could change one thing about our product, what would it be? → Walk me through a challenge you had with our product.
- What's a feature you wish our product had? → Describe something that is missing from our product.
- How would you feel if you couldn't use our product anymore? → Talk me through a workaround you used to do X.
- If you could wave a magic wand and change anything about our product, what would it be? → No to this question! Instead, ask about people's pain points and needs.
- How much would you pay for this product? → Hire a pricing expert.
- What would you do instead of that task? → Describe how you've done this in the past.
- Under what circumstances would you like to use the X feature? → Explain a time when you've used the X feature in the past.

LEADING QUESTIONS

Participants can fall into the trap of social desirability bias, which is the tendency to answer questions in a manner that will be viewed favorably by others, an interviewer for instance. All people fall into this trap.

Leading questions are easy to ask but can lead to detrimental data that truly misdirects your team. They set participants up for failure and also set you on course to misunderstanding people's true reactions and perceptions of our products. These questions seem to leave out the negative side of whatever they are exploring and focus on a positive outcome.

The best thing you can do is neutralize your questions by not including any subjective or polarizing words. For example, if you want to specifically learn about satisfaction, you shouldn't ask, "How satisfied are you with X?" Instead, you would include both extremes by asking, "How satisfied or dissatisfied are you with X?"

This opens the door for constructive feedback, which is the type you need to improve and innovate! Let's rewrite the leading questions.

- How satisfied are you with our product? → How satisfied or dissatisfied are you with our product? I wouldn't ask this in an interview, but you could in a survey.
- How happy are you with the product? → Describe how you feel about the product.
- How much does the product help you? → Talk me through how you use the product.
- What value do you get from the product? → Walk me through how the product impacts your day-to-day.

Take out leading language and go as neutral as possible while still trying to ask a valid question. The only time to ask about specific feelings/sentiments is when we lean into pain points and problems.

POSITIVE QUESTIONS

Positive questions are similar to leading questions. User research shines in negative, constructive feedback. As a researcher, participants telling you things are "great" and "fine" is a colossal disappointment. You want them to tell me all their pain points, problems, frustrations, annoyances, fears, etc.

Focusing on the positive (what we are already doing well) isn't particularly actionable for teams. If you spend an entire interview asking people what we are doing well, what is the point? What will the report say?

Innovation and improvement come from negative feedback, so focusing on the bad is actually useful when it comes to qualitative user research. The only time sentiment is relevant for research is while bringing up pain points, frustrations, problems, and barriers. Focusing on "negative" experiences is amazing data for insights. You and your team improve by understanding what is wrong or dissatisfactory with the current experience. So, let's bring some negative feelings into these questions.

- What do you love most about our product? → Tell me about the last frustrating experience you've had with our product.
- What do you like most about this feature? → Describe a challenging moment you've had using X feature.
- Why do you like our product? → Explain a time when our product disappointed you.
- What would you miss the most if we took it away? → Describe one thing that is missing from the product. (Follow up with why.)
- What do you like about how you currently solve the problem? → Walk me through a time when you couldn't use our product.
- What is the best experience you've had with our product? → Talk me through a time when you had to reach out to customer support for a problem you encountered.

Although it can be tough to focus so much on the negative, it really is where user research is great at improving products and elevating the experience.

PRIORITIZING RESEARCH QUESTIONS

Now that you have nicely rewritten questions, you can prioritize them so that the scope of the project is manageable and gets you the exact information your team needs.

A great way to prioritize your research questions is to dump them into a spreadsheet, and for each question, look at the following criteria:

- the original research question the stakeholder submitted;
- whether or not user research could answer that question;
- the rewritten research question;
- the priority of the research question;
- if the question needs a qualitative, quantitative, or mixed-methods approach;
- the method for the question;
- the complexity of answering such a question;
- previous research done on the question;
- alternatives if research can't answer the question;
- supporting notes/links.

This question prioritization process can make it easier to determine, right away, if user research is the best approach (sometimes it isn't, such as with A/B testing) and how to sort through the questions stakeholders had.

Another amazing outcome from this process is being able to see across multiple teams who had similar questions. With this knowledge, you can plan strategic research that spans several teams.

SETTING GENERAL TIMELINES

Project timelines can be a bit like a puzzle, with each piece representing the unique dynamics of your organization: audience, budget, and tools. While there's no universal timeline that fits all scenarios, there are strategies to set clear expectations with stakeholders and navigate project schedules effectively. Give yourself some buffer time. After all, everyone loves it when a project ends on time, and no one appreciates delays.

Instead of prescribing timelines, use the term "negotiate." Research project timelines may not always align with stakeholder expectations. Maintain clarity regarding the timeline you anticipate for the research study. If stakeholders request tight or unrealistic deadlines, consider suggesting an alternative timeframe. Here's a general guideline for research project timelines:

- Generative Research: six to eight weeks.
- Evaluative Research: two to four weeks.
- Hybrid Research (Combining Generative and Evaluative): three to five weeks.

To illustrate these timelines, let's explore some examples of project goals, methods, and associated schedules.

GENERATIVE RESEARCH IN A B2B SETTING

Goals:

- Understand participants' current journey through the platform and their perceptions.
- Uncover pain points and frustrations in daily platform usage.
- Identify unmet needs and areas lacking support in daily usage.

Method:

- 1×1 60-minute interviews with 15 participants (one segment).

Timeline:

- Week one: Planning and kick-off (recruitment in parallel).
- Week two: Recruitment.
- Week three: Continued recruitment, sessions, and debriefs.
- Week four: Sessions and debriefs.
- Week five: Remaining sessions and debriefs.
- Week six: Overall synthesis and report building.
- Week seven: Sharing and workshops.

EVALUATIVE RESEARCH IN A B2C CONTEXT

Goals:

- Understand people's perceptions of the account area and its usage.
- Uncover pain points and frustrations within the account area.
- Evaluate reactions to the prototype.

Method:

- 60-minute usability tests with 7 participants.

Timeline:

- Week one: Planning and kick-off (recruitment in parallel).
- Week two: Recruitment and sessions.
- Week three: Remaining sessions, synthesis, and report-building.
- Week four: Sharing and workshop.

HYBRID RESEARCH IN A B2B2C SCENARIO

Goals:

- Understand how academics currently incorporate interactive components in published journals.
- Uncover pain points and unmet needs of academics regarding interactive components in publications.
- Evaluate participant perceptions and reactions to the concept/prototype.

Method:

- 1×1 60-minute interviews with 15 participants, including a generative and evaluative phase (one segment).

Timeline:

- Week one: Planning and kick-off (recruitment in parallel).
- Week two: Recruitment.

- Week three: Sessions and debriefs.
- Week four: Remaining sessions and debriefs.
- Week five: Synthesis and report-building.
- Week six: Sharing and workshop.

SURVEY RESEARCH IN A B2B SETTING

Goals:

- Understand the broader applicability of insights from qualitative research.
- Prioritize insights from previous qualitative research.

Method:

- Opportunity gap survey to 150 people.

Timeline:

- Week one: Planning and survey-building.
- Week two: Send out the survey and collect responses.
- Week three: Collect responses and perform analysis.
- Week four: Analysis, synthesis, and report-building.
- Week five: Sharing and workshop.

Remember: these timelines are flexible guidelines and may not fit every situation perfectly. If you're uncertain about your project's timeline, consider running a few studies and tracking their durations. This data can help you establish timelines that align with your organization's specific circumstances, ensuring efficient project management.

DESIGN A RESEARCH ROADMAP AND BACKLOG

Demonstrating impact is critical to our jobs as user researchers, especially now. Everywhere you look, it's all about impact. Showing impact, proving impact, sharing impact.

Often the impact gets tied to the output of user research. Were the insights impactful? Did they spur action? What about the product changed? How did the stakeholders feel about the report?

I played the dangerous game of waiting until the insights came from the research to see how impactful the project was. This approach led me to hope my research would impact teams and the organization, rather than knowing I was conducting the most influential research possible.

At one point, I ran several studies in a row that had landed on my desk, without really thinking about how they tied back to the larger goals of the team and the organization. When it came to performance review time, I had done a lot of stuff, but there wasn't much to show. It was disappointing for me, but a fantastic lesson.

A few months before, I had started a user research roadmap and backlog to organize my upcoming projects better and share them with my stakeholders. I'd "grown up" with product roadmaps being important, so I simply took the same concept to apply to my research projects. However, over time, I saw my research roadmaps fall into the same trap many product roadmaps do—they became like "feature factories" filled with projects focused on outputs rather than outcomes. I simply threw research projects on the roadmap, not thinking too much about how the project tied back to the outcome or the business.

While this worked for a while, it ended up not serving me. I was frustrated, churning out projects as teams churned out features. The work felt disjointed from the "bigger picture," but I didn't want to let go of my roadmap. Although it wasn't the most ideal, it gave me such a great place to plan from and was so helpful in transparency with what I was working on.

WHAT'S AN OUTCOME-BASED RESEARCH ROADMAP?

An outcome-based user research roadmap is a living, ever-evolving document that shows the work a user researcher (or user research team) is focused on and how it specifically relates to a larger business objective. It mainly includes projects the team will work on in the next quarter, half-year, or year.

The biggest difference between a general roadmap and an outcome-based roadmap is that, instead of feeling like a feature factory, all of the projects on the roadmap are tied to a specific outcome. The roadmap demonstrates the different outcomes the team will work on and how they will achieve them.

WHAT DO YOU MEAN BY OUTCOME?

Outcomes can be difficult to measure in user research, but it is essential to consider how our work ties to larger team or company-based objectives/goals. When simply putting projects on my roadmap without thinking about the larger goal, I spun my wheels doing the same work repeatedly and always failed to answer the question, "How does user research relate to business?"

When it comes to outcomes, you have to look to your colleagues, teams, and organizations to help you. User research is a support system for decision-making and risk mitigation, so the outcomes of your research should support teams in the decisions they have to make and the risks they might be taking. This concept can be tough to understand, so let's look at some examples.

EXAMPLE ONE

Imagine we are working with the retention team at Pokemon TCG Live (add me if you play—my username is nicolerothier), and the team's outcome is to "improve our day-7 app retention rate by 10%."

Essentially, when people sign up for the live Pokemon Trading Card Game, we want them to return to our app within seven days because, once they pass that seven-day threshold, they are more likely to play for longer and purchase more cards from the store. There are a million ways that we could likely brainstorm how to do this. This means there are a million risks they could take to try and move this metric. That's where user research comes in, and where we can start tying it back to an outcome.

Our research project becomes about mitigating the risks the team is taking when they work to improve this metric. It gives them more of a path or guidance toward making better decisions that resonate with users. So, within this project, our outcome would be:

"Reduce the risk of wasted time/energy when creating solutions to improve our day-7 app retention rate by 10%."

You could also just tie the project directly to the team outcome, but I always like mentioning risk mitigation, helping with decision-making, or reducing choice because it really is the essence of user research.

EXAMPLE TWO

For this example, I will demonstrate the difference between a more feature-based research project versus an outcome-based research project.

Imagine we are working with a conversion team (focused on increasing conversions in our product) at a company called Spooky World, where we sell year-round Halloween decorations. The team's questions are:

- "Should we add a quick buy button?"
- "Should we add product reviews and photos?"

- "Should we include tips on how to decorate? Or maybe create a blog?"
- Should we let users connect with each other and talk about tips? Should we create a Spooky Community?"

These questions focus on features rather than an outcome or users. They can lead to many usability tests that don't add much value to an organization or a product. When you go into a performance review, these types of projects can sometimes feel low impact while still being a good amount of work.

Instead, you can reframe these questions to a larger outcome. Let's take the quick buy button and the product reviews and photos feature. Instead of just talking about features, we could approach it this way: "Improve conversion rate by 5% by simplifying the purchase process."

Or, if we take the blog and community idea, we could tie it to a much larger objective, "Increasing customer basket size by 10% by helping customers understand how to use decorations together."

Either way, we aren't focused on "adding a button" or "creating a community," but rather, we are mitigating risk by helping users and moving business metrics.

EXAMPLE THREE

The final example I want to share is when you run into research projects that feel like they aren't particularly tied to an outcome, such as generative research. Frequently, generative research can be lofty and abstract or could have a lot of potential outcomes across multiple teams.

For this example, let's imagine we are working at Lego, and we are trying to understand our customers better by doing generative research to uncover their pain points, goals, and needs. We're focusing primarily on parents because…money.

Within this context, what is our outcome? There are a few things we could tie this to.

- Break down exactly how this project could impact the current outcomes/goals your teams are working on. Generative research helps you gather a lot of useful information that could help all the major metrics (AARRR metrics, as an example). For instance, generative research could absolutely help with improving retention rates by understanding unmet needs.
- Look further than team-based metrics toward higher-level organization metrics. Generative research helps identify avenues for growth and innovation, which tend to be larger company goals.
- Take into consideration internal outcomes for your team/yourself. You could have a goal of conducting more generative research (e.g., balancing evaluative and generative research better), so that could be an outcome you could include in the study.

- Try not to tie it to a deliverable, because that's an output rather than an outcome. So, if you are looking to create an output, what is the outcome it will achieve? For example, the output of a project is a persona. The outcome of the project is what that persona helps the team do. If we created a persona at Lego, we would want to tie it to an outcome such as creating user-centric product roadmaps or increasing retention rates by understanding and addressing unmet needs.

WHAT'S IN AN OUTCOME-BASED RESEARCH ROADMAP?

There are many different ways you can structure outcome-based research roadmaps, and there isn't necessarily one golden rule to follow. As always, a lot of these components depend on your organization and context, so make sure to take what you need and leave behind what you don't. Also, remember that this is a living, breathing document, and ideally, you are asking for feedback and iterating on it based on your team's needs.

ROADMAP COMPONENTS

Project Name

A name for the project that everyone has agreed on that makes it easy to search for and find later.

Project Goals

Provide a brief overview of the project goals and focus.

Need/Problem

Identify the need for the research and the problem that will be solved from a user-centric point of view.

Outcomes

What are the outcomes that will be achieved when the project is over? These can be broken down into:

- business outcomes, such as the ones we defined above that relate back to concepts like the AARRR metrics;
- internal/research outcomes, such as conducting more generative research.

Project Type

In this section, I typically note the type of product through methodology.

Priority Level

In my roadmap, I have low, medium, high, and critical levels. I put the project through this template to help me determine the priority level.

Support Level

Decide on the level of support you (or the researcher) will give the team. Here are examples of support levels I use.

1. Full support indicates that you are doing everything to run the research project, from script development to recruitment, analysis, and (lean) report writing. The team needs to be present in the interviews and analysis for this to be effective.
2. Medium support means that you are conducting around 50% of the interviews, reviewing the documents (such as the interview guide), and helping with 50% of the synthesis sessions. At medium support, encourage the team to write the report and invite you to double-check it to ensure they interpreted the insights correctly.
3. Minimum support implies that you are doing very little active work. At this level, you can recruit and review the interview guides, but you are not conducting any of the interviews or synthesis sessions. I always recommend taking a look at the report, however, to ensure it is sound. You should reserve this level of support only for teams with a high degree of experience in user research.

Team/Stakeholders

Note the team and stakeholders involved in the research. You can use the RACI model here (responsible, accountable, consulted, informed).

Current Status

Keep the current status of the project updated. I typically do this by the research phase it is in.

Approximate Timeline

Give an approximate timeline of the project. If you want to get into the details here, you can break down the timeline into phases, or you can give a more general timeline of when the project can be done.

Incentive Amount

I always include the incentive amount for the study because it can help with budgeting in the future.

Resources

Any necessary or helpful links to things like the intake document or research plan, which has all the relevant information for the study, including a script, deliverables, and a report. I recommend putting these into whatever software your team is currently using for roadmaps or tracking work. If you want a starting point, you can use this and adapt it to your software.

HOW TO BUILD AN OUTCOME-BASED RESEARCH ROADMAP

Outcome-based research roadmaps are similar to standard roadmaps, but you go a few steps further to ensure the roadmap is aligned with the team and business objectives. Here are the steps I go through when building out this type of research roadmap.

STEP ONE: UNDERSTAND THE ORGANIZATIONAL VISION AND GOALS

In the most ideal world, the organizational product vision and strategy are already clearly defined by others (such as the C-suite or executive-level leadership). A product vision is essentially about the reason your product exists and where you want it to be in five years. It should give the organization a cohesive North Star to work toward so that everyone is aligned on the overarching goal of the organization.

Next, there are goals that break that product vision into specific and measurable components. These goals will help you achieve the larger product vision. Ideally, they are written using the SMART format: Specific, Measurable, Achievable, Relevant, and Time-Bound.

The product vision and goals will be your jumping-off point for research work. They give you a concrete idea of where the organization wants to go and can help you understand the most impactful research you can do to support these goals.

I typically sit down with a product leader to get an understanding of the organizational product vision and goals. As they explain it to me, I ask different questions, like why that particular vision, what the main metrics they are looking to achieve are, the timeframe of the goals, and any prioritization of projects or initiatives of which I should be aware.

WHAT IF THERE IS NO PRODUCT VISION OR GOALS?

Unfortunately, sometimes companies lack a clear vision and goals. Try to help your organization get started with these types of conversations. A huge caveat for this is to ensure that YOU don't take this on. It's not the responsibility of a researcher to define a product's vision and goals. You could, however, help with facilitating a workshop on the topic.

STEP TWO: GET FAMILIAR WITH TEAM GOALS

Ideally, the teams you are working with also have clear and straightforward goals that are aligned with the overarching product vision and goals. Whenever you are working with a team, it is super important to remember that you are their support system. You are there to mitigate the risk of the choices they make, narrow the scope of potential solutions, and help them make better decisions that move metrics in a positive way.

My favorite thing to do at this point is to sit down with each of my product managers and designers (depending on how many teams I'm working with at once) and go through their goals. I use a stakeholder interview technique at this point to gather this information by asking questions like:

- Tell me about your team's focus area.
- What is your team working on right now? How about in the next 6 months?

- Is there a roadmap and backlog I can see?
- What are the team's current goals/metrics/OKRs/KPIs?
- How do you plan and prioritize projects?
- How do you measure success in your team?
- What is your number one priority right now? How would that be successful?
- What are some metrics/OKRs that you would like to improve? Why?
- What would the ideal outcome be by the end of this quarter? The end of the year?
- What areas are you struggling with when it comes to achieving these goals?
- What are some of your ideas to achieve these goals/OKRs/metrics?

This conversation usually gives me a clear understanding of what the team's goals are and how I can help support these goals through research, which makes tying my projects back to outcomes much easier.

WHAT IF MY TEAMS DON'T HAVE CLEAR GOALS?

This question gets a bit harder than the product vision/goal question. If your teams don't have goals or metrics on what they're working toward, it becomes impossible to tie your work back to them. If this is the case, I would highly recommend creating your own (or your team's) OKRs/goals so that you still have something to tie your work back to. If you are struggling to come up with these team OKRs, I highly recommend listening to where I outline clear ways to do this.

STEP THREE: GATHER YOUR RESEARCH PROJECTS/REQUESTS

If you already have a bunch of research projects that you need to put into a roadmap and backlog, you can skip to step four and start mapping your projects to the different outcomes. If you don't have a large list of projects or requests, there are a few things you can do.

- Ask your stakeholders to submit their requests through intake documents.
- Run a question-gathering workshop to identify large questions across your teams.

- Sit down with your stakeholders to interview them, and review their backlog to get an idea about their research needs.

Whatever place you are in, it's important to have a potential list of projects you will be working on. User research does its best when it is ahead of what's coming, especially generative-based research.

STEP FOUR: MAP THE PROJECTS/REQUESTS TO OUTCOMES

Now comes the fun part…well, fun for some. This part will be worth it when you step into your performance evaluation and can see directly how your research has impacted a team or organization.

For each project, it's time to sit down and map it to the outcomes you determined for each team you are working with and the organization as a whole. Think about the metric you will impact based on the team's goals. For instance:

- reducing bounce rate from the sign-up page by 10%;
- increasing first-time ticket purchases by 5%;
- increasing repeat order rate by 15%;
- increasing sign-ups through a bonus referral program by 10%;
- increasing basket size/average order value by 10%.

Refer back to the team's OKRs/goals and use those (or the organization's goals) to map to each project.

If you can't map an outcome to a project, I would consider it lower priority. However, you can also use success criteria.

Success criteria don't have to do with things like UX metrics or the product necessarily, but rather look at how you would deem the project as a success by the end. Ideally, your success criteria should be measurable and should relate back to your research goals. A great question to ask is, "What would determine this research project a success in the end?" The answer could be anything from.

- It identified and clearly articulated the top five pain points.
- It discovered the top three most frustrating moments of users.
- You completed three ideation workshops.

For this part, really think about what would make you and your team sit at the end of a project and say, "That was a success."

STEP FIVE: PRIORITIZE THE ROADMAP BASED ON THE HIGHEST-IMPACT PROJECTS

Once you have all the outcomes mapped, it's time to look at the highest-impact projects. You can ask yourself:

- What are the projects that will help the teams the most?
- What are the projects that have the biggest potential impact on the organization?
- What are the projects that I feel user research can impact the most?

Not every project you do will have the highest impact on a team or organization. Sometimes we need to do some low-level usability tests because it will help a team move forward with an idea. So, keep in mind that you won't always be able to do super high-impact projects; however, they should be closer to 60% of your work.

Once you prioritize this, make sure to share with your stakeholders how the prioritization came about so they can understand your decision-making process. If you are struggling with balancing different levels of impact work, you could potentially start a rolling research program.

AN EXAMPLE OF BUILDING AN OUTCOME-BASED RESEARCH ROADMAP

Because building a roadmap can be a difficult concept (and often feel abstract), let's look at an example of how I've built an outcome-based research roadmap in the past. This example is from when I was working at a travel company. I am going to use similar data from the actual company and projects, but it isn't 100% the same because I don't have that documentation. The reason I can share this is due to the fact that the company went under, so I am not sharing anything confidential.

STEP ONE: UNDERSTAND THE ORGANIZATIONAL VISION AND GOALS

We had a bit of a fuzzy product vision and goals, so if you are struggling with this part, I feel you. A bit of context: we were a ticketing platform where you could search for your destination, and we would give you different combinations of routes you could take to get from your starting to ending point. This could include different modes of transport such as buses, cars, trains, and planes.

Our big product vision was to be the go-to ticketing platform for people planning and purchasing trips throughout Europe. Some of our organizational goals included:

1. To implement a seamless and intuitive booking process, reducing the time it takes to complete a booking by 20% within the next 12 months.
2. To be used monthly by 50% of European target markets within the next 12 months.

There were a million ways that we could get to those goals, so it was time to go to my team.

STEP TWO: GET FAMILIAR WITH TEAM GOALS

I was working across several different teams, but I will highlight the goals from two particular teams.

Acquisition

I sat down with my product manager and designer in the acquisition team to understand the particular goals they were working on that would help achieve the larger organizational goals. One of those goals was to increase the number of monthly user registrations on the platform by 30% within the next six months.

Retention

I then sat down and did a more formal interview with my product manager and designer in the retention team because the team was newly formed and we hadn't worked together yet. I asked the questions I mentioned above about what they were focusing on and what kinds of metrics they were looking to use. One of those goals was to increase the percentage of users who make repeat bookings within 12 months by 20%.

STEP THREE: GATHER YOUR RESEARCH PROJECTS/REQUESTS

I was newer to the organization at this point, so I didn't have a long list of research projects or requests. With this in mind, since I was in a start-up setting, I ended up sitting with my respective teams to discuss the type of research they needed. I did this because I thought a big question-gathering workshop would be too overwhelming. In these meetings, I asked things like:

- How could you imagine user research helping you with [goals they mentioned]?
- Tell me about your research needs.
- What are the gaps in our knowledge?
- What do you wish you knew about users that would make your decision-making easier?
- What is a problem users are facing?
- How do we know this is a problem?
- Why is this problem important?

When I left this meeting, I had a list of questions from both teams that included topics and questions like the following.

- How did people actually navigate through the platform?
- What are the top five pain points people encounter when searching and booking?
- How do people decide to use us over our competitors? And vice versa?
- What are the unmet needs of our users? Where are we not supporting them in their searching/booking journey?
- What do people think of loyalty programs?
- Why don't people come back after their first purchase?

STEP FOUR: MAP THE PROJECTS/ REQUESTS TO OUTCOMES

The first thing I did was look at the different questions that came from the workshop and start to map them to the outcomes. I changed these from questions to projects, which means some of them rolled into each other.

1. Navigate the platform → Better understand how users navigate the platform, including what pain points they encounter and unmet needs they have while searching/booking.
2. Loyalty program → Better understand people's mental models around loyalty programs in general and when it comes to travel.
3. Competitve research → Better understand how people think about searching/booking travel and how they choose their platform.
4. Retention research → Better understand why people come back for repeat purchases and what is still missing from the platform.

Then I went back to the two main goals I focused on:

- increase the number of monthly user registrations on the platform by 30% within the next six months;
- increase the percentage of users who make repeat bookings within 12 months by 20%.

With these in mind, I was able to map the projects to the different outcomes.

1. Navigating the platform → Increase the percentage of repeat bookings. This is because we would identify pain points and unmet needs during this particular project that could lead to improvements, causing people to come back.
2. Competitive research → Increase the monthly user registration. This would help us uncover people's mental models behind why they choose certain platforms and potentially give us insight into how to acquire more customers.
3. Loyalty program → Increase the monthly user registration. This one was a bit more of a gamble because, although it might increase our user base, this was a bit too specific for right then. I wanted to first understand how people navigated the platform and their pain points before moving forward with this.
4. Retention research → Increase the percentage of repeat bookings. By understanding why people stayed and what they were frustrated by, we could potentially get rid of these pain points and encourage people to stay.

All of these also felt like they aligned with the below goals:

- implement a seamless and intuitive booking process, reducing the time it takes to complete a booking by 20% within the next 12 months;
- be used monthly by 50% of European target markets within the next 12 months.

STEP FIVE: PRIORITIZE THE ROADMAP BASED ON THE HIGHEST-IMPACT PROJECTS

I sat with my product managers and designers to help prioritize this list of projects. We did have more than we listed that were less relevant, such as looking into sustainable travel decisions, rebranding our website, and redesigning the look of a ticket. However, for the quarter, we decided on:

- navigating the platform, because this would help us with creating a more seamless and intuitive booking process while also helping increase the percentage of repeat orders;

- competitive research, because this would help us with being used by more people within our target market and increasing monthly registration.

We put retention research and the loyalty program in the backlog because retention research is really complex, and I believed we could get more from the platform navigation, and the loyalty program felt too specific.

Since these projects were quite large, the roadmap also included a few smaller projects, such as a few usability tests on features we had discovered last quarter.

ITERATE AND IMPROVE

Building an outcome-based roadmap is definitely not something you can immediately do perfectly. They take some patience and practice, but they are so incredibly worth it. You can easily tie your work back to a huge impact and have "evidence" of this right in your roadmap. You can also share all the work you are currently doing, which enables people to see that they need to engage with you early and plan research in advance.

I recommend building a roadmap but keeping very open to iterating on it, gathering feedback, and improving it over time. My first roadmap was just the name of the project and the team, so it took me a few years to get into the habit of outcome-based roadmaps. However, it was well worth the effort!

Create a Research Framework 7

Now that you have set up the core operations of your research practice, it is time to put a user research framework into place. To be impactful, you must align user research with the business and your teams. This means we look at the overarching strategy and goals of your company and at ensuring your projects are directly related.

There are a lot of processes and frameworks out there when it comes to user research. For example, we have design thinking, lean user research, sprints, Jobs to be Done, and product development processes. As a user researcher, what is your process? How do you execute different research projects? Which elements of design thinking do you mash together with product development phases? When do you throw away lean research for an in-depth study?

What are your boundaries? Your colleagues could come to you with questions that break any template. What do you do if stakeholders don't care about parts of the process, or they want the research to go quicker?

It is critical to build a framework for your user research team—even if you are a team of one. A framework gives you direction and purpose and helps you make transparent decisions on project priority. A user research framework is the glue that holds together all the work you did to set up your core operations. It gives meaning to what you do within an organization.

WHY A USER RESEARCH FRAMEWORK IS IMPORTANT

As researchers, we often find ourselves caught in the whirlwind of trying to conduct research in a rush, striving to meet deadlines that seem to have passed yesterday. This reactive approach can leave us feeling overwhelmed and disconnected from the broader goals of our research practice. This disarray is particularly frustrating when we yearn to engage in more strategic and impactful work.

Every research project and initiative should have a well-defined set of goals and outcomes, and the creation of a user research framework is no exception. Your research framework should be accompanied by a clear set of goals, answering the fundamental question: "What do we aim to achieve?" It's essential to remember that your research framework doesn't only serve you; it's also a roadmap for your colleagues. Including them in the process is paramount, and conducting stakeholder interviews can provide valuable insights into their expectations.

COMPONENTS OF A RESEARCH FRAMEWORK

Once you've defined your goals and outcomes, you can begin crafting your framework. A productive starting point is to draw inspiration from framework documents within other departments of your organization. Engage in conversations with colleagues, who have previously created impactful strategies, to understand their approach and rationale. Deconstruct their strategies to discern what makes them effective, and gain insights for shaping your own.

It's perfectly okay for this phase to take time. Brainstorming and developing strategies, especially if you're new to the process, can be time-consuming. Consider involving others, such as your manager, in this process if you encounter challenges. When outlining your research framework, consider incorporating the following elements.

- Mission: Define the mission of your research team or function and how it contributes to the organization. Specify the levels within the organization that user research impacts and the value it provides at each level.
- Vision: Break down the mission into smaller components and articulate how you plan to realize and achieve each part.
- Goals: Establish short-term goals for three, six, and twelve months. Align these goals with the teams you work with and the overarching business objectives.
- Roadmap and Backlog: Develop a roadmap and backlog to provide transparency about ongoing research projects and their timelines.
- Prioritization Process: Implement a clear prioritization process to determine which projects are most impactful and should take precedence when resources are limited.
- Impact Measurement: Devise a method for measuring the impact of user research over time, both externally (product metrics, strategic changes) and internally (team and process improvements).
- Resource Tracking: Maintain a resource tracking sheet that includes budgetary requirements, team capacity, necessary tools, and potential hiring decisions.

As you can see, you already have some of these components covered from previous sections of the book, such as a roadmap, backlog, and a prioritization process. Of course, you can pick and choose what works best for your user research framework, but I do recommend thinking through the above pieces.

CREATING YOUR USER RESEARCH FRAMEWORK

Developing a user research framework is a gradual process that requires continuous refinement. Feedback and the evolving nature of research within your organization will necessitate ongoing iterations. It's essential to remember that everyone has to start somewhere. Here's a structured process for creating your user research framework.

Define the Mission

The mission within your user research framework is all about the value the team currently provides the organization and what that team is at its core. When defining the mission, you can think about the different levels of an organization that user research impacts:

- individuals
- teams
- cross-departmental
- organizational.

Then, brainstorm how research is valuable to that particular level. For example, user research can support designers in their choice of how to design something, help customer support teams surface important bugs, or help create an innovative product through personas or customer journey maps.

Once you have this information, synthesize it into a concise mission, about one or two sentences. An example of a previous mission I've used is:

> To deliver high-quality insights and findings that help individuals and teams make more user-centric decisions, and to ensure we are solving real problems while saving time and money for the organization.

In this mission, you are impacting individuals and teams to make user-centric decisions through high-quality insights, and you are also highlighting real problems while saving time and money. These are all extremely important parts of user research and how it can impact different spaces within a company. Ideally, your mission showcases that you can effectively help those different areas.

Create the Vision

The vision breaks down the mission into actionable steps that align with your goals. Deconstruct each part of the mission and determine how research can tangibly impact those areas. For example, the above mission includes:

- high-quality insights and findings;
- teams making more user-centric decisions;
- ensuring we solve real problems;
- saving money and time for the organization.

How, as a research function, can you tangibly impact those areas? So, for instance, helping teams make more user-centric decisions means you need to:

- know what teams are working on;
- align your research efforts with their work and expected outcomes;
- conduct research that informs whatever gaps in knowledge or questions they have;
- meet with your teams regularly to align with their work.

Some other examples include:

- biweekly or weekly meetings with colleagues to understand what they are working on in terms of projects and team goals;
- aligning your research roadmap/backlog with the product roadmap/backlog so you can get ahead of projects and do proactive research;
- quarterly question-gathering workshops that allow you to understand what gaps are in your knowledge to fill them through generative research.

Again, do this for each part of the mission until you have a vision with several parts that would help you achieve your created mission.

Break Down Goals

Develop goals for the short, medium, and long term (e.g., three, six, and twelve months). Use Objectives and Key Results (OKRs) to align with the teams you work with and the overarching business objectives. Regularly engage with stakeholders to understand their goals and metrics by asking these questions:

- What are your goals for the next three to six months?
- What are you hoping to achieve in the next three to six months?
- What metrics are important to you in the next three to six months?

Once you have these conversations, utilize the information to create OKRs for the research team. There are two types of goals you can focus on:

1. External goals, which focus on product- or company-based goals. These goals primarily look at moving metrics, such as increasing acquisition, decreasing time on task, or understanding users on a larger scale.
2. Internal goals, which include optimizing the current user research practice by increasing stakeholder satisfaction, decreasing the time between research requests and research start, and decreasing recruitment time.

Remember to meet with stakeholders biweekly to ensure you are supporting them with their most relevant goals.

Set Up a Roadmap and Prioritization Process

If you haven't already set up a roadmap and prioritization process, now is the time to do it. Remember that these key parts of your process allow you to ensure project transparency, track the work you're doing, understand your capacity, and balance the type of research you're conducting.

By aligning your roadmap and prioritization process to your mission, vision, and goals, you make sure you are doing the most impactful research possible in a consistent manner.

Track Your Impact over Time

Tracking the impact of research over time can be difficult. For example, so many teams contribute to a product's or feature's success, so it can be challenging to understand how user research contributes to this. I recommend categorizing your impact:

1. External impact, which looks at areas such as product metrics or strategic change for the product or organization.
2. Internal impact, which looks at your team and processes and how they affect user research value and perception across the organization.

Every time user research impacts an individual, team, multiple departments, or organization, write down the impact so you can track this over time to see what we are affecting and at what level.

Define Your Principles

Articulate the principles that guide your research practice. These principles should embody your team's values and beliefs, serving as a moral compass for your work. The best step is to brainstorm with your team (or with your manager/trusted colleague if you are on your own). Below are some examples of principles I've used in the past:

- User-Centeredness: Prioritize the needs, preferences, and behaviors of users in all research activities. Ensure that research outcomes directly contribute to improving the user experience.
- Empathy: Cultivate empathy for users by actively seeking to understand their perspectives, challenges, and emotions. This empathy informs research design and interactions with study participants.
- Inclusivity: Strive to include diverse user groups representative of the intended audience in research studies. Recognize and respect individual differences in backgrounds, abilities, and circumstances.
- Ethical Conduct: Adhere to ethical research practices, including informed consent, data privacy, and the protection of participants' rights. Maintain the highest level of integrity in research processes and outcomes.
- Transparency: Be transparent about research objectives, methods, and findings. Communicate research limitations and uncertainties to stakeholders and participants honestly.
- Collaboration: Foster collaboration between cross-functional teams, integrating user research into the design and decision-making processes. Share insights and collaborate effectively with colleagues to drive user-centered solutions.
- Continuous Learning: Embrace a culture of continuous learning and improvement. Seek opportunities to refine research methods, stay updated on industry trends, and incorporate feedback into research practices.
- Usability and Accessibility: Prioritize usability and accessibility testing to ensure products and services are usable and inclusive for all users, including those with disabilities.
- Rigorous Methodology: Apply rigorous research methodologies appropriate to the research objectives. Maintain consistency and validity in data collection and analysis.
- Actionable Insights: Focus on generating actionable insights that directly inform design decisions and product improvements. Avoid conducting research for research's sake.
- Iterative Approach: Embrace an iterative approach to research and design, continuously refining solutions based on user feedback and evolving needs.
- Empirical Evidence: Rely on empirical evidence and data-driven insights rather than assumptions or personal biases when making recommendations and decisions.
- User Advocacy: Act as advocates for users within the organization, ensuring that their needs and concerns are considered at all stages of product development.
- Impact Orientation: Evaluate the impact of research efforts by measuring how they contribute to business goals, user satisfaction, and product success.

- Communication Skills: Develop effective communication skills to convey research findings and insights in a clear, compelling, and actionable manner to both technical and non-technical stakeholders.
- Flexibility: Adapt research approaches and methodologies to suit the specific context, constraints, and objectives of each project. Avoid a one-size-fits-all approach to research.

Make a Budget

Depending on your organization's budgeting cadence, create a budget for user research. Consider both a lean budget and a strategic budget over the budgeting period. Present these options to stakeholders, highlighting the pros and cons of each approach to facilitate informed decision-making. After you choose the cadence, calculate two types of budgets (this example uses biannual budgeting):

1. A lean budget—The absolute bare minimum of research you should do over six months and the fewest amount of tools/team members.
2. A strategic budget—The most user research you could do over six months and the ideal number of tools/team members.

The strategy of adopting a dual-budget approach, while not always essential, can be particularly valuable depending on your organization's context. For instance, in my experience working with startups and smaller companies that often have limited budgets for user research, this approach can provide a practical solution to a common question: "How low can we go?"

Instead of repeatedly addressing this question, consider creating two distinct budgets and aiming to strike a balance between them. This method offers transparency in your decision-making process and can enhance trust among stakeholders.

When presenting these two budgets, it's crucial to articulate the significant differences between the lean and strategic approaches, along with their associated advantages and disadvantages. For instance, focusing on a strategic budget can bring several benefits.

1. Holistic Customer Insights: A strategic budget allows you to gain a more comprehensive understanding of your customer base, paving the way for testing multiple features across various teams.
2. Enhanced Customer Engagement: With a strategic budget, you can foster more frequent and meaningful interactions between your teams and customers, thereby gathering valuable input.
3. Establishment of a Rolling Research Program: This approach facilitates the extension of research support to teams beyond the product domain, ensuring that customer input is available where needed.
4. Diverse Customer Reach: A strategic budget enables outreach to a wider array of customers, fostering a deeper understanding of the market space and enabling the creation of deliverables like personas and journey maps.

5. Informed Decision-Making: By prioritizing a strategic budget, you empower your organization to make decisions based on a more extensive customer base, leading to more informed and effective choices.
6. Streamlined Research Processes: With a strategic budget, you can invest in tools that streamline and optimize the user research process, ultimately making projects more efficient and effective.

By clearly elucidating the advantages and drawbacks of each approach, you enable your colleagues to make well-informed decisions. They will have a precise understanding of what to anticipate from research efforts in the forthcoming six months.

Once you have determined the budgeting cadence and the type of budget you require, you can proceed with the following steps to calculate the exact funding needed.

CONDUCTING RESEARCH

- Projects: Begin by estimating the total number of research projects planned for the next six months. Collaborate with stakeholders to ascertain project requirements.
- Methodologies: For each project, identify the methodologies to be employed and estimate the time required for each (e.g., 90-minute interviews, 45-minute usability tests). Timing is critical for determining participant incentives and the required number of participants.
- Participant Numbers: Determine the number of participants required for each project and calculate the average cost per participant.

Using this information, apply the following calculation:

(Total Cost of Projects) * (Number of Participants) * (Cost per Participant).

For instance, consider four projects:

- two 45-minute usability tests with seven participants each (14 total);
- one 60-minute one-on-one interview project with fifteen participants;
- one unmoderated card sort with twenty-five participants.

Each participant's cost varies (e.g., $45, $60, $35). Calculate the total research cost by multiplying these factors:

- usability Test Total: 14 * $45 = $630;
- interview Total: 15 * $60 = $900;
- card Sorting Total: 25 * $35 = $875.

Thus, the total research cost amounts to $2,405.

TOOLING

Categorize tools into planning research, recruitment and scheduling, conducting research, analysis and synthesis, and sharing research. Ideally, have at least one tool (or a few for each category) that enhances efficiency.

When budgeting for tools, consider the aspects of your research process that consume the most time and identify significant pain points. Addressing these specific pain points can be an effective way to justify the addition of tools, highlighting benefits such as increased study numbers, faster research timelines, reduced recruitment efforts, or broader participant pools. When proposing tool budgets, particularly within constraints, explore multiple options at different price points and present these choices for consideration.

HIRING

Determine whether hiring is a necessary component of your budget. If so, emphasize the value that an additional team member can bring to the organization. The pitch for hiring can encompass these points:

- Building an empathetic, user-focused company that aligns product and business strategies with user needs.
- Improving the understanding of how users perform tasks to design a more effective and enjoyable user experience.
- Reducing development time and avoiding costly fixes by gaining a clear vision upfront.
- Ensuring a cohesive user experience across different teams and products/services.
- Resolving disagreements through user testing, fostering a culture of evidence-based decision-making.
- Creating products that address relevant user problems and motivate teams.

When budgeting for hiring, conduct thorough research on market salaries and average compensation for the role, considering the level and location. The key is to provide colleagues with a clear rationale for the chosen numbers.

By meticulously following these steps and offering transparent explanations, you can develop a well-structured budget that aligns with your organization's goals and resources. This approach not only facilitates effective financial planning but also enhances communication and understanding among stakeholders.

While crafting your user research framework, remember that it's a dynamic document that evolves alongside your organization's needs and research practices. Embrace the iterative nature of this process, seeking continuous feedback and making refinements as you learn and grow.

PART FOUR

Define Your Playbook

Introduction to the Five Phases

8

When first creating a research process, I wanted to build something that would apply to many companies, so I took the general product development process (which has a million variations) at its most basic form:

- discovery;
- definition;
- design;
- development and implementation.

I modeled my process after the product development process because I wanted something that stakeholders would be familiar with. If I created an approach based solely on what I wanted to do as a researcher, it might not match the reality of how a product works at an organization. And this framework gave me a starting point, rather than just sitting and staring at a blank page for hours.

After writing the four areas of the product development process, I realized I wanted to elaborate on some of them, so I chose the following stages:

- problem discovery, which looks at your users' problems and needs with a broader lens;
- problem definition, which narrows the scope of the project to dive deeply into understanding a particular pain point or need;
- design refinement, which helps you know if the team is going in the right direction with solving that problem;
- testing and execution, which allows you to decide on whether the solution is ready to launch;
- measuring and iterating, which enables you to measure the success of the solution and continue iterating on it based on feedback.

These steps don't always happen linearly. Sometimes, if you've already done the research, you might skip to design refinement. Or if the product is live and you never set up success criteria, you might start with measuring and then return to design refinement if things need to change (or even to problem definition if you need a deeper understanding of the problem).

I recommend going through the normal process for writing down the different phases you encounter—almost like a customer journey map. Through this process, you can define your steps if the above don't make sense for your organization. Feel free to also start with the phases above and tweak them based on feedback and iteration.

Once you have defined your phases, the next step is to detail the information you are going to include in each phase to build out your exact approach. You can use the following to get started:

1. goal, including what you are trying to achieve with that particular phase of the process;
2. activities that happened before any actual research took place;
3. approximate timeline of that phase;
4. potential methodologies that make sense in that phase;
5. approaches to analysis in that phase;
6. ways to synthesize within that particular phase;
7. expected outcomes/deliverables for the phase;
8. post-research activities (activation) that bring your insights to a solution;
9. how to lean out the phase;
10. your boundaries for that phase.

With these in mind, it's time for you to build out your playbook. Each chapter will detail one of the five phases. I recommend reading through all of them and then going back through each as you create your playbook.

Phase One
Problem Discovery

9

Problem discovery is all about learning the problems your users might be encountering, for uncovering those juicy "unknown unknowns." It is hugely based on longer, broader discovery work as the topics can be general. You are diving into your user base, simply trying to understand them. It's an exciting part of the process, but can feel overwhelming due to being so loosely defined.

When it comes to problem discovery, it is important to have a playbook in mind, because it can help descope the research from getting too out of hand. Here is how I structure the first phase of the research playbook.

GOAL

To discover the range of our users' problems and needs through a broad lens.

PRE-RESEARCH ACTIVITIES

- Intake. When a request comes through, do your best to send an intake form to them to get as much information as possible, even if it a shortened version of the one previously discussed. Review this with stakeholders, and reframe any questions to properly scope the project.
- Question gathering workshop with stakeholders. If the stakeholders are unsure about their questions OR you aren't starting with an intake form, a question-gathering workshop is the best step for you to understand their needs.
- Research plan. Once the project questions are user-centric and defined, it is time to create your research plan to ensure everyone is on the same page with expectations.
- Define participant segments and plan recruitment. Ensuring you get the right participants is absolutely critical before you start researching. Check out pages X and X for more information on segmentation and recruitment.

- Success criteria. Defining success criteria is critical to knowing and proving whether or not the project was successful. For the broad approach of problem discovery, your success criteria may not be as pointed as in other projects. Some great success criteria for a problem discovery project include:
  - finding and prioritizing X amount of insights from the project;
  - following up with X studies to dive deeper into each prioritized problem space.
- Kick-off meeting to align expectations, goals, and outcomes right before the project begins. I typically don't hold these meetings anymore, since I've replaced them with the intake document and the research plan. However, if you feel like another meeting is necessary to ensure everyone is aligned, this is a great step. In this kick-off meeting you can review:
  - research goals and outcomes;
  - recruitment criteria and participants;
  - methodology;
  - discussion guide/questions;
  - deliverables;
  - timelines.

APPROXIMATE TIMELINE

Problem discovery is often a larger project, because the goals tend to be more loosely defined than something like solution design. Because of the larger scope, I recommend giving yourself more time for these types of projects. Here is a breakdown of a problem discovery project timeline:

- Total time: Eight weeks (for one or two segments)
  - planning: one week;
  - recruitment: two weeks;
  - conducting research: two weeks;
  - analysis and synthesis: one week;
  - reporting: one week;
  - activation: one week.

For each additional segment, add one or two weeks.

SAMPLE SIZES

- one-on-one interviews: 15–25 participants per segment. For personas or other similar deliverables, aim for 20 participants per segment;
- diary studies: 15 participants per segment;

- contextual inquiry: 12–15 participants, per segment;
- mental model interviews: 15–20 interviews, per segment;
- participatory design: 10–12 participants, per segment.

POTENTIAL METHODOLOGIES

Primary Research

- Generative research one-on-one interviews. Generative research one-on-one interviews are your go-to for problem discovery. They allow you to dive deeply into understanding humans and their needs, goals, and pain points. You don't take them down a particular path, but rather explore the space and topics with them. At the problem discovery stage, these conversations can often be product-agnostic.
- Jobs to be Done (JTBD)—See resource appendix. There have been plenty of books written just on JTBD, so I am not covering this in my book. The best resource I have for you to learn JTBD is Jim Kalbach's Jobs to be Done Playbook, which you can find in the resource appendix. He gives a fantastic in-depth guide beyond anything I could create. JTBD is a fantastic way of understanding user needs in a product-agnostic sense within the problem discovery phase.
- Mental model interviews—See resource appendix. Indi Youngs book Mental Models is the most fantastic resource I've read, when it comes to properly understanding Mental Models in user research. This approach is ideal for the problem discovery stage, because it allows you to dive deeply into how your audience thinks about and perceives the world around them, both inside and outside of a product perspective. You can dive deeply into the problems they encounter and needs they have.
- Customer Journey interviews—See resource appendix. Mapping Experiences by Jim Kalbach will give you everything you need to know about customer journey mapping. Using customer journey maps for problem discovery is a fantastic mechanism for understanding how your audience moves through an overarching journey, and the associated needs, goals, and pain points to each stage. A journey map can give you a great representation of what problems your audience is encountering, so that you can dive more deeply into each.
- Contextual inquiry. Contextual inquiry is the ultimate tool for understanding how your audiences' environments impact their decisions, thoughts, and perceptions. You can gain so many insights into the problems your audience runs into, while interacting with their environment—some of which they might not even be aware of themselves!

Secondary Research

- Literature review. A literature review is an extremely important part of the discovery research process because it gives you the opportunity to think through the scope of your research and find what you truly don't know. Literature reviews are a go-to first step, especially when starting out with such broad topics and concepts as we do in problem discovery research.
- Triangulating data. Looking for clues of potential problems in different resources (e.g., customer support tickets) is a great way to start problem discovery research. Through triangulating data from multiple sources, you can already start to get an idea of what types of problems your audience may be encountering. If you want to experiment with an explanatory sequential research design (quantitative research followed by qualitative research), triangulating data is a fantastic approach.

FOLLOW-UP RESEARCH

- Opportunity gap survey. During problem discovery, you can often find many problems or insights, which can make it difficult for teams to prioritize. The opportunity gap survey gives you a mechanism to measure the current importance and level of satisfaction for each problem. This survey can help you and your team determine which problems to focus on first.

ANALYSIS

- Transcribing the session. Depending on what tools and budget you have available, you might not have to transcribe your research sessions. Typically, this looks like listening to the session and creating a transcript, which you can then analyze and synthesize. This step is optional, especially if you are overwhelmed with interviews and data.
- Creating tags. You can either create tags from the ground up (which we will talk about in the grounded theory section) or use pre-determined tags. When it comes to problem discovery, a great approach is to let the problems surface, and then create tags based on what you are seeing in the data. This ensures you aren't missing major themes by using pre-determined tags.

- Tagging the transcript. If you did transcribe your session, you can then tag the different parts of your transcript with either your ground-up or pre-determined tags. This stage is optional, as you could skip tagging the transcript and go directly to affinity diagramming.

SYNTHESIS

- Grounded theory. This approach to synthesis is great for problem discovery because you are creating the tags based on the data you are hearing. Using this bottom-up approach means you are less likely to miss a major theme or skip over an important insight. When doing problem discovery, I generally use a grounded approach, unless I am pressed for time.
- Affinity diagrams. These are the bread and butter of synthesizing research to see patterns and trends across your data. I recommend using affinity diagrams to help you organize large amounts of data that tend to come from problem discovery research. This will allow you to organize your data into meaningful information that you can more easily share with your team.
- Debrief sessions with the team. If you are lucky enough to have others involved in your research process, debrief sessions are the best way to engage others in the synthesis process. Using debrief sessions in problem discovery is a fantastic way to make sure colleagues are familiar with the sessions and are getting the most out of your research.

OUTCOMES/DELIVERABLES

- Report. Problem discovery research tends to have a lot of information and data come out of it. A report is a fantastic way to give everyone the depth of information they need to make the decision for their next steps. You can have several different reports with different depth of information, depending on your audiences.
- Summaries of each session. Because each problem discovery session can be so intense and filled with amazing goodies, you can create a brief summary of each interview/session you have with a participant. This is a great way to not only organize your thoughts, but also to include others alongside the research project.
- Ecosystem maps. These are a great way to visualize how your audience is interacting with the world around them when it comes to other people or systems. This visual can help you highlight potential problems they

encounter, as they are trying to achieve their goals and can show your team where people are running into issues.
- Journey maps—See resource appendix. These are another great visual for the problem discovery phase, because they show your audience going through a particular journey and all the associated problems, needs, and goals within that journey. Journey map visuals can give your team a clear understanding of what is happening, when it is happening, and how well your product/service is (or isn't!) serving people during their journey. This deliverable can also help you prioritize which points are most painful!
- Job statements—See resource appendix. These come directly from the JTBD framework and help you understand what your audience is trying to accomplish. You can then prioritize these job statements (through the opportunity gap survey) to understand which goals are most important to your audience, and which they are least satisfied with. Then, you can start to come up with meaningful solutions!
- Mental model diagrams—See resource appendix. These diagrams are perfect for visualizing how your audience perceives the world around them, and the activities they do. This is especially helpful during the problem discovery phase, as you can deeply understand how your audience is interacting with the world around them and where the friction lies.
- How Might We (HMW) statements. HMW statements are extremely important in taking all those fantastic insights and problems you learned about and moving them into a solution. These statements show us the problems people are encountering, and invite the team to collaborate to come up with solutions.

ACTIVATION

- Ideation session. One of the best follow-ups to big research projects like problem discovery are ideation sessions. These sessions are where you take the insights (and HMW statements) and turn them into potential solutions that you can then test through concept or usability testing (the most ideal cycle of user research!).

HOW TO LEAN OUT THE STAGE

- If there are too many segments to do in an appropriate timeline, prioritize one or two segments and save the others for later. It is okay to do "phased" research and save other segments for another time.

- Recruit while you conduct the research, so these two activities overlap, saving you some precious time.
- Once clear patterns and trends emerge, stop the rest of the interviews (no fewer than ten interviews) OR send out the survey, even if there are some interviews left (e.g., send out the survey after ten interviews).

EXAMPLES OF BOUNDARIES

- No fewer than 12 participants per segment.
- The sample size for a survey must be correctly calculated. You can use to correctly determine your sample size depending on your needs.
- No more than three generative interviews a day, so you avoid overwhelm and burnout.
- The team must be present for at least 50% of the debriefs.
- Analysis takes no less than five working days, as you are dealing with a high amount of qualitative data.
- If time runs out, pause the study entirely and go back to it later. It is really important to not derive insights from the incomplete study, as this can lead to misdirection and unreliable data.

Phase Two
Problem Definition 10

Once you understand the different problems your users encounter, it is time to dig deeper into those particular problems. When you are in phase one, you typically discover a multitude of issues, rather than getting depth on a particular problem. Phase two allows you to dive into one problem to fully understand it.

Again, with phase two, you are still in the midst of generative, discovery-based research, but you are now more focused on defining and more deeply understanding a particular problem. Let's dive into the playbook for problem definition.

GOAL

To dive deeply into understanding a particular pain point or need.

PRE-RESEARCH ACTIVITIES

- Intake. When a request comes through, do your best to send an intake form to get as much information as possible, even if it a shortened version of the one previously discussed. Review this with stakeholders, and reframe any questions to properly scope the project.
- Question gathering workshop with stakeholders. If the stakeholders are unsure about their questions OR you aren't starting with an intake form, a question-gathering workshop is the best step for you to understand their needs.
- Research plan. Once the project questions are user-centric and defined, it is time to create your research plan to ensure everyone is on the same page.
- Define participant segments and plan recruitment. Ensuring you get the right participants is key, so this step is critical before you start researching. Check out pages X and X for more information on segmentation and recruitment.

- Success criteria. Since you are now looking more deeply into one (or two) problem spaces, your success criteria can be more descriptive. Examples of success criteria in this stage include:
  - number of deliverables that are activated through presentations and workshops;
  - stakeholders using [deliverable] to prioritize roadmap and backlog;
  - increased generative research insights on the roadmap and backlog;
  - increased language using [persona name] to write user stories or prioritize work during planning;
  - a number of prioritized insights to be worked on.
- Kick-off meeting to align expectations, goals, and outcomes right before the project begins. In this kick-off meeting you can review:
  - research goals and outcomes;
  - recruitment criteria and participants;
  - methodology;
  - discussion guide/questions;
  - deliverables;
  - timelines.

APPROXIMATE TIMELINE

Problem definition is more narrow in scope that problem discovery because you've focused on one particular problem. However, it can still be quite a long project, so make sure to give yourself enough time. Here is a breakdown of a problem definition project timeline:

- Total time: six weeks (for one or two segments):
  - planning: three days;
  - recruitment: two weeks;
  - conducting research: two weeks;
  - analysis and synthesis: one week;
  - reporting: one week;
  - activation: three days.

For each additional segment, add one or two weeks.

SAMPLE SIZES

- one-on-one interviews: 15–25 participants per segment. For personas or other similar deliverables, aim for 20 participants per segment;
- diary studies: 15 participants per segment;

- contextual inquiry: 12–15 participants, per segment;
- mental model interviews: 15–20 interviews, per segment;
- participatory design: 10–12 participants, per segment.

POTENTIAL METHODOLOGIES

Secondary Research

- Literature review. A literature review can really help you in the problem definition phase, because it can highlight information that's already there on different problems you may have encountered and where you have to dig deeper. Starting with this literature review will help ensure you aren't doing research on problems or questions that you already have enough information on to make a decision.
- Triangulating data. Using other data sources to see whether certain problems have come up before is a great way to help bolster your insights. Through triangulating data from multiple sources you can get an idea of how much weight each problem has, depending on how often it's surfaced in other areas.

Primary Research

- Generative research one-on-one interviews. Generative research one-on-one interviews are your go-to for diving more deeply into your participants' needs, goals, and pain points to further define them. With these interviews, you can get a deep understanding of how your audience is feeling and thinking through the problems you identified, and get really into their needs.
- Customer journey interviews—See resource appendix. Diving into a customer journey after you have identified problems can be really helpful, as it can narrow the scope of your journey. Instead of looking at a huge, holistic picture, you can zoom into particular parts of the journey to better understand what problems users are encountering, and what associated needs they have.
- Persona interviews—See resource appendix. Although you can do personas during the problem discovery phase, I recommend saving them for the problem definition phase, because it can be much easier to segment your audience once you have a better understanding of them. With that, it is easier to see the potential differences between them and focus on creating personas based on the areas you want to prioritize.
- Contextual inquiry. You can also conduct contextual inquiry after you identify particular issues or topics you want to dive deeper into. With

this, you narrow the scope of your contextual inquiry, and go into it with a more pointed goal of observing certain interactions or particular moments you want to understand better.
- Diary studies. Technically speaking, you can use a diary study in a problem discovery project, but I prefer to use them in problem definition because they really help to narrow the scope if you have a clear topic in mind. You can use them to get deeper information on particular needs, goals, or pain points of your audience, and understand how they are feeling in certain situations.
- Walk the store interview. While I usually steer clear of product-based methods during these phases, I had to bring up walk the store interviews. These interviews allow you to go through your product/service with your participants to see where they are getting stuck (ideally based on a real, previous situation). Again, ideally you would stay product-agnostic, but if you need to get into the nitty gritty of product problems, this is your go-to!

FOLLOW-UP RESEARCH

- Opportunity gap survey. During problem definition, you still may be stuck with lots of insights as there is typically a lot of information still coming in, although it might be more cohesive. The opportunity gap survey can be helpful during this phase by giving you a mechanism to prioritize your insights into what your team should work on first.

ANALYSIS

- Transcribing the session. Depending on what tools and budget you have available, you might not have to transcribe your research sessions. Typically, this looks like listening to the session and creating a transcript, which you can then analyze and synthesize. This step is optional, especially if you are overwhelmed with interviews and data.
- Creating tags. When it comes to problem definition, you can use either tags or pre-determined tags. It really depends on the amount of time you have to dedicate to this phase. Ideally, if you have time, go ground-up, but if you don't, it is okay to use pre-determined tags.
- Tagging the transcript. If you did transcribe your session, you can then tag the different parts of your transcript with either your ground-up or pre-determined tags. This stage is optional, and you can go directly to affinity diagramming.

SYNTHESIS

- Grounded theory. This approach to synthesis is also great for problem definition, if you have the time. Again, it allows you to ensure you are creating insights and patterns that are really relevant and based on what you are hearing. If you don't have the time, it is okay to use those pre-determined tags and skip to affinity diagrams.
- Affinity diagrams (either by tags or goals of the research). These are also helpful when organizing the large amounts of data that tends to come from problem definition research.
- Debrief sessions with the team. Again, if you have your team involved, these debrief sessions are fantastic for getting them engaged with the research and for breaking up synthesis into bite-sized pieces.

OUTCOMES/DELIVERABLES

- Report. Reports can be fantastic for problem definition research because, again, you can be dealing with a lot of in-depth data. Think about varying the depth of data and reports based on your audience.
- Summaries of each session. Because each problem definition session can be so intense and filled with amazing goodies, you can create a brief summary of each interview/session you have with a participant. This is a great way to not only organize your thoughts, but also to include others alongside the research project.
- Personas for B2B persona. Personas are a fantastic representation of a segment of your users, as long as you make sure they are filled with the necessary information for the team. During the problem definition phase, you can really hone into particular segments or users that are a high priority to your organization.
- Journey maps—See resource appendix. Again, journey maps are a wonderful visualization of the journey your audience is going through. During the problem definition phase, they can help you really showcase specific journeys, flows, or situations that need to be improved (or created)!
- HMW statements. As you see, HMW statements are hugely valuable almost at every phase, because they allow you to take insights and turn them into opportunities to collaborate on solutions. They are great for problem definition, as you get to hone into potential ideas to focus, solutionize, and ideate on.

ACTIVATION

- Ideation session. Ideation sessions during problem definition allow you to focus even more deeply on the problems, needs, and goals you have prioritized. Since you will have even more insights, you and the team will be better equipped to start creating concepts or solutions that help your users achieve what they need with minimal friction.

HOW TO LEAN OUT THE STAGE

- If there are too many segments to do in an appropriate timeline, prioritize one or two segments, and save the others for later. It is okay to do "phased" research and save other segments for another time.
- Recruit while you conduct the research, so these two activities overlap, saving you some precious time.
- Once clear patterns and trends emerge, stop the rest of the interviews (no fewer than ten interviews) OR send out the survey even if there are some interviews left (e.g., send out the survey after ten interviews).

EXAMPLES OF BOUNDARIES

- No fewer than 12 participants per segment.
- The sample size for a survey must be correctly calculated. You can use to correctly determine your sample size depending on your needs.
- No more than three generative interviews a day, so you avoid overwhelm and burnout.
- The team must be present for at least 50% of the debriefs.
- Analysis takes no less than five working days, as you are dealing with a high amount of qualitative data.
- If time runs out, pause the study entirely and go back to it later. It is really important to not derive insights from the incomplete study, as this can lead to misdirection and unreliable data.

Phase Three
Solution Design and Refinement

11

User research allows your teams to take insights from the problem space into a solution. But before your team fully designs a solution, it's important to understand if the solution is aligned with users' mental models.

Phase three allows you to realize how aligned your team's ideas are with how users think, as well as how the ideas meet their needs and alleviate their pain points. This is a critical step in the process that is often skipped for time, or because colleagues don't know it exists. I highly recommend sitting in this space as much as you can and feeling comfortable with the ambiguity of it.

Let's dive into it.

GOAL

To helps us understand if we are going in the right direction with solving the problem and, if not, how to course correct.

PRE-RESEARCH ACTIVITIES

- Intake. When a request comes through, do your best to send an intake form to get as much information as possible, even if it's a shortened version of the one previously discussed. Review this with stakeholders and reframe any questions to properly scope the project.
- Question gathering workshop with stakeholders. If the stakeholders are unsure about their questions OR you aren't starting with an intake form, a question-gathering workshop is the best step for you to understand what they need.

- Research plan. Once the project questions are user-centric and defined, it is time to create your research plan to ensure everyone is on the same page with what to expect.
- Define participant segments and plan recruitment. Ensuring you get the right participants is key, so this step is absolutely a critical before you start researching. Check out pages X and X for more information on segmentation and recruitment.
- Success criteria. Now that you are moving on to more tangible and concrete ideas, your success criteria for the project will reflect that. Examples of success criteria in this stage include:
  - prioritized list of improvements to concepts from the research;
  - increased confidence in the direction of the product/feature/service;
  - follow-up usability test on the finalized concept.
- Kick-off meeting to align expectations, goals, and outcomes right before the project begins. In this kick-off meeting you can review:
  - research goals and outcomes;
  - recruitment criteria and participants;
  - methodology;
  - discussion guide/questions;
  - deliverables;
  - timelines.

APPROXIMATE TIMELINE

Solution design and refinement narrows down the scope even more, as you are now traveling from the problem space to the solution space, which can make research faster to conduct. Here is a breakdown of a solution design and refinement project timeline:

- Total time: Five weeks (for one or two segments):
  - planning: three days;
  - recruitment: one-and-a-half weeks;
  - conducting research: one-and-a-half weeks;
  - analysis and synthesis: three days;
  - reporting: three days;
  - activation: two days.

For each additional segment, add one to two weeks.

SAMPLE SIZES

- Concept testing
  - moderated: at least eight participants, per segment;
  - unmoderated: at least 15 participants, per segment, in case you get messy data;

- Card sorting: 20–30 participants, per segment;
- Tree testing: 20–30 participants, per segment.

POTENTIAL METHODOLOGIES

Secondary Research

- Internal testing with stakeholders. Dogfooding, or testing ideas with internal colleagues, is a great way to get preliminary insights and feedback on ideas. You can use this method to make sure ideas generally make sense, and that you don't have any glaring issues or bugs. A huge caveat with internal testing is that it is not a replacement for external research with your audience.

Primary Research

- Concept testing. This phase is perfect for concept testing, because your team is navigating that in-between area where you don't have one solution, but rather a few potential ideas. Concept testing shines when you need to understand how your audience reacts to the different ideas you have. You can even end up with a Frankenstein concept at the end, pulling components from several different ideas.
- Card sorting. Card sorting, especially open, is a great approach for solution design, because it can give you a beginning indication of how your audience categorizes and structures information. This is ideal to do in the beginning phases, because redoing large portions of design like categorization or navigation can take a lot of effort.
- Tree testing. Similar to card sorting, tree testing really helps you with the structure of your product/service, and how people perceive that it should be structured. Conducting tree testing during solution design helps you understand how your audience thinks through the information and content of your product/service, and ideally, how you should best organize to fit their mental models.

FOLLOW-UP RESEARCH

- Unmoderated testing for larger sample size, especially if you are struggling with conclusive findings, or feel like you need more feedback to understand how to move forward with designs.

ANALYSIS

- Transcribing the session. When it comes to solution design, this step is really optional, as you might lose the context of the session through your transcription. If you have time, you can transcribe these sessions to ensure you didn't miss anything during synthesis, but it isn't necessary.
- Creating tags. When it comes to tags for solution design, you can use a mix between pre-determined and ground-up tags. This means that you can pre-determine some tags you think might be helpful to the project (e.g., pain points and needs), and also use a ground-up approach to understand what big themes are coming through from the data.
- Tagging the transcript. Again, super optional, depending on if you have a transcript and have the time. To be honest, with solution design, I typically dive right into affinity diagrams.

SYNTHESIS

- Affinity diagrams. This approach becomes hugely helpful with solution as you can quickly see patterns and trends through your data. When it comes to this phase, you can include photos of the concepts, and actually annotate them within the affinity diagramming session, if that makes it easier to see patterns for you and your team.
- Debrief sessions with the team. Again, debrief sessions, when you can hold them, are hugely helpful with any phase, but especially when it comes to participants actually commenting on and interacting with something the team created. By attending these sessions, your team will have an easier time understanding the feedback and creating an ideal solution based on it.

OUTCOMES/DELIVERABLES

- Report. With solution design, your reports will naturally become more visual. You can use photos and annotations to help visualize the findings from the research sessions. This could mean annotating a concept, what resonated with participants or did not, or any sort of charts and graphs that come from card sorting and tree testing.
- Summaries of each session. Depending on how much time you have, it might be helpful to create summaries of concept testing sessions.

These summaries can help you down the line with your reporting, and help the team be more involved with the research.

ACTIVATION

- Ideation session. Ideation sessions are critical for this stage, because they allow you to take the immediate feedback you've received on your concept(s) and ideate on them. You should ideally hold an ideation session after ever solution design test. It gives your team the opportunity to put the feedback into action.

HOW TO LEAN OUT THE STAGE

- If there are too many segments to do in an appropriate timeline, prioritize one or two segments and save the others for later. It is okay to do "phased" research and save other segments for another time.
- Recruit while you conduct the research, so these two activities overlap, saving you some precious time.
- Try unmoderated testing if you are struggling to get moderated tests, have less time, or don't have a budget for moderated testing. A great hack is to do three to five moderated tests, and the rest can be unmoderated.

EXAMPLES OF BOUNDARIES

- No fewer than eight participants per segment (depending on methodology, refer to the sample sizes for this chapter).
- The sample size for a survey must be correctly calculated. You can use to correctly determine your sample size depending on your needs.
- No more than three tests a day do ensure you don't get overwhelmed and burnt-out.
- The team must be present for at least 50% of the debriefs.
- Analysis takes no less than five working days, as you are still potentially dealing with a good deal of qualitative data, especially with concept testing.
- If time runs out, pause the study entirely and go back to it later. It is really important to not derive insights from the incomplete study, as this can lead to misdirection and unreliable data.

Phase Four
Testing and Execution

12

When you understand the general concept, and idea of a solution is heading in the right direction, it's time to test a hugely important part of the experience, its usability. Usability is fundamental to a successful product, so it deserves it's own phase.

In phase four, you are testing the different solution your team created to understand their usability, and iterating to make the experience more usable. Within this, you might end up combining several different solutions (a Frakenstein of a solution), so that your end product is as efficient, effective, and satisfactory as possible. Let's dive into this extremely important step.

GOAL

To understand whether the solution is ready to launch.

PRE-RESEARCH ACTIVITIES

- Intake. When a request comes through, do your best to send an intake form to get as much information as possible, even if it a shortened version of the one previously discussed. Review this with stakeholders, and reframe any questions to properly scope the project.
- Research plan. Once the project questions are user-centric and defined, it is time to create your research plan to ensure everyone is on the same page with expectations.

- Define participant segments and plan recruitment. Ensuring you get the right participants is key, so this step is critical before you start researching. Check out pages X and X for more information on segmentation and recruitment.
- Success criteria. Since you are now in a testing phase, your success criteria will become more entwined with the product and its experience. By tying your criteria to this, you are able to better show the progress and positive impact of research on the experience. In this stage, it is important to also align your success criteria with the metrics your team is working on. Examples of success criteria in this stage include:
  - x% increase in task success;
  - x% decrease of time on task (assuming you want a decrease);
  - x% increase/decrease in [important team metric] (e.g., click-thru rate, conversion rate, retention rate, drop-off rate);
  - x% increase in satisfaction;
  - x% increase in usability (as measured by the System Usability Scale, UMUX/UMUX-Lite, or Single Ease Questionnaire).
- Kick-off meeting to align expectations, goals, and outcomes right before the project begins. In this kick-off meeting you can review:
  - research goals and outcomes;
  - recruitment criteria and participants;
  - methodology;
  - discussion guide/questions;
  - deliverables;
  - timelines.

APPROXIMATE TIMELINE

Testing and execution are the narrowest scope, as you are looking to really understand how usable your solution is, and identify what needs to be fixed to align with users' expectations and mental models. Here is a breakdown of a testing and execution project timeline:

- Total time: Four weeks (for one or two segments):
  - planning: three days;
  - recruitment: one-and-a-half weeks;
  - conducting research: one week;
  - analysis and synthesis: three days;
  - reporting: three days;
  - activation: two days.

For each additional segment, add one to two weeks.

SAMPLE SIZES

- Usability testing
  - moderated: five to seven participants, per segment;
  - unmoderated: at least 15 participants, per segment, in case you get messy data;
- Content testing: 15 participants, per segment;
- Benchmarking/quantitative usability testing: 25 participants, per segment;
- Open or closed word choice: 25–50 participants;
- Aesthetic explanation: 25–50 participants;
- Five-second tests: 25–50 participants;
- Quality ranking: 25–50 participants.

POTENTIAL METHODOLOGIES

Secondary Research

- Triangulating data. Because this phase of testing and execution can call for a smaller sample size (which is okay and normal!), having other data that demonstrates similar findings can be really helpful in further validating your findings.
- Internal testing with stakeholders. Again, testing your ideas and prototypes with internal stakeholders can be a great way to find weird flows or bugs before showing them to users. This step can be especially helpful if your product is something your stakeholders actually use. But, remember: it isn't a replacement for primary research and speaking to users!

Primary Research

- Usability testing. Usability testing is your go-to for this phase of testing and executing on solutions! By this phase, you're at a point where you have a solution or two in mind, and testing the usability of said solutions is the next logical step. Usability testing will help you determine how satisfactory your solution will be because usability = satisfaction, effectiveness, and efficiency!
- Comparative usability testing. The biggest pitfall of testing multiple solutions is asking your audience which one they prefer. Preference testing is highly subjective and not particularly reliable. Instead, you can

usability test both solutions to see which flows/components are the most usable. At this stage, you might end up with another Frankenstein, and that is okay.
- Content testing. If you are also interested in testing the actual content of your prototype, content testing is supremely helpful. It gives you an indication on how your audience is reacting and understanding the content of your product/service. You can do this as early as this phase, or you can wait until the product is further along.

FOLLOW-UP RESEARCH

- If you are feeling unsure about your moderated sample size and seeking more feedback, conducting a follow-up unmoderated test could be a great fit for you.
- Beta testing. If the product/service is in an advanced state and actually usable, you can set up a beta test to get ongoing feedback from participants, who are using your product/service on a regular basis. This is a great next step regardless, as it helps you iron out any issues before releasing to a wider audience.

ANALYSIS

- Creating tags. When it comes to testing and execution, I typically use a set of pre-determined tags, such as pain points, needs, and bugs. However, you can create whatever tags you find to be most helpful to synthesizing the information you need with your team. Additionally, you can also analyze by screen. In this approach, you analyze the feedback and data you received screen by screen.

SYNTHESIS

- Affinity diagrams. Within this phase, you can dive straight into affinity diagramming. I recommend annotating visuals of the prototype to help aid in the synthesis (and your report!). You can either use your pre-determined tags, the research goals, or each prototype screen. Use whatever approach feels easiest to digest the information.

- Debrief sessions with the team. Again, when it comes to participants interacting with or using something your team created, it is essential to get them involved as much as you can. Debrief sessions are a great way to do this, and they make the end synthesis more efficient.

OUTCOMES/DELIVERABLES

- Usability report. As with solution design, your testing reports will likely be heavily visual. You can use annotations to describe the feedback you received on different screens, and highlight what did/did not work.
- UX Scorecard. This is a clear way to showcase how your product/service compares to others and to highlight the top problems.

ACTIVATION

- Ideation session. Ideation sessions are, again, key for moving to the next iteration and continuing on the iterative cycle based on research findings. Your ideation sessions might be shorter, if your team has a pretty solid idea that just needs some fixing. But you should still hold that space for them to address any pain points or unmet needs that came up in the sessions.
- Usability bingo. See resource appendix. This is a really fun way to share the findings from your study with colleagues. You set up clips from the session, ideally of pain points or unmet needs, and create a bingo board. Then, your colleagues play bingo! You don't have to use this step, as it is time consuming, but if you have the space, try it!

HOW TO LEAN OUT THE STAGE

- If there are too many segments to do in an appropriate timeline, prioritize one or two segments and save the others for later. It is okay to do "phased" research and save other segments for another time.
- Recruit while you conduct the research so these two activities overlap, saving you some precious time.
- Try unmoderated testing if you are struggling to get moderated tests, have less time, or don't have a budget for moderated testing.

EXAMPLES OF BOUNDARIES

- No fewer than six participants per segment (depending on methodology).
- The sample size for a survey must be correctly calculated. You can use to correctly determine your sample size depending on your needs.
- No more than three tests a day to avoid overwhelm and burnout.
- The team must be present for at least 50% of the debriefs.
- Analysis takes no less than three working days, as you still might have some qualitative data to handle.
- If time runs out, pause the study entirely and go back to it later. It is really important to not derive insights from the incomplete study, as this can lead to misdirection and unreliable data.

Phase Five
Maintain and Iterate

13

User research can continue to have a huge impact on a product/service/feature even after it has shipped. You can continue to be a part of the project and monitor important metrics (usually those you defined at the beginning of the project) to see if things need to be improved and iterated on.

As someone conducting user research, you can continue to have an impact on all parts of this process, so it is important to save time in your schedule for monitoring past projects. If you have any downtime, which can sometimes happen, going back through old projects to look at usage data or any other metrics can be a great use of your time. You might uncover something that needs to be improved!

Also, the concept of continuous improvement and iteration is critical for an organization to succeed, so being able to be a part of that process can help demonstrate your value. Let's dive into the last phase.

GOAL

To measure the success of the solution and continue iterating on it based on feedback.

PRE-RESEARCH ACTIVITIES

- Reviewing success criteria. Now that the product/feature/service is out in the world, reviewing the success criteria that you originally stated is critical. You want to understand if your metrics have changed in a positive way and identify any other changes, or metrics to continue to monitor, such as usage metrics.

- Reviewing usability and satisfaction metrics. One of the best concepts you can put into place during this stage is continuous testing of the usability and satisfaction of the product/feature/service. You can do this through continuous benchmarking and continuous UX surveys. By reviewing and monitoring these important metrics, you can highlight what has been improved through research, and any additional projects that need to take place.

APPROXIMATE TIMELINE

- Since this is an ongoing task, your timeline depends on regular team check-ins or the cadence you choose to check-in and measure the metrics you originally determined. I recommend partnering with a data analyst and your product manager to figure out the best cadence for monitoring the metrics.

POTENTIAL METHODOLOGIES

- Quantitative usability testing. When it comes to quantitative usability testing (such as measuring task success and time on task), I typically recommend waiting until you have a working product and, more importantly, a product that can go wrong. When you use quantitative usability testing on a prototype, you are testing something that usually only has one path, so there is less likelihood of things going wrong. Quantitative usability testing is trying to get to as real of an experience as possible, so I recommend waiting until the beginning of the monitoring phase.
- Continuous benchmarking. When you think about ways to show your impact, continuous benchmarking is a fantastic approach. You conduct quantitative usability testing over time, as your team makes improvements to the product/service. This benchmarking can demonstrate improvement in important areas, like task success and time on task.
- Continuous UX surveys. UX surveys are a wonderful tool to use during this phase, as you are able to track and see improvements in certain areas, like usability over time. Similar to benchmarking, using these surveys can help demonstrate how you've positively impacted the product development process through research.
- Walk the store interview. As I mentioned before, you can do a walk the store interview earlier on in the research process, but the monitoring and maintaining phase is a fantastic time to do so, as you have a "finished" product/service and can walk through how your audience is using it.

VISUAL TESTING

- Open or closed word choice. Open or closed word choice helps you understand what your audience thinks of your brand. With this approach, you are trying to understand how people perceive a brand or a design by having them point out and describe their perceptions.
- Aesthetic explanation. Similar to open or closed word choice, aesthetic explanation is a great approach when you want to know how people would describe your brand or design.
- Five-second tests. Five-second tests are hugely helpful in understanding if a design or brand effectively communicates a message. This is a great approach if your team is struggling to understand how impactful their messaging is, or if your audience might be confused on certain parts of your product.
- Quality ranking. If you need to dive deeper into how your audience perceives your brand or design, then quality rankings enable you to understand how certain brand attributes resonate (or don't) with your audience.

FOLLOW-UP RESEARCH

- Unmoderated testing for larger sample size, especially if you are struggling with conclusive findings or feel like you need more feedback to understand how to move forward with designs.
- A/B tests—See resource appendix. The A/B test is all about testing really small, incremental changes on your product/service and understanding how that impacts certain metrics. I highly recommend partnering with a product manager or data analyst to help you with setting up A/B tests, because they can be difficult to get right!

OUTCOMES/DELIVERABLES

- Report on analytics and metrics. If you are continuously benchmarking or using surveys, creating a report on these results is a fantastic way to share findings with your colleagues. You can report on these every quarter or six months (or sometimes more), depending on how often you are monitoring your products/services.

- Dashboards. Partnering with someone from the data team, if possible, can help in the creation of dashboards that track important metrics, such as quantitative usability metrics, or whatever success criteria you and your team set up at the beginning of a project.
- Additional research studies. Sometimes during benchmarking, walk the stores, or surveys, something might come up that needs digging into. This is how the cycle of user research continues, because if you spot a problem, you can head back to phase two for problem definition!

ACTIVATION

- Follow-up meeting with stakeholders to determine next steps to dive deeper into any unexpected or surprising metric changes.

Now that you have defined and built your playbook, it's time to get comfortable with the different methodologies and activities in each phase.

PART FIVE

Methodology Breakdown

Problem Discovery Methods

14

LITERATURE REVIEW

Literature reviews have their roots in academia. Many people in user research come from an academic background. Although sometimes academia can be considered too slow for the fast-paced nature of product and tech companies, there are many valuable pieces you can take from academia. Literature reviews are one of those pieces. They give you a fantastic way to understand your topic more deeply, before diving into a project.

Before we dive into what a literature review is, it's important to distinguish between primary and secondary research:

- Primary research is research that you conduct to directly answer a research question.
- Secondary research is research that others conducted or that you previously conducted.

This is important because literature reviews (also referred to as lit reviews) are a secondary research method. This means that, when conducting a lit review, you are collecting, analyzing, and synthesizing research that others have conducted or that you previously conducted. Now, let's get to what a literature review actually is:

In a literature review, the researcher collects information via academic papers, journals, websites, or previous research on a particular subject area. These resources are brought together to summarize the trends or patterns based on research already conducted on a particular topic.

There are technically four types of literature reviews.

1. Systematic literature reviews aim for an exhaustive, comprehensive appraisal of as much relevant and existing research as possible on the topic, with little to no bias. It is a very rigorous and well-defined approach. This review can take one to two years to complete.
2. Rapid literature reviews assess what is already known about a topic within a time-constrained setting. Rapid literature reviews also follow a structured research protocol, but employ methodological "shortcuts" (e.g., limiting the scope of the literature review) at the risk of introducing bias. This type of review can take up to six months.
3. Scoping literature reviews are a preliminary assessment of the potential size and scope of available research on a particular topic. This type of review looks at the nature and extent of research already done (and sometimes ongoing). Within this review, the researcher seeks to identify gaps, identify key concepts and characteristics of the literature, and/or examine how research is conducted on a topic of interest. This can take anywhere from two weeks to two months, depending on the scope of the review.
4. Narrative literature reviews summarize the body of literature relevant to a particular research question. Within the narrative review, the researcher also draws conclusions about the topic and identifies gaps or inconsistencies in a body of knowledge. You need to have a sufficiently focused research question to conduct a narrative literature review. This review can take anywhere from a week to a month.

Since some of these timelines may look scary to you, this is a great time to point out that user researchers typically focus on scoping and narrative literature reviews. Starting with a narrative literature review is the quickest way to learn how to gather, synthesize, and summarize relevant data.

WHY ARE LITERATURE REVIEWS IMPORTANT?

For a while, I didn't do literature reviews at the beginning of my projects. I was working at start-ups in fast-paced environments. I didn't have time to spend on the literature reviews I used to do before an academic research project. It was that stigma toward lit reviews that stopped me from doing them.

Then I was faced with a massive project. On this particular project, I was working as a freelance user researcher. But I say that it is just as important for a full-time or contract researcher to incorporate literature reviews into their process.

The company I was working with wanted to understand the different factors that impacted teenagers' inclination to become a cyberbully. I remember first hearing about the project. I was immediately overwhelmed by how I was going to start. Not only was I not familiar with cyberbullying, but I also had no idea where to begin. My mind spun with how I could possibly tackle this immense project—seriously, it kept me up at night.

Luckily, I had been reading some academic research books, and I made the connection: I should start this particular project with a literature review. I am so glad I did. I truly believe writing that lit review made my freelance project a success, and without it, I'm uncertain if I would have been able to properly tackle the project.

Literature reviews can help you in so many different ways:

- Find the gaps in previous research. It's fascinating to look through previous projects and highlight your continued gaps in knowledge, which can lead to amazing studies. Literature reviews are a great way to comb through any internal or external resources to see what questions have been left unanswered.
- Understand (and potentially reduce) the scope of our research question. When you are tasked with an overwhelming research question, a literature review can help ground you and potentially reduce the scope of it. For instance, the above research question, "What factors impact teenagers' inclination to become a cyberbully?" is a massive project. By using a lit review, you could potentially find research that demonstrates certain factors, and reduce the scope of your project to the specific gaps in previous research.
- Ensure you are not redoing work. Standing on the shoulders of giants is an important part of research, in general. Whether externally or internally, one of the biggest wastes of resources is redoing research that's previously been conducted. A literature review helps ensure you aren't reinventing the wheel and, instead, doing new research that addresses gaps in knowledge.
- Help to formulate hypotheses. Literature reviews give you the context and knowledge to form strong hypotheses. Instead of basing our hypotheses on assumptions or what you hope to learn, a lit review allows you to base your hypotheses on real data. This can help you ask better and more informed questions during the project.
- Make research findings more valid/reliable. Data triangulation is key in user research, and literature reviews can serve as a great source of evidence. If your research outcomes are aligned with those that have come out of similar studies, you have an additional data source to point to.
- Gain inspiration for further studies. If you have downtime, conduct literature reviews to understand general industry trends within the area you are working. Going through other researchers' studies can give you amazing inspiration for further studies you could conduct to help your organization.
- Reduce time and cost. One of the biggest hurdles for researchers is the time and cost of research. Conducting a lit review before a more extensive study can help reduce the time and cost of your project. For instance, instead of doing a large-scale survey or many interviews on a topic, you can review previous research, utilize the findings within your project, and reduce redoing any unnecessary work.

188 Impact

Not every study needs a literature review! For example, some evaluative research (such as usability tests) would not benefit from a literature review. Typically, the projects that are best suited for lit reviews are those with broader, generative questions.

HOW TO CONDUCT A LITERATURE REVIEW

Now that you are excited to start conducting literature reviews, here is a step-by-step guide on how to approach one.

1. Choose your research topic and question. Like any other research project, you must ensure you have a clear topic and question you are trying to answer, or your literature review will take months and lack focus. You can do this in two different ways, depending on who else is involved with the research project:
    a. Identify the question based on a research question you have identified as important to answer.
    b. Hold a question-gathering workshop with stakeholders to understand the types of questions they need help answering, and pick the most impactful one.
2. Decide on the type of literature review. As mentioned, there are four types of literature reviews, but most user researchers focus on scoping or narrative lit reviews. By choosing the type of literature review, you are also determining the scope, such as the timeline of the lit review and the number of resources you will include. I recommend doing this before starting the review, because these reviews can be rabbit holes: you can lose hours spiraling on resources. Putting a cap on the time and number is essential.
3. Identify your reliable sources and ensure they are based on primary research (e.g., not opinion-based pieces). There are two main types of resources you can focus on:
    a. Internal resources, which focus on gathering all the relevant information and studies previously conducted within your organization, such as study reports, customer service logs, stakeholder interviews, deliverables, or workshop outcomes.
    b. External resources, which focus on sources outside of your organization, such as journals, libraries, papers, articles, etc. Some fantastic external resources include:
        i. Google Scholar: A great source of academic papers or reports by universities;
        ii. ResearchGate: A handy resource for scientific or academic papers;
        iii. ACM Digital Library: Has many scholarly peer-reviewed journals, particularly on information technology disciplines;

iv. Springer: Filled with scientific documents and books on many different topics;
v. Wiley Online Library: Scientific and academic journals, articles, and books on a wide range of subjects;
vi. Forrester: Has insights on trending and essential marketing topics;
vii. Baymard: Filled with UX articles, UX Benchmarks, and research that help make more informed design decisions;
viii. Voicebot: Trends and reports specifically on AI and Voice;
ix. Journal of Usability Studies (JUS): A publication dedicated to exploring usability and other research-related topics;
x. Stanford d.school: Brings sources on a variety of topics when it comes to design and research;
xi. MIT D-Lab: Dives into topics related to humanitarianism and other social causes.

When doing a scoping or narrative review, I recommend choosing three to five of the best resources you find, which means you might initially look through more.
4. Review your sources. Go through each of your sources, and fill out the criteria you initially picked out. I recommend spending 30–60 minutes per source. Identify if the source is relevant to your lit review, and if it is relevant, review it and extrapolate important information you identified.
5. Analyze the data. Once you review all the sources and filled out your spreadsheet, use affinity diagramming to combine the patterns and trends across the different sources. For literature reviews, you can use an inductive method. I recommend this because each lit review is so different, that using pre-defined global tags can introduce too much bias. As you organize the content, you'll start to see similarities between articles—create themes/categories around these similarities.
6. Write the literature review. Once you've reviewed your resources, it's time to start reviewing what you've collected. At this point, themes and high-level conclusions will be evident. Here is an example of a literature review structure:
   a. the literature review question and topic;
   b. approach—why a literature review? What type of literature review, including what is/is not included;
   c. summarize the trends and patterns you found with regard to your question and topic;
   d. demonstrate gaps in the knowledge and remaining questions;
   e. refine your research question and what still needs to be uncovered in a further summary.

The best way to start incorporating this into your toolkit is by practicing! A great approach is to do a literature review on a particular topic you've previously investigated, to summarize your findings and see what questions still remain for future projects.

EXAMPLE OF A LITERATURE REVIEW

Let's imagine we are working at a life insurance company, and we want to investigate:

How are family dynamics impacted by a chronic illness diagnosis, and how does this impact their decisions for life insurance?

The reason we are looking into this is to help understand how family dynamics are impacted when a member of the family gets diagnosed with a chronic physical or mental illness, to provide appropriate support and resources to these families. Let's go through the steps above:

The research question: Since we've been "given" a research question, this one is pretty easy. However, I would probably narrow the scope slightly because "family dynamics" is a huge potential concept with many different varieties (e.g., what is considered a "family?"). I would rework it to narrow it down.

How are those with a chronic illness treated by their families post-diagnosis, and how does this impact their decisions for life insurance?

This way, we are focused more on the individual with the chronic illness rather than the dynamic of the family.

1. Decide on the type of literature review. For this, I would likely do a narrative literature review in which I pick out several sources, summarize the patterns/trends, and then point out gaps for a future study.
2. Select your criteria. For this, I would use all the criteria above, and also probably select some project-based topics such as:
   a. type of chronic illness (physical, mental, both);
   b. relationship within the family: people who are married, people who are dependents, people living alone, or parents;
   c. chronic illness type;
   d. age range of the diagnosed participants;
   e. life insurance impact.
3. Identify your reliable sources. Using the sites mentioned above, I would choose about five resources that are relevant to the context and understanding of our research question. I would likely search for resources on topics like:
   a. family relationships and chronic illness;
   b. familial coping strategies with chronic illness;
   c. family stories of surviving chronic illness;
   d. family caregivers and chronic illness;
   e. family interactions and chronic illness;
   f. chronic illness and life insurance.
4. Review your sources. As mentioned, I would go through each source to first identify if it was relevant. Then, once I identified five great sources, I would fill out the spreadsheet with the criteria I originally selected.
5. Analyze the data. Now it's time to assemble an affinity diagram of the patterns I found across the different resources.

6. Write the literature review. Finally, we get to the literature review. This can come in the form of a document or a presentation, depending on what you think is best. Below is a short example.
   a. The literature review question and topic: How are those with a chronic illness treated by their families post-diagnosis, and how does this impact their decisions for life insurance?
   b. Approach—why a literature review? What type of literature review, including what is and is not included?
      i. This will show us pre-existing research on the topic, allowing us to narrow our scope to the relevant gaps in knowledge and answer the questions that haven't yet been answered.
   c. Summarize the trends and patterns you found with regard to your question and topic:
      i. There are some key differences between how physical and mental chronic illness patients are treated by their families.
      ii. Marriage has a large impact on both physical and mental chronic illnesses.
      iii. Narratives in a physical chronic illness can help dictate the success of the patient and the family.
      iv. The family role plays a big part in how physical chronic illness impacts the patient.
      v. Parent-child relationships in chronic mental illnesses can be very difficult. Parents of children with a chronic mental illness grieve about ambiguous losses, like the child's loss of self or identity. Parents with chronic mental illness need to be very clear with the child about what to expect.
      vi. Communication in families with both physical and mental chronic illnesses is key to patient success.
      vii. Chronic illness patients, regardless of the type, need to feel accepted and comfortable in their familial space through clear and constant communication. This communication allows patients to truly process where they are, and helps them make more informed decisions on things like life insurance.
   d. Demonstrate gaps in the knowledge and remaining questions:
      i. We need to further investigate how this ties to decisions on life insurance.
   e. Refine your research question and what still needs to be uncovered in a further summary:
      i. How are those with a chronic illness treated by their families post-diagnosis, and how does this impact their decisions for life insurance? → "How does being in a safe or unsafe familial space impact those who are diagnosed with chronic illness's ability to make decisions about life insurance?"

It is important to note that literature reviews are not substitutes for primary research! It's typical to conduct a literature review during the planning process, to help you better understand the context behind the topic and pose a relevant question. Always follow up with research if the question you set out to answer hasn't already been answered within the literature review.

TRIANGULATING DATA

In the realm of user research, triangulating data is a valuable technique to attain a deeper and more comprehensive understanding of your research problem or user base. Triangulation involves the integration of multiple data sources, perspectives, theories, and methods to enhance the validity and credibility of your findings. There are four main ways you can leverage triangulation in user research and delve into concrete examples of its application.

1. Data Triangulation: This approach involves gathering data from different times, spaces, or people. For instance, conducting a longitudinal study or comparing data from various locations can provide valuable insights. Imagine you're assessing the adoption of a new feature on your platform. By examining user behavior data from different time periods, you can identify trends and changes in user interactions, helping you understand how the feature's usage evolves over time.
2. Investigator Triangulation: This technique entails involving multiple researchers in collecting and analyzing data, and subsequently comparing their code sheets or findings. While investigator triangulation is more common in larger research teams, it can yield diverse perspectives that enrich your analysis. For example, when studying user preferences for a mobile app, having multiple researchers independently analyze user interviews can uncover nuanced insights and reduce the risk of individual bias.
3. Theory Triangulation: Theory triangulation involves employing different theoretical frameworks to investigate a particular phenomenon. Consider a scenario, where you aim to understand user motivation for engaging with an e-commerce platform. By applying various psychological theories related to motivation, such as Maslow's hierarchy of needs or self-determination theory, you can gain a multifaceted perspective on the driving forces behind user behavior.
4. Methodological Triangulation: This approach entails using diverse research methods to explore the same topic. For instance, combining survey data with in-depth interviews can provide a richer understanding of user experiences. Suppose you're studying user satisfaction with an e-learning platform. By employing both surveys and interviews, you can collect quantitative data on overall satisfaction levels, and gather qualitative insights into specific pain points or areas for improvement.

Triangulation proves especially beneficial in the following scenarios.

- Gaining a Holistic Picture: When striving to comprehend a complex research problem or user behavior holistically, triangulation allows you to collect multiple perspectives, unveiling the intricacies of why individuals think, feel, or act in a certain way.
- Enhancing Validity: By blending complementary methods and cross-checking different data sources, triangulation bolsters the validity of your study. It mitigates biases or limitations inherent in a single method, ensuring that your conclusions are well-founded.
- Credibility of Insights: Cross-referencing information from various sources enhances the credibility of your research findings. When you're unsure about the accuracy of your results, or when faced with ambiguous outcomes, triangulation can validate your insights.

Let's explore concrete examples of how triangulation can be applied in user research.

TO SEE A COMPLETE PICTURE

Suppose you've sent out a System Usability Scale (SUS) on your platform to assess usability and satisfaction. Unfortunately, you've received low scores without clear explanations. To gain a more holistic understanding, consult account managers and the customer support team. They can highlight areas where issues frequently arise, either from customer conversations or tickets.

Subsequently, conduct usability tests to pinpoint underlying issues. This combined approach reveals both the "what" (low SUS scores) and the "why" (specific usability problems), offering a comprehensive view of the problem.

TO ENHANCE VALIDITY

In a persona study involving 15 participants, you've collected a wealth of qualitative insights. To ensure the validity of your findings and prioritize key insights, administer a follow-up opportunity gap survey to a larger user population.

Additionally, leverage data analytics to confirm user-identified pain points. This triangulation of methods validates the significance of your qualitative data and helps in prioritization.

TO GIVE INSIGHTS MORE CREDIBILITY

While usability testing a new feature, you notice that four out of seven participants struggle with a particular task. However, this data seems inconclusive on its own. To enhance credibility, analyze user analytics data, revealing a high drop-off rate at the same problematic point.

Furthermore, reach out to customer support, uncovering a surge in complaints related to the feature. Combining these data sources strengthens the case for addressing the issue.

There are myriad ways to incorporate triangulation into your user research, and most of these approaches are readily accessible to researchers. Experimenting with triangulation methods in your next study, particularly when faced with complex or uncertain situations, can help mitigate risks and lead to more robust and insightful findings.

ONE-ON-ONE GENERATIVE RESEARCH INTERVIEWS

In the realm of user research, generative research interviews are an invaluable tool for uncovering deep insights into user motivations, goals, needs, and pain points. These interviews involve open-ended conversations that encourage users to share their experiences, both within and beyond the context of your product.

GETTING STARTED WITH GENERATIVE RESEARCH

To embark on generative research, follow these steps:

1. Define your users: Determine the participants you want to recruit for generative research. This could be current users of your product, users of a competitor's product, or a mix of users and potential users.
2. Set clear goals: Define the objectives of your research. What questions do you aim to answer, and what outcomes do you expect? Establish a clear purpose for your research efforts.
3. Create a research plan: Outline the logistics of your research, including the number of participants, session durations, and timelines. Ensure you have a realistic schedule that aligns with your project's deadlines.

4. Develop a discussion guide: Prepare a guide or script that contains open-ended questions and conversation starters. This guide will serve as your roadmap during interviews.
5. Recruit participants: Based on your defined user base, initiate the participant recruitment process. Consider conducting interviews while recruiting to expedite the overall study timeline.
6. Conduct the research: Prior to conducting interviews, practice using your interview guide internally. This rehearsal with colleagues will help fine-tune your approach. When it comes to generative research, practice truly enhances the quality of insights.

Generative research interviews empower you to uncover the "whys" behind user behavior, fostering a deeper understanding of your users and their needs. By embarking on this journey from the problem space, you can develop products that genuinely address users' real-world challenges, ultimately leading to more meaningful and user-centric solutions.

WRITING A GREAT GENERATIVE INTERVIEW SCRIPT

What Makes a Generative Research Discussion Guide Different

When it comes to generative research, it's all about playing the conversation by ear. Coming from conducting mostly evaluative research, having a discussion guide that wasn't a step-by-step indication of exactly what I would ask participants was really challenging for me. I was so used to writing down all of the tasks I'd use and then the subsequent follow-up questions I'd ask.

Generative research was completely different. I had a short list of open-ended questions, but they were just conversation starters. It was as if as soon as I started a generative research session, I forgot how to have a conversation and ask natural follow-up questions. I was so scared of asking the wrong thing or sounding stupid, it stopped me from actively listening and blocked my natural curiosity.

I struggled so much with having a loose interview script. Whenever my mind went blank, which happened quite a lot while I was learning this skill, I had nothing to ground myself with. At least with evaluative research, you have more of an outline, while with generative research, it can feel a lot more like improv.

I truly believe the lack of prediction can make writing a sparse discussion guide so scary—for a long time, my discussion guide was my security blanket and told me exactly what I needed to be asking at what time. When that got taken away, I struggled with how to write an effective one. However, over time, I learned some tips and tricks which I am excited to share with you!

How to Write a Generative Research Discussion Guide

When it comes to writing an impactful and effective generative research discussion guide, I have one piece of advice: start with your research goals. The reason I approach generative research guides this way is because, when it comes down to it, we are trying to get specific information to help support our teams in making more informed decisions and mitigating risk.

When I create my research goals, I always work together with the team to understand exactly what information they need in order to move forward, or feel more confident with whatever decision they are trying to make. I ensure these are aligned on and documented in a research plan. By starting with your research goals, and using those as a way to craft interview questions, you are much more likely to get the information your teams need. Let's go through an example of what I mean by using your goals to write interview questions.

Imagine we were working at an HR company, and we wanted to deeply understand how small companies think about choosing HR software. Here's how we might structure a generative research interview guide via goals:

Let's take another example. Imagine we are working at a food delivery takeaway, and we are trying to understand the reasons behind why certain customers are reordering at a higher frequency, as well as the barriers encountered by customers that prevent them from reordering on the platform.

Goals:

- discover users' motivations behind reordering, both inside and outside of the app;
- uncover other websites/apps customers are using to order takeaway and what their experience is like;
- learn about any pain points users are encountering during their process.

INTERVIEW QUESTIONS

Goal one: discover users' motivations behind reordering, both inside and outside of the app.

- Think about the last time you ordered takeaway on our app. Walk me through the entire process, starting with what sparked the idea.
- Explain how you made the decision to reorder food on our particular website/app.
- Describe why you decided to reorder takeaway rather than cooking your own dinner and/or going out to eat.
  - Who were you talking to?
  - What time of day was it?
  - How were you feeling?

- What else were you doing?
- What other websites/apps did you have open?

Goal two: learn about any pain points users are encountering during their process.

- Describe the last time you struggled with reordering food; what was that like?
  - How did you solve the problem?
- Walk me through another frustrating experience you had reordering food.
- Explain what is currently missing from the experience of reordering food.
- Talk me through the most confusing part of the experience.

Goal three: uncover other websites/apps customers are using to order takeaway.

- Talk me through the other websites/apps you have used multiple times to order takeaway (or even groceries).
  - Describe your experience with these other websites/apps.
- What are the other websites/apps you use to help you make a decision about whether or not to order takeaway?

As you can see here, using your goals as a starting point for writing your discussion guide is a great way to ensure you are asking the key questions during your interview, but also keeping those questions open-ended.

A QUESTION-WRITING FRAMEWORK

The art of writing open-ended generative research interview questions takes some time to learn. We really want to ensure that our questions are as open-ended, yet specific, as possible. The beauty of generative research is that it really helps with getting users to open up with a specific story, so ideally, our questions should prompt that type of information from them. When it comes to writing generative research interview questions, I always use the TEDW framework.

- T = "Tell me about…" or "Talk me through…"
- E = "Explain…"
- D = "Describe…"
- W = "Walk me through…"

These phrases help us open up into a conversation. Let's look at the difference between questions I commonly see asked versus a TEDW question.

Non-TEDW version: "What are some frustrations you've encountered while using our product?"

There are a few things that aren't ideal with this question.

- A "what" question is typically better suited for quantitative research, because if we are looking for what is happening, we want a larger sample size than qualitative research.
- More likely than not, you will get a list of some things participants are frustrated by. If you report on this list, you will have frustrations, but no understanding of their context. This question can lead to shallow information and not understanding why something is frustrating.
- We get minimal detail on how someone has worked around the frustration or other ways they've seen it done.

TEDW version: "Describe the last time you experienced a frustration with our product."

WHY IS THIS A BETTER VERSION?

- This question prompts an actual story/memory, giving you rich contextual data for teams to act on what went wrong.
- You could get information about how this participant has seen it done better on other tools or hacks they used, which can lead to innovative improvements.

If you are concerned about only getting one pain point, you can follow up with questions like:

- "How often has this particular problem occurred?"
- "Describe another frustration you've encountered."

Here are a few more examples.
Non-TEDW version: "When was the last time you used the product?"
TEDW version: "Walk me through the last time you used the product, starting from the beginning."
Non-TEDW version: "How did you decide you needed HR software?"
TEDW version: "Talk me through your decision-making process when finding an HR software, starting from when you felt you needed it."
Non-TEDW version: "What did you feel during the demo?"
TEDW version: "Explain how you were feeling during the demo."
As you can see, these phrases prompt more specific examples and stories from participants. They also aim to take subjective, biased language out of our questions, so we can truly focus on how the participant feels.

Another really key component of this structure is asking for one specific experience. When we ask for generalities, or questions like, "What are some frustrations?" or "What are some reasons you are using this software?" we will typically get a shallow list of responses we don't want from qualitative research. By focusing on one or two specific experiences, we will get much more detailed information, leading to very meaningful insights.

Let's look at a few more common questions that we can rewrite into TEDW versions.

- What's a problem that our product has helped you solve recently? → Tell me about the last time you had a problem and used our product to fix it.
- Are there any features that you don't use in our product? If so, why? → Describe a feature you don't use in our product.
  - Explain why you don't use X feature.
- Which feature helps you solve problems the most? → Describe a time when our product helped you solve a problem.
- Can you use our product well? → Walk me through, step-by-step, how you use our product.
- What's something you've learned from using our product? → Explain something you've learned since using our product.
- Are you satisfied with our product? → Describe how you feel about our product.
- What tools are most important to help you accomplish your key responsibilities? → Walk me through a tool you use to help you achieve X goal.
- Does our product fit into your workflow? → Talk me through how our product impacts your workflow.
- What are some alternatives to our product you've used or considered? → Describe another similar product you've used.

Some other types of questions to avoid in your generative research guides include:

- leading questions, which may prohibit the user from exploring a different avenue:
  - V1: "What makes this product helpful?"
  - Better version: "Describe how this product impacts your day-to-day life."
- asking about future behavior, instead of focusing on the past/present:
  - V1: "Would you use this feature?"
  - Better version: "Describe a time you used something similar."
- double-barreled questions, asking two questions in one sentence:
  - V1: "Are you more interested in visiting historical landmarks or experiencing local cuisine when you travel?"
  - Better version: "Describe the types of experiences you look for when traveling."
- preference-based questions, which is asking about preference instead of usability or pain points:
  - V1: "Do you prefer to explore exotic destinations or relaxing beach vacation?"
  - Better version: "Describe the overall experience of the platform/service/app/website."

By avoiding certain question types, using open-ended conversation-starters, and using our goals to prompt our questions, we can write a super impactful discussion guide that gets us the information we need.

OTHER COMPONENTS TO INCLUDE IN A DISCUSSION GUIDE

We've covered questions in discussion guides, but there are other very important components to include as well:

- an introduction, which sets the stage and the expectations for the research session;
- a warm-up which gives you a chance to build some rapport with the participant before diving in;
- a section for questions that might be outside of the scope, but the team may be interested in if you have time;
- a wrap-up, where you conclude the research session.

HOW TO "PROBE"/CONDUCT IMPROV RESEARCH

One of the hardest parts of generative research is the fact that a lot of it is steered by the participant. Of course, you have guardrails (your research goals), so the conversation doesn't get too out of hand, but it is nearly impossible to plan for an open conversation. This part of generative research was the hardest part for me to learn and took the most practice. Incidentally, because asking probing questions is so incredibly contextual, it is one of the hardest things to teach. However, I do have some tips you can follow, when learning to have these more "improv-based" conversations.

USE ACTIVE LISTENING AND MIRRORING

Active listening, during a session, can be skillfully accomplished through the technique of mirroring. Mirroring, in its essence, is the art of imitation. Humans unconsciously mimic each other as a means to connect, provide comfort, and establish trust. This mimicry extends to body language, tone of voice, speech patterns, and vocabulary.

The psychological impact of mirroring is profound. It conveys to the other person that you share similarities, thus fostering trust more rapidly. We are naturally drawn to what is familiar and inclined to avoid what is not. When you mirror someone, you're essentially signaling that you're a trustworthy ally on the same wavelength.

Mirroring also proves invaluable when crafting questions subtly, without the need for explicit queries. It can be especially useful when you find yourself experiencing a sense of frustration or curiosity.

Participant: "I was uncertain how to complete the onboarding process."
Researcher: "You were uncertain…"
Participant: "Yes, I felt confused because the final screen kept redirecting me to a verification page, but I wasn't receiving the confirmation email."
Researcher: "You weren't receiving the email…"
Participant: "Exactly, I checked my email multiple times and retried the process, but the email never arrived. It was really frustrating."
Researcher: "It was frustrating…"
Participant: "I just wanted to get it done and over with!"

By repeating what the participant is saying, you are subconsciously establishing trust, and asking them to open up more fully to explain what they mean.

PROBE SUBJECTIVE OR VAGUE WORDS AND PHRASES

When it comes to follow-up, a smart strategy is to delve deeper when someone uses words and expressions open to interpretation, rooted in personal experience. But what do we mean by subjective? Let's take a closer look. Imagine I mention the word "scared"—what's the first thing that pops into your mind? And what about "barking dog?" I bet we each have our own unique definitions and associations when it comes to being scared, just as we possess distinct mental images of barking dogs.

For me, the concept of being scared immediately brings back memories of a nighttime break-in, which tends to make me jittery and anxious, replaying the scenario in my mind.

Now, let's shift to the phrase "barking dog." Before I welcomed Poncho into my life, this would have conjured up images of a cute dog joyfully barking during playtime. However, my perspective has since evolved, thanks to Poncho's nightly barking habit. Now, "barking dog" triggers feelings of irritation when he disrupts my sleep with an untimely bark. That sudden bark can even stir up worries about a potential intruder…

Do you see how this experience can vary significantly from one person to the next? How would you have grasped all this context if I hadn't shared it with you? So, whenever participants introduce words or phrases that leave room for interpretation, don't hesitate to ask for clarification. This approach helps us reach a mutual understanding of a feeling or reaction.

But what are some of these subjective words to watch out for? They are mostly emotions that can take on a multitude of meanings, depending on the individual and circumstances. Here are a few examples:

- happy;
- frustrated;
- annoyed;
- angry;
- excited;
- confused.

When you encounter these types of words, you can ask the following probing questions:

- "Describe what you mean by [subjective word]."
- "Tell me more about what [subjective feeling] felt like."
- "Explain what you mean by [subjective word]."

RELIABLE FOLLOW-UP PHRASES

There are a few other follow-up phrases you can use when you want to dig deeper into the topic or what the participant mentioned. Here are the ones I most commonly use.

"Describe How [Experience] Made You Feel."

We're on a mission to uncover vivid stories and treasured memories from our participants. These narratives are like gold, enriching our understanding of customers beyond our wildest expectations. When it comes to experiences, having tangible examples of what a particular encounter was like, and the emotions it stirred in a participant, is absolutely crucial.

It's often a breeze to stop at a participant mentioning a specific experience, but that's precisely when we should keep the conversation flowing. The simple phrase, "Tell me about how [experience] made you feel," works wonders. It's open-ended and naturally prompts engaging conversation.

And if you prefer, you can even opt for a more general approach with, "Share your thoughts on [the experience]." This choice comes in handy if you'd like to backtrack a bit, and gain a broader perspective on the overall experience before diving into the nitty-gritty details.

Participant: "I had to wait forever in line at the bank, even though I had an appointment."
Interviewer: "Describe how waiting in line made you feel."

"Why?"/"How So?"

The good old "why." There's a reason why "why" is so popular: it's a quick and easy way to probe deeper into someone's thoughts and meanings. Another way to ask why is the phrase "How so?"

Participant: "I didn't want to reach out to customer support."
Interviewer: "Why?"
Participant: "I didn't think they would be able to help with the problem easily..."
Interviewer: "How so?"

You can continue asking why or how until you hit a core value, or get deep enough that the participant can't explain anymore.
"In What Sense?"
"In what sense?" is a great way to follow up without having to form a question fully. It is also a great alternative to "why." This phrase is a great tool to use when you're met with those vague terms that could mean a million different things to anyone listening or trying to interpret results.

Participant: "Trying to get a hold of customer support was a nightmare."
Interviewer: "In what sense?"

GET INTO THE MINDSET

No matter how many questions you do or don't have, when it comes to generative research, your mindset is key. The most effective change I employed during my generative research interviews—aside from having TEDW and certain questions to follow up with at hand—was to get into a super curious mindset. Everyone always says empathy is the bedrock of user research, and while I agree that empathy is hugely important for our job, curiosity enables us to foster that empathy.

As I mentioned, when I first started conducting generative research interviews, I got super nervous that I would say something wrong or ask a stupid question. This mindset really inhibited my sense of curiosity. Instead of opening my mind and listening, I clammed up, trying to think of the next thing to say before the participant had even said anything at all.

Over time, and with practice (I practiced a lot internally rather than on participants), I let go of those fears. The wonderful thing about generative research is that the participant is meant to be the expert, and the researcher is meant to understand the topic from the participant's perspective deeply. Which means, there really are no stupid questions.

When I started to understand that I just had to listen to the person in front of me and get genuinely curious about what they had to say, it became much easier to have that conversation. I went from being nervous and self-conscious to just wanting to fully understand everything about that topic from the participant's perspective.

I stopped caring about how I sounded, and started to care more about unraveling the participant's mental model and thought process. Now I can honestly ask questions and feel comfortable running a generative research session on any topic, because I know it has nothing to do with me and everything to do with the participant. As long as you use open-ended and unbiased language that gets their experiences and stories, you are doing great!

I highly recommend practicing these types of interviews on colleagues, friends, and families—TEDW and the other probing questions are great to use in pretty much any conversation!

TWO EXAMPLES OF GENERATIVE RESEARCH DISCUSSION GUIDES

Example One

This first example of generative research script is from a B2C travel company I used to work for. In this example, I show you my introduction, warm-up, discussion guide, and wrap-up. In the discussion guide, you can see some of my prompts for follow-up questions, which are there to remind me to probe into the questions.

Hi there, I'm Nikki, a user experience researcher at X. First off, thank you so much for being willing to participate in this session. We really value your feedback, and use what we learn from you within our product team to help us make customer-focused decisions.

For the next 90 minutes, we are going to be talking about how you planned your last leisure holiday. I would love for this to be a conversation based on what is most important to you. Imagine I am trying to make a documentary of your step-by-step process when planning your last leisure holiday—tell me everything!

Feel free to stop this session at any time if you need to take a break or feel uncomfortable.

Do you mind if I record this session? It is for notetaking purposes and will only be used internally; all of your answers will be kept confidential.

Do you have any questions before we begin?

Let's get started!

Warm-up:

- What is your favorite thing to do in your spare time?
- What is your favorite hobby?
- Describe anything really interesting that you've either read or seen recently.
- Tell me about the number one place you wish you could travel. Why there?

Journey:

Remember, the questions I'm asking aren't just about your experience with X website, but also outside of that!

- Tell me about the last time you traveled, and walk me through the experience from when you started planning.
- Describe your main motivation for traveling.
- Why did you decide to take the trip?
- Who else was on the trip?
- When did you plan the trip? How far in advance, and why?
- How did you plan? Tell me about the tools you used for each part.
- Where did you plan the trip?

First experience:

- Describe how you first heard about X?
- Walk me through the last time you used the X website, starting with what prompted your decision to take a trip.
  - Describe how you felt during the experience.
  - Walk me through what you were trying to accomplish when you first used X.
  - Show your screen and walk me through what you did, step-by-step.
    - On each screen: Who, what, where, when, why, how.

Final details:

- Remember a time when X website didn't work for you, or you had a negative experience, describe what happened.
  - Tell me about another frustrating experience you had using X website.
- Talk me through your last experience contacting customer care.
- Describe another tool that you have used to help you plan travel.
  - Walk me through your experience with it.

Things to listen for (from other teams):

1. Ads on website.
2. Newsletter subscription.

Wrap-up

Thank you so much for participating today. We really appreciate your time. This session was extremely helpful for us. Again, all of your answers will be kept completely confidential. I will send you your compensation by the end of today/tomorrow. Since this session was so valuable, would it be okay for me to contact you again, in the future, to participate in another research session? Do you have any other questions for me? Thank you again!

Example Two

This next example is from a B2B company I worked at, and is a much more stripped-down version of a discussion guide, with more bullet points and vague questions. Many of the questions aren't even in the TEDW format because I translated them during the session (this was when I felt much more comfortable with generative research). If you want to give it a go, you can translate some of these questions into TEDW versions.

- Ask for permission to record.
- Mention screen sharing.
- Hard stop (an hour and a half).
- Introduce any necessary people on the call.
- If you have any questions or want to stop at any point, just let me know.
- I want this to be conversation with all your details—tell me everything.

Warm-up:

- What is your current role?
- How long have you been in that role?
- How long have you been in the field?
- What are your top three day-to-day responsibilities?
- Describe some other roles you work with outside of your immediate team.

Journey:
This isn't just about inside X platform, but also about how you do things in general, outside of the platform as well*

For this conversation, I'd love to hear about your entire journey when it comes to UCG and content management, starting all the way from when you noticed a particular problem to solve. If you weren't involved in a stage, just let me know, and we will skip over it. Let's get started.

- Awareness—When did you first think about getting a solution? What problem were you trying to solve?
- Onboarding—Involved when X was brought into the company? First time using X?
- Collect—Involved in finding content? Content sources? Where are you getting it? Professional photographers?
- Curate—Go through and decide what to use and what not to. When? Strategy-based?
- Activate—How do you activate? Which channels? When would you choose to use UGC versus owned content?
- Analyze—How are you measuring results?
- Integrate—With other tools?

*If they skip over a portion of the journey because they don't work in that area, ask if we can speak with someone who does.

Wrap-up

- Thank you for participating.
- Incentive.
- More research (if participant was good).
- Anyone else you'd recommend for these sessions.

Practice Makes Progress

When it comes to generative research, both crafting the discussion guides and holding the sessions, it takes a lot of practice to feel comfortable. It took hours and hours of practice for me to gain that confidence and shake the self-consciousness that comes with the improv part of generative research. If you're feeling defeated or like this is tough, just give yourself the time and space to practice! I promise that it is a skill that gets easier over time!

CONTEXTUAL INQUIRY

Crafting a compelling contextual inquiry involves navigating a realm where participants recount their experiences. However, it's crucial to recognize that users can inadvertently omit essential details, and this limitation is by no means a fault of our participants or the user research field. Human memory is intricate, and relying solely on self-reported data has its constraints. Sometimes, we yearn to witness firsthand the user's journey, to see it with our own eyes.

Enter contextual inquiry—a nuanced research approach that marries structured interviews with unobtrusive observations within the participant's natural environment. What sets contextual inquiry apart are two key elements:

1. A Delicate Balance: Contextual inquiry strikes a delicate balance between interviewing and observing participants.
2. In Situ Exploration: It unfolds within the user's native surroundings, making it uniquely suited to uncovering insights that might remain concealed in other research methods.

Mastering this method requires finesse, because you're essentially an unobtrusive observer in the participant's habitat. Participants may expect questions or modify their behavior in your presence, necessitating a well-crafted strategy to establish expectations and blend seamlessly into their environment. Let's embark on the journey of conducting a contextual inquiry, a challenging yet immensely rewarding approach that promises rich insights to empower your team.

How to Conduct Contextual Inquiry

Conducting a contextual inquiry may seem challenging, but the treasure trove of insights it offers is well worth the effort. It's an exhilarating journey that allows you to delve into users' real-world experiences, and brings invaluable information back to your team. Before delving into the nitty-gritty of conducting a contextual inquiry, it's essential to grasp the two modes of these sessions:

- Active Inquiry: In this mode, participants actively engage in answering clarifying questions and discussing the tasks they perform, providing context throughout the session.
- Passive Inquiry: Conversely, passive inquiry entails the researcher's silent observation of tasks and the environment. Clarifying questions are postponed until after the observation concludes.

Both approaches are entirely valid, and your choice depends on your objectives and the participant's comfort level. Initially, you might find an active approach more suitable, and as you become more proficient with the method, you can transition to a passive stance. So, let's dive into the intricate process of conducting a contextual inquiry and uncover the steps to master this complex methodology.

Introduction and Explanation

Contextual inquiry demands a more thoughtful and deliberate introduction than conventional research sessions. Here's a comprehensive breakdown.

Introduce Yourself: Begin by introducing yourself. Building rapport is vital, so consider warming up with questions like, "How's your day?" or "What's your favorite hobby?" Establishing a friendly atmosphere paves the way for a smoother interaction.

Set the Stage: Delve into how the session will unfold. Communicate your expectations and what participants can anticipate from you. For instance, you might explain,

> Today, I'll observe your natural work process. I may interject for context or clarifications, after which you can resume as usual. Please let me know if interruptions are inconvenient. Pretend I'm not here—I aim to understand your daily workflow.

Remind of Commitment: Inform participants about the expected session duration and reassure them that they can halt the process at any time if they feel uncomfortable. Encourage them to ask questions before commencing observation.

Permission to Record: If recording is warranted, seek participants' consent and have them sign necessary consent forms. Additionally, inquire if it's acceptable to capture photos of their workspace to provide an accurate environmental context.

Optional Interview Start: If preliminary questions are necessary, commence with an interview phase. These queries can address roles or any other aspects requiring clarification.

Observation

The observation stage varies according to whether you're conducting an active or passive contextual inquiry.

Active Contextual Inquiry: Observe and meticulously document the participant's actions and behaviors, focusing on facts without interpreting thoughts or motivations. Interrupt occasionally with clarifying questions, to gain context or understand the participant's mental model. Sample questions include, "Why did you do X?" or "What led to your decision to try Y?"

Passive Contextual Inquiry: Similar to the active approach, observe and document actions without making assumptions. Create a list of questions for post-observation clarification. Ask these questions after the observation concludes, to delve into specific actions or mental models. An example inquiry could be, "When you navigated to X, can you explain your thought process?"

Wrap-up

The wrap-up phase serves several purposes:

- Address Remaining Queries: It's an ideal time to pose any lingering questions and solicit feedback from participants. This step ensures accurate interpretation of observations.
- Summarize Key Insights: Recap main takeaways to validate your understanding and eliminate misreporting risks. For instance, if you observed a participant struggling with a task, seek clarification by asking, "What were your emotions when attaching those documents to the email?"

With your meticulously compiled notes and newfound insights, you're well-prepared to report back to your team. Conducting contextual inquiries is a craft that demands practice and finesse. Yet, the rewards are profound, unveiling the intricate tapestry of user experiences, and empowering you to shape your product's future with an unparalleled depth of understanding.

OPPORTUNITY GAP SURVEY

I remember the first time I ran a very successful generative research study. I had spent months practicing my skills and finally felt like I had achieved a rhythm and depth that got us deep and meaningful data from our participants. I had uncovered information beyond what we had imagined. Not only did I answer the study's goals, but the data we received included innovative, never-before-heard insights that surprised us. The "wows" we said topped those of Owen Wilson.

Never had I gathered quite as much qualitative research and so many insights. At the end of the study, I had to bring my report down from over 50 pages to something more manageable, but I had no idea which insights to prioritize. Of course, I started with the study goals and made sure I shared the information the team needed to move forward with the decisions they'd been struggling with. But I had so much more deep data and interesting information for them.

Since I hadn't had this kind of "problem" before, I wasn't sure what to do, so I roped my entire team into the process of understanding all the insights and trying to decide which ones we should focus on first. While I was thrilled that the study had such an impact and gave us so much data, I soon saw how this could be a substantial problem. Outside of the direct insights we needed for the study goals, we had a very hard time trying to determine what else to focus on from the learnings.

After three workshops of trying to prioritize the insights, I threw my hands in the air, frustrated by our lack of progress. We had gone around in circles trying to determine which of the fifty insights were now, next, and later. We'd tried various prioritization models, such as RICE (Reach, Impact, Confidence, and Effort) and the Kano Model, but none of them seemed to help. We walked out with questions and doubts.

When that last workshop ended, instead of scheduling another, I decided to take a step back. We had put so much effort into this study and got everything we asked for and more, but now it felt like it was all being wasted. I could predict that, soon, people would give up on this exercise, and the insights would be stuck somewhere in a Google Drive folder like I'd seen happen before.

I researched how I could potentially solve this prioritization problem and stumbled across something called the Opportunity Gap Survey.

What Is the Opportunity Gap Survey?

Officially, the opportunity gap survey is part of the Jobs to be Done framework and the Opportunity-Driven Innovation framework created by Anthony W. Ulwick. However, when I found out about this opportunity survey, despite not using Jobs to be Done for this study, I thought I could possibly use it to help us make some decisions.

The opportunity gap survey analyzes the gap between how important each insight is and how satisfied people are with current solutions. The "gap" between the perceived importance and the perceived level of satisfaction is your opportunity score. The bigger the gap between how important something is to the person and how satisfied they currently are, the bigger the potential opportunity. Let's look at an example to make this more concrete.

Imagine we were doing a study on students going through medical school—I asked my best friend about this since she went through this process a few years ago. We're trying to understand their different needs during the process of "surviving" medical school.

During this generative study, we uncover the following needs and goals of medical students:

- pass STEP exams;
- find research and paper publication opportunities;
- discover a mentor;
- find cheap accommodation;

- study for in-person interactions with patients;
- find time for exercising;
- overcome impostor syndrome.

There is quite a lot of variety within these learnings, so where do we place our focus, and where do we start? This situation is when the opportunity gap survey can become a very handy tool. For each of these points, we'd create two questions, one focused on the level of importance and the other on the current satisfaction. These questions each follow the below model:

How important is it to you that you are able to [outcome/goal/need]?

- 1 to 5 scale, 1 = "Not at all important," 5 = "Extremely important."
  When using [current solution], how satisfied are you with your ability to achieve [outcome/goal/need]?
- 1 to 5 scale, 1 = "Not at all satisfied," 5 = "Extremely satisfied."
  So, for each of the above points, we'd fill in the goal, need, or outcome, for the two questions, and it would look like this:
  How important is it to you that you are able to pass the STEP exam?
- 1 to 5 scale, 1 = "Not at all important," 5 = "Extremely important."
  When using your current solution, how satisfied are you with your ability to pass the STEP exam?
- 1 to 5 scale, 1 = "Not at all satisfied," 5 = "Extremely satisfied."
  You'd set up these two questions for each of the bullet points above.

It might be that you've uncovered the solutions participants are using, so you can specify in the question if that's the case, or you can even ask about the satisfaction of your own product as a solution (if the participants are users).

Once you send this out, you will start to receive opportunity scores, the delta between importance and satisfaction, which will help you to prioritize your learnings. We'll cover analyzing the score in a second, but first, let's walk through what creating an opportunity gap survey looks like.

How to Create an Opportunity Gap Survey

The entire point of this survey is to help you prioritize findings and insights from generative research, so the first and most essential step of creating an opportunity gap survey is to conduct some generative research. Basing your survey on results from this type of research is critical to ensuring you get the most accurate information from your participants.

Setting Up Your Study

Whenever I know I'm going to use a generative research approach, I automatically assume that I will be sending out the opportunity gap survey at the end of the study to help us prioritize insights and needs. By knowing I will send out this survey, I can ensure I get the most relevant information from participants, setting us up for success. The first step to a successful study is setting up a research plan with incredibly clear research goals.

Research goals are the in-depth areas we want to explore in our research project that will help us answer what we are trying to learn. These goals are the things we want to be able to gather information about by the end of the study. They aren't posed as questions, but we want to be able to "answer" them in the sense of getting enough data on them to feel comfortable making decisions. When it comes to a generative research study that has an opportunity gap survey, my goals usually consist of:

- Discover the unmet needs of our participants and where we don't support them in [topic].
- Identify participant's goals and their current process to achieve those goals.
- Uncover the different tools participants are currently using to achieve their goals and what their experience is like with them.

Through this study, I am hugely focused on goals and needs, which is the exact information I need to put together an opportunity gap survey. The opportunity gap survey will only be as helpful as it is relevant to the information you get. If you don't have information on goals and needs, the opportunity score won't be as helpful in prioritizing what you focus on. As always, make sure the approach makes sense given the goals of your study and the information you collect from participants.

Creating the Survey Questions

As covered above, for each need, goal, or outcome you uncover, you use both the importance and satisfaction questions to get the opportunity score:
How important is it to you that you are able to [outcome/goal/need]?

- 1 to 5 scale, 1 = "Not at all important," 5 = "Extremely important."
  When using [current solution], how satisfied are you with your ability to achieve [outcome/goal/need]?
- 1 to 5 scale, 1 = "Not at all satisfied," 5 = "Extremely satisfied."
  Let's look at a few more examples of putting these together.
  Need: Keep track of my eating habits
  How important is it to you that you are able to keep track of your eating habits?
- 1 to 5 scale, 1 = "Not at all important," 5 = "Extremely important."
  When using MyFitnessPal, how satisfied are you with your ability to keep track of your eating habits?
- 1 to 5 scale, 1 = "Not at all satisfied," 5 = "Extremely satisfied."

Need: Minimize Time Inputting Expenses

How important is it to you that you are able to minimize your time inputting expenses?

- 1 to 5 scale, 1 = "Not at all important," 5 = "Extremely important."
    When using Xero, how satisfied are you with your ability to minimize your time inputting expenses?
- 1 to 5 scale, 1 = "Not at all satisfied," 5 = "Extremely satisfied."
    Need: Give specific package delivery instructions
    How important is it to you that you are able to give specific package delivery instructions?
- 1 to 5 scale, 1 = "Not at all important," 5 = "Extremely important."
    When using UPS, how satisfied are you with your ability to give specific package delivery instructions?
- 1 to 5 scale, 1 = "Not at all satisfied," 5 = "Extremely satisfied."
    Need: Minimize the time it takes to research where to stay on a trip
    How important is it to you that you are able to minimize the time it takes to research where to stay on a trip?
- 1 to 5 scale, 1 = "Not at all important," 5 = "Extremely important."
    When using Expedia, how satisfied are you with your ability to minimize the time it takes to research where to stay on a trip?
- 1 to 5 scale, 1 = "Not at all satisfied," 5 = "Extremely satisfied."

As you can see, this survey is extremely adaptable and, as long as you have the right information to put into it, can be relatively simple to put together. Whenever it comes to surveys, however, always make sure you take into consideration the number of questions. Since, essentially, each need is two questions, these can add up very quickly. Typically, once a survey response time exceeds seven minutes, you may start to see a significant drop-off in responses.

I like to keep my surveys shorter—around 15 questions (I count each of the two questions as one in the case of the opportunity gap survey—which might mean you can't include all of your needs in your opportunity gap survey. In studies where I've had more than 15 needs, goals, or outcomes to prioritize, I've had to sit with my team and try to work out the ones that are most important to ask in our given context.

Another option is to send out several surveys in different phases. Obviously, this takes longer, but it can be a good compromise. You still need to prioritize which questions you're sending out first.

For this, we typically use the RICE model to help us understand which are the most important questions to send. Another way I've prioritized the questions is by the weight of the need, goal, or outcome. What I mean by this is how often that need, goal, or outcome came up across participants. The more participants who mentioned the given need, goal, or outcome, the higher it went on the list of questions.

Sending the Survey

Once you have your questions set, it's time to send out your survey. This part prompted some questions, such as, "Who should I send the survey to?" and "How many people should I send it to?" Typically, with generative research, you have a smaller sample size, such as 15 or 20 participants. Unfortunately, that number is a bit too small of a sample size for a survey, and limiting to only that group of users may skew your results.

Ideally, when it comes to this type of survey, you would send it out to similar participants to those you interviewed, whether this means a particular persona, segment, or demographic. Make sure the survey participants are similar to those you interviewed and would have the same needs, goals, or outcomes, or use the same solutions. If you aren't sure whether they've used those solutions or not, make the satisfaction question more generic by saying "your current solution."

For this particular survey, we aren't looking at comparison, so we can use a confidence interval around sample means, which in this case, are average satisfaction and average importance. So, we must determine our comfortable margin of error and confidence interval. The most common of these is a 5% margin of error and 95% confidence interval. Calculate your necessary sample size by understanding your population size and popping that into a calculator like.

Once you have all of that set, plug your survey into the many survey-based tools and send it out to more people than necessary in your sample size. Remember, not everyone will respond to your survey. Typically, you can expect a 10%–20% response rate, unless you have a very engaged customer base, in which you can expect closer to a 50%–60% response rate.

If you are new to surveys, the best thing you can do is test out your response rates and which medium (e.g., email, pop-up) gives you the best response. It might take some time to understand your numbers, but it's great to experiment and iterate on this process!

Also, as a tip, always send a dry run of your survey internally to make sure there are no problems with it and to see approximately how long it will take, as one of the worst feelings in the world is to have to resend a survey because of an error. Trust me, I've been there.

How to Analyze Your Opportunity Gap Survey

Once you receive your responses, it's time to analyze your survey. In general, the criteria are relatively straightforward. Any insight with a high importance and low satisfaction is a potential opportunity that will bring a high ROI. This score indicates people find the goal, need, or outcome important but are currently dissatisfied with the solution. So, if the team were to make a better solution that addresses that need, goal, or outcome, the higher likelihood the person would use it and be more satisfied. The other scores include:

- low importance and high satisfaction;
- high importance and high satisfaction;
- low importance and low satisfaction.

These insights become deprioritized because there is either already a satisfactory solution or the insight isn't important for users.

To score the test, you can use the following formula.

Importance + (importance − satisfaction) = opportunity.

So let's go back to one of our examples:
Need: Minimize the time it takes to research where to stay on a trip
How important is it to you that you are able to minimize the time it takes to research where to stay on a trip?

- 1 to 5 scale, 1 = "Not at all important," 5 = "Extremely important"
    When using Expedia, how satisfied are you with your ability to minimize the time it takes to research where to stay on a trip?
- 1 to 5 scale, 1 = "Not at all satisfied," 5 = "Extremely satisfied"
    Let's say that a participant responded with the following data:
- Level of importance is 4
- Level of satisfaction is 2

We would then have:

$4 + (4 - 2) = 6$

The highest opportunity score for the survey is 9 (an importance level of 5 and a satisfaction level of 1), so an opportunity score of 6 is fairly significant.

Now let's look at a different example.

Need: Give specific package delivery instructions
How important is it to you that you are able to give specific package delivery instructions?

- 1 to 5 scale, 1 = "Not at all important," 5 = "Extremely important"
    When using UPS, how satisfied are you with your ability to give specific package delivery instructions?
- 1 to 5 scale, 1 = "Not at all satisfied," 5 = "Extremely satisfied"
    Let's say that a participant responded with the following data:
- Level of importance is 2
- Level of satisfaction is 4

We would then have:

$2 + (2 - 4) = 0$

Compared to 6, this is not a great opportunity to focus on. The participant does not find this insight important and is satisfied with their current solution.

For me, this has always been a relatively manual process since each participant has several scores (one for each insight). Once you have scored each participant's responses, it's time to take the average opportunity score. To make this easy (using small numbers), let's say we had five respondents to the insight of minimizing the time it takes to research where to stay on a trip. We got the following opportunity scores from the five participants.

- 6
- 5
- 7
- 8
- 6

We would then take the average of these scores and get an opportunity score for this insight of 6.4. We would do this for each insight so we understood the average opportunity score across all participants. As I said, I've done this fairly manually on a spreadsheet (not the most fun), but there are some templates out there, but they have slightly different setups to what I've used in the past.

How I've Used the Opportunity Gap Survey

I've used the opportunity gap survey quite a few times in my work to help with prioritizing qualitative research insights, especially when we were overwhelmed with the amount of information and no other prioritization model helped us.

An Example

We had just finished an extensive project, with 25 diary study participants answering daily questions and then quite a few follow-up interviews to clarify some of the data. When I looked at our Miro board, I cringed at the amount of information on it. Everything was supremely interesting, and a lot of information was new. We'd looked at a new segment and how they found inspiration in fashion.

Since we'd rarely spoken to this segment in the past, we uncovered insights we'd never imagined, but, again, the team felt stuck. We had information and no idea how we could begin to prioritize what was most important to our customers, especially since we still didn't know them well enough.

We had about thirty insights, which were too many to put into the opportunity gap survey. To narrow down which we would use, I facilitated a prioritization workshop. In that workshop, we went through all the insights, and we assigned a weight to each of them. That weight was based on how many participants had mentioned the given insight.

Once we'd weighed all the insights, we used part of the RICE prioritization model to predict our perceived reach, impact, and confidence of each of the insights. We left off the effort piece because there was no solution to base an effort level on. We used the weight of each insight to predict our confidence in it. In the workshop, we went through each insight and plotted it on an RIC matrix.

We ended up deciding on ten insights that we felt would have the biggest reach and impact for that segment. I turned those insights into survey questions:

We sent the survey via qualtrics. Luckily, we had a really large panel and had the budget to use our platform to recruit even more of our particular segment. We ended up with 500 responses to the survey, which was right around where we were targeting (we had a significantly large target population).

I then scored the different insights and plotted their scores on a graph:

The insights that had a high average level of importance and a low average level of satisfaction are those we decided to focus on right away.

We sent out two subsequent phases of the survey to include the other 20 insights we'd found and added to the graph and continued to reprioritize if we found another underserved insight or unmet need, based on the opportunity scores.

I shared this graph with my teams to help them visualize the scores and it hugely helped us with taking all that wonderful data and figuring out the best place to start, based on our users' perceptions rather than our own.

Problem Definition Methods

15

DIARY STUDIES

Diary studies are a qualitative, longitudinal method that allows participants to record their thoughts, experiences, and perceptions through activities. These activities can come in many different forms, such as writing text, recording audio or video, screen recordings, or taking photos.

Typically, with these types of studies, you are getting participants to respond to activities within their environment in more natural ways than something like a one-on-one interview. Although diary studies don't replace contextual inquiry—literally nothing can—they are still a great tool to use if you want to get a remote understanding of participants' context, environment, and reactions in a real-world setting.

When to Use a Diary Study

As fantastic as they are, diary studies have a time and a place. Since they are qualitative and longitudinal, they can take a long time to get the results, and are geared toward more of a generative understanding of your participants' and their context. Certain goals are best suited for this method. The goals I most commonly use for diary studies include:

- Discover people's current processes/decision-making about [research subject], and how they feel about the overall experience.
- Understand what [research subject] means to people (how they define it) and why it is important to them.
- Learn about people's perceptions of [research subject].
- Uncover how people interact with or experience [research subject] in their day-to-day lives.

- Discover resources people interact with when it comes to [research subject].
- While diary studies can be hugely impactful, and powerful, there are times where they aren't the best choice of method, such as:
- Quick insights. If you are looking for super quick insights on something, diary studies are not the best option for you because they are meant to span over a certain amount of time.
- Product-focused questions. For really product-focused questions or usability testing responses, I don't recommend diary studies since they are meant to focus more on participants' perceptions, context, and environment in a product-agnostic sense. For these types of questions, usability testing is your best bet.
- Quantitative data. While diary studies typically require a larger sample size (we'll get into that later), they are a qualitative method. Of course you can always follow up with a survey, but the actual diary study looks at qualitative type responses.
- Limited resources. Diary studies produce a lot of qualitative data to sift through. Not only that, but they can also be difficult to set up and maintain. If you have limited capacity, budget, and time, diary studies might not be the best approach. It took me a few weeks to get through and make sense of all of my qualitative data for one of my studies.
- Hard to reach/niche participants. Niche participants are tough to get regardless of methodology, but diary studies require participants to respond multiple times over a set period. So, if you have a participant base that is time-poor or won't engage regularly, you might be better set up for a one-time approach.

Again, make sure you look at your goals, outcomes, and constraints when thinking about which method is best for your study!

Let's Set Up a Diary Study

When I've set up a diary study, it felt very overwhelming and complex. Since I had never done it, I was confused about all the moving parts and components I should add. I was also unsure how to set up the activities properly.

To make it easier, I will use an example from a project I conducted with dscout (which is why you will see screenshots of their tool). You can also do this manually, and I will share screenshots of how I planned a diary study without a tool as well.

This sample project is about body positivity, body neutrality, and health at every size. Not only are these movements and ideas highly relevant right now, but they also gave us a deeper understanding of how people got into, and thought about these concepts.

Previous research has focused specifically on the intersection of social media and body positivity/neutrality, or the impact of body positivity/neutrality on body image. Little research is done into understanding how people discover, explore, and get inspired by body positivity/neutrality daily. With this project, we aimed to explore participants' philosophy, the path into, and everyday experiences with the body positivity and body neutrality movement.

Writing a Research Plan

We started with a research plan and the most basic components, which included the research statement and goals. The first thing we did was ask ourselves:

- What do we want to learn about body positivity, body neutrality, and health at every size?
- What type of experiences do we want to learn?
- What information do we want at the end of the study?

When asking these questions, if you can, brainstorm together with your team. User research is a team sport, and is often a support system for your teams to make better decisions. If you include them in this step, you make it more likely for the research to succeed as well as be actionable for your team.

With these questions, we crafted the following goals:

- Discover the paths people take to get into the body positivity, body neutrality, or health at every size movement.
- Learn about people's philosophies of body positivity, body neutrality, and health at every size.
- Uncover how people interact with or experience body positivity, body neutrality, and health at every size in their day-to-day lives.
- Discover resources people interact with to gain inspiration from body positivity, body neutrality, and health at every size.

These goals screamed diary study in particular because of goals three and four.

Could we have achieved these goals in an interview? Yes, probably. However, with these goals, there would be a lot to cover in the interview. We'd have to get through the path, the philosophies, the interactions, and the resources. Even for a 90–120 minute interview, that was a lot to cover. And since this could lead to sensitive topics, it would be a high cognitive load for the participant and for the interviewer (I have a sensitive relationship with food and body image, so I knew this would be a challenging yet fulfilling project).

Instead of shoving all these goals into an interview format, we decided a diary study would be best, followed by some qualitative interviews and, later on, a survey to help prioritize any insights.

Here is the beginning of our research plan:

Recruitment

Recruiting the right participants makes or breaks a research study. Using a screener survey is one of the best ways to ensure you are intentionally getting the right participants, who can give you the exact information you need to accomplish your study's goals.

For this process, the first step is to brainstorm the criteria your participants must have to answer your study goals. You can do this by asking yourself a few different questions:

- What are the questions your users have to answer to get you meaningful information?
- What gaps in knowledge do you have that you need your participants to fill in?
- What behaviors do you need to understand more?
- What habits are you trying to target?
- What are the goals the user is trying to accomplish?

For this project, we asked ourselves the above questions and came up with the following criteria:

- People who are directly involved in the body positivity, body neutrality, or health at every size movement through a variety of ways.
- People who have heard about and are knowledgeable about the body positivity, body neutrality, or health at every size movement.
- People involved in nonprofits or in a career inside these movements.
- People impacted by body positivity, body neutrality, or health at every size.
- People who practice body positivity, body neutrality, or health at every size.

We crafted our screener questions to target participants with these particular characteristics. We decided on a mix of closed- and open-ended questions because we wanted to see how participants reacted to the open-ended questions. Through the video screener and the open-ended questions, we got a much better idea of how people might participate in the study and the level of detail we could expect.

Sample Size

Regarding the number of participants we wanted for this diary study, we agreed on no less than 20 participants (with an ideal of 25) to help us meet data saturation. Data saturation occurs when additional data collection does not yield significantly new insights or themes. Once you reach data saturation, further participants may not be necessary for achieving your research goals.

Since diary studies are often time-intensive for participants, there can be some drop-off, so we recruited 32 participants and ended up with 26. I always recommend over-recruiting for diary studies. The worst thing that can happen is that you get extra data!

Compensation

Diary studies require your participants to come back to your study multiple times (sometimes more than once a day) over an extended period of time. Although each of your activities might be short, which I highly recommend, it is still a lot to ask people to remember and return to those tasks. I usually pay more than I would for a 60-minute interview.

For this ten-day diary study, we offered $110 at the end of the ten days. This was to a US audience. Of course, compensation always depends on:

- the complexity of your tasks and how long each takes;
- how often you are asking for tasks to be done (e.g., every day, every other day);
- how long your diary study is;
- the area of the world you are recruiting from.

You can take a look at tools like Ethnio's incentive calculator to give you a starting point for thinking about incentives for your study and area. Remember that calculators like this are just a starting point, and it's best to do additional research or use past research projects to figure out the best compensation.

Diary Study Logistics

Now, this is where diary studies can get overwhelming. There are so many logistics to think about when it comes to diary studies, such as:

- length of the diary study;
- logging protocol;
- tools;
- the device(s).

Length of the Diary Study

The length of your diary study will vary depending on what kind of information you need from your participants, and how frequently your participants encounter that information. For example, if you are talking to someone about how they choose an outfit to wear daily, you could make your diary study shorter, because they are doing the task of choosing an outfit every day and, thus, encountering the information you need more frequently.

However, if you are asking about purchasing books, depending on your participant recruitment criteria, they might only do this once or twice a month. So your diary study has to be longer to gather this information.

And finally, something that is very important is to ensure your diary study coincides with the events you need to capture. For instance, if you are talking to teachers about how they prepare for the upcoming school year, you don't want to ask them in the middle of the year. Or, if you are talking to accountants prepping taxes, the best time to do so would be in April as they take on this work.

Of course, you can always "force" certain questions and events on to your participants. For instance, our diary study was simply information gathering on how participants got into these movements. We didn't have any particular date range or frequency—we just needed to make sure we gave enough time to get the information we needed to achieve our goals. We chose ten days because it was enough time to ask all the questions we wanted without overwhelming our participants. The most common length for diary studies that I've seen is about two weeks long, but always think about the above considerations when determining length.

Logging Protocol

Logging protocol refers to how frequently participants will respond to your activities or prompts. It is super critical to set up clear expectation and framework for your participants, especially if you aren't using an automated tool. It takes away the headache for them, and also for you, if everything is super clear. There are a bunch of different ways you could categorize your logging protocol, but these are the most common.

- Time-based logging asks participants to record their experiences and activities at specific time intervals (e.g., every hour, at the end of the day). This protocol provides a structured timeline of events and helps capture changes and patterns throughout the day.
- Event-based logging asks participants to log their experiences and thoughts whenever specific events or activities occur. For example, they might record entries after using a particular product or encountering a specific situation. Event-based logging allows for capturing immediate reactions and context-specific information.
- Trigger-based logging is when the researcher provides participants with pre-defined triggers or prompts that signal when to make diary entries. These prompts can be based on specific events, times, or cues. Trigger-based logging ensures that participants focus on particular moments or experiences of interest to the researcher.

You can also have participants log when they change location or context, track emotion/mood changes, or give a summary of their day. It is all up to the information you need from your participants and how you can get it most naturally.

For our particular project, we used trigger-based logging, which means that we provided the participants with certain prompts that signaled what each entry had to be about.

If you use a diary study tool, there could be two options on how you present the prompts to participants.

- Manual: In this mode, you control when prompts or activities appear to your participants. The first part will open on launch. Subsequent parts will be in draft mode; you can edit them until they are published and launched.
- Automatic: Automatic prompts or activities give participants more control and require less work on the researcher's part. The first part will open on

launch, and all subsequent parts will be locked from being edited. Once a participant submits the minimum number of entries required for a part, the next part automatically opens up for them.

Since we used dscout for this project, we decided to go with the automatic approach, giving our participants the flexibility of answering the questions whenever they wanted during the ten days. If someone wanted to sit down and finish the entire diary study in one sitting, they could. Or, they could decide to split it up over ten days. This method afforded our participants more freedom and stopped us from bottlenecking their responses. Whenever I haven't had a tool, I've had to send participants each activity manually.

Tools

As I mentioned above, I used dscout for the sample project. I've also used Indeemo as a diary study tool. Both have pros and cons that highly depend on a study/organization's needs, so I won't get into that right now. I highly recommend doing a demo for any tool you are thinking about using, and asking all your questions there to ensure it's a great fit.

If you don't have the tools, diary studies become tricky. Usually, this means pulling many tools together for planning, sending, receiving responses, etc. Here are some combinations I've used:

Planning the Tasks

- Google docs
- Google sheets

Sending the Tasks

- WhatsApp
- Facebook group (community style)
- Email
- Actual diary with prompts written in it

Recording Tasks

- Loom
- Zoom
- Quicktime
- Phone
- Google Forms

Receiving the Tasks

- Google drive folder
- Dropbox folder
- Email

Analyzing and Synthesizing the Tasks
- Miro
- Mural

I ended up creating a Facebook community (it was a common place for that niche to congregate) where I listed the tasks and reminded people, and then they used either their phone to take photos or screen record, Loom to record videos, and Google Forms to fill out actual text to questions. They uploaded all video/audio/photos to a Google Drive directly, so they didn't need to worry about emailing me anything.

It's totally doable to do an entire diary study manually with no set diary study tool—I've done this more often than I've used tools. Of course, tools make it easier and streamline parts of the process that can become burdensome.

The Device(s)

When planning the diary study, it's important to consider the device(s) the participants will have to use to ensure they have access to them. When it comes to text-heavy questions, I like to ask people to complete those on a desktop or laptop because it's easier to type. However, if I need them to record a screen, I might ask them to do something like that directly on their phone. Keep in mind that some tools require you only to use one device during the diary study, so always make sure to look this up ahead of time!

Writing the Activities/Prompts

Next comes the fun (and sometimes difficult, but still exciting!) part of writing your actual activities and prompts! Before we dive into the actual activities/prompts, it's important to start with the overview of what the participants can expect from the study, kind of like an introduction to it.

Writing the Overview

The overview of the diary study is something you can send to participants to share what to expect. This is another step to ensure you are getting the best participants that align with what you need.

I also recommend sending this overview to the participants that you "accept" after the screener surveys come through—you might have more screener survey applications than you need, which is what I mean by accept—as this helps remind your participants what they should expect.

This introduction is very similar to one you might use in an interview, and it gives an indication of what the participant needs to do during the diary study. It includes:

- how the diary study works;
- what the diary study is about;
- dates of the diary study (including the deadline);
- compensation.

Here was our overview:

Welcome to the Body Positivity and Neutrality mission. We are so excited to learn from you. This mission consists of six parts that you will need to complete to earn the $110 reward:

1. Your philosophy on body positivity/neutrality and/or health at every size.
2. How technology plays a role in body positivity/neutrality and/or health at every size.
3. Your path into body positivity/neutrality and/or health at every size.
4. Your day-to-day experience with body positivity/neutrality and/or health at every size.
5. Resources or inspiration on body positivity/neutrality and/or health at every size.
6. Any parting wisdom or advice you have for others about body positivity/neutrality and/or health at every size.

As you complete a part, another will open on the mission page. Tap it to begin. Just tap the message bubbles in the upper right corner if you have any questions!

Some parts ask for multiple entries, while others, just one. Be sure to read the part description before beginning carefully. After you complete all six parts, you may be asked to take place in a one-on-one interview with us to dive deeper into your answers and thoughts on body positivity/neutrality and/or health at every size.

As a reminder, answers to this mission may be published to a wide audience or be used to teach a class. If you are not comfortable with this, please decline the mission! But if you're willing/interested in sharing your story with a wider audience, we're excited to have you here.

You Have until Saturday, October 23rd at 5PM Central to Complete All Six Parts!

As you can see, we gave a clear indication of what the diary study was about, how it worked (within the tool), the deadline for this particular study, and what they would get when they completed it. Since we also did one-on-one interviews within this project, we mentioned it in the project overview, so participants were aware they might get contacted for this.

Writing Diary Study Prompts

Writing diary study prompts is kind of a combination of writing a one-on-one interview questions and a usability testing task, which is a really hard balance to accomplish. While there is no one right way to write a diary study task, I use the following formula to help me.

1. Start with clear instruction. Begin your prompt with clear and concise instruction that tells participants what you want them to do. This includes what type of response you are looking for, such as a video or photo, and how long or how many you need. Example: "Using [medium + length/number] please describe…"
2. Specify the time or event you want them to recall. Next, specify the time, event, or trigger that participants should focus on when writing their entry. This is really important because qualitative data is best gathered from specific memories and stories. Example: "…how you first got into body positivity/body neutrality/HAES, thinking back to the first time you ever heard about it."
3. Use open-ended language. Use open-ended questions to encourage participants to provide detailed and reflective responses. Avoid yes/no questions and aim for questions that prompt participants to share their thoughts, emotions, or experiences. Example: "Talk through how you first discovered it."
4. Optional: Include probing questions or follow-ups. To elicit deeper insights, consider adding probing questions or follow-up prompts encouraging participants to expand on their initial responses. These can help uncover underlying motivations or factors. Example: "Describe what that feeling was like. Explain what resonated with you."

Putting It All Together, Here's an Example of a Diary Study Prompt Using the Formula

Prompt: In a 1–2 minute video, please talk us through (clear instruction) how you first got into body positivity/body neutrality/HAES, thinking back to the first time you ever heard about it (specific time/event). Talk us through how you first discovered it (open-ended language). Describe what that feeling was like. Explain what resonated with you (probing questions/follow-ups)." As you can see here, there is a lot of specificity in what we are looking for. If you wanted to, you could break up the probing questions/follow-ups into subsequent questions, you don't have to include it all in one prompt. Using this formula will help you ensure that you include all the information you need while being specific but also open-ended.

Not every question needs to be a long, open-ended prompt. You can also have multiple choice or surveys. I always recommend varying the types of questions you ask in your diary study, such as survey-based or open-ended, so that you have different types of data to choose from when reporting.

Here are some other examples using the above formula and framework to write diary study tasks (outside of the one in this study).

Travel Experience

- Clear instruction. "In a 2-minute video, please share your thoughts…"
- Time or event you want them to recall. "…thinking back to your most recent holiday abroad (outside of the US/EU/whatever country)."
- Open-ended language. "…describe the most memorable experience on this trip."
- Probing questions or follow-ups. "Explain why this was the most memorable experience on your trip."

Prompt: In a 2-minute video, please share your thoughts by reflecting on your most recent holiday abroad (outside of the US/EU/whatever country). Describe the most memorable experience on this trip. Explain why this was the most memorable experience on your trip.

Productivity Tool Study

- Clear instruction. "Using three screenshots, we'd like you to share…"
- Time or event you want them to recall. "…the most recent tool you used to stay productive today."
- Open-ended language. "…Using text, please describe the most unhelpful part of this tool."
- Probing questions or follow-ups. "Explain what made this part of the tool unhelpful."

Prompt: Using three screenshots, we'd like you to share the most recent tool you used to stay productive today. Using text, please describe the most unhelpful part of this tool. Explain what made this part of the tool unhelpful.

Social Media Usage

- Clear instruction. "In this one-minute screen share, please show us…"
- Time or event you want them to recall. "…what you were browsing the last time you logged onto Facebook."
- Open-ended language. "Describe what motivated you to log on to Facebook at that moment."
- Probing questions or follow-ups. "Walk us through any emotions or reactions that came up while you were browsing the content."

Prompt: In this one-minute screen share, please show us what you were browsing the last time you logged onto Facebook. Describe what motivated you to log on to Facebook at that moment. Walk us through any emotions or reactions that came up while you were browsing the content.

Using the above framework to experiment with writing diary study tasks will definitely help you structure the more qualitative and open-ended tasks, which are typically the hardest to write!

When it comes to organizing the prompts, think about the most natural order or a funnel approach. For instance, start with more broad information and funnel down to more specific information. Or, you can theme every day/few days around a specific topic, similar to what we did with the different parts.

Don't forget to run a pilot test/dry run or, to have a few colleagues look over the study to ensure it makes sense, before sending it out to participants.

WALK THE STORE INTERVIEWS

Walk the store interviews are a unique research method that combines the generative power of contextual inquiry with the evaluative aspect of usability testing. They allow you to observe participants, as they naturally interact with a product or service in their real-world environment.

Walk the store interviews grant participants complete control, as they guide you through their product or service interaction from their perspective. These sessions strike a balance between generative research, where you observe behavior, and evaluative research, where you assess pain points and issues.

The primary goals of walk the store interviews encompass a combination of observation, learning, and evaluation.

- Evaluate Product Use: Understand how users interact with a product or service in their day-to-day activities.
- Identify Pain Points: Recognize pain points and obstacles users encounter during their interactions, potentially leading to improvement ideas.
- Comprehend User Needs: Gain insights into the needs and goals of users when utilizing the product or service.

How to Conduct a Walk the Store Interview

Imagine you're collaborating with a prominent hospital that relies on an internal system for managing patient information, notes, and rounds. The hospital is eager to pinpoint areas for product enhancement and prioritize new feature development. In this scenario, we'll dive into the step-by-step process of conducting walk the store interviews tailored to the healthcare setting.

1. Define Clear Research Goals

Begin by establishing research goals:

1. Evaluate Daily Usage: Understand how doctors utilize the internal system in their daily routines.
2. Identify Pain Points: Uncover challenges doctors face when using the system and brainstorm potential improvements.

3. Comprehend User Needs: Gain insights into doctors' needs and goals, pinpointing areas where the product falls short.

2. Determine Expected Deliverables

Outline the expected deliverables for your project:

- Comprehensive Report: The report should include annotations and video clips that highlight areas of frustration and opportunity.
- Journey Maps: Create common journey maps illustrating the daily usage of the system.
- Visualization of Pain Points: Develop a visualization that showcases the top pain points and provides recommendations for the next steps.

3. Participant Recruitment

Select your participant pool based on the unique requirements of the healthcare environment.

- Sample Size: Opt for a substantial sample size, aiming for 24 doctors, with a balanced distribution of 12 emergency department doctors and 12 neurologists. This distribution aligns with the hospital's patterns of system usage.
- Diverse Representation: Ensure a diverse mix of participants in terms of gender, ethnicity, and age.

4. Create a Customized Discussion Guide

Tailor your discussion guide to address the most critical areas of the healthcare system.

- Patient check-up notes
- Tracking rounds
- Monitoring patient medication
- General usage

5. Starting the Interview

Walk the store interviews follow the natural sequence of how participants typically use the system or start with general system usage to begin the conversation. Participants often organically introduce different aspects of the system during the interview, so your questions won't follow a linear format.

6. Sample Interview Questions

Utilize the TEDW principle (Tell me more about, Explain, Describe, Walk me through) to gain comprehensive insights into participants' experiences:

Overall Usage

- "Show me the last time you opened the system. Describe what triggered you to open it."
  - "How typical is it for you to start from this area?"
  - "Walk me through your most recent experience using the system. How did it feel for you?"
  - "Describe a recent negative experience you had with the system."
- "What steps did you take to address and 'fix' that negative experience?"
- "In an ideal scenario, how would you have expected your interaction with the system to go?"
- "Explain what you are trying to accomplish when you access the system?"

Patient Notes

- "Let's delve into the last time you wrote patient notes. Walk me through which steps you took."
- "Explain your main goal when writing patient notes."
- "Talk me through the most frustrating experience you've had while writing patient notes."

Tracking Rounds

- "Walk me through how you typically track rounds."
- "Describe your main goal when tracking rounds."
- "Tell me about the most frustrating experience you've recently encountered while tracking rounds."

Patient Medication

- "Walk me through the last time you monitored patient medication? What was the experience like?"
- "Explain your main goal when monitoring patient medication."
- "Describe the most frustrating experience you've had while monitoring patient medication recently."

These questions aim to encourage participants to relive their experiences, offering in-depth insights and stories about their interactions with the hospital's internal system. The ultimate goal is to gain a profound understanding of their experiences and interactions to inform future product enhancements.

16 Solution Design and Refinement Methods

INTERNAL TESTING WITH STAKEHOLDERS

Internal testing with employees often faces skepticism due to concerns about data skewing, the introduction of biases, and employees potentially presenting inauthentic reactions. These concerns are valid, but it's essential to recognize that internal user testing can have its advantages when employed correctly. Let's explore the pros and cons, and provide insights on when and how to leverage employee user testing effectively.

Challenges of Employee User Testing

- Brand Loyalty: Employees tend to have loyalty to their company, which can influence their feedback. Their feelings about the company might overshadow their objective evaluation of a prototype or feature.
- Familiarity: Internal participants may know each other or even be friends. This familiarity can impact their willingness to provide honest feedback. They might opt for white lies to avoid insulting colleagues.
- Bias: Employees often have internal motivations and opinions aligned with the company's interests. Testing a feature that corresponds with these motivations can lead to overly positive feedback, while opposing views may garner criticism.
- Technical Focus: Technical employees may provide extremely technical feedback, making it challenging to receive innovative insights. They may struggle to break free from the company's established technical norms.

Internal Knowledge: Employees possess prior knowledge about the study and the company's inner workings. They are familiar with the company's jargon and perspectives, potentially influencing their performance and comprehension.

It's important to acknowledge these challenges, as they highlight the difficulties of achieving authentic user research within the organization. Authenticity is the essence of user research, and these challenges can hinder that.

Benefits of Employee User Testing

Despite the challenges, there are certain situations where internal user testing can offer valuable insights.

- Cost-Efficiency: Conducting user research typically involves significant time and monetary investments. In contrast, internal user testing is cost-effective, as employees are readily accessible and willing to participate.
- Ease of Recruitment: Recruiting external users can be time-consuming, but employees are more accessible and inclined to contribute their time to the company's cause. Quick recruitment facilitates timely feedback collection.
- Promotion of UX Research: Involving employees in testing prototypes or concepts raises awareness of user research within the organization. It provides firsthand experience of the research process and fosters support for UX initiatives, potentially leading to increased budgets.
- Cross-Functional Feedback: Employees from different departments may offer unique perspectives. They might understand users differently from the product team, leading to valuable insights that bridge communication gaps within the company.
- Testing Your Flow: Internal testing allows you to run a pilot test of your research script, identifying and addressing any flaws or awkwardness before engaging with external users.

When to Use Internal User Testing

While internal user testing should not replace external user testing, it can be beneficial in specific scenarios:

- Testing Research Scripts: It's ideal for rehearsing your research script in a semi-realistic setting, allowing you to fine-tune the interview flow.
- Product for Employees: If your product targets employees, internal user testing becomes an integral part of the user testing process.
- Gathering Feedback on Confidential Concepts: When dealing with sensitive, confidential concepts, internal testing can mitigate confidentiality concerns, as employees are already bound by NDAs.

Setting Up Internal User Testing

Here are some approaches to kickstart internal user testing within your organization.

- Monthly Test Sessions: Establish recurring testing sessions where teams can sign up to have their ideas tested internally. This regular practice helps teams receive feedback on prototypes or concepts promptly. During these tests, you would also try out the script you would use on users, to practice and ensure the flow of the session was sound.
- Speed Testing: Organize speed testing events, akin to speed dating, to gather quick feedback on multiple prototypes or concepts in a short amount of time. Colleagues rotate through each prototype/concept, getting ten minutes to try it and give feedback. You provide each person with a form they take with them during each round, prompting them on areas you needed input.
- Demo Desk: Create a designated area, a demo desk, where employees can interact with and provide feedback on current prototypes or concepts at their convenience. To do this, put your mobile testing devices and a spare laptop in the area. You then set up instructions on accessing the prototypes and a form to fill out with the feedback you are looking for. This form can ask questions like, "How does the prototype feel?" or have specific tasks you want colleagues to complete, with follow-up questions on how they found each task.

While internal user testing cannot replace the invaluable insights gained from external users, it has its merits when used judiciously. Always consider its limitations, and remember that employees aren't a substitute for your actual users. The key is to utilize internal user testing as a supplementary tool to complement your user research efforts effectively.

CONCEPT TESTING

Concept testing can sometimes feel like a mystery. There were quite a few times in my career when teams put an idea in front of me and asked me to test it with users (well, to validate or ask for preference, which we don't do, of course). And for some time, I felt incredibly stuck when my teams made these requests.

> The ideas weren't solid enough to conduct a usability test.
> They weren't basic enough for me to conduct generative research.
> These concepts were in the in-between (or the upside-down, if you will).

Whenever a team came to me with these concepts, I cringed. I had no idea how to get them the information they needed without leading the participants and asking biased questions. I knew I shouldn't be asking things like:

"Do you like this idea?"
"Would you use something like this?"
"How would you make this better?"
"Is this going in the right direction?"
But I wasn't sure how else to engage with participants.

So, I tried to conduct usability tests on concepts. That ended as a major failure. The ideas were too early to test. Participants got lost and confused because there wasn't a flow. And, to be honest, I had no idea what I was trying to test. My goals for those research projects were vague, and the findings were unhelpful.

We understood that people had a hard time navigating a loosely defined concept, but we still had no idea whether or not we were heading in the right direction. Each of those reports ended up disappointing not only my teams but also me.

It was by chance that I heard about the concept of concept testing (very meta, I know). At first, I wasn't sold. How were we meant to evaluate concepts in an unbiased way? And how were we meant to investigate their reactions without relying too heavily on future-based data?

But, after some more disappointing results and failed usability tests on ideas, I finally decided to give concept testing a whirl. Admittedly, I wasn't very skilled at conducting those tests, but with some practice and guidance, I finally understood the importance of concept testing. And, from there, I never looked back.

What Is Concept Testing, Anyway?

Concept testing is one of those elusive methods that, I believe, we don't discuss nearly enough, as it can be an extremely powerful tool to use early in the discovery process. Because it can be such an "in-between" method, we often skip it, going straight from generative research to usability testing.

However, concept testing definitely has its place in our process. The way I define it is:

> Concept testing is a way to engage with participants to more deeply understand a specific problem and their current process through a stimuli (concept). Through concept testing, we gather feedback that allows us to gauge how aligned we are (or not) with participants' mental models regarding an idea.

Within the scope of this definition, we are looking for immediate reactions and perceptions from our participants. We are looking to see how participants respond to the idea and where there are gaps or confusion about what we've put in front of them.

This is the crux of the definition and often where I can see concept testing go wrong (and where I've done it incorrectly before).

Where Concept Testing Goes Wrong

As I mentioned, it took me a good amount of practice to hone my concept testing skills. Because it is a less-discussed methodology, I struggled with finding the proper resources on how to conduct a concept test and what exactly I was looking for as an outcome.

Unfortunately, I see concept testing used a lot for things like:

- Product/idea validation
- Preference testing
- A/B testing
- Asking about future-based behavior

When I first started concept testing, I made these mistakes. I wanted the concept test to tell me whether or not participants liked the concept, if they would use it or not, and if I tested multiple concepts, which one they preferred.

The problem with all of the above is that concept testing is still a qualitative method. And with qualitative methods, we can't answer these types of questions. Qualitative user research isn't set up for success to answer "whether or not" or "if" or "preference" questions.

Qualitative research involves uncovering reactions, perceptions, feelings, and mental models. Concept testing should be no different.

When I first started conducting concept tests, I asked many of those questions, and the results were more disappointing than the usability tests I had attempted to run on the concepts.

What did it mean if people liked or disliked a concept? What did preference mean when it came to the concepts? How would we know people would actually use the product in the future? Not only that, but usually, during these tests, there can be social desirability bias present, where participants will tell you what you want to hear.

So, when I delivered my results, my teams weren't always sure what actions to take. We knew that people liked the concept and which they preferred, but there was so little depth to the answers and so little action within the data that the teams ended up feeling just as stuck as before.

From there, I changed how I thought and approached concept tests, ensuring that I got my teams the data they needed without asking participants questions that could skew our decision-making.

How to Conduct a Concept Test

Realizing that my current way of concept testing wasn't helping teams, I shifted away from that mindset. I had to be much more intentional with exactly what I was testing, why I was using this approach, and the research outcomes. I also had to clarify what concept testing was and what it wasn't for myself and my teams.

A Preamble

Something that I believe can happen often when it comes to concept testing or more in-between-type tests is that we can expect the user to come up with solutions or ideas for us. I fell into this trap when I started conducting concept tests.

I would go into a session with a few different ideas and place them in front of the user, hoping they would come up with a different solution or idea or something better we could do.

The participant's role in any research session is NOT to develop solutions. It is to scope the problems the users are having and understand how that concept helps (or doesn't) solve the identified problem. So, sitting down with several concepts and asking participants if they like them, would use them, or how they would improve them won't get you very far.

Concepts are a stimulus. They help trigger thoughts and get participants thinking about their problems and processes, not to think about solutions or give opinions on the ideas. With this, the concept needs to be designed in a way that isn't about opinions but rather more about exploring the problems and the current process people are navigating through that problem.

So, when you are looking to conduct a concept test, keep in mind that the concepts aren't there for you to gather opinions about (e.g., whether participants like them) but to explore problems more fully so that you can get information for the designers to continue to create a more robust solution.

Another idea I highly recommend that helped me was to talk to my designers after the concept tests to understand what kind of information was helpful for them and what wasn't—this led me to ask better questions that got at what my team needed to know to make better decisions.

Before a Concept Test

The entire basis of concept testing is understanding how your early ideas align (or don't) with the users' mental models of how they might solve a given problem. You use the concept as a stimulus to dig deeper into the problem and get more insights on creating something that can help your users with their pain points and needs.

However, one big issue I've encountered is when I skip generative research before a concept test. Generative research allows us to deeply explore the problems people are having, regardless of the products or solutions we might want to create for them (those niggly shower ideas that lots of people tend to have).

If we skip generative research, we skip the fundamental basis of creating a concept: identifying an important problem. Without knowledge of a problem, how can we even begin to create a stimulus that addresses a problem?

It is imperative to conduct generative research (or pull from previous generative research) before creating concepts because this type of data gives us the basis for the concepts we could create to engage participants in talking through their specific problems more deeply.

Concept testing sits much closer to generative research than evaluative because, at this point, you are still exploring the problem space. Instead of the more broad approach of generative research where you explore different problems and needs, with concept testing, you are deeply diving into a more specific problem through the stimuli of the concept you created.

So, before you dive into concept testing, conduct generative research to identify the important problems (the opportunity gap survey is great for prioritizing these) and create relevant concepts to help you dig deeper into the specific problems your users are encountering.

If you find you are conducting many concept tests with very little foundation behind them, take a step back and mention to your team that it would be better to start with generative research to inform the types of concepts that would be best to focus on.

Setting Up Your Concept Test

If you've done your generative research and identified a specific problem you want to dive deeper into, a concept test might be the perfect methodology for you. One caution I will say before getting into set-up is that you don't always need a concept test. Some problems out there have clear and obvious solutions, which means you might go straight to evaluative research, such as usability testing.

Now, I want to caution against my caution because…well, making decisions can be difficult.

When I say "obvious," I mean things like:

- A bug that needs to be fixed.
- A usability issue that has a clear solution.
- A heuristic violation that can easily be fixed.
- A problem that has a clear fix based on industry standards.
- You have additional past data that helps point toward a solution.
- A simple/basic need or pain point that doesn't require additional digging.

As researchers, we sometimes get caught up in doing extra tests because we want to ensure we aren't leading participants or skipping too quickly into solution land. However, consider whether you need a concept test or the solution can be created without one.

For example, when I was working at a travel company, users had many problems with our sidebar filters. They were clunky, unusable, and generally frustrating. We identified that problem, and I could have run a concept test (in fact, I was tempted to). However, there are pretty standard and clear ways of creating usable and effective filters out there. Running an entire concept test on something that "obvious" felt like a waste of time.

On the other hand, when we were trying to understand how people thought about sustainable travel, I decided to run a concept test because we didn't fully understand the idea and the process people go through when making that decision, and there wasn't too much out there at the time in terms of industry standards or benchmarking.

Concept Testing Goals

As always, you first start with goals (and a research plan) because they help focus your projects and indicate if you've chosen the correct methodology to achieve them. The best way to develop research goals is to talk to your team because, ultimately, they will use the information to make better decisions. To do this, I ask them a few different questions:

- What questions do you have?
- What information are you looking for from the study?
- What decisions are you trying to make with the information?
- What types of outcomes are you hoping for at the end of the study?

If you want to try a different approach, you can have your team fill out the following:

I need [X information] to make [Y decision] that will impact [team/organizational goal]. Then, by the end of the study, I need [Z ideal outcome].

By collaborating with your team early on, you can get them the exact information they need from the study and confirm that the methodology you are considering is the best for getting that type of information.

Some examples of concept testing goals I've used in the past are:

- Probe more deeply into [problem space] to better understand [specific problem].
- Uncover the users' current process in navigating [problem].
- Understand users' reactions to concept stimuli and anything confusing within the concept stimuli.

Based on these goals, you are looking to use the concept as a stimulus to understand the identified problem more deeply so that your team can brainstorm solutions relevant to users' needs and pain points through an ideation workshop. Again, you aren't looking to see if people like the idea or whether they would use it, but rather, you are using the concept as a basis for exploring the problem so your team can generate effective solutions.

Example from Lego

For many years, Lego was mainly regarded as a toy for boys, which is something Lego wanted to change. They conducted research and found that boys and girls interacted with Lego much differently. Boys liked stand-alone structures, while girls were more concerned with the backgrounds and environments.

To understand how girls played, Lego ran concept tests, using stimuli to understand how girls interacted with different Lego elements, the problems they had with them, and the unmet needs associated with the current Lego pieces. They used the stimulus as a way to explore participants' mental models and the problem space more deeply.

With this research, Lego launched Lego Friends in 2012 with a product range including stylized boxes of Lego to build a pop star house, a cupcake café, a hair salon, a supermarket, and so on. This proved to be a resounding success, with the brand's average annual growth of 15% since its launch.

Lego didn't ask participants what they wanted or if they liked something. Instead, they used the concepts as a jumping-off point to better understand interaction and to help stimulate conversation with participants, leading to a deeper comprehension of how girls thought about Lego, giving the team the information they needed to create effective and impactful solutions.

Type of Concept Test

There are four main types of concept tests for you to choose from:

1. Monadic testing
2. Sequential monadic testing
3. Comparative testing
4. Protomonadic testing

Monadic testing

Monadic testing means that you are testing just one concept at a time. You show participants one concept without comparing it to others—the concept stands completely alone and you are using just that concept as a conversation starter. Monadic testing is the most simple form of concept testing and I highly recommend starting here if you are new to concept testing and want to get a taste of using a stimulus to dive more deeply into a given problem.

Sequential monadic testing

In sequential monadic testing, participants see one concept at a time, but each person sees multiple concepts (one after another). The concepts might be similar to one another and each can be used as a new conversation starter about the given problems they are trying to solve.

This type of test can become more complex when participants instinctively compare the concepts. However, in sequential monadic testing, we aren't looking for any comparison and just looking to more deeply understand the problem through different angles (concepts).

If you are ever showing more than one concept, make sure to vary the order of the concepts for each participant to reduce the bias of everyone seeing them in the same order.

Comparative testing

Comparative testing is actually my least favorite of the concept testing types because I see it done incorrectly (and have done it incorrectly myself). The reason I don't like comparative testing is because it is a slippery slope toward preference and answering the terrible question of:

"Which idea/concept do participants prefer?"

As we discussed, concept testing is not about evaluating the concepts and getting validation or preference. It is about exploring the important problem that was discovered and diving more deeply by using the concept as a stimulus.

When we think of comparing two different concepts, it is easy to jump to solution land. I honestly try to avoid comparative testing within the scope of concept testing and, instead, much prefer to compare things at a larger scale with A/B testing.

However, if you have two concepts, make sure you use each to explore the problem space deeply rather than compare one solution to the other. You can see if each concept brings up different problems, processes, or needs during the conversation. Let's say you have three concepts; you could ask participants to identify two concepts that are different from the third and describe why they are different and how this relates back to the problem you identified. This process helps you understand what might be important to users when solving their problems.

Protomonadic testing

Protomonadic testing combines sequential monadic and comparative testing in that each participant sees multiple concepts (one at a time) and then compares all the concepts at the end. This is the most complex of the concept tests, and it takes a lot of practice and skill to get this right because it is so easy to slip into preference and solution-based questions.

Again, I tend to shy away from protomonadic testing because I feel it takes away from delving more deeply into the problem space and gets much more into evaluating ideas and coming up with solutions.

However, if you have to conduct protomonadic testing, make sure that you take the time to explore each concept deeply and then, in the end, talk through the different needs/problems based on each concept and understand how different concepts bring up different needs, problems, and processes.

I know there are quite a few different ways of concept testing, but I do really highly recommend monadic testing as one of the best because you really focus on the problem with one given stimulus. However, if you do need to approach the problem from different angles (and through different concepts), then sequential monadic would be a great choice.

As you get more comfortable, you can begin to go into comparative and protomonadic testing!

Fidelity of the Concept

When it comes to using a stimulus in tests, I always go for low fidelity because it helps the participant see the idea as a rough sketch rather than a fully fledged feature or product. A low-fidelity concept can help reduce social desirability bias and encourage participants to give more genuine (and critical) feedback on the concept. It also helps to encourage talking about the problem space without putting participants into a given box of a solution.

In contrast, high-fidelity prototypes are great for evaluating products through methods like usability testing.

Writing Questions

If the whole point of a concept test is to explore the problem space more deeply with a stimulus, what types of questions are you meant to ask participants? This very question is why having goals is so important. Your goals will greatly help you determine which questions you need to ask to get the information you need.

So, if you were to look at the general goals for a concept test, you would have:

- Probe more deeply into [problem space] to better understand [specific problem].
- Uncover the users' current process in navigating [problem].
- Understand users' reactions to concept stimuli and anything confusing within the concept stimuli.

Now, you can develop questions that help you achieve these goals. And, since concept testing is a more generative-based methodology, you would use the TEDW framework for writing questions to ensure you are asking open-ended, story-based questions:

- T = "Tell me about…" or "Talk me through…"
- E = "Explain…"
- D = "Describe…"
- W = "Walk me through…"

Let's look at some examples for each of these goals.
Probe more deeply into [problem space] to better understand [specific problem]

- Tell me about the last time you encountered [specific problem].
- Explain what happened, step-by-step when you encountered the problem.
- Walk me through another time you had [specific problem].
- Describe what happened.
- Describe what was missing or confusing when encountering [specific problem].

Uncover the users' current process in navigating [problem]

- Describe what you did to get around [specific problem].
- Explain what happened, step-by-step, as you tried to resolve [specific problem].

- Walk me through another way you've solved [specific problem] in the past.
- Walk me through how you've used [another product] to solve [specific problem] in the past.
- Tell me about a time when you looked for an alternate solution to [specific problem].

Understand users' reactions to concept stimuli and anything confusing within the concept stimuli

- Walk me through how this concept relates to the problem we discussed.
- Describe anything confusing or missing within the concept, especially when it comes to [specific problem].
- Tell me about how this concept compares to how you currently solve [specific problem].
- Explain your first thoughts when looking at this concept.

Another method you could employ when trying to understand better how someone is feeling about a concept is using Benedek and Miner's Microsoft Product Reaction Cards. They developed a set of adjectives research participants could use to describe their reactions to a concept.

You can show the concept and have each participant pick three to five of these adjectives to describe the concept. But the most important part is following up on why they picked those adjectives.

There aren't many questions when it comes to concept testing discussion guides, and that is because concept testing is about the deeper conversation you have relating to the problem! Keep your questions focused on the problem, and always follow up on participants' responses!

The Run of Show

Usually, I start by briefly talking with the participant about the problem space we identified, asking them more broad questions about how they encountered the problem and what happened, as I mentioned above.

After this conversation, I will show them the concept (stimulus) and use that to explore the problem more deeply.

Typically, my concept tests are around 60–90 minutes, depending on how many concepts I share with the participant. I tend to recommend sharing no more than three concepts because each concept has a high cognitive load, and participants will quickly get tired of deeply exploring the problem space (as will you!).

Here is an example agenda for a 60-minute test:

- Introduction: 3 minutes about the test, who I am, signing an NDA/consent form, and instructions.
- Warm-up: 5 minutes for asking general questions to get the participant in the mindset of conversation. My favorite warm-up questions are, "What

hobbies do you love?" "What do you do in your free time?" or "What have you watched recently that you loved?"
- General questions: 10 minutes to focus on the problem space of the concepts. For example, if we were testing different meal kit plans, we would use this section to ask about meal kits or cooking habits in general.
- Concept A: 20 minutes focusing on concept A and how it relates to the problem space we discussed before.
- Concept B: 20 minutes focusing on concept B in the same way as above.
- Follow-up (optional): A 5-minute buffer to follow up on the concepts and check if the participant has anything else to discuss or add.
- Outro: 2 minutes of thanking the participant, answering any of their questions, and explaining any next steps, such as when they can expect the incentive.

Sample Size

Once you set your goals and plan, it is time to recruit. Ideally, you're targeting people who have had the problem you are exploring through the concept in the past because, as always, we want to focus on past behavior rather than future-based behavior (which is all hypothetical). They can be users of your current product/service or people who have identified they have the problem your concept is highlighting.

Creating a screener survey is the best way to ensure you get the right people. Within the screener survey, you will try to target people who have the problem you initially identified so that you can dig deeper into their experiences and so that the questions are relevant to them. For example, if we were looking at people who have struggled to find a dog walker in their area, we want to screen for that information so that we can dig more deeply into how they currently navigate the problem and what their needs are.

When it comes to sample size, it can really depend. I typically follow the rules for generative research (e.g., 1x1 interviews) because concept testing is such a similar format. With this in mind, I recommend talking to 15–20 participants per segment regarding concept tests.

Moderated versus Unmoderated

Personally, I don't think concept tests suit unmoderated studies because the entire point of a concept test is to understand a problem more deeply. It is very difficult to achieve that depth and concept testing goals through an unmoderated approach. This is where concept testing can again get confused with concept/product/idea validation, comparative usability testing, or A/B testing.

Concept testing is all about more deeply understanding the user and is a generative approach, while methods like comparative usability testing or A/B testing are much more evaluative and can definitely be used through an unmoderated approach.

I highly recommend using a moderated approach when doing true concept testing because it will yield much better results and get you the depth of information you need.

Analyzing the Data

Because I view concept testing as a generative method, I use my go-to generative research analysis method of coding and affinity diagramming whenever I analyze and synthesize the data.

Coding and Concept Testing

When it comes to coding, there are two main ways to create them:

1. Inductive method: With the inductive method, you don't create any codes until you have gone through some data. You then find the codes in your data.
2. Deductive method: You develop codes before synthesizing your data.

When it comes to concept testing, I typically employ a deductive method, and I recommend starting with this. I use global tags in a lot of my research synthesis. The global tags I use are:

- Goal: What the person is trying to accomplish as an outcome.
- Need: Something a person needs to fulfill a goal.
- Motivation: Why is the person trying to achieve that goal?
- Task: Something a person does to achieve a goal.
- Pain point: A barrier or difficulty toward accomplishing a goal.
- Tools: A tool a person uses to try to accomplish a goal.

For concept testing, and since it is all about trying to understand people's problems and needs more deeply, I tend to focus on the following:

- Pain points
- Needs
- Goals
- Motivations

Affinity Diagramming

Affinity diagramming is the process of combining all of your data into groups using your codes. If you used global tags, these could serve as broad categories. For example, you would bring participants' pain points under one section.

Once you have all the pain points from all the participants, you can begin to cluster similar pain points across participants. We do this because we want to get to more specific recommendations. We can have more apparent action items if we break the data down into similar, smaller points. We can then name these clusters based on the content inside of them.

Now you have clusters, or patterns, of information that you can review with our teams. Instead of presenting them with all of these goals, you can say, "how might we help alleviate the anxiety of changing prices and when it is best to book a ticket?"

By having these clusters of information, we can effectively go into the action step of outcomes.

The Outcomes

When it comes to a concept test, you aren't going to have a yes/no, go/no go kind of answer for your team. Instead, the action will come after the research is done through something like an ideation workshop. Holding a workshop is absolutely critical for turning the data from the research into action because it will give the team a chance to take the findings into solution land.

Whenever I conduct a concept test, I automatically schedule an ideation session at the end of the study. Within this ideation session, I will present the synthesis of the results (which ideally everyone is already familiar with either from coming to the sessions or synthesizing with me), and then we will go into a brainstorming exercise such as Crazy 8s.

The whole point of this workshop is to take a deeper understanding of the problem through the concept and, finally, create solutions that help the participants overcome pain points and achieve their needs. This is the magical time when your data goes from research data to tangible results in the form of ideas.

Several ideas might emerge from the workshop, and the team will decide on which to turn into a prototype so that you can begin usability testing with your participants. With this process, your research has come full circle from deeply understanding the problem space to now creating a relevant solution that will be effective and impactful for the user and the business.

CARD SORTING

Card sorting is excellent for understanding mental models and how people categorize information. It also serves as a way to visualize the skeleton of a product/service. However, as with many qualitative user research techniques, many questions arise when creating one. Card sorting can be an extremely subjective process.

Card sorting is an activity in which you give "cards" to a participant and organize them in the order makes sense to them. These cards can have information written on them, be blank, or be a combination of the two. There are three different card sorting techniques you can use in your research.

1. Closed-card sorting. Closed-card sorting is when each participant gets a set of cards with information already written on them. They are limited to using these cards. This approach is very evaluative, and is best when the terminology or concepts are well-defined and established. It can give you apparent patterns on the cards. However, the significant cons of this are that you might not fully understand the user's mental model, as they have to conform to what you wrote on the cards.
2. Open-card sorting. Open-card sorting is the opposite of closed-card sorting. Participants create categories and concepts of their own and then organize them. Open-card sorting is great for exploratory work, and understanding how users relate to, organize, and define different concepts. It can lead to a better understanding of terms and definitions. However, the con of this approach is that the patterns are usually not as straightforward as in closed sorting.
3. Mixed (or hybrid) card sorting. Mixed-card sorting includes cards with predetermined information, but allows the participant to create new categories or concepts that may be missing. With mixed-card sorting, participants can "edit" the pre-written information. Mixed-card sorting is a great approach because it allows for both evaluative and generative work, although you may still run into the same cons of fewer distinct patterns. The mixed-card sort generally calls for a more significant number of participants.

How Do You Choose between Card Sorting Techniques?

First off, determine if you are in a generative or evaluative phase of the project by asking yourself:

- Would you feel comfortable and confident in defining terms, concepts, and categories for your users?
- Have you conducted previous research that would help you correctly identify those terms, concepts, and categories? If yes, you can then use closed-card sorting to evaluate the patterns better.

If you are starting from scratch, or don't feel confident in creating cards, I recommend going with either open- or mixed-card sorting to first understand how users define these areas. You can follow up with a closed-card sorting. If you have already done research on certain concepts, but not others, then go for the hybrid. If you want to go all out discovery, open method will suit you best. Regardless, make sure you always capture the running commentary as the participants are placing, writing, or organizing cards.

Moderated versus Unmoderated Card Sorting

Moderated card sorting involves a researcher being present in the room while the user participates in the card sort. The researcher will encourage the participant to think aloud during the process and probe into why they are making certain choices. Another way is to interview users post-test to gain extra insight into their decisions and ask questions about specific cards, if necessary.

On the other side, unmoderated card sorting is when the user does the card sort alone. Users typically perform unmoderated card sorting online, with the help of a card sorting tool. Some design teams employ this method, since it tends to be a quicker, cheaper option.

Let's Go through an Example

There are a few uses for card sorting. The most common goals that align with card sorting as a methodology are:

- evaluating a users' mental model on the information architecture of a product/service;
- understanding how concepts relate to each other in the mind of the user and the hierarchy of them;
- uncovering definitions, terms, or ideas that might be missing or misunderstood.

As an example, say you work at Google, and the team from Google Shopping wants to re-imagine the Google Shopping page. There is little usage of the page, with a high bounce rate and low click-through rate.

These metrics result in a lower commission rate and revenue for Google. Something isn't working for users, and we believe it has to do with the current experience and design of the page.

This opportunity is perfect for a card-sort exercise. You want to understand how users categorize and organize different information on a page.

Closed versus Open versus Mixed

You already have a live website for the project, but it isn't performing as well as the team had hoped. Some elements exist that may serve well in future iterations. However, you don't know how to organize them, and you also don't know what's missing.

With this in mind, you recommend a mixed-card sort. This way, you are keeping the old components for participants to organize, edit, or discard, while also allowing them to add anything you are missing.

Online versus In-Person

Paper-card sorting is the traditional version of this research method. As the name suggests, users take physical cards with topics or concepts and organize them into various piles on a large table. The main advantage of paper-card sorting is that there is no learning curve from technology.

The other option is digital-card sorting, which requires the user to perform the card sort on a website or service. The main advantage of this method is that you capture each card sorting exercise digitally, reducing the amount of work for synthesis. For this example, we'll go through an online card sort. Some tools you can use are:

- Trello
- Optimal workshop
- XSort
- Miro
- Mural

Just make sure to provide detailed instructions for the participant on how to use the software. Also, leave time at the beginning of the interview for the sign-in and learning curve.

Unmoderated versus Moderated

Since you're conducting a mixed-card sort, you'll need to recruit more participants. Ideally, you'll recruit 10–15 participants for open-card sorting, and about 30–50 participants for closed and hybrid sorting variations. In this case, you settle for 40 users for the hybrid card sort.

Since 40 is a large number to recruit and host, you can mix moderated and unmoderated card sorting. In this situation, you decide to start with ten moderated card sorts, followed by unmoderated testing with the other 30 to confirm the initial results. You can always choose to do more moderated before the unmoderated card sorts, in case you feel you don't have sufficient data.

Creating the Cards

If you are doing a closed- or mixed-card sort, you have to write the cards. Knowing what to include in a card sort is the tricky part. What you write on the card depends on the website or app you are looking to improve. The most important part is not to include more than 40 cards in your card sort.

The best way to start creating cards is to get a site map or overall information architecture visual of your website. The site map will lay out all navigation categories, such as header navigation, primary navigation, secondary navigation (sub-categories), footer navigation, footer and sub-categories. You can also include filters that are on the side and not nested under any categories.

So, taking a look at Google Shopping, there is quite a lot of information. Let's tackle it one area at a time.

Header and Primary Navigation

The header consists of a few elements. We could include all of them:

- All
- Images
- Maps
- Shopping
- More
- Videos
- News
- Books
- Flights
- Finance
- Settings
- Search bar

For simplicity, you cut this portion out since the focus is on Google Shopping. Instead, you decide to include:

- Shopping
- Search bar
- Secondary navigation

In the secondary navigation, you have some words, as well as icons. Instead of drawing out the figures, consider using the words that describe them. You can easily find this out by hovering over the image and using that text. For the secondary navigation, you decide to include:

- Your location
- List
- Grid
- Default
- Reviews
- Price—low to high
- Price—high to low
- Bookmarks
- Sponsored
- Relevant searches

- Previous page
- Next page

Filters and all the options that come with them are where the card sort can get tricky. You can either include the filters and also each sub-filter, or just the filter name. Remember, you don't want more than 30–40 cards, so you need to judge based on the number of cards you already have and will end up with. For this example, you choose to include the filter names:

- Price
- Style
- Gender
- Brand
- Size type
- Size
- Material
- Condition
- Shipping
- Seller

The footer navigation is at the bottom of a website. For this, you include:

- Help
- Send feedback
- Privacy
- Terms
- Information for merchants
- Report a violation
- Content

With just filter names, plus the other cards, you have 32. I would recommend stopping here and allowing users to add clarifying cards, such as price ranges or style, during the card sort. If you want to include sub-category filters, I recommend not putting in every single brand or size.

Since this is an e-commerce website, you could include actual content on the page. This step is optional. The way you can approach this is by printing out the cards and having them available. Having the content cards can help participants structure the look of the website in their minds, leading to less confusion.

Since you are conducting a hybrid card sort, you include blank cards for the participants to create their own content as well.

Setting Up the Card Sort

Usually, card sorts last 60 minutes, so plan for that amount of time. Ensure there is enough space, either physically or digitally, to spread out all of the cards for the participant to see easily. If you're conducting your card sort online, make sure you have sent the link to the participants and told them they will need internet access.

Get someone to help you during the session to take notes and observe what you might miss. Practice the session with a colleague to make sure everything makes sense before inviting the participants. Always record the meetings (with permission, of course)!

Moderating the Card Sort

Give the participant the set of cards (or have them out on a remote tool). Walk them through what the session will be like and explain what you are looking for them to do. In each scenario, mention that any cards that are confusing can be put to the side.

For a closed/mixed-card sort, explain that you are looking to understand how all of the items on the cards relate to each other. Tell them to group the information in a way that makes the most sense to them.

For an open-card sort, tell the participant that you're trying to understand what should be in your product/service. Then explain, once they've finished naming the cards, that you want them to group them in a way that makes sense to them. Once grouped, ask the participant what they would call the grouping. Explain that you will ask for a name for each group of cards once the participant has arranged them.

Request that the participant thinks aloud during the session to fully understand their thought process behind their categorizations. If the participant struggles with thinking aloud, be sure to prompt them regularly.

Thank the participant, give them a chance to ask any questions, and provide your contact information. Be sure to mention the timeline for any incentive.

Finally, email the participant within 24 hours to thank them for their participation in the study with any incentive you offered.

Analyzing the Card Sort

After you have compiled all of the card sorting results, it is time for analysis and synthesis! This part can be quite complicated, especially in an open-card sort. There are four steps to take when manually analyzing card sorts. Of course, digital tools, can make your life easier. However, let's assume you don't have the luxury of a tool.

As a disclaimer, this is the way I have approached card sorting analysis. There are a few different ways to approach it, so I encourage you to find the best technique for you.

Step 1: Identify Patterns

For a closed-card sort, you've already predetermined the categories. However, for an open-card sort, you need to identify the most commonly suggested categories from the responses. To do this, you'll want to look for items that users frequently sort together under the same groups. Those are your categories.

Also, remember to check the cards that users frequently leave in an unknown or discarded pile. If users don't know what to do with cards, those components may not belong in this section of the website.

Step 2: Create a Spreadsheet or Rainbow Chart

There are two ways to go about this step: the less complicated version or the more complicated version. Naturally, the more complex analysis will yield better results, but it depends on your workload and timeline.

Rainbow Chart

The less complicated way of approaching card sorting analysis is to create a rainbow chart. A rainbow chart visualizes the cards each participant used and shows the most commonly used ones. I recommend this method of analysis if you have little to no sub-categories and simple navigation. Read more about creating a rainbow chart.

Spreadsheet Matrix

Now, the more complicated route. I would recommend this analysis technique for the project, with sub-categories and filters. Create a spreadsheet with all the cards you wrote in the rows and each common group you identified in the columns. From your card sort results, count how many times each card appeared under the group and add that number.

Step 3: Delete the Smaller Numbers

Once you've entered the data, keep the substantial groups. To quickly determine the meaningful results, set a threshold for importance. If a card appears a small number of times in a group, you could delete it. You can determine a percentage threshold as well if that is easier. For this card sort, remove any data under 15%, or appearing six times.

Step 4: Highlight and Sort the Cards

After deleting the additional data, go through and highlight the cards that appear most often in a group. Also remove groups that don't have a significant number of cards (e.g., no highlights). Delete all the unhighlighted data and re-sort the cards. These cards would now belong to the groups where they occur most often.

Make Decisions

After analyzing the results of all your card sorting sessions, you'll be in a much more informed position about the shape your information architecture should take, and how to best structure the content hierarchy. Decide where to place content and what content needs to be changed. For instance, if many participants edited one card name (e.g., style type to length), then include them in your final decision-making.

TREE TESTING

Most companies' customers aren't extremely dependent on their products or services. Those businesses cannot afford for their users to have a bad experience, failing to find what they are looking for. If most people can't find something, they are looking for another product or service that's easier. And that's where tree testing comes in.

Tree testing is an evaluative research method that helps you understand the findability of your product. During this evaluation, you show the participant your site's hierarchy, and ask them how they would find certain content. Tree testing is almost like usability testing the skeleton of your product. It allows you to highlight findability issues and mismatched expectations.

Generally, with tree testing, you are looking to:

- set a baseline findability of the navigation of your product to understand what needs to be improved;
- understand how a recent change in navigation impacts the findability;
- discover how well users can find necessary and important information effectively and efficiently.

Sometimes there is confusion between tree testing and first-click testing. As its name suggests, first-click testing is all about the first click. In first-click testing, we want to ensure the user knows where to start with a task, so we ask them to complete a goal and see where they start. With tree testing, the participant continues to click until they reach the goal (or destination).

When to Use a Tree Test

Tree testing is useful whenever you want to find:

- how users perceive the understandability of labels and structure of the information on your website, intranet, or app;
- how easy or difficult it is for users to find information on your website, intranet, or app;

- how well the labels and structure of your website align with users' mental models;
- how to conduct a tree test.

Tree tests can be really fun to conduct because they can be relatively low effort, and yield quick and effective results. You know all those times stakeholders ask you for super concrete answers to questions? Tree testing is one of those methods that can really demonstrate findability and understandability clearly. It's fun to have that in your toolkit!

The best way to illustrate tree testing is to walk through an example. For this, we're going to use a homewares website that we often frequent in Jersey called B&Q.

Defining the Tree

The first step is understanding what specific parts you want to test and prioritizing those particular scenarios. Can you test everything? Sure, but your tree test will be huge and the cognitive load on the participant might be too much. Instead, prioritize what you need to focus on and what the most important tasks are for your participants. There are a few ways to do this.

- Look at data analytics for the most used areas or clicked-on links. You could assume that these are the most important areas people are trying to access, so you would want to test those.
- Talk to your team to understand what they might prioritize, and look at the relevant data to see what's happening in that area. For instance, if you are trying to get more people to sign up for a newsletter, you would prioritize that flow and any associated tasks.
- If you are testing something completely new, let's say some sort of virtual assistant to help you with designing a new bathroom, you would prioritize that flow and any associated tasks.

Let's say that the team wants to prioritize your new line of bathroom products and understand how people navigate through that area.

Creating the Map

Now you have to compile the information you want to test. You can first put your tree test into a spreadsheet to help you visualize it in a site-map way, but you could also use other tools like Miro, Figjam, etc.

Keeping in mind that you are looking at our new bathroom products, you can map out the prioritized areas of showers, baths, and basins into a spreadsheet.

Once you have this, you can usually copy and paste it into a tree testing tool (my favorite is TreeJack by Optimal Sort—no sponsorship, just genuinely love the tool).

A/B Testing Labels

Imagine you had a few different ideas for what "basins" should be called, and you wanted to test which was more effective. We could send out more tests with variable names, so some participants got "basins" while others got "sinks."

Ideally, you would have completed card sorting beforehand, which could help avoid this question, but sometimes there are mixed results, and you want to see how the labels perform in action.

Writing the Tasks

Now that you have your labels, it is time to write some tasks. You should base your tasks on the information you gathered above, regarding priorities. Your tasks could target:

1. finding information or areas that help increase conversion, revenue, or acquisition;
2. potential problem areas, such as drop-off areas or less used links;
3. new ideas, such as a new area or structure.

For this example, you come under the third section as you are testing the findability of the team's new bathroom products.

Task Phrasing

Each task evaluates a category and the findability of information within that category. You want to think about the goal and end result without priming the user by including language that tells them what to do.

Let's say you want someone to find a wall-hung basin:

- Leading: Find a wall-hung basin.
- Wordy and leading: You are trying to renovate your bathroom and having difficulty finding the right basin for your project. You need a basin that hangs directly on the wall. Find a wall-hung basin.
- Ideal: You are considering a bathroom renovation. See if there are basins that attach directly to a wall.

Sometimes you can't avoid all the language because you risk it becoming convoluted and confusing. If you tried not to use the words basin and wall, it might end up being confusing. Just do your best with using as few direct and leading words as possible.

Let's look at a few other potential tasks:

- You're looking to purchase a new bath, but want one that includes a shower. Where would you go to find one?

- The doors on your new guest bathroom shower are broken. Where would you go to find a new one?
- Your shower head doesn't match your updated bathroom. Where would you go to find one?
- Sample size.

Since tree testing comes under the evaluative side, and tends to show metrics like task completion, time on task, and directness, it's important to think about sample size. MeasuringU has a great table that shows the different sample sizes for a tree test, depending on the confidence interval you're interested in.

Analyze the Results

The great thing about tree testing is that you can get fairly straight-forward results that give clear answers about the findability of information. Typically you look at:

- Task success: how many people were able to successfully find the item.
- Time on task: how long it took people to find the item.
- Directness: the percentage of users completing the task without hesitation, those who are getting the correct answer from the first attempt.

Using this data, you can make vast improvements by understanding where people failed in finding certain information. For instance, if the directness is low on certain tasks, even if participants ultimately succeed, there must be confusion on how to reach the end result. If participants are failing tasks, you need to go back and understand labeling through card sorting or even first-click tests.

Testing and Execution Methods 17

USABILITY TESTING

For me, quantitative usability testing was always super straightforward. I put a high-fidelity design or live product in front of someone and asked them to do certain tasks, which I then measured through metrics like task success, time on task, and surveys like the Single Ease Questionnaire.

There was very little room for asking qualitative-based questions or for introducing bias. We were there to truly understand the effectiveness, efficiency, and satisfaction of what we put in front of the participants. Straightforward. Easy, dare I say. In fact, I could even set up an unmoderated test to get even more participants.

However, I felt uncomfortable when it came to qualitative usability testing. I never seemed to be able to strike the right balance and constantly felt like I was asking leading and biased questions. I hated the standard questions like:

- "What would you expect to see?"
- "What do you think of this?"
- "What would you change?"
- "Explore the interface and tell me what you would do."

I hated those questions because they were so hypothetical and future-based. I felt like I was asking the participant to develop ideas and design the website or app. The data I got from those questions was skewed and unhelpful.

Very rarely, if ever, as a user, do I sit on a website and think, "What am I expecting to see?" I can't remember the last time I went to a website or app to explore the interface. And, although sometimes I do have opinions on websites/apps, my opinions likely wouldn't be helpful or actionable to teams trying to make changes.

"This is dumb" is not a very actionable quote.

So, how do you make qualitative usability testing useful and ensure you are asking the best questions for the best data? Let's dive in.

What Is Qualitative Usability Testing?

Before we get into forming the best questions, it's important to define what qualitative usability testing is and to explore why it's different from approaches like quantitative usability testing or concept testing.

Having the word usability in the approach is what makes things confusing. When we are doing usability testing, we are testing the usability of a product/service. And, to me, this makes total sense when looking at quantitative usability testing because you are directly measuring and observing the product's usability via effectiveness, efficiency, and satisfaction.

However, the usability part becomes difficult to understand regarding qualitative usability testing. With qualitative research, can we really test the usability of a product/service?

To me, qualitative usability testing isn't actually about testing the usability of a product/service but a state in between concept testing and usability testing in which you are trying to get feedback on the direction of designs.

Qualitative Usability Testing Versus Quantitative Usability Testing

Quantitative usability testing is all about observing and measuring a participant's experience when interacting with the product in as much of a "real-world" context as possible. With this approach, you aren't chatting to the participants and asking them what they think about the experience or designs.

Instead, you are 100% focused on measuring the effectiveness, efficiency, and satisfaction of the product/service. You have the pre-determined tasks you need participants to complete, ask them to do so, and then move to the next scenario.

Ideally, for quantitative usability testing, your product/service is either a *very* high-fidelity prototype that allows people to make mistakes or a live product.

Qualitative Usability Testing Versus Concept Testing

Concept testing is a way to engage with participants to understand a specific problem and their current process more deeply through a stimulus (concept). Through concept testing, we gather feedback that allows us to gauge how aligned we are (or not) with participants' mental models regarding an idea.

You use a very low-fidelity sketch/prototype to help you stimulate the conversation with the participants to dive further into what and how they think about a certain problem. With this approach, you are still trying to understand the problem space better rather than looking at solutions.

Where Does This Leave Us?

Now that we've defined qualitative usability testing as neither quantitative nor concept testing, where does that leave us with the definition?

To be honest, I wish we could rename qualitative usability testing to something like a "qualitative feedback session." The reason is that qualitative usability testing almost gives the wrong impression and is a misnomer for what we really get out of it. We can't qualitatively test the usability, but we can gather feedback on people's experience.

So, to me, qualitative usability testing is about gathering qualitative feedback on the current mid-fidelity experience, not necessarily looking to measure the usability but rather understanding how someone perceives the product/service and their experience with it.

In a way, it is more like experience feedback sessions than usability testing—maybe we should start calling it that.

Common Qualitative Usability Testing Goals

As you may know, I am obsessed with starting every project or approaching every method by understanding the goals and writing a research plan. By knowing your goals, you can make a much more informed decision on who you need to recruit and the best methodology for your study.

Every project and organization can be different, but there are certain models you can use for goals to understand if certain methods are better suited to your study than others. These goals are points, ideas, or areas you are trying to learn more about in your study. They set your study up for success and ensure you get the information you need to help your team make better decisions.

You can ask yourself the following questions when defining study goals:

- What is my team trying to understand better?
- What information does my team need to move forward?
- What decisions are we trying to make?
- What are we trying to learn by the end of the study?

Since not every study is exactly the same, your answers may vary, but here are a few examples that indicate a qualitative usability test is the right methodology for your study:

- The team has developed an idea but wants feedback on the mid-fidelity experience and how it aligns or doesn't with how people are currently achieving their goals or meeting their needs.

- The team wants to understand what potential pain points their idea might have for the user.
- The team is looking to understand what is confusing or missing about the experience they've created.
- The team is trying to refine an idea further and move it to a higher fidelity but needs more data on how people perceive the experience.

So, as you can see here, the information your team needs and the decisions they are trying to make aren't really about usability but rather about getting feedback on the experience they've created to see what needs further improvement.

As I mentioned, qualitative usability testing falls so much into an in-between state. You aren't trying to explore a completely new concept but aren't ready for actual usability testing. A qualitative usability test is a likely candidate whenever you find yourself in this weird middle state.

With that, the most common goals I have used in the past to set my qualitative usability tests up for success include:

Discover the pain points within the proposed experience, potentially comparing it to the current experience.
Uncover confusing or missing portions of the proposed experience.
Understand how participants perceive the proposed experience and how it relates (or doesn't) to their needs and goals.
Compare the proposed experience to how people are currently achieving their needs and goals.
Understand how the proposed experience aligns (or doesn't) with participants' mental models.

You don't have to have all of these goals in your qualitative usability test. For instance, sometimes, you don't have to compare the proposed experience with the current one if you've explored that previously. Pick the most relevant goals for your team's needs to move forward.

Creating Qualitative Usability Test Questions

Once you have your goals and have determined a qualitative usability test is best for your study, it's time to develop questions for the session. As a reminder, I always recommend filling out a research plan to help keep you and your team aligned on expectations and outcomes for the study.

The next part I struggled with so much when it came to qualitative usability tests was creating impactful, non-leading, and unbiased questions. I realized, over time, a lot of my questions had become future-based or super hypothetical. There were a lot of:

- "What do you imagine the next screen to look like?"
- "What do you expect to see here?"

- "What do you think of this?"
- "What would you change to make this better?"

It frustrated me to ask these questions because they were vague and superficial, leading me to gather shallow and unhelpful feedback. For a time, I went back and forth on whether to use scenarios/tasks that were similar to what I'd use for quantitative usability tests.

However, I kept hitting a snag with the tasks because whenever I created them for quant usability tests, it was to measure the usability. But, again, I wasn't really looking to measure usability because the mid-fidelity ideas weren't ready for that level of exploration. There weren't incorrect paths for the participants to go down, and nothing was built out enough to evaluate the usability properly.

Additionally, asking people to do tasks on a mid-fidelity prototype/design didn't lead to meaningful feedback. Participants kind of bumbled around—since the prototype wasn't fully designed or developed, it was no surprise that participants sometimes had difficulty navigating through an experience. So, when it came to gaining insight into the usability, the results showed that the experience was obviously clunky.

This information did not help the team because, of course, a mid-fidelity prototype/design would be clunky. There is nothing I hate more than delivering results where everyone says, "Duh, we already knew that." It then feels like research was a complete waste of time.

Instead, I tried a different approach that is more similar to how I structure my generative research discussion guides. I created questions based on the agreed-upon goals using the TEDW method. The only time I now use a scenario is to kick-off the session.

Let's look at some examples of how you can develop questions by using the goals from above:

Discover the pain points within the proposed experience, potentially comparing it to the current experience.
- Walk me through the number one problem you encounter using a similar product/service.
- Explain why this has been a problem.
- Describe how you currently work around the problem.
- Talk me through some problems you notice about this current experience.
- Describe how these problems differ from the current experience.

Uncover confusing or missing portions of the proposed experience.
- Talk me through something that you notice is missing about this experience.
- Explain why [missing thing] is important to you.
- How have you used [missing thing] in your past experience?
- Describe something that you notice that is confusing about this experience.
- Explain what makes it confusing.
- Talk me through a recent, similar experience that wasn't confusing.

Understand how participants perceive the proposed experience and how it relates (or doesn't) to their needs and goals.
- Tell me about what you are trying to achieve when using a product/service like this.
- Describe your top two needs when using a product/service like this.

- Walk me through how this experience could stop you from reaching [mentioned goal].
- Describe how this experience could help you reach [mentioned goal].

Compare the proposed experience to how people are currently achieving their needs and goals.
- Describe how this experience compares to a product/service you've used recently.
- Talk me through the top two differences.

Understand how the proposed experience aligns (or doesn't) with participants' mental models.
- Describe the main way you have used similar products/services in the past.
- Walk me through your most recent experience using a similar product/service.
- Explain one of the biggest disappointments of using similar products/services in the past.
- Talk me through a disappointment you notice in this particular experience.

Rather than a generative research session, which doesn't typically have any stimuli, with a qualitative usability test, you have a design in front of you to ask questions based on the screen the participant is viewing.

The Overall Setup

Introduction + Warm-up

The introduction to the session is about you introducing yourself and asking some warm-up questions to get the participant familiar with answering qualitative-based questions in depth. An example introduction looks like:

> Hi, I'm Nikki! Thank you for participating in this research session for Gap. We are looking for your in-depth feedback on a new experience we're trying out. I will give you some context of what we will do and then have you look through the next experience while asking some questions. We are really looking for in-depth, critical feedback on how to improve the experience and how it might differ from your current experience, so please share everything with us. Remember that this isn't a test; we genuinely want to understand what's going through your head! Let me know if you have any questions.

And some of my favorite warm-up questions (you don't have to ask all of these, just two or three):

- Tell me about your favorite hobby.
- Tell me about your favorite book or TV show.
- Describe why it is your favorite.
- Tell me about your absolute favorite moment while traveling.

You can also get into more relevant warm-up questions if you'd like. So, if you are looking at fashion or clothing e-commerce:

- Describe your favorite outfit.
- Tell me about your favorite clothing shop.
- Describe why it is your favorite.

Either way, these questions prime the participant to answer open-ended TEDW-based questions and get them comfortable opening up.

Describe the Overarching Scenario

Give the participant some context about what they are looking at through a more overarching scenario (not a specific task). For example, if you want to gauge the perception of the team's new experience of how people can purchase jeans online, you would want to set the stage with that information so the participant understands what they are looking at. An overarching scenario for this might look like:

For the next 60 minutes, we will focus on how you purchase jeans online, and we will have you look over some screens that will show you a new experience we are considering. We'd love your honest and open feedback on these screens, focusing on the experience rather than design and how it might help or hinder how you purchase jeans online. For this experience, we will have you imagine you are trying to find a pair of jeans and determine the best size for you.

Now, the expectations for the participants of what they will be doing and what you expect of them are straightforward and clear. Again, this is vastly different than quantitative usability tasks because it is just context rather than assigning them to do an actual task.

Go Screen by Screen

Since you have a stimulus, you will likely go screen by screen to ask some of the above questions we have already determined. Not every question will be relevant for every screen; ideally, you are customizing the questions for every screen.

For example, if you have a screen with search results that are filtered by body type, you would ask about pain points within that experience. And then, if the next screen has an experience in which you input your previous sizes to determine the best fit for the jeans, you ask about that experience.

As an example:

Screen One: Filtering by Body Type
- Talk me through the last time you used a website that filters jeans by body type.
- Walk me through the number one problem you encounter when filtering jeans by body type.

- Describe a disappointing moment you encountered when doing this.
- Talk me through something that you notice is missing about this version of filtering jeans by body type.
- Explain why [missing thing] is important to you.
- How have you used [missing thing] in your past experience?
- Describe something that you notice that is confusing about this version of filtering jeans by body type.
- Explain what makes it confusing.
- Talk me through a recent, similar experience that wasn't confusing.

Screen Two: Inputting Similar Brand Sizes
- Describe a similar website where you've had to input your size for similar brands.
- Describe how this experience compares to a product/service you've used recently.
- Talk me through the top two differences.
- Tell me about what you were trying to achieve when doing this on the other website.
- Walk me through how this experience could stop you from reaching [mentioned goal].
- Describe how this experience could help you reach [mentioned goal].

If you need to, you can use the same questions for each screen to hit on pain points, confusing and missing content, goals, and needs. It's really up to you, and what your team determines is important to understand about each screen!

Wrap-up

My wrap-up consists of any larger questions, and then I conclude the session by ensuring the participant doesn't have any questions for me and that everything, such as incentives, is clear to them. My wrap-up usually looks like this:

Now, I just have a few more overall questions for you:

- Talk me through your overall impression of this new experience.
- Describe the most painful part of this new experience.
- Explain one thing you might change about this new experience and why you would change that.

Thank you so much for your time today. We really appreciate it, and your feedback was extremely helpful. I'll send over [incentive] via email later today, so you should receive it by the end of the day. Since this was such a productive session, would you be willing to talk with us again?

- Do you have any questions for me?
- Thank you again! Enjoy your day!

Analyzing the Data

Since qualitative usability testing is focused on gathering qualitative feedback, I use my go-to generative research analysis method of coding and affinity diagramming whenever I analyze and synthesize the data.

Coding and Qualitative Usability Testing

When it comes to coding, there are two main ways to create them:

> Inductive method: With the inductive method, you don't create any codes until you have gone through some data. You then find the codes in your data.
> Deductive method: You develop codes before synthesizing your data.

I typically employ a deductive method when it comes to qualitative usability testing, and I recommend starting with this. I use global tags in a lot of my research synthesis. The global tags I use are:

- Goal: What the person is trying to accomplish as an outcome.
- Need: Something a person needs to fulfill a goal.
- Motivation: Why is the person trying to achieve that goal?
- Task: Something a person does to achieve a goal.
- Pain point: A barrier or difficulty toward accomplishing a goal.
- Tools: A tool a person uses to try to accomplish a goal.

I use the goals from my qualitative usability testing to help inform the best global tags to use for my study. For example, from the goals above, you could use:

- Pain points
- Needs
- Goals
- Mental models
- Current versus proposed experience

Affinity Diagramming

Affinity diagramming is the process of combining all of your data into groups using your codes. If you used global tags, these could serve as broad categories. Regarding qualitative usability testing, I like to use affinity diagrams by the screen for each screen I share. I do this for each participant.

Once you have done this for each participant, you can begin to cluster similar pain points across participants. We do this because we want to get to more specific recommendations. We can have more apparent action items if we break the data down into similar, smaller points. We can then name these clusters based on the content inside of them.

To do this, I give each participant a different colored sticky and bring similar pain points, needs, goals, and comparisons together across different participants for each screen. You can note the participant number on each sticky if you don't have enough colors.

Now that you have clusters or patterns of information, you can review them with our teams. Instead of presenting them with all of these goals, you can say, "How might we help alleviate the confusion of what body shapes mean?"

By having these clusters of information, you can then help your team act on how to improve the current experience to meet users' needs and goals and help them overcome their pain points.

A Quick Note on Some Logistics

Sample size

Since you are gathering qualitative data, I usually recommend talking to 10–15 participants per segment. Generally, you must speak to more participants to find saturation within qualitative data.

I know this goes against the 5–7 participants per segment advice that is super prevalent online. While I have seen patterns after 7 participants, I aim for 10–15 participants to ensure the patterns are clear and relevant.

Moderated versus Unmoderated

Personally, I don't think qualitative usability tests suit unmoderated studies because it is extremely difficult to gather meaningful qualitative data through an unmoderated setting. You cannot follow up, ask why, probe on perceptions, and get to the level of depth necessary to help your team move forward—trust me, I've tried.

I highly recommend using a moderated approach when running qualitative usability tests because it will yield much better results and get you the depth of information you need.

Session Length

I usually recommend 60-minute sessions for qualitative usability testing, especially if you have many screens to walk through. With 60 minutes, you get enough time so you don't feel like you have to rush through the screens, and you can get in-depth data. If you have to, you could minimize the amount of screens you show and conduct a 45-minute session, although you might feel tight for time.

The Outcomes

When it comes to a qualitative usability test, you aren't going to have a yes/no, go/no go kind of answer for your team. Instead, the action will come after the research is done through something like an ideation workshop. Holding a workshop is absolutely critical for turning the data from the research into action because it will give the team a chance to take the findings into solution land.

Whenever I conduct a qualitative usability test, I automatically schedule an ideation session at the end of the study. Within this ideation session, I will present the synthesis of the results (which ideally everyone is already familiar with either from coming to the sessions or synthesizing with me), and then we will go into a brainstorming exercise such as Crazy 8s.

The whole point of this workshop is to understand the gaps or problems in the proposed experience so that we can improve it to a point where we can then usability test it. With this process, your research has come full circle from understanding how the proposed experience needs to be improved so you can then create an impactful and positive experience for the user and the business.

COMPARATIVE USABILITY TESTING

Comparative usability testing stands as a distinctive approach in the realm of usability testing. It diverges from other methodologies, as it revolves around the evaluation of different designs, placing a significant emphasis on two fundamental pillars: effectiveness and efficiency. These two cornerstones are the bedrock of usability testing, shaping the way we understand and enhance user experiences.

Effectiveness and efficiency are the North Stars guiding comparative usability testing. Yet, it's crucial to note what this method doesn't focus on—namely, user preference and overall performance. Instead, it delves into the realm of task completion and goal achievement. The primary aim is to discern which prototype empowers users to accomplish their objectives most seamlessly.

In this approach, designers craft several diverse designs, all aimed at facilitating the same task or goal. Low-fidelity prototypes often shine in this context, as they encourage valuable participant feedback. However, it's also feasible to test live code, provided the variations in designs remain sufficiently distinguishable.

The key is to ensure participants can make meaningful comparisons among the different solutions. For instance, if you're exploring multiple ways for users to achieve a specific goal, allocate each prototype to address one of these solutions. This approach enables you to discern what resonates most effectively with participants. Comparative usability testing offers multiple avenues for comparing designs.

- Task Success: Evaluate the ability of participants to successfully complete tasks across different designs.
- Error Analysis: Keep track of the number of errors participants encounter within each design.

- Time Efficiency: Measure the time participants spend on tasks in each design, providing insights into efficiency.
- Satisfaction Ratings: Gather participants' satisfaction ratings for each design, capturing their overall sentiment.
- Usability Metrics: Employ standardized usability metrics to assess the usability of each design systematically.
- General Feedback: Encourage participants to provide open-ended feedback on their experiences with each design.

To navigate this approach effectively, it's helpful to establish success criteria for each task. For instance, if you're examining how individuals decide whether to purchase a product, your criteria might encompass factors like the sufficiency of information on the product page, clarity and accessibility of reviews, and ease of locating the "add to cart" button.

The ultimate goal of comparative usability testing is to identify the design that outshines the others in facilitating task accomplishment during the test. As the test concludes, you'll be equipped to guide the designer toward the most effective design, while pinpointing specific strengths and weaknesses within each iteration. Armed with these insights, designers can refine their designs iteratively, based on participant feedback.

While conducting comparative usability studies, it's essential to remain attuned to the nuances of this approach.

- Steer Clear of Subjectivity: Avoid the use of subjective terms like "prefer" or "like" when interacting with participants. These terms can introduce bias and skew results.
- Combat Bias: Mix up the order in which participants encounter different designs to mitigate any order-related biases. Ensure that no two participants view the designs in the same sequence.
- Limit the Number of Designs: Restrict the number of designs under consideration, typically to no more than three. Testing an excessive number can overwhelm participants, leading to diminished insights.
- Diversity in Design: Ensure that the design variations under scrutiny are distinct enough to yield meaningful comparisons. It's counterproductive to employ comparative testing for minor design nuances.
- Functionality Over Preference: Always remember that the primary focus is on functionality, not personal preferences. The goal is to determine which design is most effective, irrespective of aesthetic preferences.
- Potential Blend: In some instances, you might not witness a single design emerging as the undisputed winner. In such cases, consider amalgamating positive aspects from various designs into one or two, which can then be retested in a follow-up study.

Comparative usability testing is a potent tool in your usability testing arsenal, honed to pinpoint the designs that excel in empowering users to achieve their goals efficiently. By adhering to its principles and best practices, you can wield this method to make informed design decisions, ultimately delivering user experiences that shine.

CONTENT TESTING

The first time I was tasked with assessing website content, I found myself in a perplexing predicament. I grappled with the challenge of evaluating information and text on a webpage beyond simply asking participants for their opinions. Without knowing how to properly run content tests, I decided to conduct usability tests in these scenarios. If users struggled to complete tasks, it indicated that something was amiss with the content. So, I employed this strategy to assess content for quite a while.

While this approach wasn't inherently flawed, it often failed to yield optimal feedback for my teams. I would present the usability issues we had uncovered, and we could conclude that the website's information was somewhat lacking. However, I couldn't offer more precise guidance.

Whenever a content test loomed on the horizon, I felt a sense of trepidation, and my team seemed disheartened by the absence of clarity. It became evident that I couldn't evade content tests indefinitely. So, I embarked on a deep dive into the realm of dedicated content testing.

Through extensive research and experience, I swiftly discovered more effective ways to assess content and provide teams with concrete answers.

The crux of our organizations' success lies in users achieving their goals. Whether it's acquiring new customers, retaining existing ones, or boosting conversions, a user's success is a business success. If users cannot readily locate the information they seek, their likelihood of signing up, making a purchase, or remaining loyal to a company diminishes significantly.

Content testing serves as the best approach for ascertaining whether users can efficiently access and comprehend critical information. It plays a pivotal role in shedding light on these insights and settling debates regarding textual changes.

Content testing transcends the mere assessment of information clarity within your interface. It delves into whether the tone of voice aligns with your brand, and if users can effortlessly grasp and digest the text. When a visitor encounters your website and struggles to discern the value of your product or is confronted with excessive jargon, the likelihood of them making a purchase dwindles.

Below are three primary approaches I've used when evaluating content.

Cloze Tests

Imagine a cloze test as a sophisticated version of the "Mad Libs" game. In this evaluative technique, a segment of text is carefully selected, and specific words within it are systematically removed. Participants are then tasked with filling in these blanks, using their contextual comprehension and knowledge of your product or content.

Cloze tests shine as a formidable tool for assessing the appropriateness and comprehensibility of text, particularly when dealing with intricate subjects like legal or healthcare information. Nevertheless, their utility extends beyond such domains, making them a valuable resource for evaluating the understandability of any website's content. Here's a step-by-step guide to get you started.

1. Select Your Text: Begin by choosing a snippet of text from your website, roughly around 250 words in length. Opt for text that has raised uncertainties or historically prompted inquiries from users. For instance, if your customer support team frequently fields calls regarding how your product functions, focus on the textual content pertaining to that subject.
2. Create Blank Spaces: Once you've pinpointed the text, systematically remove every fifth word, substituting it with a blank space. The aim is to have approximately 25 blanks within your text, with a cap not exceeding 50. Avoid overburdening participants; excessive blanks can be mentally taxing.
3. Participant Involvement: Invite participants to partake in the cloze test. Their task is to populate the blank spaces with the words they believe fit logically and contextually.
4. Scoring the Test: After collecting participants' responses, scoring is straightforward. Calculate the number of correct answers and divide it by the total number of blank words. Convert this figure into a percentage. For example, if your test contained 25 blanks, and a participant correctly filled in 15, their score would be 60%.
5. Interpreting the Results: Now that you have the scores in hand, you can rely on the following benchmarks to gauge the effectiveness of your text:
    a. A score of 60% or higher signifies that the text is well-comprehended by the audience.
    b. Scores falling within the 40%–60% range suggest that readers may encounter challenges in grasping the content.
    c. Scores below 40% indicate that the text is inadequately understood, implying that users will likely struggle to digest the information.

Incorporating cloze tests into your evaluation toolkit can provide invaluable insights into the clarity and effectiveness of your website's content. With this method, you can empower your team to refine text, ensuring that users can easily access and understand the information you provide.

Recall-Based Tests

A recall-based test is a powerful method to evaluate the memorability and comprehensiveness of content. It delves into the two distinct cognitive processes involved in reading: decoding and comprehension.

Decoding is the initial step, where readers identify and combine letters to form words. Comprehension, on the other hand, involves understanding the meaning of words in the context of the entire text. Ever experienced reading a sentence, reaching the end, and realizing you didn't grasp what you just read? This is where recall-based testing becomes invaluable.

It's crucial to distinguish between understanding and comprehension. Understanding simply asks if the reader "got" what they read, while comprehension delves into the deeper meaning and implications of the text. Recall-based testing can help bridge this gap and provide more nuanced insights. Here's a detailed guide on how to conduct a recall-based test.

1. Select Relevant Content: Choose a piece of text that is either known to be confusing to users, or contains new content you wish to evaluate. For instance, if you're testing a car dealership website and want to assess comprehension of a crucial payment plan option, select that specific content.
2. Formulate Factual Questions: Craft factual questions that will assess participants' comprehension of the selected text. These questions should be designed to test their ability to recall essential information accurately. In the car dealership example, you might ask participants to recall details about the payment plan.
3. Present the Content: Show the chosen text to the participants and allow them to read it thoroughly. Depending on the length of the text, this reading phase may take from a few seconds to several minutes. Encourage participants to take as much time as they would need if they were reading the content at home or in a non-testing environment.
4. Administer Recall Questions: Once participants have finished reading, follow up with factual questions about the content. You can ask these questions verbally or provide a survey for participants to complete. These questions should assess their ability to recall specific details, ensuring that they comprehended the content accurately.
5. Analyze Participant Responses: Analyze how well participants were able to recall and comprehend the information presented in the text. If many participants struggle to recall essential details, it may indicate that the content needs revision.
6. Post-Test Feedback: After the recall-based test and survey, consider asking participants open-ended questions about how they think the content could be improved. This additional feedback can provide valuable insights into potential content enhancements.

By following these steps, you can effectively use recall-based testing to assess content comprehension, identify areas for improvement, and ensure that your content resonates with your target audience.

Highlighter Tests

One of my favorite techniques for testing content is the "highlighter method." This approach allows users to pinpoint what's clear and unclear within text by highlighting specific portions. It serves as a precise tool to identify areas that require rewriting, and can streamline content to focus on what truly matters to the user. The highlighter test is particularly effective for gauging a value proposition, and determining the essential information needed to help users achieve their goals. Here's a step-by-step guide on how to conduct a highlighter test, along with an example.

Step 1: Select Your Content

Choose the content you want to evaluate. It can be a webpage, a product description, an article, or any text that you believe needs assessment. Make sure the content is relevant to your goals.

Example

Let's say you're a travel website looking to improve your destination guides. You've selected a draft of a guide about a popular tourist destination.

Step 2: Define Highlighter Colors

Establish a color code that participants will use to highlight the text. Ensure participants understand the color code before proceeding.

Example

- Green: Highlight information that you find useful or helpful for planning your trip.
- Pink: Highlight any sections that seem confusing or irrelevant to your travel needs.

Step 3: Present the Content

Provide the selected content to the user. Instruct them to read through it without making any marks initially. Ask participants to take as much time as they would, when reading such content outside of a testing environment. This ensures a realistic reading experience.

Example

Give the participant the draft destination guide and ask them to read it thoroughly.

Step 4: Conduct the Highlighting

After participants have read the content, explain the color code again and instruct them to use highlighters to mark sections based on their understanding. They should use the defined colors to highlight what they consider useful or confusing.

Example

"Now, please use the highlighters to mark the sections of the guide. Remember to use green for information you find useful, and pink for sections that confuse you or seem unnecessary."

Step 5: Follow-Up Questions

Allocate some time for follow-up questions. Ask participants why they highlighted specific sections in a certain way. This provides qualitative insights into their thought processes and helps you understand their perspective.

Example

"Why did you highlight this section in green? What did you find particularly useful about it? And why did you choose to mark this part in pink? What made it confusing or unnecessary for your trip planning?"

Step 6: Score and Analyze

Review the highlighted sections and participants' explanations. Identify the most frequently highlighted areas in green and pink. Also, consider the qualitative comments provided. These insights will guide you in making improvements to the content.

Example

You notice that participants frequently highlighted details about local transportation in green, indicating its usefulness. On the other hand, they highlighted lengthy historical background information in pink, signifying it was confusing and potentially unnecessary for trip planning.

By conducting a highlighter test and analyzing the results, you can pinpoint areas that require revision, and gain a better understanding of what content resonates with your audience. This valuable feedback will help you enhance the clarity and effectiveness of your written material.

ALPHA AND BETA TESTING

Alpha and beta testing are pivotal stages in product development, enabling you to fine-tune your offering before a full-scale release. In this section, we explore the nuances of alpha and beta testing, when to employ each, how to set them up effectively, and their importance in fostering user-centricity.

Alpha Testing: Shaping the Initial Vision

Alpha testing is your opportunity to assess a product internally, to collaborate with a select group of individuals to ascertain if your product aligns with your vision, and to pinpoint any significant issues, particularly bugs. It offers insights into whether you're crafting a solution that genuinely aids users in achieving their objectives, while helping you identify and rectify glitches.

Alpha testing is most beneficial in the following scenarios:

- Early Development Stage: Conduct alpha testing before design and ideas become too concrete. It's an ideal phase for identifying major flaws in the user experience (UX) and addressing them swiftly.
- Bug Identification: Alpha testing is excellent for tracking and fixing bugs within the product.
- Specific Flows Testing: Use alpha testing to scrutinize defined product flows. Avoid vague instructions like "explore the product/feature" and focus on specific tasks.
- Feedback Utilization: Alpha testing is valuable when teams are ready to employ the feedback to enhance the user experience.

Here are some successful methods to implement alpha testing in your organization.

- "Speed Testing": Like speed dating, allocate 15-minute slots to evaluate different ideas or aspects of your product.
- Demo Desk: Set up an accessible station in your workplace (or virtually) where colleagues can provide feedback on ongoing projects. Reward participation with small incentives.
- Weekly Testing Sprints: Organize regular testing days, allowing employees to sign up for convenient slots using a scheduling tool like Calendly.

Since alpha testing can rely heavily on getting colleagues to interact with your test, consider some best practices:

- Recruit employees who have minimal involvement with the product, as they offer a fresh perspective.
- Consider small incentives, such as snacks or gift cards, to encourage participation.
- Develop a straightforward feedback form to structure and gather actionable insights.

Beta Testing: Engaging Your User Community

Beta testing extends your testing reach to a select group of external users, who get access to a specific product or feature. It serves as an invaluable source of consistent qualitative feedback before rolling out the product or feature to a wider audience.

Beta testing is most beneficial when:

- Product or Feature Is Live: It is suitable for products or features that are already live and need refinement.
- Feature-Specific Learning: You want to understand how users engage with specific features within a product before a full-scale release.
- Data-Driven Decisions: You require comprehensive analytics on usage patterns before launching to a broader user base.
- Bug Detection: Beta testing helps identify issues and glitches in the flow of new features or products.
- Feedback Integration: You plan to actively incorporate user feedback into ongoing improvements.

Typically, it is great to start with alpha testing, and then set up a beta testing program, so you have both types of testing covered. Here is how you can set up a beta program.

1. Define Beta Program Goals and Rules: Determine the scope, frequency, and expectations of your beta program. Decide how often users must provide feedback.
2. Create a Beta Program Sign-Up: Encourage users to join the beta program by highlighting the benefits, such as early access and influencing product development.
3. Invite Participants: Reach out to potential beta testers, considering input from account management, marketing, and previous research sessions.
4. Conduct Beta Testing: Provide users with access to the feature or product. Encourage exploration, but clarify your availability for questions and feedback.
5. Gather Feedback: Hold feedback sessions, gather data, and document user experiences. Share insights with relevant teams for action.

Continuing the Cycle

Beta testing serves as a gateway to continuous user research. By nurturing a community of engaged users through alpha and beta programs, you gain access to ongoing insights that enhance your product's user-centricity. Utilize this wealth of data to guide your organization toward delivering the best possible user experience.

By employing alpha and beta testing, you streamline your development process, minimize usability issues, and refine your product iteratively. Getting this early user feedback positions your organization for long-term success in delivering valuable solutions to your audience.

Monitor and Iterate Methods 18

BENCHMARKING AND QUANTITATIVE USABILITY TESTS

Usability tests, as a whole, are about having participants attempt to do the most common and important tasks on a product/service. While you conduct the test, you as a researcher, are looking to find problems the participant runs into during the test. You then take these problems to your team and brainstorm to find ways to fix the usability issues—which are sometimes simple and other times complex.

With qualitative usability tests, you are talking to the participants and describing the different reactions, perceptions, or issues they encounter. However, with a quantitative usability test, you can still describe the problem, but you also measure:

- how many people encountered a problem;
- how many people were able to complete the tasks;
- the time it took them to complete tasks;
- how many errors participants ran into;
- what types of errors participants encountered;
- participants' perceptions of usability.

With quantitative usability testing, you can find out a lot of important information that can help you generate the impact of your research. For instance, when I was working at a travel company, we conducted a quantitative usability test on our checkout flow. We found that people were taking a long time to fill out information that ultimately wasn't that relevant and, thus, dropping off and abandoning the flow for a competitor that was easier to use.

Based on these results, we made some significant changes and retested the flow after the improvements were made. We reduced the time it took to fill out information by 50% (which was faster than people could do on the competitive product as well), and we reduced abandonment by 35%. This meant that we increased revenue by £75,000 annually.

That Is a Big Impact

When it comes to measuring usability, we can break that down into three major areas.

1. Effectiveness: Whether a user can accurately complete tasks and an overarching goal.
2. Efficiency: How much effort and time it takes for the user to complete tasks and an overarching goal accurately.
3. Satisfaction: How comfortable and satisfied a user is with completing the tasks and goal.

Each of these areas owns metrics you can use to quantify them.

Effectiveness

- Task Success: This simple metric tells you if a user could complete a given task (0=Fail, 1=Pass). You can get fancier with this by assigning more numbers that denote the difficulty users had with the task, but you need to determine the levels with your team before the study.
- The Number of Errors: This task gives you the number of errors a user committed while trying to complete a task. You can also gain insight into common mistakes users run into while attempting to complete the task. If any of your users seem to want to complete a task differently, a common trend of errors may occur.
- Single Ease Question (SEQ): The SEQ is one question (on a seven-point scale) measuring the participant's perceived task ease. Ask the SEQ after each completed (or failed) task.
- Confidence: Confidence is a seven-point scale that asks users to rate how confident they were that they completed the task successfully.

Efficiency

- Time on Task: This metric measures how long it takes participants to complete or fail a given task. This metric can give you a few different options to report on, where you can provide the data on average task completion time, average task failure time, or overall average task time (of both completed and failed tasks).
- Number of Errors: With this metric, you count the number of errors participants encounter while trying to complete a given task. After the test, you can also categorize the types of errors participants encountered to understand if there are trends and patterns across the errors.

- Subjective Mental Effort Question (SMEQ): The SMEQ allows the users to rate how mentally tricky a task was to complete.

Satisfaction

- System Usability Scale (SUS): The SUS has become an industry standard, and measures the perceived usability of user experience. Because of its popularity, you can reference published statistics (e.g., the average SUS score is 68).
- Usability Metric for User Experience (UMUX/UMUX-Lite): The UMUX has slightly taken over the SUS as an industry standard, as it is shorter and easier to administer. It also measures the perception of usability.

There are a lot of metrics in this list, and I don't recommend measuring them all during one test, especially if you are just starting out, and doubly so if you are running moderated tests. I learned the hard way, trying to juggle a stopwatch, understanding if someone was successfully completing a task, and counting the number of errors. It was a mess.

But before we dive into how to run a quantitative usability test, let's talk through when they are useful.

When to Run a Quantitative Usability Test

There is a time and a place for everything, including quantitative usability testing. How do you know when it's appropriate to run a quantitative usability test, rather than a qualitative one? Quantitative and qualitative usability tests have different goals, and are appropriate for different parts of the product development process.

Qualitative versus Quantitative Usability Tests in the PDP

Qualitative usability tests are much more about exploring people's feelings, reactions, and perceptions of an idea/prototype. The goals of this type of study are to explore and get early feedback, and the ideas are usually less defined.

On the other side, quantitative usability testing is about evaluating the efficiency, effectiveness, and satisfaction of the product/service. You can absolutely ask questions about perceptions, but it is usually at the end of the study after the measurements are complete. If you already have a solid idea of the solution, and you are ready to measure the actual usability, quantitative usability testing is the perfect approach.

How to Run a Quantitative Usability Test

Now that we're clear on what quantitative usability testing is and when to use it, it's time to go through how to run one of these fantastic tests. We're going to go through a step-by-step guide with an example of how to run a quantitative usability test effectively and efficiently.

Create a Plan

The most important artifact to create at the beginning of any research study is a research plan. This plan is critical because it enables you and your team to align exactly on what you're trying to achieve in the research project and how. It also helps clarify the project, and lets you focus as a researcher. Within the plan, you will explore the goals of the research study. This is where the above component about when to conduct a quantitative usability test becomes important.

The outcome of this type of study is clear measurements of the usability of a product/service. In this, your goals are to:

- understand how a product/service is progressing over time through iterations and improvements;
- identify the effectiveness, efficiency, and satisfaction of the most important and critical tasks on the product/service;
- discover the main pain points, errors, and usability issues of the product/service.

Ensure the Fidelity Makes Sense for Quantitative Testing

One of the biggest mistakes I made was attempting to conduct a quantitative usability test on a prototype. Why was this a mistake? When you think about the point of quantitative usability testing, it is about really assessing efficiency and effectiveness. Now, with the prototype I was testing (and many prototypes out there), we generally design a happy and clear path. There aren't as many distractions as with a real product. There isn't as much of an opportunity to get lost.

If you are using a prototype to test usability, there might only be one path for your participants to go down in this testing scenario. Whereas, once the product is live, there are multiple paths your participants could get lost on.

What happened when I tested the prototype? We had high task success and a relatively good time on task. The problem was the prototype was unrealistic, and when we tested again on the live product (with all the bells, whistles, and distractions), our task success fell, and our time on task rose.

I highly recommend, if you want to do a quantitative usability test, to do it on either an already live product, or one that is as close to what it will be like live as possible, and use the rough prototype phase to get qualitative feedback.

Choose Your Metrics

The metrics you choose will differ depending on one main factor: moderated versus unmoderated testing. If you are running a moderated study, and you don't have anyone there to help support you, I would recommend only tracking:

- time on task;
- task success;
- the SUS or UMUX.

I recommend this because it is extremely challenging to keep track of this all at once alone. As I mentioned, I have tried to juggle tracking way too many metrics and, in the end, I lacked confidence in my data. I wasn't sure if I could trust how many errors I counted, or if I started a stopwatch at the right time.

If you have someone else (or multiple people) helping you during your moderated study, you can give each person a metric or two to track. That way, the entire test isn't on you. However, if you are running an unmoderated study and using a tool, it usually has predefined metrics that you can choose or automatically measure.

This is hugely helpful, and I do recommend running a few moderated studies to make sure everything is okay, and that your tasks are clear and straightforward, and then leaving the rest to run unmoderated whenever possible.

If you have help, and are running a moderated test, you can measure:

- task success;
- time on task;
- number and type of errors;
- SEQ;
- SUS or UMUX;
- confidence.

With these metrics, your team can get a really comprehensive understanding of the usability of your product/service, which also allows us to continue to track how our improvements change these metrics over time. The one metric that can get tricky is task success. Task success can either be measured as binary—the participant passed or failed—or it can be measured across a spectrum. For the latter, you and your team have to decide, for each task, what passing versus struggling versus failing means.

Identify the Tasks

The next step is about understanding what you want to test. Regarding quantitative usability testing, I recommend picking the most critical tasks a user has to perform to achieve their primary goals. The best way to do this is to sit with your team and use previous research and usage data to understand the primary goals people have and the top tasks people are performing on your product/service.

Let's take Booking.com, for example. I have never worked at Booking.com, so I don't know if these are true, but wanted to use an easy example. The top tasks for the website might be:

1. searching for a hotel;
2. filtering for a specific type of hotel;
3. comparing different hotels;
4. choosing a hotel room;
5. viewing the booking details.

I often get asked how many tasks to include in a usability test, but it really depends on the session length and the complexity of your tasks. I recommend taking anywhere from 60 to 90 minutes for a quantitative usability test, and within that time, testing anywhere from 5 to 15 tasks.

However, if you are using an unmoderated tool, this might differ because you don't have to take as much time to do an intro, outro, or all the other human things that come with moderated tests. Usually, unmoderated tests take closer to 20–30 minutes, but it still depends on the number of tasks and complexity of your tasks.

I recommend taking no longer than 90 minutes and testing no more than 15 tasks—beyond that, it becomes cognitively overwhelming for both you and the participant. If you happen to have extra time, I recommend having a backlog of deprioritized tasks that you can test.

Write the Tasks

When I first started conducting usability tests, I had some pretty outlandish and funny tasks. No one trained me in task writing, and as a fiction writer, I have quite an overactive imagination, so I ran wild with usability testing tasks. I dug deep into the pits of my previous work and had a range of horrendous tasks such as:

- Find how to download the brochure.
- Book a trip you would love to go on.
- Imagine you are booking a holiday and really looking forward to lying on the beach with a piña colada and a great book, listening to the waves crashing. How would you find the perfect holiday?
- Imagine that you really want to adopt a dog. What dog would you adopt?

These make me laugh, but we all have to start somewhere. So, how do you write great usability testing tasks? First, let's define two important concepts:

1. User goal: This is the end goal for the participant.
2. Task scenario: Describes what the participant will do through relevant details and context.

For example, here is the difference between a user goal and a task scenario.
User goal: Make a doctor's appointment.

Task scenario: Make a doctor's appointment for October 31 at 10 a.m. with Doctor Anderson.

A user goal is the basic goal your user needs to accomplish on your platform (which you ideally listed above), while the task scenario gives relevancy and context to the task that allows a participant actually to do something meaningful on your platform.

One more example:

1. User goal: Find a restaurant to eat.
2. Task scenario: Find a pizza restaurant in the West Village to book for October 31 at 6 p.m. for two people.

If you just told someone to find a restaurant to eat at, they would likely ask many questions, which is not great for a quantitative usability test because talking during tasks skews your data.

How to Write a Task Scenario

Before we get into a step-by-step of how to write an effective task scenario, let's first look at the things we should avoid.

- Using words in the interface. If you are trying to get users to click a button that says: "sign up for our newsletter," try not to tell them to "sign up for our newsletter." Try to avoid including words in your UI in your task. Using words in your interface makes tasks easier for participants, as it leads them to the correct answer.
- Creating elaborate scenarios. As you saw above, I have created some elaborate scenarios. While they can be fun to write, they can really break the realistic nature of your test. Keep your scenario realistic, simple, and straightforward.
- Offending or triggering the participant. Do your best to steer away from personal information that may be triggering. I once saw a usability test that said, "You've really put on the pounds recently and are feeling bad about your weight. How would you find a nutritional guide?" If you can't avoid these topics, do your best to ensure the task scenarios are neutral.
- Using marketing/company jargon. It can be easy for us to slip into company or marketing jargon in our tests. But it's important to make sure we're using participant's language. Don't ask them to select the "most awesome discount" (biased language).

For each user goal/critical task you identified, write a task scenario. Let's explore how to construct them.

1. Start with your user goal/critical task. Take one of the user goals/critical tasks you identified above and start with that.
2. Include some context. Rather than just giving the user the basic task, you now briefly describe the context the person is in, so that they can understand

why they are performing the actual task. This gets the participant into a more realistic state of mind.
3. Give them relevant information. When recording metrics, you don't want people guessing what type of information they should be inputting. For example, if you just tell someone to book a trip to NYC and don't give any context, your time on task might be hugely skewed. This is especially important with unmoderated tasks, when there is no one who can clarify directions.
4. Specify the starting point. If there is a particular place you need the participant to start from, make sure that's very clear in your instructions.
5. Ensure there is an end the user can reach. Ensuring there is a reachable end is not only satisfactory to the participants, but also gives you an indication of whether or not the participant successfully completed the task.

Once you have this information for each goal, it's time to write your task scenarios. Let's look at the example from above on Booking.com. The most critical user goals were:

1. searching for a hotel;
2. filtering for a specific type of hotel;
3. comparing different hotels;
4. choosing a hotel room;
5. viewing the booking details.

Here is how I would write task scenarios for this particular test.

- User goal: Searching for a hotel.
- Context: Going on a holiday with your friend to Paris for a four-day trip and looking for a hotel in the city center.
- Relevant details: No more than a 30-minute walk to major tourist destinations (Louvre, Notre Dame), from October 28 to 31.
- Starting point: Booking.com homepage.
- Endpoint for task scenario: Search results page.

Task scenario: Imagine you're planning a four-day trip to Paris with your friend. You are using Booking.com to find a hotel in the city center (no more than 3 km away from the center) for your stay from October 28 to 31.

- User goal: Filtering for a specific type of hotel.
- Context: You're looking for more specific hotels.
- Relevant details: Looking for only 4-star hotels with free WiFi.
- Starting point: Booking.com search results page.
- Endpoint for task scenario: Search results page with filters.

Task scenario: You and your friend are looking for slightly more specific hotels in Paris. You want to find only 4-star reviews with free WiFi.

If you want another formula to follow, you can use:

Action Verb + Object + Context + Goal + (Optional) Constraints + Endpoint.

Let's break down each component.

- Action Verb: This is the specific action you want the participant to perform.
- Object: What the participant is interacting with (e.g., a button, a menu, a webpage).
- Context: The scenario or context in which the action is taking place. This sets the stage for the task.
- Goal: The purpose or objective of the task. What do you want the participant to achieve or find?
- Constraints: Any limitations or conditions that apply to the task.
- Endpoint: Where the participant is meant to end (mostly to ensure there is an endpoint for the task).

If you look at the above tasks from this lens, they would look like this.

- User goal: Searching for a hotel.
- Action: Find a hotel.
- Object: Booking.com search.
- Context: Four-day trip to Paris with friend, city center, October 28–31.
- Goal: Planning a trip.
- Constraints: No more than 3 km away from the center.
- Endpoint: Search results page.

Task scenario: Imagine you're planning a four-day trip (goal) to Paris with your friend. Using Booking.com (object) to find a hotel (action) in the city center, no more than 3 km away from the center (constraint), for your stay from October 28 to 31 (context).

It might take some time for you to write your tasks, but I promise it will be well worth the effort, especially if you are running a moderated study!

Conduct a Dry Run

Do yourself a huge favor and run a dry run or two with your colleagues to ensure you get all the kinks and bugs out of your script before moving on to your participants. There is nothing worse than wasted sessions!

Run the Study

If you are running an unmoderated study, this is pretty straightforward. Depending on the tool you are using, all you have to do is input your tasks and choose whatever measurements that you need, or add survey responses (e.g., SEQ or UMUX) that aren't already there. In terms of a moderated study, here is how you can structure the session with the example from Booking.com.

Hi there! My name is Nikki, and I am a user researcher at Booking.com. First off, thank you so much for being willing to participate in this session—we really appreciate your time.

For the next 60 minutes, I will ask you to perform five different activities. I will give you all the relevant information you need for the activities, and you can tell me when you're done with the activity. The purpose of this session is to understand how you interact with our website and identify any areas that may need improvement. Remember: this isn't a test, so there is no one right way to do anything. Feel free to stop this session at any time if you need to.

Do you mind if I record this session? It is for notetaking purposes and will only be used internally; all of your answers will be kept confidential. Do you have any questions before we begin?

Warm-up Questions

- When was the last time you went on holiday? What was it like?
- What's your favorite holiday destination and why?

Tasks and Surveys

For each task:

Read and send the task scenario. Imagine you're planning a four-day trip to Paris with your friend. Find a hotel in the city center (no more than 3 km away from the center) for your stay from October 28 to 31. Go to Booking.com to start.

- When the user begins, start the timer and continue the timer until:
  - the user completes the given task;
  - the user indicates they would give up (failed task).
- Count the number of errors, if any, and record them at the end of the task.
- Record the task success or failure (or struggle).
- Ask the user the SEQ:
  - Overall, how difficult or easy was the task to complete?
    - 1 = very difficult, 7 = very easy.

Ask the UMUX or SUS at the end of the tasks.

- [This system's] capabilities meet my requirements.
  - 1 = strongly disagree, 7 = strongly agree.
- Using [this system] is a frustrating experience.
  - 1 = strongly disagree, 7 = strongly agree.

- [This system] is easy to use.
  - 1 = strongly disagree, 7 = strongly agree.
- I have to spend too much time correcting things with [this system].
  - 1 = strongly disagree, 7 = strongly agree.

Follow-up Questions

Thank you so much for completing those activities; that was very helpful. I just have a few follow-up questions to ask you based on your overall experience.

- Talk me through your impressions of the overall experience.
- Describe the most confusing part of the experience.
- Explain one thing that was missing from the experience.
- Walk me through one thing you would change to improve the experience?

Wrap-up

Thank you so much for participating today; we really appreciate your time. This session was extremely helpful for us. We will be analyzing the data from this test and making improvements based on your feedback. This will help us create a better user experience for everyone.

Again, all of your answers will be kept completely confidential. You will receive [compensation and when they will receive it].

Since this session was so valuable, would it be okay for me to contact you again in the future to participate in another research session?

Do you have any other questions for me? If any come up, you can contact me at [email]. Thank you again!

Analyze the Results

Depending if you are using a tool, such as something for unmoderated testing, you might have an easier time analyzing your results, as many of these tools can do it for you. If you are looking for a way to visualize results, especially if you are stuck in the more manual, moderated world, you can use something called a stoplight chart.

A stoplight chart, also known as a red-yellow-green chart, is a visual tool used to analyze and communicate the severity of usability issues identified during a usability test. It categorizes issues into three levels of severity:

1. critical (red);
2. important (yellow);
3. minor (green).

Here's a step-by-step guide on how to use a stoplight chart to analyze usability test results.

Step 1: Prepare Your Usability Test Results

Gather all the data and observations from your usability test. This includes video recordings, notes, and any metrics you decided to track. Make sure you have sat down with your team to define what task success and failure are (and what a struggle is if you aren't measuring binary task success), as well as your error types.

Step 2: Create the Chart

You can create a stoplight chart using spreadsheet software like Microsoft Excel or Google Sheets. If you're having a hard time getting started, check out this template.

Step 3: Assign Task Completion Colors

For each task, assign colors to make it clear what the task success was for each participant and the average per task:

- red = failed task;
- orange = struggled with the task;
- green = succeeded with the task.

Step 4: Populate the Chart

For each participant and task, record the task completion, time on task, and any other metrics you tracked.

Step 5: Categorize Issues

Review the usability issues you've identified during the usability test, and categorize each issue into issue types.

- Critical: These are issues that severely hinder or prevent users from completing essential tasks or achieving their goals. They can result in a high level of frustration or abandonment of the task or system.
- Important: These issues are significant but may not be as severe as critical ones. They can cause user frustration or confusion, but are not complete showstoppers.

- Minor: These are minor issues or suggestions for improvement that don't significantly impact the user experience. They may be cosmetic or inconsequential.

Step 6: Describe Each Issue

You can put this in your chart or have it in a supplemental report. Provide a brief but clear description of each issue you've categorized. Be concise and specific, so that anyone reviewing the chart can understand the problem.

Step 7: Prioritize and Plan Action

After creating the stoplight chart, review it to identify patterns and prioritize which issues to address first. Critical issues should be addressed immediately, as they have the most significant impact on usability and user satisfaction. Important issues should also be addressed after, while minor issues can be tackled whenever there is space in the roadmap.

Present

Once you have your stoplight chart, you can go about presenting your findings in a few different ways, depending on the needs of your team. For many quantitative usability tests, I just sit with my team to review the videos of the task failures and most critical issues. With this, we brainstorm ideas or solutions to fix the issues. If you need to, and (sometimes it's necessary!) you can create a usability testing report where you go into more detail with annotations and text.

CONTINUOUS BENCHMARKING TO SHOW THE IMPACT

The beauty of quantitative usability testing really comes through when you do it continuously. If we go back to the original question that spurred on my usage of quantitative usability testing—"how do we know these changes are improving the usability?"—we get to continuous benchmarking. This means that, over a certain amount of time, you are conducting these quantitative usability tests, either over a set period of time (e.g., every quarter or six months) or when changes are made.

For each study, you can create a new stoplight report that can visually show you the improvements that you're making over time. You can also use this information to calculate the types of impact as I mentioned above, on important metrics like acquisition, retention, revenue, etc.

UX SURVEYS

These scales help uncover discrepancies between user anticipation and actual experience.

Here is an example scale.

- How was your experience with [X]?
  - 1 = Much worse than I expected, 4 = About what I expected, 7 = Much better than I expected.

While less common, disconfirmation scales can provide valuable insights into user satisfaction, particularly regarding how a product either exceeds or falls short of expectations.

Performance Satisfaction Metrics

Single Ease Questionnaire (SEQ):

The Single Ease Questionnaire (SEQ) focuses on task-specific performance satisfaction. Administered immediately after users complete a usability test task, it gauges their perception of task difficulty. The SEQ has one question:

- Overall, how difficult or easy was the task to complete?

SEQ employs a seven-point response scale ranging from very difficult to very easy (1 to 7). By targeting specific tasks, SEQ helps pinpoint performance-related satisfaction issues.

After Scenario Questionnaire (ASQ):

The After Scenario Questionnaire (ASQ) offers an alternative approach to measuring task efficiency, effectiveness, and user satisfaction in a usability test. It assesses the user's perceived ease of task completion through three statements:

1. Overall, I am satisfied with the ease of completing the task in this scenario.
2. Overall, I am satisfied with the amount of time it took to complete the task in this scenario.
3. Overall, I am satisfied with the support information (online help, messages, documentation) when completing the task.

Respondents rate their agreement on a seven-point scale (1 = Strongly disagree, 7 = Strongly agree) for each statement. ASQ provides a more holistic view of user satisfaction during task execution.

Confidence Rating:

Confidence Rating measures user confidence in successfully completing a task within the product. It probes beyond task completion to gauge user self-assurance. The confidence rating is one question:

- Overall, how confident are you that you completed the task successfully?

With a seven-point response scale (1 = Not at all confident, 4 = Not sure, 7 = Extremely confident), Confidence Rating helps uncover instances where users may be confident despite task failure, highlighting potential usability issues.

Each of these customer satisfaction metrics plays a pivotal role in providing nuanced insights into the user experience. Depending on your specific research goals and the context of your product or service, you can strategically employ these metrics to collect targeted feedback and drive meaningful improvements.

How to Set Up a Customer Satisfaction Practice

Setting up a customer satisfaction practice within your organization involves a series of thoughtful steps to ensure you collect actionable insights effectively. Here's a more in-depth look at how to establish a robust customer satisfaction practice.

Understand user journeys

Begin by comprehending the general journeys users take when interacting with your product or service. Recognize key touchpoints and interactions they have while using your product or service. Identify where users often struggle or encounter. In the quest for meaningful insights beyond the limitations of Net Promoter Score (NPS), I embarked on a journey to redefine customer satisfaction. I aimed to extract actionable data that would empower teams to make informed decisions. Over time, I honed a more precise definition of customer satisfaction, one that delves into a product's efficiency, effectiveness, functionality, and reliability.

Customer satisfaction, as I see it now, scrutinizes a solution's ability to align with customer needs, eliminate pain points, and facilitate goal attainment. In essence, it measures the degree to which a product or service caters to customers' requirements and aspirations.

The traditional NPS approach no longer resonated with this refined definition. It begged for more versatile methods, that would offer richer insights to teams.

Customer satisfaction is a multi-faceted concept, and one-size-fits-all metrics no longer suffice. Instead, a combination of metrics helps you unearth actual problems. You can categorize these metrics into two primary types:

1. performance satisfaction, which assesses a user's contentment with specific tasks;
2. perceived satisfaction, which gauges overall satisfaction with a product.

Perceived Satisfaction Metrics

System Usability Scale (SUS):
The System Usability Scale, known as SUS, is a battle-tested 10-point questionnaire widely utilized for assessing the perceived ease of using a website, application, or platform. Its strengths lie in simplicity and effectiveness. It includes the following.

- I think that I would like to use this system frequently.
- I found the system unnecessarily complex.
- I thought the system was easy to use.
- I think that I would need the support of a technical person to be able to use this system.
- I found the various functions in this system were well integrated.
- I thought there was too much inconsistency in this system.
- I would imagine that most people would learn to use this system very quickly.
- I found the system very cumbersome to use.
- I felt very confident using the system.
- I needed to learn a lot of things before I could get going with this system.

SUS is typically administered after a usability test or independently, to gauge participants' general experience with a platform. This makes it a potent perceived satisfaction metric. SUS provides an overarching view of perceived ease of use, which directly correlates with overall satisfaction.

Usability Metric for User Experience (UMUX and UMUX-Lite)

UMUX and UMUX-Lite offer a streamlined alternative to SUS. These metrics emphasize efficiency, effectiveness, and satisfaction while reducing the number of questions, making them ideal for shorter usability tests. The UMUX is four questions, with two positive and two negative items, with a seven-point response scale (1 = Strongly disagree, 7 = Strongly agree):

- [This system's] capabilities meet my requirements.
- Using [this system] is a frustrating experience.
- [This system] is easy to use.
- I have to spend too much time correcting things with [this system].

The UMUX-Lite is a further improvement on the UMUX, containing only two questions with a seven- or five-point response scale (1 = Strongly disagree, 7 = Strongly agree):

- [This system's] capabilities meet my requirements.
- [This system] is easy to use.

Satisfaction Scales:
General satisfaction scales employ a bipolar structure to assess overall user satisfaction or dissatisfaction. These scales provide a straightforward and effective means to capture overall user sentiment. Here is a sample scale:

- How satisfied or dissatisfied are you with [X]?
  - 1 = Very dissatisfied, 4 = Mixed (equally satisfied and dissatisfied), 7 = Very satisfied.

These scales offer a straightforward yet comprehensive view of user satisfaction, and are often employed for broader product assessments.

Disconfirmation Scales

Disconfirmation scales measure how closely a product meets—or falls short of—user expectations. Low scores highlight gaps between expectations and reality, pointing to likely sources of dissatisfaction.

Choose appropriate metrics

Decide which satisfaction metrics align best with your research objectives. Perceived satisfaction metrics provide an overall sentiment, while performance satisfaction metrics offer task-specific insights. For perceived satisfaction, consider metrics like SUS, UMUX, UMUX-Lite, satisfaction scales, and disconfirmation scales. For performance satisfaction, utilize SEQ, ASQ, and Confidence Rating.

Determine data collection methods

Select how you'll reach out to users for satisfaction assessments. Common methods include in-platform surveys, email surveys, or dedicated studies. Decide on the frequency of data collection, which can vary from continuous measurement, periodic intervals (quarterly or semi-annually), or project-based intervals (following specific usability tests).

Segment and group users

Categorize users into meaningful groups or segments based on their interaction patterns, preferences, or attitudes. This segmentation can help you tailor your satisfaction assessments and identify specific user needs. Grouping users within their different segments or personas can guide you in selecting participants for particular tests, making the outcomes and insights more focused and actionable.

Combine qualitative and quantitative data

Recognize that satisfaction metrics provide data on what's happening, but not why it's happening. Complement quantitative metrics with qualitative insights from interviews or open-ended survey responses. Qualitative data helps uncover the underlying reasons behind satisfaction or dissatisfaction, and provides context for making improvements.

Implement a feedback tracking system

Establish a central repository or tracking system for recording and monitoring user feedback over time. This could be a digital dashboard, a collaborative tool like Miro, or a dedicated feedback database.

Use this system to analyze satisfaction scores, qualitative feedback, and evidence from usability tests.

Iteratively improve

Continuously analyze the feedback collected through your satisfaction practice to identify recurring issues or trends. Prioritize areas where improvements can enhance user satisfaction. Conduct ideation workshops or internal hackathons to brainstorm and implement solutions to address identified problems.

Measure progress and showcase impact

Track changes in satisfaction scores over time, especially after implementing improvements. Document the impact of these changes to showcase the value of your satisfaction practice. Develop case studies highlighting how user satisfaction improvements have positively affected the user experience and contributed to organizational success.

Establishing a customer satisfaction practice is an ongoing process that involves data collection, analysis, and action. By aligning your practice with organizational objectives and continually seeking to understand and meet user needs, you can enhance the user experience and foster a customer-centric culture within your organization.

VISUAL TESTING

Visual testing plays a pivotal role in design and user experience research, but it's essential to clarify what it isn't before diving into its various strategies and methods. Visual testing doesn't focus on:

- Comparing Design Preferences: It doesn't aim to determine which design users prefer over another. Asking users to pick their favorite design isn't the primary goal.

- Liking or Disliking Designs: It doesn't solely explore whether users like or dislike a design. Subjective opinions don't provide actionable insights.
- Color Preferences: Visual testing doesn't revolve around gauging users' color preferences or choices.

Qualitative user research isn't suited to answer these questions effectively. Here's why:

- Sample Size Limitations: Qualitative user research typically involves a small sample size. Relying on a handful of opinions for yes/no or preference-based questions isn't representative or reliable.
- User Uncertainty: Users often struggle to express their design preferences clearly. Questions like: "Which color scheme do you prefer?" can be challenging for users to answer meaningfully. Focusing on user needs is more productive.
- Opinions versus Perceptions: Gathering opinions on design preferences provides limited value. Instead, visual testing aims to understand user perceptions, reactions, needs, goals, and pain points, which offer more actionable data.

When Visual Testing Makes Sense

To leverage visual testing effectively, align your goals with its capabilities. Visual testing is suitable for objectives such as:

- Discovering Initial Reactions and Impressions: Visual testing excels at capturing users' immediate responses to a design or brand.
- Evaluating Visual Impact: It helps understand how visuals influence user experiences and behaviors.
- Assessing Brand Attributes: Visual testing can provide insights into how users perceive and describe brand attributes in relation to design.
- Analyzing User Perceptions: It's valuable for exploring how users view and describe your brand in the context of design.

However, it's crucial to manage stakeholder expectations. Visual testing won't yield definitive answers like "this design is the best." Instead, it provides insights into how users react to and describe different designs, enabling informed decision-making.

Usability Testing First

Usability testing takes precedence over visual testing. Before delving into aesthetics, ensure your product meets the essential user needs.

1. Functional: The product must serve its intended purpose and perform its core functions effectively.

2. Reliable: Users should trust that the product will perform consistently and without errors.
3. Usable: The product must be user-friendly, ensuring users can navigate and achieve their goals efficiently.

Only when these fundamental requirements are met should you focus on aesthetics and visual appeal.

Visual Testing Methods

Once usability is established, you can employ visual testing methods aligned with specific goals.
Goal: Discover Initial Reactions and Impressions of a Design or Brand
Method: Five-Second Tests

- Measure how effectively a design conveys its message within seconds.
- Assess users' understanding of the main message, trustworthiness perception, and comprehension of the primary product or service.
- Implement by defining a problem, brainstorming designs, creating variations, writing a script of questions, and presenting variations to users.

Scenario: Imagine you are designing a travel booking website. You want to assess how effectively different landing page designs convey trustworthiness and encourage users to explore vacation packages.
Setup: Create variations of your landing page designs, each with different visual elements like images, color schemes, and layout. Then, present these variations to users for five seconds each.
Questions after showing each design:

- "What message or impression do you get from this landing page?"
- "How would you feel using this website to plan your travel?"
- "What aspects of this landing page stand out to you? Why?"

Method: Aesthetic Explanation

- Understand how users would describe their initial impressions of a design or brand.
- Collect insights into what users focus on during their initial encounter.
- Set up by defining your objectives, creating variations, scripting questions, and presenting designs to users.

Scenario: You're developing a travel app, and you want to understand how users describe their initial impressions of the app's interface and branding.

Setup: Prepare different versions of your travel app's interface, including variations in color schemes, typography, and imagery. Present these versions to users.

Questions after viewing each version:

- "How would you describe the overall look and feel of this travel app?"
- "What aspects of the app's design caught your attention?"
- "If you had to describe this app to a friend, what words or phrases would you use?"

Goal: Understand How People Perceive Brand or Design Attributes
Method: Open Word Choice

- Grasp users' views and descriptions of your brand.
- Allow users to freely describe your brand, identifying strengths and weaknesses.
- Select designs for assessment, present them to participants, and prompt them to list descriptive words.

Scenario: Your travel agency is rebranding, and you want to gauge how users perceive the new brand elements.

Setup: Show users the rebranded elements, including logos, color schemes, and taglines.

Questions after viewing the elements:

- "Please, list several words or phrases that come to mind when you see our new logo and branding."
- "How would you describe the style and personality of our rebranded travel agency?"
- "Are there any specific emotions or impressions you associate with our new branding?"

Method: Closed Word Choice

- Determine users' agreement with specific brand attributes as they relate to your design.
- Assess which brand attributes resonate most with users.
- Brainstorm brand attributes, choose or create designs embodying these attributes, and ask users to select relevant terms while viewing the designs.

Scenario: You've introduced new brand attributes for your travel booking platform, and you want to assess user agreement with these attributes as they relate to the platform's design.

Setup: Present users with different versions of your platform design, each emphasizing specific brand attributes such as "Adventure," "Reliability," and "Luxury."

Questions after viewing each version:

- "Please select the brand attributes that you believe align with this design."
- "On a scale of 1 (not at all) to 5 (completely), how well does this design embody the 'Adventure' attribute?"
- "How much does this design reflect the 'Reliability' attribute, from 1 (not at all) to 5 (completely)?"

Method: Quality Rankings

- Evaluate how users rate your design and brand against specific attributes.
- Gain insights into the alignment between users' perceptions and brand attributes.
- Select attributes, choose designs, and ask users to rate attributes while viewing the designs.

Scenario: You want to evaluate user perceptions of the quality of experiences offered by different travel tour packages on your website.

Setup: Display various travel tour package listings, each with a distinct design, images, and descriptions.

Questions after viewing each package:

- "Please, rate the quality of this travel tour package on a scale of 1 to 5."
- "How does this package design convey the quality of the travel experience?"
- "To what extent does this package description align or not align with your expectations of a high-quality travel experience?"

Goal: Learn How Visuals Impact Experiences and Behaviors
Method: First-Click Tests

- Measure users' ability to efficiently and effectively perform specific tasks on your site.
- Assess task completion, efficiency, and ease of task initiation.
- Measures the amount of time it takes for a user to identify where they would click when prompted with a particular task.

Scenario: Your travel blog website aims to provide users with quick access to popular destinations. You want to ensure users can efficiently find their desired destination using the site's navigation.

Setup: Create multiple designs for the website's homepage, each with different navigation layouts and labels.

Instruct users with tasks like:

- "Find information about the top-rated hotels in Paris."
- "Locate flight booking options for a trip to New York."
- "Discover travel tips and recommendations for a visit to Tokyo."

Incorporate visual testing strategically within your research process to enhance the user experience and inform design decisions effectively.

PAIRWISE COMPARISON

If you know me, you know that I absolutely hate asking people for their preferences.

Understanding user preferences can be tricky because they are so subjective and influenced by many factors. Imagine asking someone if they prefer chocolate or vanilla ice cream. They might say chocolate because they love the taste, while another person might choose vanilla because it reminds them of childhood memories.

The same complexity arises in design choices. If we ask users whether they prefer a blue or purple website background, it's a decision they usually don't make. Or, consider asking if they prefer a large image banner or a smaller one with text. These are not typical choices users face, and their responses can be inconsistent and hard to interpret.

I actually tried this with my mom while she was trying to purchase furniture online for their new house. I showed her two different furniture websites and asked her which she preferred. She told me she preferred the second option more because it had fewer sponsored/ad-based search results. I then proceeded to watch her browse for a little bit, pick a sponsored search result and buy that product. Huzzah.

Plus, preferences might not align with best design practices. Someone might like a large image banner, but it could pose accessibility issues. This makes designing solely based on user preferences challenging, as it's hard to understand the reasons behind their choices and ensure those choices work well for everyone.

When it comes to comparing different versions of ideas or products, I tend to go with usability testing. The version that is more effective and efficient will generally be the one that people end up using more...

However, as we've been asked hundreds of times as researchers, sometimes we have to compare certain aspects without the aid of usability testing.

Sometimes we have to understand a degree of preference—as much as I hate writing those words.

But that doesn't mean that we have to ask people whether or not they prefer something. Instead, introducing: Pairwise comparison.

What's Pairwise Comparison?

Imagine I gave you a list of ten songs you've listened to recently and asked you to rank them in order of preference. You, like most people, might really struggle to fill out this survey accurately.

I love Taylor Swift's "Love Story," but do I like it more than Queen's "Bohemian Rhapsody" or The Beatles' "Hey Jude?" And then where does Adele's "Rolling in the Deep" sit within all of this?

You might struggle, trying to decide if you like Taylor Swift's "Love Story" more than Queen's "Bohemian Rhapsody" or if The Beatles' "Hey Jude" tops Adele's "Rolling in the Deep." But if I give you two songs at a time and ask which one you like more, it becomes much easier.

This is pairwise comparison in a nutshell. This method simplifies decision-making by breaking down complex choices into manageable comparisons, which then become a series of head-to-head votes. It's rooted in the idea that humans find it easier to make decisions when faced with two options rather than many.

Pairwise comparison is a fantastic technique for ranking, prioritizing, and comparing options efficiently and effectively.

Let's look at an example:

Food for a Party

Imagine you are planning a party and trying to figure out the best food to serve your guests. One way you could figure it out is by having people force-rank all the different options. However, as mentioned above, force ranking gives people a lot of different options to choose from, whereas pairwise comparison makes these rankings easier for users.

Let's look at the options for food:

- Pizza
- Chips
- Chocolate cake
- Sushi
- Fruit Salad
- Chicken wings

We would then go on to create survey questions to compare each option:

- Pizza versus Chips
- Pizza versus Chocolate cake
- Pizza versus Sushi
- Pizza versus Fruit salad
- Pizza versus Chicken wings
- Chips versus Chocolate cake
- Chips versus Sushi
- Chips versus Fruit salad
- Chips versus Chicken wings
- Chocolate cake versus Sushi
- Chocolate cake versus Fruit salad
- Chocolate cake versus Chicken wings
- Sushi versus Fruit salad
- Sushi versus Chicken wings
- Fruit salad versus Chicken wings

The total number of possible pairwise comparisons from a list of options is $n(n-1)/2$, where "n" stands for the number of options in the set. In the above example, we have six examples, so the formula would look like $6(6-1)/2$. Therefore, there would be 15 combinations to ask about, so there would be 15 total survey questions.

In a pairwise comparison survey, one participant can be tasked with voting on every possible pair combination or a bunch of people can each be given a sample of pairs to complete that can later be used to calculate the group's overall combined ranking.

Different Types of Pairwise Comparison Tests

Pairwise comparison fundamentally involves head-to-head voting, but there are several ways to customize your survey to suit different needs. These formats can be used independently or combined for more flexibility.

Complete Pairwise Comparison

In a Complete Pairwise Comparison, each respondent is shown every possible pair from the list of options. This method provides a detailed and accurate representation of an individual's preferences. The total number of possible pairwise comparisons is calculated using the formula $n(n-1)/2$. For example, if there are 10 options, the total number of pairs is $10 \times 9/2 = 45$. This then means the respondent is going through 45 survey questions.

> 45 survey questions?! That is way too much.

That's what crossed my mind the first time I heard about this approach. I try to limit my surveys to 10 questions, or at least surveys that take less than seven minutes to account for increased attrition if you hit the seven-minute mark. 45 questions felt like the participant would be there all day taking the survey, or, worse, that no one would take it.

However, pairwise comparison is pretty fast—I recommend you try taking a pairwise comparison survey to see just how quickly questions can go—and since the participant is only choosing between two options at one time, the amount of time and cognitive load for each question is fairly low.

Example

Imagine a small team of designers choosing their favorite colors for a new logo. With only 10 colors to choose from, each team member compares every pair to express their preferences clearly.

Complete Pairwise Comparison is ideal for small groups, individual preference ranking, or surveys with a limited number of options (usually up to 15–20).

Partial Pairwise Comparison

In Partial Pairwise Comparison, each participant sees only a sample of all possible pairs, which is useful for larger surveys or when there are many options. The general guideline is to ensure the dataset gets votes equal to 3 times the total number of possible pairs. This is calculated with the formula $3n(n-1)/2$, divided by the estimated minimum number of participants.

> **Example**
>
> A company wants to prioritize new features for their software from a list of 25 options. Instead of overwhelming participants with 300 comparisons, each participant might see only a subset, ensuring sufficient data is collected while keeping the survey manageable.
>
> Partial Pairwise Comparison is common in larger surveys with more than 20 options, allowing researchers to gather robust data without overburdening participants.

Forced Pairwise Comparison

Forced Pairwise Comparison eliminates the "skip" option, requiring participants to make a choice for each pair. This ensures every pair is evaluated, which can be useful when all options are relevant.

> **Example**
>
> A university conducting a survey to choose the best academic programs to expand must ensure that every participant makes a choice for all comparisons to get comprehensive results.

Image Pairwise Comparison

Image Pairwise Comparison uses images or GIFs instead of text options. This format is particularly effective for visual concept testing where visual comparisons are critical.

> **Example**
>
> An advertising agency tests different billboard designs by showing participants pairs of images and asking which one stands out more. This method helps determine the most visually appealing design.

Adaptive Pairwise Comparison

In Adaptive Pairwise Comparison, the survey adapts based on previous responses. Using principles like transitivity (if A>B and B>C, then A>C is assumed) or balancing the overall dataset, the survey selects the most informative pairs for each participant.

Example

An online retailer wants to understand customer comparisons for new product categories. The survey adjusts the pairs shown to each participant based on their earlier choices, ensuring efficient data collection and reducing redundant comparisons.

Types of Comparisons

Comparison might feel like an obvious word, especially in this context. We are comparing two things. But what are we actually comparing? What are the criteria by which we compare the two ideas, concepts, features, etc.?

It is really important to think about how we are comparing the two things in a pairwise comparison test because it will determine the type of language we use in the survey question and the outcome we get as a result.

Typically, there are five different ways to compare two things in this type of approach:

1. Value—what is worth most to them?
2. Motivation—what is the biggest thing that drives them?
3. Pain point—what is a bigger obstacle to achieving their goal?
4. Unmet needs—what is a bigger unmet need?
5. Risk—what is their biggest concern?

Some people run a pairwise comparison to understand the importance of the two options. However, I am generally more inclined to run an opportunity gap survey because it generally yields better results when understanding the gap between importance and satisfaction.

Here are some examples of how these comparisons translate into survey questions:

Value

- Which feature do you find more valuable in a smartphone?
    - Long Battery Life
    - High-Resolution Camera
- Which is worth more to you in a streaming service?
    - A large library of movies and shows
    - Ad-free experience

Motivation

- Which is a bigger motivator for using a fitness app?
    - Tracking your progress
    - Access to personalized workout plans
- What drives you more to purchase online?
    - Fast shipping
    - Discounts and offers

Pain point

- Which is a bigger obstacle to achieving your fitness goals?
  - Lack of time
  - Limited access to equipment
- What is a more significant barrier to your productivity at work?
  - Frequent interruptions
  - Inefficient software

Unmet need

- Which need do you feel is more unmet in your current job?
  - Opportunities for professional growth
  - Work-life balance
- What do you feel is a bigger unmet need in your community?
  - Access to healthcare services
  - Availability of public transportation

Risk

- Which is a bigger concern when considering a new financial product?
  - Risk of losing money
  - Complexity of the product
- What concerns you more about sharing personal data online?
  - Privacy breaches
  - Misuse of data by companies

Get super clear on the type of comparison you are trying to understand since that will lead to the language you use in the survey question and the type of information you get from respondents.

Ways to Analyze a Pairwise Comparison Test

The most common way to analyze a pairwise comparison test is through win rate (it sounds like a video game, doesn't it?).

Win rate is how often an option won out of all pairs it appeared in, and it is displayed as a percentage or a simple 0–100 number. It represents the proportion of times an option "wins" in all the comparisons it appears in.

Imagine you are participating in a survey where you need to choose between pairs of smartphone features. For each pair, you select the feature you value more. The win rate for each feature is calculated by looking at how many times that feature was chosen over others relative to the total number of comparisons it was part of.

In mathematical terms, the win rate is calculated as:

Win Rate = (Number of Win / Total Comparisons) * 100

This gives a percentage that shows how frequently an option wins.

The win rate is crucial because it simplifies the results of potentially complex pairwise comparisons into an easy-to-understand metric. It tells you at a glance which options are most preferred overall and it helps with:

- Quantitative Measure: It provides a clear, numerical value representing preference, making it easy to compare different options.
- Relative Comparison: It reflects the relative comparison of one option over another within the context of the survey.
- Decision-Making: High win rates indicate strong preferences, guiding product development, feature prioritization, and other strategic decisions.

A GUIDE TO WRITING SURVEYS

Surveys can feel like a simple methodology—write a few questions, send the survey to a bunch of people, and, voila, we have insights. If surveys were that easy, we'd all be swimming in deep and rich insights and, likely, surveys would be the only method we need.

But that isn't necessarily the case because surveys, while a great research method, can be difficult to assemble to get appropriate information. There have been many times when I've used a survey when I should have used another method, such as 1×1 interviews, diary studies, or looking into quantitative data.

I remember desperately trying to ask five open-ended questions in a survey to get qualitative information. That was back when I thought surveys could solve pretty much anything. I got my heart broken several times over trying to use surveys incorrectly (and for everything).

Now, I am very intentional and thoughtful when I choose surveys as a method.

What Are User Research Surveys (and How Are They Different)

Imagine you are throwing a party for your friends, and you want to understand what your friends need to make the party enjoyable for them. You might need to understand the types of food to get for the party, the kind of music people listen to, the games they play, and a bit about different parties they've enjoyed in the past and what made them enjoyable. You are throwing out feelers to make the night successful. To make it a good experience for your guests.

A user research survey is similar. You are asking questions to understand, at scale, the pain points, habits, behaviors, and needs of your users. With a survey, you are looking to broaden your understanding of an audience, specifically around what they are doing and feeling.

Because of this "what" caveat, a great way to use surveys is to supplement with other "why" methodologies, such as 1x1 interviews. For example, surveys are fantastic at telling you, on a larger scale, what people are doing or what tools people are using, but they don't go a great job telling you why a person is acting in a certain way or using a particular tool. Or how the experience is for someone beyond a rating.

It is super important to keep this in mind as you decide whether or not surveys are the right approach for your study.

How Are They Different?

There are a lot of different surveys out there, so it can sometimes be confusing to delineate which one is best for what you need. Here are ways you can differentiate them:

Market Research Surveys: These surveys look at the big picture of your market or audience. They tend to have a much broader question or scope, such as looking at the entire audience to understand what type of party to throw, rather than getting into the nitty-gritty of people's experience.

Customer Satisfaction Surveys: These are quick check-ins post-purchase or interaction, seeing how the experience was for the user, typically surrounding their satisfaction. These focus a lot on post-experience, so people can tell you what actually went wrong and recall from a particular usage. This would be like asking people how satisfied or dissatisfied they were with the snacks at your party.

Feedback Forms: These are even quicker, often just a few questions or a rating scale about a specific concept or thing, like the new dip you tried out at your party. They're super focused and don't dive deep into the whole experience but rather look at a small slice or moment.

Where Can They Fail?

Many companies rely solely on survey data to make data-driven decisions. They include comment boxes with the hope users will leave a message explaining their survey response—but most users don't.

The truth is surveys don't drive better decisions on their own. Too many companies sometimes use surveys to convince themselves they are customer-centric. But when you only use one method of user research or use only quantitative or qualitative data, you are missing other pieces of the puzzle that give you a more robust and empathetic understanding of your users.

It is super important to weigh surveys' pros and cons, such as:

Lack of Depth: Surveys may not provide the depth of insights that can be gained from qualitative methods like interviews or ethnographic studies. The predefined answers can limit the range of responses, potentially missing nuanced feedback.

Low-Response Rates: Depending on the survey's design and distribution method, achieving a high-response rate can be challenging, leading to sample bias if only certain users are more likely to respond.

Misinterpretation of Questions: Users might misunderstand survey questions, leading to inaccurate responses. The lack of interaction with respondents means there's no opportunity to clarify questions or probe deeper as you can in interviews.

Over-reliance on Self-reported Data: Surveys rely on users' perceptions and self-reported data, which can be biased or inaccurate due to memory recall issues or the desire to present oneself in a favorable light.

Surveys can be a really great tool when used properly. Let's dive into how to know a survey is the right fit and, once you determined that, how to write an effective survey.

Where to Start with Your User Research Survey

Starting with understanding

I often see a problem when people try to create a survey, and they don't know the meaningful answers to put in as choices for participants. For example, when working at a hospitality start-up, I sent a survey to understand people's top pain points with our software.

The issue? I had no idea what to list as the multiple-choice or ranking options. For half of those answers, I guessed what might be the pain points they were experiencing. This is obviously not ideal because, when it comes to surveys, people might just choose an easy answer that isn't 100% fit or the one that is closest to what they are experiencing rather than the actual experience they are having.

What Are Your Goals?

Defining and setting your goals (like with every other project) are so incredibly important for the success of your survey. They give you a super clear focus on what exact information you need from your survey and can help you define whether or not a survey is the right fit for your study. These goals will also help you develop questions that get you the information you need by the end of the study.

Creating goals is always the first step that I take because it honestly sets the entire project up for success, no matter what approach, method, or problem you are trying to solve.

I usually define goals for surveys into three distinct buckets:

1. To look at usability
2. To better understand your user base
3. To prioritize information

However, this is only the surface of creating goals and, sometimes, they can be tricky to create, especially if you aren't used to writing them. So let's go step-by-step into how you can determine your survey goals.

Define the overarching why. The best way to start this process is to understand what you are trying to achieve through the survey. This will help you determine if a survey is, in fact, the right method to use. In this step, you can ask yourself:

- What are you trying to achieve with this survey?
- How will this survey help you/the team?
- What do you expect from the results (assumptions)?
- What do you expect to do with the results?
- How does this survey fit into any business/organizational goals?

Specify your needs. Next, defining what exactly you are trying to get from your survey is critical. I recommend drilling down on these questions to know whether a survey is the right approach for what you are trying to get. These questions will also help you develop screener questions.

- What are you trying to learn about your users?
- What information are you trying to get from your users? Does a survey make sense, given that information?
- What kind of information do your users have to be able to give you?
- What gaps does the information from this survey aim to fill?

List the criteria of your ideal participant. Once you better understand your needs and if a survey is the right fit, you can start thinking about who you want to recruit. I tend to do this before finalizing survey goals because it gives me another opportunity to ensure a survey is the best way to get the information I need from users.

- What are the questions your users have to answer to get you meaningful information?
- What gaps in knowledge do you have that you need your participants to fill in?
- What behaviors do you need to understand more?
- What habits are you trying to target?

Write your goals. Now that you've gathered all this information, it is time to write your goals for the survey. As I mentioned above, I use certain models for writing survey goals that go into one of those three buckets:

Usability goals. These are all about understanding the usability of a product or service and often include UX metrics such as the SEQ, SUS, and UMUX-lite. You can read more about this process here! Here are some example goals:

- Evaluate people's perception of the ease of use of [product/service].
- Identify the task- or product-based satisfaction of [product/service].
- Understanding goals. These goals focus on understanding different behaviors, actions, tasks, or tools people use and the frequency of that information.
- Identify behaviors and actions people are taking on [product/service].

- Uncover the different tools participants are currently using to achieve their goals and what their experience is like with them.
- Uncover people's perceptions/feelings regarding certain actions/tasks on [product/service].

Prioritization goals. Whenever you have a large amount of qualitative data, it is important to prioritize the data to allow your team to take action. Prioritization surveys, such as the opportunity gap survey, are perfect for this situation.

- Prioritize qualitative insights based on the current level of importance and satisfaction.
- Understand the most impactful unmet needs/pain points to solve.

I highly recommend working with stakeholders on defining your goals to ensure everyone is aligned on the expected outcomes and information from the study!

Formulating Effective Survey Questions

With your goals clearly articulated, writing survey questions becomes much easier. When formulating your questions, I recommend listing your goals and writing up a few questions per goal. Let this be a brain dump, and, at this stage, don't worry about the number of questions until later.

Before translating your goals directly into survey questions, let's review some survey best practices and get comfortable with the most common survey question types.

Best Practices

There are a few ways to optimize your survey questions to get the best information possible. Let's look at how you can write better surveys by ensuring they are delightful for users and allow them to tell you their stories.

Keep It Simple

The average literacy rate is around 5th grade, so use direct language. This means avoiding industry jargon, advanced wording, or unknown abbreviations. If you must use complicated words or abbreviations, include directions or explanations on what they mean. Also, keep the questions short. The fewer words, the more direct and easily understood they will be.

Ask about Past Behavior

The best predictor of future behavior is past behavior, so it is vital to use this method regardless of the type of survey question.

Asking users about the past forces them to answer with what they did, instead of projecting potential future behavior in a given scenario or opinions.

For example:

- Future-based question (that I see way too often): "Would you purchase this gym membership package?"
  - Follow-up question: "Why would you?" OR "Why wouldn't you?"
  - Follow-up question: "What would make you?"
- Past-based question: "In the past, have you ever purchased a gym membership package?
  - Follow-up question: "Why did you purchase?" OR "Why did you not purchase?"
  - Follow-up question: "If you did purchase, did you use the membership package?"
  - Follow-up question: "Why did you?" OR "Why didn't you?"
  - Follow-up question: "What was missing from this membership package?"
  - Follow-up question: "What was a frustrating moment you had with the membership package?" AND "What was a positive experience you had with the membership package?"

The past-based items allow you to understand how a person responded in a scenario. You are allowing them to recall particular memories and explain real-life examples. You are not asking them to extrapolate or simulate future behavior.

People cannot accurately describe their future behavior, and this includes whether or not they will use or buy a product/service.

By seeing how they responded in the past, you can construct a story of how they might act in the future. You can also ask them what was missing from their previous experience to fill in those gaps.

First-Person Questions

First-person questions are cool and always make me smile when I see them on a survey. These replace the standard third-person survey questions with a more personal touch.

For example:

- Third-person question: "What is the hardest part of our check-out process?"
- First-person question: "The hardest part I encountered during the check-out process was…"

Using the first-person question writing technique, you can increase the chances of gathering authentic and personal responses through a survey.

First-person questions are a great technique to turn a survey from an impersonal form to something more comfortable and personable for users to fill out. I now use this technique in most of my survey designs.

Avoid Double-Barreled Questions

Double-barreled questions can be challenging to spot because we naturally ask them in conversations. A question like this includes asking two questions at once, which makes it impossible for a participant to respond appropriately. Go through each item and ensure there is only one answer, and be sure not to include and/or questions. For example:

Double-barreled question: "How do you feel about the information and/or functionality on this website?"

Two separate questions: "How do you feel about the functionality of this website?" AND "How do you feel about the information on this website?"

Leave Out Loaded Questions

Loaded questions make many assumptions about a person's feelings or context. They force the respondent to answer in a way that may be untrue and could cause drop-out or skipping. Avoid these questions by introducing logic to your survey.

For example:

- Loaded question: "Where do you enjoy drinking beer?"
- Unloaded question sequence: "Do you enjoy drinking beer?"; If yes, "Where do you drink beer?" with the follow-up: "Is there a particular place you enjoy drinking beer?" If yes, "Where?"

Give Your Surveys a Mix of Questions

The best surveys I have seen include multiple types of questions. They achieve the delicate balance of closed- and open-ended questions.

It is essential not to write every survey question as an open-ended question and also to include the opportunity for respondents to express themselves. I typically use the rule of 60/40.

For example, your survey might have 70% closed questions and 30% a mix of different open-ended questions. Forty percent may seem like many open-ended questions, but not each is a stand-alone.

Question Types

There are different overall types of survey questions that you can use to get the best information possible. The general buckets I put them into are:

Closed questions. These prompt participants to answer from a fixed number of possible responses. Examples of closed questions include:

- Yes/No questions
- Multiple-choice type questions (radio—only choose one option)

- Multiple-choice type questions (checkbox—select more than one option)
- Rating questions

Open-ended questions. These allow users to respond however they want. Examples of open-ended questions include:

- Stand-alone questions
- Follow-up questions
- The "Other" option on a multiple-choice question

Choosing which one to use depends on the type of data you are trying to get. Here are the advantages of each:
Closed questions:

- Have a higher-response rate
- Are easier to analyze
- Can provide statistical significance
- Can be used to "quantify" qualitative findings

Open questions:

- Can provide insight into "why" users are answering in a specific way
- Allows for responses you may not have expected
- Are much more abundant in qualitative detail
- Gives respondents the chance to express themselves fully

Closed Question Types

Since open-ended questions are a bit more self-explanatory and typically used as a follow-up, let's focus on the different types of closed questions:

Likert scale questions. This type of question is a statement where participants can rate their experience level or agreement. There are two main characteristics of a Likert scale:

- There is an odd number of responses, which allows for a neutral response
- There is a spectrum of feelings on which a user can rate a level of agreement or experience
  - For example: After using the X product, I found the navigation to be [1 (very bad) to 7 (very good)]
- Semantic differential scales. This type of question pairs opposite adjectives at either side of a scale. It helps you understand the emotional attitude of a respondent toward a concept, organization, product, or service. For example:
  - Love → Hate

- Powerful → Weak
- Likely to return → Unlikely to return
- Multiple-choice questions. The most common type of question is where a respondent is presented with a question and has to choose from a predetermined list of questions. For example:
  - How many times did you exercise last week?
    - Zero
    - One
    - Two
    - Three
    - More than three
    - Other

Open Question Types

Open-ended questions

Open-ended survey questions might make people slightly skeptical, and for a good reason.

How often have you zoomed past a "Please let us know if you have any other comments" box on a survey? It's hard to get qualitative data in a survey, but I highly recommend including these questions.

Why are these so important? They can give you a small insight into why people are responding in a particular way to your "closed" survey questions. There are three ways you can incorporate open-ended questions into your surveys:

- A stand-alone question
- Follow-up questions
- An "other" option for each (relevant) question

Then there's the most difficult open-ended question: the stand-alone. This question is completely free from other survey questions and requires users to think and write down their thoughts.

A way to call more attention to and make these questions more appealing is to use the first-person questioning approach. You would turn the above into, "What I am missing from the current gym membership package is…" This approach won't guarantee more answers, but it helps catch people's eyes and make the survey more personal.

Turning Goals Into Questions

Now, let's look at translating research goals into survey questions.

Questions for the Goal of Usability

Every survey question I use regarding usability is already pre-defined, so it can be relatively easy to create a usability-based survey. I break up the questions into three buckets:

1. Effectiveness: Whether a user can accurately complete tasks and an overarching goal
2. Efficiency: How much effort and time it takes for the user to complete tasks and an overarching goal accurately
3. Satisfaction: How comfortable and satisfied a user is with completing the tasks and goal

Effectiveness questions:

- Single Ease Question (SEQ): The SEQ is one question (on a seven-point scale) measuring the participant's perceived task ease. Ask the SEQ after each completed (or failed) task.
- Confidence: Confidence is a seven-point scale that asks users to rate how confident they were that they completed the task successfully.

Efficiency questions:

- Subjective Mental Effort Question (SMEQ): The SMEQ allows the users to rate how mentally tricky a task was to complete.

Satisfaction questions:

- System Usability Scale (SUS): The SUS has become an industry standard and measures the perceived usability of user experience. Because of its popularity, you can reference published statistics (e.g., the average SUS score is 68).
- Usability Metric for User Experience (UMUX/UMUX-Lite). The UMUX has slightly taken over the SUS as an industry standard as it is shorter and easier to administer. It also measures the perception of usability.

Questions for the Goal of Understanding/ Identifying Behavior

How do you purchase board games?

- In-store
- Online
- Other

Logic: Why do you prefer to purchase board games that way? (open text)
With which stores have you purchased board games online?

- Multiple choice with "other" option

How often do you purchase board games online?

- 1–2 times a month
- 3–4 times a month
- 5+ times a month

Why do you purchase board games online?

- Either: Multiple choice with answers from previous research and "other" option OR open text

What is your main goal when visiting an online board game shop?

- Multiple choice with "other" option

Is there anything you look for on an online board game store that is missing?

- Yes
- No

Logic, if yes: what are you looking for?
Have you ever returned a board game you purchased online?

- Yes
- No

Logic, if yes: Why did you return it? (open text)

Questions for Gathering Feelings/Perceptions

Think about a time when you purchased a board game online. How was your experience?

- Scale: Very good, good, neutral, bad, very bad
- Why (open text)

Think about a frustrating experience you had purchasing a board game online. What happened to make that experience frustrating?

- Open text

What is the most difficult part of buying a board game online?

- Either: Multiple choice with answers from previous research and "Other" option OR open text

What do you look for when going to an online board game store?

- Open text

What would make you purchase a board game online?

- Open text

How would you improve the experience of purchasing a board game online?

- Either: Multiple choice with answers from previous research and "Other" option OR open text

What do you like about purchasing board games online?

- Either: Multiple choice with answers from previous research and "other" option OR open text

Questions for Prioritizing Qualitative Data

Whenever it comes to prioritizing qualitative data, I rely on the opportunity gap survey, which uses the following set of questions:

- How important is it to you that you can achieve [outcome/goal/need]?
  - 1–5 scale, 1 = "Not at all important", 5 = "Extremely important"
- When using [current solution], how satisfied are you with your ability to achieve [outcome/goal/need]?
  - 1–5 scale, 1 = "Not at all satisfied", 5 = "Extremely satisfied"

Don't forget that before running an opportunity gap survey, you must conduct generative research to uncover these needs, goals, and outcomes.

Follow-up Questions

Follow-up questions can also be difficult to place correctly in a survey. These tend to come in the form of logic-based questions.

For example: "On a scale of 1–5 (1 = bad, 5 = excellent), how do you feel about your current gym membership package?"

If someone answers with a 1 or 2, we can ask, "Why do you feel that way about your gym membership package?" You could also do this if someone responds very positively with a 5.

Follow-up questions allow the respondent to explain their answer, which is especially helpful for a rating scale.

Finally, always include an "other" option with an open-text field. I have seen many surveys with precise answers to questions, which can be great, but they didn't have a relevant option.

Including an "other" option with an open-text field allows respondents to answer in a way most relevant to them. This also gives you insight into the types of answers you are not aware of that you could include in future surveys.

The Dreaded Sample Size

Surveys

When you are creating a survey to send, you need to look at a few different metrics:

Population Size

How many people are you trying to generalize your findings to? You can segment your users into smaller groups and send them surveys, but know that your conclusions will only apply to that group. It's okay to have a range, not an exact number.

If you are working on a product that doesn't exist, look toward your competitors to estimate population size.

Confidence Intervals/Margin of Error

This concept popped up again! What margin of error do you feel comfortable with? I usually set this to 5% or 10%.

Confidence Level

How confident do you want to be that your findings fall within that certain margin of error? Usually, you see this at 95% or 90% confidence. I usually set this to 80%–85% when dealing with fast-paced product teams but have dipped as low as 70%.

Standard Deviation

Standard deviation looks at the amount of variation in your data. Think of the famous bell curve (normal distribution) in statistics. A low standard deviation means most data points will be close to the mean (the middle), and a high standard deviation means the data will be spread out across the bell curve.

Don't worry too much about this as a safe choice for the standard deviation of a survey is 0.5.

If you are feeling overwhelmed by all of these steps and terms, don't worry. There are plenty of online calculators that can help you step-by-step. Two of my favorites are:

1. Qualtrics
2. Survey Monkey

Let's say I ran a qualitative study on people who travel. In my fifteen 1x1 interviews, I found that traveling for business was less stressful than traveling for leisure. I want to know if this is true across a broader population that uses my app. I would then plug in the above:

- Population size (my user base) is around 50,000 people.
- I want to have a margin of error of 7%.
- I want to be 90% confident of my findings.
- My standard deviation would be 0.5.

If I plug these into a calculator, I would see my ideal sample size is sending the survey to 138 people.

Quantitative Usability Test Surveys

For quantitative usability studies, a common guideline is to aim for around 40 participants to ensure trustworthy predictions about user behavior. If you want to learn more about where this number comes from, check out this detailed article.

Getting Engagement and Responses

I have a researcher's guilt so I often answer surveys when I see them on websites or apps since I know there is a human on the other side counting down the number of responses they need. However, most people ignore surveys, which is why it can be difficult to hit that sample size. Here are some ways you can help up that engagement and response rate:

Engagement

A key factor for engagement is relevance. Ensure that every question feels applicable to the participants. For example, if you're surveying about vintage clothing preferences, tailor questions to the specifics: "Which decade's fashion inspires you the most?" rather than a broad "Do you like vintage clothing?" This specificity makes respondents feel understood and increases their willingness to engage. This can also make for a fantastic screener survey, while avoiding the yes/no question, to see if the participant is relevant for the study.

Survey Length and Fatigue

Survey length directly impacts participant fatigue. I've seen surveys with 30+ questions that stakeholders thought were perfect because of the thoroughness of information. However, if you've ever taken a long survey, you know how exhausting and overwhelming they can be—if you haven't, I recommend trying some because there's no better way to understand participant's experiences than by living them! It's important to find a sweet spot. For instance, instead of asking separate questions about each aspect of a shopping experience (website navigation, checkout process, product range, etc.), use a well-designed matrix question that covers all these aspects succinctly. This approach respects the respondent's time while still collecting comprehensive data.

Personalization

Personalization is difficult but can make a big difference. Whenever possible, I recommended finding ways to add in people's first names. For instance, "John, your thoughts on our latest eco-friendly vintage collection can help us tailor our future offerings to your preferences." Also, consider the timing of your survey; sending it out when your audience is most active online (but not super busy) increases visibility and participation rates.

Ideal Survey Length

The ideal survey length typically ranges from five to ten minutes. This duration strikes a balance between gathering enough data and respecting the respondent's time. Consider the complexity of the topic as well; more involved subjects might warrant a slightly longer survey but be cautious of exceeding the 10-minute mark. Offering a clear indication of the time commitment upfront ("This survey will take approximately 7 minutes") helps set expectations.

Balancing Survey Length and Complexity

Starting with your survey goals as we did above can help you avoid unnecessary questions. Use branching logic to tailor the survey experience; if a respondent indicates they haven't used a particular service, skip the detailed follow-up questions related to that service. Instead of multiple open-ended questions that require lengthy responses, use a mix of rating scales, multiple-choice questions, and limit open-ended questions to those where detailed feedback is crucial.

Conduct a Pilot Test

Pilot testing (or dry run) are critical for literally every single method out there, including surveys. Since messing up several surveys (and other methods too), I quickly learned the importance of pilot testing before engaging with participants. I once sent a survey out to over 500 people with a few incorrect questions. Not only did we have to resend the survey, but we also had to beg people to fill it out all over again. Womp womp.

From that moment, I always conduct a dry run of my surveys, both internally with colleagues and externally with a smaller, representative sample of our audience. Here's how I conduct my survey pilot tests:

- Select a small, diverse sample from your target audience. Use the criteria you identified above to pull together your ideal participants. Pick a small sample of those participants.
- Distribute the survey to this group and ask them to complete it as if they were participating in the actual research.
- Collect feedback on the survey experience. This can be done through follow-up interviews or an additional open-ended question at the end of the pilot survey asking for their thoughts on clarity, length, and any difficulties they encountered.

What to Look For:

- Question Clarity: Are there any questions that were consistently misunderstood or skipped?
- Survey Flow: Is the sequence of questions logical and does it maintain respondent engagement?
- Technical Issues: Look for any technical glitches, such as problems with loading, saving responses, or navigating between questions.
- Time to Complete: Ensure the survey can be completed in a reasonable amount of time. Adjust based on feedback if it's too long.

Incorporating Feedback:

Use the feedback to make necessary revisions to your survey. This might mean rewording confusing questions, adjusting the order of questions for a better flow, fixing any technical issues, and shortening the survey if it takes too long to complete.

For example, suppose you're developing a survey for a new app that connects vintage clothing enthusiasts with local sellers. Your initial pilot test reveals that respondents are unsure about what constitutes "local." Based on this feedback, you revise the question to specify "within a 50-mile radius."

A second pilot test might then reveal that the revised question is clear, but now respondents want an option to define their own radius. Incorporating this feedback leads to a more user-friendly question, enhancing the quality and relevance of the data collected from the survey.

Taking all of this into account helps you develop a survey that not only collects meaningful information given your goals, but can also help you hit that goal sample size more efficiently.

Analyzing the Survey

When I went to analyze my first user research survey, I was unbelievably overwhelmed. Luckily, I had some experience with analyzing surveys in my graduate program, so I applied similar steps to this experience. Over time I've iterated on those steps and made them into a process that reduces that overwhelming feeling. Here are the steps I take when looking at quantitative survey data.

Step 1: Compile Your Data

Gather all your survey responses in one place, typically in a spreadsheet or statistical software. Most survey tools offer the option to export data directly. Since I did a lot of work in start-ups with low budget, I usually exported directly to Google Sheets.

Within my spreadsheets, I typically put columns for each question with rows representing individual responses.

Step 2: Clean Your Data

Before analysis, ensure your data is clean. This means checking for and removing any duplicate responses, incomplete entries, or outliers that don't make sense. For example, you might find that some responses to a numerical question might contain text responses by mistake. Remove or correct them so they make sense.

Step 3: Descriptive Statistics

Start with descriptive statistics to get a general sense of your data. This includes calculating means (averages), medians (middle values), modes (most frequent values), and standard deviations (measure of data spread).

For example, if we bring through the example of vintage clothing, you could calculate the average number of vintage clothing items purchased per year by respondents. Or you can look at the most frequent types of vintage clothing participants buy. This can give you an insight into their habits and behaviors.

Step 4: Analyze Individual Questions

Look at each survey question individually to interpret the responses. I usually do this depending on the question type. For example:

Categorical Data (Multiple Choice, Yes/No, Likert Scale, etc.):

What to Do: For each question, calculate the percentage of respondents who selected each available option. This gives you a clear view of behavior or tendencies within your respondent group.

How to Do It: Count the number of responses for each option and divide by the total number of responses to that question. Multiply by 100 to get a percentage.

Why It's Important: Percentages make it easier to compare the popularity or preference between options, especially when the number of respondents varies.

Numerical Data (Ratings, Scales, Quantities, etc.):

What to Do: Calculate average (mean) values to understand the central tendency of responses. You can also calculate the median and mode for a more comprehensive view.

How to Do It: Add up all the numerical responses for a question and divide by the number of responses to find the average. Use statistical functions or software to find medians (the middle value when all responses are ordered) and modes (the most frequently occurring value).

Why It's Important: Averages provide a snapshot of the overall response trend, while medians and modes can offer insights into the distribution and commonality of responses, respectively.

For example, let's say you've conducted a survey for your online vintage clothing store, and one of the questions asked is, "Which era of vintage clothing do you most purchase?" with options including "1920s," "1950s," "1970s," and "1980s."

Step 1: Compile Responses: Gather all responses to this question.

Step 2: Calculate Percentages:

If out of 100 respondents, 20 chose "1920s," 30 chose "1950s," 40 chose "1970s," and 10 chose "1980s":

- 1920s: $\frac{20}{100} \times 100 = 20\%$
- 1950s: $\frac{30}{100} \times 100 = 30\%$
- 1970s: $\frac{40}{100} \times 100 = 40\%$
- 1980s: $\frac{10}{100} \times 100 = 10\%$

Step 3: Analyze and Interpret:

The data reveals that the "1970s" era is the most purchased among your audience, with 40% of respondents selecting this option. The "1950s" follows, indicating these two eras are particularly popular for your customer base.

Step 4: Cross-tabulation

Cross-tabulation is a tool to help you analyze and compare the relationship between two or more variables by creating a table. With this table, you can see how different categories (or responses) intersect, revealing patterns or trends that might not be obvious from looking at the data separately.

Imagine you've asked your customers two questions: their age group and how often they purchase vintage clothing. The goal is to understand purchasing frequency across different age groups.

With this, you can see that younger shoppers (age 18–34) seem to purchase vintage clothing more frequently than the other age groups, although there seems to still be some interest in the 35–44 age group as well.

Step 5: Analyze Anything Open-Ended

Analyzing open-ended survey questions can be daunting—I know I struggled with this quite a lot and actually avoided using open-ended questions in most of my surveys because I didn't want to go through the analysis of them. Here are some techniques I use now to analyze open-ended data questions:

Thematic Analysis: Thematic analysis involves examining qualitative data (like open-ended survey responses) to identify patterns, ideas, or themes. You categorize the data based on these themes and then analyze the frequency and the context of these themes to gain insights. I write more in-depth on thematic analysis in this article.

For example, you have open-ended responses to a question about why customers like vintage clothing. As you read through responses, you notice recurring mentions of "unique style," "quality of craftsmanship," and "sustainability." You code these mentions under respective themes: Style Uniqueness, Quality, and Sustainability. Upon further analysis, you find that "Style Uniqueness" is a dominant theme across all age groups, indicating a key driving factor for purchasing vintage clothing.

Content Analysis: Content analysis is more structured than thematic analysis and focuses on quantifying the presence of words, themes, or concepts within textual data. This method allows you to systematically categorize text data and draw statistical inferences from it.

For example, in the feedback section of your survey, you ask customers what they look for in vintage clothing. Using content analysis, you might use software to count the frequency of specific words like "authenticity," "era-specific," "condition," and "price." Discovering that "authenticity" and "era-specific" are the most frequently mentioned, you deduce that authenticity and historical accuracy are significant factors in your customers' purchasing decisions.

Comparative Analysis: Comparative analysis involves comparing different segments of your survey data to uncover trends, differences, or similarities. This comparison can be based on demographic factors, behaviors, or responses to different questions.

For example, you decide to compare purchasing frequency between two age groups within your survey respondents: 18–24 and 45–54. You find that the younger age group purchases vintage clothing more frequently, citing fashion and uniqueness as key reasons. In contrast, the older group purchases less frequently but places a higher emphasis on quality and nostalgia. This comparison reveals distinct motivations and needs between the age groups.

Helpful Tools:

It is not always fun (or really, it never is fun) to deal with a lot of open-ended responses, so I always encourage using tools whenever possible. Some that I have used include:

- NVivo: Useful for qualitative data analysis, allowing you to code, sort, and identify patterns in large sets of text data.
- Atlas.ti: Another powerful tool for qualitative analysis, providing robust options for coding and visualizing connections between themes.
- Microsoft Excel or Google Sheets: While more basic, spreadsheets can be incredibly useful for organizing, coding, and performing simple quantitative analysis of open-ended responses.

Step 6: Bring Together the Data to Identify Trends and Patterns

The next step is about bringing your data together so you can see the themes and patterns that your research has surfaced. Here are some approaches to this step:

Combining Data Points

One great place to start is by reviewing the results of your survey at a super high level and looking at how responses to different questions relate to each other and to demographic information.

For example, if your survey included questions about vintage clothing eras, reasons for purchasing, and demographic details like age and location, you could look for correlations. Perhaps younger demographics purchase more recent vintage eras (e.g., 1980s–1990s) for reasons of fashion and uniqueness, while older demographics favor earlier eras (e.g., 1950s–1960s) for quality and nostalgia.

Segment Your Data

Another way to approach trends is to break down your data by demographic groups (e.g., age, location, gender) or by respondents' answers to specific questions (e.g., frequency of purchases, vintage eras).

For example, you could segment your data to compare purchasing behaviors between age groups or to explore how purchasing vintage clothing eras vary by gender.

Look for Correlations

You can also investigate whether there are any correlations between different variables. For instance, you could see if there's a link between the time of the year and the frequency of purchases to identify any seasonal trends in purchase behavior.

Statistical software like SPSS or R can be used to run correlation analyses, but simpler tools like Excel can also provide insights through conditional formatting and pivot charts.

Explore Changes over Time

If you have longitudinal data (data collected at different points in time), from something like a diary study or asking respondents survey questions multiple times, you can compare the results to identify any changes or shifts in behavior and preferences over time.

For example, you might identify that, over time, your audience learns more about vintage clothing and their purchasing patterns change or become more specific.

Step 7: Draw Conclusions and Report

Based on your analysis and your original research goals, it's time to compile your findings into a report or presentation. Again, the most important findings that you can include in your report are the ones that relate back to those original goals you created, and the ones that help the team move forward with any decisions they have to make.

I always structure my survey reports based directly on the goals we originally set up. The report would look something like:

- Research goal one title
- Finding summary, which includes bullet points of the one to three findings relevant to the goal
- Finding one directly related to the research goal
  - Evidence of finding one
- Finding two directly related to the research goal
  - Evidence of finding two
- Finding three directly related to the research goal
  - Evidence of finding three

Tools for Analysis:
I'm definitely not a tools expert, but here are some that I have used the most frequently:

- Excel or Google Sheets: Great for basic analysis and visualizations.
- SPSS or R: More advanced statistical software for in-depth analysis and testing hypotheses.

Ethical Considerations and Accessibility

Once you've started to design your survey, it is absolute necessary to ensure the survey is accessible and inclusive. I am not at all an expert of accessibility and inclusivity, but here are some areas I am very mindful of:

- Use clear and simple language to avoid confusion and misunderstanding.
- Avoid leading questions that could influence participants' responses.

- Ensure your survey is compatible with assistive technologies, such as screen readers, for visually impaired users.
- Include alternative text (alt-text) for visual content to aid screen reader users.
- Test your survey for accessibility using tools like Qualtrics' Check Survey Accessibility feature
- Recruit a diverse range of participants to represent various demographics and perspectives.
- Be aware of unconscious bias and strive for inclusivity throughout the entire process.

Bonus 19
Uncommon Methods

While usability tests and one-on-one interviews are beloved staples in the world of user research, occasionally you may find yourself yearning for fresh perspectives, or grappling with questions these methods can't readily address. In such moments, it's time to explore innovative research approaches.

It's not merely about diary studies or Jobs to be Done; we're delving into lesser-known techniques. These uncharted territories might seem daunting initially, but the insights they yield are well worth the journey. As a researcher, adaptability and flexibility are your greatest assets. So, what are these obscure research methods? Let's take a closer look.

FIDO (FREEHAND INTERACTIVE DESIGN ONLINE)

FIDO, coined by Fidelity, is a participatory design framework. It bridges the gap between conceptual design and prototypes, by involving participants in the creative process. Instead of merely testing prototypes, FIDO allows participants to shape the design themselves.

When to Use FIDO:

- Exploring initial concepts with participants before creating prototypes.
- Understanding participants' perceived needs within a design.
- Uncovering participants' feelings about various design elements (e.g., which components they find useful or confusing).

How to Run a FIDO Session:

1. Select an early-stage concept or design that requires feedback.
2. Break down the concept into its distinct components (e.g., navigation elements, sidebars, search bars).

3. Optionally, include components from competitors to gauge participants' opinions.
4. Transform each component into a notecard or virtual post-it.
5. Create a canvas with a browser window or platform frame, devoid of colors and components.
6. Invite participants for one-on-one sessions and ask them to build their ideal design using the provided elements.
7. After participants complete their designs, engage in discussions about their choices and the reasoning behind them.
8. Analyze the similarities and differences between participants' ideal designs, assess the popularity of each component, and prepare for usability testing to validate the design.

Example of a FIDO Study

Imagine you're designing a travel booking website. You want to ensure that the user interface (UI) elements align with travelers' expectations and preferences. Instead of creating prototypes and conducting traditional usability tests, you decide to employ FIDO.

- Step 1: You choose an early-stage design concept for the hotel booking section of your travel website.
- Step 2: You break down this concept into distinct components, such as the search bar, filter options, map view, and review ratings.
- Step 3: To gain broader insights, you incorporate elements from competing travel websites that your product doesn't currently have.
- Step 4: Each UI component is transformed into a virtual notecard.
- Step 5: In one-on-one sessions with travelers, you ask them to construct their ideal hotel booking page using these UI components.
- Step 6: After participants create their designs, you discuss their choices and the rationale behind their decisions.
- Step 7: Analysis reveals commonalities and differences in participants' ideal hotel booking pages, helping you refine the design for usability testing.

RUN OF POST

The brainchild of Caroline Jarret, the Run of Post study examines off-platform digital communication delivered by your organization to specific user groups over a defined period. This method helps evaluate the coherence and effectiveness of your communication strategies.

When to Use Run of Post:

- Gaining insights into how and what you're communicating to specific user groups.
- Identifying inconsistencies, gaps, or missed opportunities in communication strategies across different teams.

How to Conduct a Run of Post:

1. Choose a specific user group to focus on, rather than attempting to analyze all communication with all users.
2. Determine an appropriate timeframe for analysis (e.g., the past three to six months).
3. Gather all relevant communication materials into a digital platform like Miro or by printing them out.
4. Analyze the content for inconsistencies, narrative gaps, or missed opportunities in communication.
5. Develop a strategy to implement improvements based on your findings, and continue monitoring communication periodically.

Example of a Run of Post Study

Suppose you work for a travel company that communicates with its customers through emails, social media, and blog posts. You want to ensure that your messaging is coherent and effectively serves different customer segments.

- Step 1: You select a particular customer segment, such as adventure travelers interested in hiking trips.
- Step 2: You decide to analyze all communication directed at this segment over the past three months.
- Step 3: Gathering all relevant emails, social media posts, and blog articles in one place, like a Miro board, makes it easier for analysis.
- Step 4: You assess the content for consistency, narrative flow, and any missed opportunities in communication, especially regarding hiking adventure options.
- Step 5: Based on your findings, you develop a strategy to improve communication, ensuring a more streamlined and engaging approach for adventure travelers.

TRUE INTENT STUDY

A true intent study, a form of intercept survey, engages visitors to your product with questions about their experiences, needs, pain points, or goals. It provides quick data on user demographics, goals, and their ability to accomplish tasks, with a focus on multiple-choice questions to maintain respondent engagement.

When to Use a True Intent Study:

- Quickly collecting data on visitor demographics and goals.
- Assessing task accomplishment and suggestions for enhancing the user experience.

How to Run a True Intent Study:

1. Decide on the questions and product areas to focus on (e.g., cart abandonment in a checkout funnel).
2. Keep the survey concise with one to three questions, preferably multiple-choice.
3. Set triggers for survey interception, such as when users attempt to exit the website, hover over specific areas, or after a defined time on a page.
4. Determine the required duration for the survey to gather sufficient responses.
5. Implement the survey on your product, aiming for over 100 responses per intercept.
6. Analyze responses by examining the percentage of users visiting to perform specific tasks, evaluating average user experiences, and identifying commonalities in open-ended responses.

True Intent Study Example

Your travel website attracts visitors from diverse backgrounds and with varying travel goals. To better understand their needs, and how well your site serves them, you decide to implement a true intent study.

- Step 1: You choose specific questions to understand visitors' travel intent. For example, you ask about their main reasons for visiting your site, their current travel goals, and their overall experience.
- Step 2: To maintain engagement, you keep the survey short, consisting of three multiple-choice questions.
- Step 3: You set up the survey to intercept users when they attempt to exit your travel website.
- Step 4: Over two weeks, you collect responses from more than 100 visitors.
- Step 5: Your analysis reveals that a significant portion of visitors is interested in beach vacations and local cultural experiences, while some find it challenging to locate detailed itineraries. Armed with this data, you can tailor your site's content to better meet users' travel goals.

While it's easy to remain tethered to familiar research methods, the vast array of alternative approaches offers untapped potential. The next time your study calls for fresh answers, consider these methods. Remember, practice makes perfect, so conduct a few dry runs to get comfortable with these innovative techniques. Happy researching!

PART SIX

Analysis and Synthesis Breakdown

Demystifying the Synthesis Process 20

WHAT IS THE SYNTHESIS PROCESS IN USER RESEARCH?

My journey into the world of synthesis was marked by a series of trials and errors, driven by the unique challenges of roles where I found myself as a solitary user researcher, lacking the guidance of a dedicated manager. In these circumstances, I learned to rely on experimentation and iterative approaches.

Before I embarked on my first synthesis, I diligently researched the key components involved in the user research synthesis process. While many resources provided theoretical insights, I managed to extract several crucial elements that formed the backbone of synthesis.

- Note-taking and Recording: Capturing essential information during research sessions.
- Transcription: Converting the session into text to code and analyze.
- Coding and Tagging: Organizing data by assigning relevant codes and tags.
- Affinity Diagrams: Creating visual representations of data to identify patterns and connections.
- Patterns and Trends: Recognizing recurring themes or trends within the collected data.
- Writing Actionable Recommendations and Insights: Converting raw data into practical, actionable recommendations for product improvement.

We're going to cover the most important parts of synthesis in the following sections, so that you can feel comfortable and confident when bringing together your data!

HOW DO I TAKE GOOD NOTES?

In my early days as a user researcher, I grappled with the challenge of effectively taking notes during research sessions. It often felt like trying to catch a whirlwind with a butterfly net. Even though my typing speed was fairly impressive, I found myself struggling to keep pace with the participants, especially when they delved into lengthy explanations or captivating narratives. What's worse, my relentless note-taking during the sessions hindered my ability to engage in active listening, which is paramount for building rapport and truly understanding the participant's perspective.

After numerous trials and errors, I eventually decided to revamp my note-taking strategy. I realized that attempting to capture every word spoken during a session wasn't the most efficient approach. Instead, I shifted my focus to a more streamlined method that allowed me to be fully present during the session, while still ensuring that no valuable insights were lost. Here's the evolved approach I adopted.

- Active Listening: During the research session, I devoted my full attention to the participant. I listened attentively, without the constant distraction of frantic note-taking. This change not only improved the quality of my engagement, but also enabled me to ask more insightful follow-up questions based on the participant's responses.
- Minimal In-Session Notes: I restricted my in-session note-taking to jotting down only the most crucial points or specific topics that I wanted to revisit later. This minimalist approach allowed me to maintain a smoother flow of conversation, and avoided overwhelming me with excessive note-taking responsibilities.
- Post-Session Transcription: After the research session concluded, I took a systematic approach to transcribing the conversation. Depending on my available time and resources (read: budget), I either transcribed the session myself into Google Sheets or Docs, used a transcription software, or enlisted the help of a professional transcriber. This step allowed me to generate a comprehensive, accurate record of the interview, and also gave me a great review before I stepped into synthesis.

By adopting this method, I achieved a balance between active participation during the session and meticulous data capture afterward. It allowed me to truly connect with the participants, while also ensuring that no valuable insights slipped through the cracks. This approach not only improved the overall quality of my research, but also enhanced the depth and accuracy of my post-session analysis.

DEMYSTIFYING CODES/TAGS

In the realm of user research synthesis, codes and tags serve as vital tools for organizing and categorizing raw research data. Think of them as the labels you attach to various aspects of your data to turn complex insights into actionable categories. While the terms "codes" and "tags" are often used interchangeably, their primary function remains the same: to facilitate the identification of patterns and trends within your research.

Now that we've clarified their purpose, let's delve into how to choose the right codes or tags effectively. When it comes to code selection, there are essentially two approaches you can take:

- Inductive Method: This method involves diving into your research data first, without preconceived notions of what codes to use. Instead, you allow the codes to emerge naturally from the data as you analyze it.
- Deductive Method: On the other hand, the deductive method entails creating codes before you begin the synthesis process. This approach can provide more structure and direction to your analysis.

For those new to user research synthesis, the deductive method is often a more approachable starting point. Here's a breakdown of how to employ this method.

Global Tags: Start by establishing a set of global tags that can be applied broadly to various user research projects. These tags typically encompass fundamental aspects of user behavior and needs. Some examples of global tags include:

- Goal: What is the user trying to achieve as an outcome?
- Need: What does the user require to fulfill their goal?
- Motivation: Why is the user striving to achieve this particular goal?
- Task: What actions or steps does the user take to reach their goal?
- Pain Point: Are there any barriers or difficulties impeding the user's progress?
- Tools: What tools or resources does the user employ in their pursuit of their goal?

With your global tags in place, review your research data, such as interview transcripts or observation notes, and apply relevant tags to corresponding sections. Here's an example.

Suppose you're conducting research on people's mental models related to post-gym stretching, and you come across these participant statements:

- "I don't have the time to stretch at the gym, and I don't have the equipment at home to stretch properly. This means I just don't do it."
  - Tag: Pain Point (as it represents a barrier to stretching).
- "I'm trying to become more flexible, and stretching is a key part of that."
- Tag: Goal (as it articulates the user's goal of increasing flexibility).
- "I'm in yoga teacher training, so I need to be able to hit certain stretches and poses for my practical test. If I don't stretch after I go to the gym, there is no way I am going to be able to do that."
  - Tag: Motivation (as it reveals the motivation behind the user's actions).

On the other side, the inductive method has you first reviewing the data to understand what types of codes/tags come out of it. In this scenario, imagine you're conducting research to understand the needs and pain points of travelers when booking accommodations online. You'll use tags to categorize and analyze the insights gathered from your research. Here are some examples of tags and how they can be applied.

Tag: Booking Experience: Use this tag to identify insights related to the overall booking process. For example:

- "I found the booking process to be confusing and time-consuming."
- "The website's user interface made it easy to book a room quickly."

Tag: Price Sensitivity: this tag to comments that reflect users' concerns about pricing and affordability:

- "I always look for discounts or deals before booking."
- "Price is the most important factor for me when choosing accommodations."

Tag: Traveler Persona: Use traveler personas as tags to distinguish different user segments and their needs. For instance:

- "As a business traveler, I prioritize proximity to the conference center."
- "As a family traveler, I seek accommodations with child-friendly amenities."

Tag: Review and Rating Influence: Use this tag to identify feedback about the impact of reviews and ratings on booking decisions:

- "I always read reviews before making a reservation."
- "Positive ratings give me confidence in my choice."

Even if you initially opt for the deductive method, you can still adapt and refine your codes based on the data as it unfolds. Over time, as you analyze more transcripts, you'll naturally develop a deeper understanding of recurring themes, which may lead to the creation of additional, more specific tags.

Ultimately, the key to effective code and tag selection is to strike a balance between structure and flexibility, allowing your synthesis process to evolve alongside your research findings.

Running Synthesis Sessions 21

DEBRIEF SESSIONS

User research is a voyage into the minds of your users, providing invaluable perspectives to shape your products. But what happens after those insightful research sessions? That's where the often-underestimated practice of research debriefs comes into play. Let's delve into what research debriefs are, why they are vital, and how to conduct them effectively.

What Is a Research Debrief?

A research debrief is a dedicated session that takes place after a user research session. It's a moment of reflection, knowledge sharing, and collaborative learning. Think of it as a collective download of the invaluable information gathered during the research, condensed into bite-sized insights. Debriefs are hugely valuable for a number of reasons, such as:

- Immediate Reflection: Research debriefs offer an immediate opportunity to reflect on what transpired during a research session. They provide a platform to dissect, analyze, and consolidate the key takeaways while they're still fresh in everyone's minds.
- Team Collaboration: Debriefs are not solo endeavors. They bring together multidisciplinary teams, including designers, developers, product managers, and researchers. This collaboration fosters diverse perspectives and ensures everyone is aligned with the research findings.
- Multiple Perspectives: Each participant in a research debrief offers their unique perspective on the session. This diversity of viewpoints enriches the understanding of the research data, uncovering facets that might have been overlooked individually.

- Highlighting Key Information: Research debriefs help identify and emphasize essential information from each session. They serve as a lens through which you can focus on the most critical insights and findings.
- Mini Synthesis Session: Consider research debriefs as mini synthesis sessions. They set the stage for more comprehensive synthesis later in the research project, streamlining the process and making it more effective.
- Efficiency: Debriefs significantly contribute to research efficiency. They make the synthesis session shorter and more focused by providing a structured foundation of insights to build upon.
- Enhanced Engagement: Debriefs engage teams more deeply with the research. Team members begin discussing findings between sessions, elevating the importance of user research throughout the organization.

Running a Research Debrief

Before the Debrief:

1. Select Participants: Decide who should attend the debrief. Stakeholders, who observed the research session, especially those directly involved in the project, should be present.
2. Define Discussion Points: Determine what aspects you want to cover in the debrief. Common discussion points include pain points, goals, needs, surprises, lingering questions, key quotes, and overall takeaways. Select three to four topics to keep the debrief focused.
3. Timeboxing: Assign time limits for each discussion point. For instance, allocate 5 minutes for individual brainstorming and 5 minutes for group discussion.
4. Create a Visual Board: Prepare a visual template for the debrief. Whether it's a whiteboard, Miro board, Jamboard, Trello, or Mural, ensure it's structured yet flexible. Create a board for each participant.
5. Include a "Parking Lot": Designate a section for the "parking lot" on the board. This is where ideas or insights that don't fit neatly into the predetermined topics can be placed for later discussion.

During the Debrief:

1. Explain Each Section/Point: Start by explaining each section or discussion point. Make sure all participants understand the terminology and purpose behind each category.
2. Time Management: Follow your timeboxes for each section. Encourage participants to brainstorm independently before discussing as a group. Pay close attention to the timer to maintain efficiency.
3. Handling Questions: Divert questions about the debrief process itself to the "parking lot" or address them after the session. This ensures the debrief remains focused on insights rather than procedural matters.

After the Debrief:

1. Share the Board: Ensure that all participants, even those who couldn't attend the session, have access to the debrief board. This enables a comprehensive review of insights and encourages ongoing engagement.
2. Bring Insights to Synthesis: The debrief board becomes a valuable asset in the later, more extensive synthesis session. It offers a clear snapshot of key insights and helps team members understand the research findings quickly.
3. Feedback Loop: Always seek feedback from stakeholders regarding the effectiveness of the debrief. Adapt and refine the process based on their input to ensure it continues to add value.

In the realm of user research, where every insight counts, research debriefs emerge as a powerful tool to unlock the potential of your research data. By fostering reflection, collaboration, and immediate learning, these sessions ensure that the voices of your users resonate throughout your organization, ultimately shaping user-centric products and services.

An Example Debrief

Imagine you're conducting a 60-minute research study on user experiences with a travel itinerary planning app. Your dedicated team comprises a UX designer, a product manager, and three developers, all deeply invested in the project's success. You've decided to hold a 30-minute debrief session after each research interview.

Before the Debrief

1. Invite the right participants

In this context, it's essential to invite all stakeholders directly involved in the project. Their diverse perspectives will be invaluable during the debrief. This can include colleagues such as:

- Product managers.
- Designers.
- Developers.
- Marketing.
- Account management.
- Customer support.

2. Define discussion points

For this debrief, select a few key discussion points. Given the complexity of travel research, focus on pain points, surprises, and key takeaways. Additionally, create a designated section for a "parking lot" to capture any stray insights or questions.

3. Timeboxing

Efficiency is key. Allocate 5 minutes for brainstorming each section and 3 minutes for discussion. This balanced approach allows for meaningful contributions within the allocated time.

4. Create a collaborative board

Since you're working remotely, a tool like Miro offers an ideal platform for collaborative debriefing. Create a board for all participants, ensuring everyone has access and the ability to contribute. The built-in timer feature in Miro can be particularly handy.

5. Utilize the calendar trick

To maximize attendance, employ the +30-minute calendar invite trick. Extend the meeting duration to include the 30-minute debrief. For example:

- Opening questions: 10:00 am to 10:15 am.
- Prototype 1: 10:15 am to 10:35 am.
- Prototype 2: 10:35 am to 10:55 am.
- Wrap-up: 10:55 am to 11:00 am.
- Debrief: 11:00 am to 11:30 am.

During the Debrief

1. Explain each section/point

Initiate the debrief by providing a brief explanation of each section or discussion point. Dedicate 1–2 minutes for this introduction, allowing for clarifying questions.

- Pain Points: Instances where users encountered difficulties, confusion, or expressed disappointment during their travel planning.
- Surprises: Moments that challenged assumptions, altered perspectives, or introduced unexpected insights.
- Key Takeaways: High-impact findings that hold significant relevance for the travel app project.
- Parking Lot: A repository for ideas or insights that don't neatly fit into the predefined categories, including lingering questions.

2. Time management

Adhere to the time schedule diligently:

- Intro and explanation: 2 minutes.
- Pain points—brainstorm: 5 minutes; discussion: 3 minutes.

- Surprises—brainstorm: 5 minutes; discussion: 3 minutes.
- Key takeaways—brainstorm: 5 minutes; discussion: 3 minutes.
- Wrap-up and other points: 4 minutes.

During the brainstorming phase, group similar ideas together to identify emerging trends and patterns.

In the realm of user research, where every insight counts, research debriefs emerge as a powerful tool to unlock the potential of your research data. By fostering reflection, collaboration, and immediate learning, these sessions ensure that not only your stakeholders take action on your research, but it also reduces the huge cognitive load of long, arduous synthesis sessions at the end of a project.

WHAT IS AFFINITY DIAGRAMMING?

An affinity diagram is an invaluable tool for user researchers, allowing you to make sense of large amounts of qualitative data by grouping related information. These are perfect for making sense of the mess of qualitative data because they are all about bundling and grouping similar information.

Affinity diagrams give you a way to filter through all your qualitative data, and see what patterns and trends emerge. They provide a visual framework for making connections between different pieces of information, allowing researchers to identify common themes, trends, and insights. In essence, it's like assembling a jigsaw puzzle from the myriad of user comments, observations, and feedback.

Affinity diagramming is a hugely important step in your synthesis process as it brings a lot to the table.

- Clear Structure: Qualitative data from user research can be chaotic. Affinity diagramming brings order to this chaos by creating a clear structure. It allows researchers to see the big picture while not losing sight of the crucial details.
- Identifying Patterns: Human behavior is full of patterns, and user research is no exception. Affinity diagramming helps researchers spot recurring themes and trends within the data. This, in turn, aids in understanding user needs, preferences, and pain points.
- Actionable Insights: Affinity diagrams don't just highlight patterns; they help turn insights into actionable recommendations. By identifying what matters most to users, researchers can provide valuable guidance to product development teams.
- Collaboration: It's often a team effort to interpret user research data. Affinity diagramming allows researchers to collaborate effectively with colleagues, stakeholders, and designers. It fosters a shared understanding of user needs, leading to better decision-making.
- Data-Driven Design: In the world of user-centered design, decisions should be rooted in data. Affinity diagramming bridges the gap between raw data

and design decisions. It ensures that every design choice is grounded in real user insights.
- Efficiency: Without a structured approach like affinity diagramming, analyzing qualitative data can be time-consuming. This method streamlines the process, enabling researchers to reach meaningful conclusions faster.

Let's dive deeper into how you can effectively use affinity diagramming with concrete examples related to travel.

1. Gather and Review Qualitative Data

As a user researcher in the travel industry, you've conducted interviews and gathered insights from travelers. These insights cover various aspects of the travel experience, such as needs, pain points, and goals.

Depending on the type of data you are collecting, you might review things like notes, session recordings, transcriptions, or debriefs.

2. Identify Common Themes

Start by identifying common themes or topics within your data. For instance, your qualitative data might include comments from travelers about their travel goals, challenges, and needs.

3. Create Categories or Clusters

Organize your notes into clusters around these common themes or categories. In the context of travel research, you might have clusters like:

- Travel Goals: Statements from travelers about their travel objectives, such as exploring new cultures or relaxation.
- Challenges: Insights related to common travel challenges like flight delays, accommodation issues, or language barriers.
- Travel needs: Comments on travel needs, accommodation types, or pricing.

4. Refine Subgroups

Within each category, further refine the subgroups based on similarities. For example, under the "Travel Goals" category, you might have subgroups like:

- Exploring New Cultures.
- Relaxation and Stress Relief.
- Adventure and Outdoor Activities.

5. Visualize the Affinity Diagram

Create a visual representation of the affinity diagram, either using digital tools, like Miro or MURAL, or post-its. Place your categorized notes or insights within each cluster or subgroup.

Typically, I recommend picking four different quadrants to fill out, so that you don't get too overwhelmed with data. You can choose any four areas, such as needs, pain points, goals, tasks, motivations, etc. You can also include a "parking lot" for anything that doesn't fit into the four quadrants but still feels important.

6. Identify Patterns and Insights

With the affinity diagram in place, you can now bring your notes and transcriptions to life through post-it notes. I start with first filling out a quadrant for each participant. Then, once I finish each individual participant, I bring together the information from each participant and quadrant into a larger board to identify patterns and trends.

Usually, I define patterns or trends by the sample size. I typically think of a trend if 1/3 (round up) of the total sample size said something similar. So, for seven participants, if three or more said they had a need for relaxation on a holiday, I would categorize that as a pattern. If I spoke to 15, I would consider a pattern after 5 people said the same thing.

This isn't an exact science, and there can be exceptions, so you don't need to use this as a hard-and-fast rule. For example, one-off insights can be compelling. As you advance in your process, you will better judge patterns and trends, but the 1/3 rule is a nice place to start.

7. Bring in Stakeholders

Affinity diagramming can be done individually or in collaboration with stakeholders. In a team setting, bring your colleagues into the process to collectively brainstorm solutions based on the identified patterns. This is especially helpful in educating stakeholders on research, as well as bringing them along the journey of the user. It also ensures a less biased approach to synthesis, when you have multiple perspectives in the room.

By using affinity diagramming, you can efficiently organize and analyze qualitative data, uncover valuable insights, and drive informed decision-making to enhance experiences for your users.

LIGHTNING SYNTHESIS

There often comes a point when you have to accelerate your synthesis process without compromising data quality. This is where the concept of lightning synthesis comes into play, a strategic approach to expedite synthesis while maintaining research integrity. In this comprehensive guide, we'll delve into the details of lightning synthesis, using a travel-related example.

Imagine you find yourself inundated with research requests, your colleagues clamoring for expedited synthesis. You're aware that your meticulous synthesis process, designed to yield comprehensive insights, is time-consuming and may not always align with project timelines. Enter "lightning synthesis."

What Is Lightning Synthesis?

Lightning synthesis is a method that streamlines the synthesis process without sacrificing data quality. To develop this approach, we scrutinize each step of the synthesis process to identify opportunities for acceleration, while maintaining the rigor of analysis. Below, we outline a typical user research synthesis process when time allows.

- Record the Session: Capture the research session.
- Take Small Notes during the Session: Jot down key points during the interview.
- Conduct a 30-Minute Debrief: Immediately after the session, engage in a concise debrief.
- Transcribe the Session: Transcribe the session within 24 hours (approximately 1–2 hours).
- Tag the Transcript: Apply relevant tags to the transcript (about 30–60 minutes).
- Write a Summary or Snapshot of the Session: Generate a summary or snapshot of the session (generally 1 hour).
- Repeat for All Remaining Sessions: Apply the above process to all sessions.
- Hold a Half- or Full-Day Synthesis Workshop: Devote 4–8 hours to a synthesis workshop.
- Conduct Post-Synthesis That Didn't Get Done in the Synthesis Workshop: Allocate one to two days for additional post-synthesis activities.
- Create the Report: Dedicate three days to crafting the final report.

While this comprehensive process yields thorough results, it demands more than double the time investment compared to the interview sessions themselves. In a fast-paced environment, this extended timeline may not align with stakeholder expectations. This is where lightning synthesis comes into play, enabling you to meet tighter deadlines while still delivering valuable insights.

The Lightning Synthesis Approach

Lightning synthesis significantly streamlines the synthesis process, with fewer steps and less time required. Let's break down each phase.
Gather the Data: Begin by collecting data from participants. Depending on your resources, you can choose from three approaches:

1. Automatic and immediate transcription (most efficient).
2. Stakeholders attending sessions and taking notes (moderate effort).
3. Self-transcription of sessions (highest effort).

To optimize efficiency, aim for automatic transcription, or educate colleagues on effective note-taking resembling a transcript.

Create/Choose Lean Global Tags: Utilize global tags as part of the lightning synthesis process. These are broad tags that apply across projects, facilitating pattern recognition. Common global tags include:

- Goal: What participants aim to achieve as an outcome.
- Need: The prerequisites necessary to fulfill a goal (typically areas of uncertainty).
- Pain Point: Barriers or challenges hindering goal attainment.
- Tools: The tools participants employ to achieve their goals.
- Quick Fix: Immediate issues or annoyances that the team can swiftly address.

Tag Each Participant through Affinity Diagrams: After each session, allocate 35 minutes for affinity diagramming using the global tags. This phase is the core of lightning synthesis and harmonizes the entire process. Here is a sample agenda for one participant:

- Goals Brainstorm: 3 minutes.
- Goals Discussion: 3 minutes.
- Needs Brainstorm: 3 minutes.
- Needs Discussion: 3 minutes.
- Pain Points Brainstorm: 3 minutes.
- Pain Points Discussion: 3 minutes.
- Quick Fixes Brainstorm: 3 minutes.
- Quick Fixes Discussion: 3 minutes.
- Identifying Patterns: 5 minutes.
- Insights + Next Steps: 5 minutes.

Participants individually brainstorm ideas for each tag within a 3-minute time frame, followed by a 3-minute discussion to consolidate similar concepts. This rapid but focused approach optimizes efficiency.

1. Look for Patterns: Begin identifying patterns within the same tagging session. While this step may not be applicable for the first few participants, patterns often emerge after three or more interviews.
2. Write Insights: As patterns become apparent, start crafting insights. Insights are profound observations about human behavior that challenge assumptions and unveil underlying motivations.
3. Assign Next Steps: Dedicate any remaining time to establishing action items based on your insights.

Repeat this process for each participant, and by the study's end, you'll already have valuable insights in the chosen report format. While not suitable for all research projects, lightning synthesis proves invaluable when time constraints demand accelerated results. It empowers you to deliver actionable insights within challenging timelines. Balancing speed and quality, this approach ensures your research remains relevant and impactful in the ever-evolving travel industry.

An Analysis and Synthesis Process for Generative Research

22

I quickly learned that synthesis processes can look different depending on the organization and resources you have at your disposal. As a team of one who worked at low-budget start-ups and typically did research in a vacuum, my synthesis process looked like:

Step 0: Record each research session (audio or video is fine). If you cannot record, beg someone to come in and take notes for you. If no one can, apologize profusely to the participant and say that you must take notes if you can't audio record the session.

Step 1: Review each interview within 24 hours of the session. During this time, I essentially write a transcript of the interview in Excel.

Step 2: Highlight important notes or quotes. I will then timestamp these to make video/audio clips for presentations or reports easily later on.

Step 3: Create a research summary based on that individual participant

Step 4. Define the codes for the project, either through inductive or deductive methods.

Step 5: Go through each line, noting any relevant tags—not every transcript line will have a tag. Do this across all the different transcripts.

Step 6: Combine the codes/tags across the participants using an affinity diagram.

Step 7: Find the patterns that come up the most frequently across participants.

Step 8: Write insights based on the most common patterns that come up during synthesis to send and present to the team and follow up with an activation/ideation workshop.

I know there are a lot of steps in this process, and sometimes, it can feel like synthesis might take forever, but once you get more comfortable and confident with it, you will get into a good routine. Plus, there are some ways to save time, such as during code creation or by running debrief sessions after each interview.

To illustrate each step better, I will use an example from my previous experience working as a user researcher at a travel company called fromAtoB. This was a ticketing company where you could input your starting location and destination, and we would show you a combination of methods (e.g., car, bus, train, plane) to get to your destination.

I don't have the research plan anymore from this particular study, but I will outline what we were trying to achieve through this project:

Background

With generative research, we are looking to more deeply understand how our users think about making travel decisions (from inspiration to planning to booking) and how they interact, at a high level, with the fromAtoB product.

Goals

Understand how people make decisions for leisure travel, from inspiration to planning to booking, and their mental models during this process.
Discover peoples' pain points while planning leisure travel.
Uncover peoples' needs and goals that emerge when planning leisure travel.

Identify how people are currently interacting with the fromAtoB website/app based on UL1 last booking experience for leisure travel.

Methodology

Twenty-five one-on-one 90-minute interviews—for the first 60 minutes, focusing on goals one, two and three, and for the last 30 minutes, diving into the last booking experience on fromAtoB.

STEP 0: RECORD THE SESSION

My first step, beyond any other, is to record the interview in any way possible—whether that be video or audio, on your computer or through your phone (with permission, of course). Recording the session enables you to focus on the participant fully and helps reduce "busy bias," which can happen when you are trying to split your focus and write down an interpretation rather than what a participant really said.

If, for whatever reason, you can't record, ask someone to come with you so that they can take down a transcript of the interview. Notice I said transcript and not notes. Taking truly unbiased notes is difficult as we naturally put our spin and perspective on what people say/do, so simply writing a transcript is much easier.

Resources

Consent form

STEP 1: REVIEW EACH INTERVIEW

After each session, and ideally within 24 hours, I review the interview recording and type up a transcript. I typically do this for two reasons:

- No one else will do it for me (e.g., I don't have a transcriber or access to a transcription service).
- It helps me remember the smaller parts of the interview that I might have missed or misinterpreted.

So, what does this look like? I listen to the entire interview and type up the transcript using Excel. I use Excel because it is what I learned, but you can also use Word if you feel more comfortable typing in that. The whole point is writing a transcript.

I wish I could explain when exactly I make line breaks in Excel, but it isn't an exact science—usually, it is when I feel there is a new idea or sometimes a new thought, but that's not always consistent. What matters more here is that I am writing a transcript of the session and not interpreting what the person is saying but writing what they said. I usually use the first person ("I did this"), but you can sometimes see when I flip to the third person ("She said she books the best class").

There is nothing strategic about this. It is merely the fact that I am typing quickly and can sometimes make mistakes. Again, what matters is that I am relaying exactly what the person said or did rather than interpreting it.

I recommend one of two things:

- Hire someone or get access to a tool that does this for you if you have the resources available.
- Try out a few different ways to do this until you find one that feels good for you. My preferred method is Excel, but yours might be Word, Evernote, or something else. Just see what fits best.

And, if you are really tight on time, or you find this part particularly painful, you can opt to hold a debrief session instead. I typically do a debrief in addition to writing the transcript because I find it refreshes my memory very well, but I know it isn't always realistic.

A research debrief is the time you take after a session to reflect on it and encourage deep learning and complex connections.

Think of it as downloading all the information you just learned without writing the transcript. The debrief is a perfect time to reflect on what just happened during the session and bring many minds together. You can do this by holding a 30-minute debrief after each interview session.

STEP 2: HIGHLIGHT IMPORTANT NOTES OR QUOTES

I tend to do this in parallel with step one because the two work together very well. If I find a particularly interesting quote or clip of the session while I am transcribing the interview, I usually highlight it and put the timestamp in another column in Excel. This makes it super easy whenever I try to find impactful quotes or when creating video clips.

What does important mean? Typically, to me, this is a piece of information/quote/clip that directly relates to the goals of the research that I feel could help the team:

Understand users more deeply
Sympathize/empathize with people
Make a decision

Again, there is no right way to determine importance, which can vary depending on the project. It's about using your intuition as a researcher and getting comfortable understanding what your team needs from you.

STEP 3: CREATE A RESEARCH SUMMARY

The next part of the process goes one step further in analyzing and synthesizing each interview. After I review the recording, I create a research summary for each participant. I love research summaries because:

They're a nice snapshot of the essential information.

You can start to thread patterns/themes from a variety of sessions to see the most impactful information.

- They allow teams to digest the sessions through words and media efficiently.
- You can include actionable next steps and recommendations based on insights.
- They are customizable for your audience.
- You can digitize them with tags for improved "findability."

The way I see a summary is that it includes the most important and relevant information from the interview, typically based on the goals of your study. Of course, you can't include everything in a summary because then it would no longer be a summary. So, try to focus on the most important stuff you heard when reviewing the recording. For instance, if one of the project's goals is to uncover pain points, that could be a great thing to include in your research summary.

Here is the type of information I include each time:

A small description of the person you spoke to (e.g., what segment or persona that person belongs to and the percentage of customers they represent)

- What teams/squads/tribes would get the most from this summary.
- A brief background of the project to give context to the goals were.
- Notable (and verbatim) quotes that represent the user and help teams make decisions.
- Insights and themes within the session and across any previous sessions.
- Recommendations based on the insights:
  - Video on audio clips that allow people to see/hear the quote or insight. When dealing with usability testing, screenshots with annotations and video clips are essential.
  - Links to any additional documentation the team would find helpful to dig deeper.

Each of these research summaries really helps me with my synthesis process because I am able to better remember each individual participant and the small details or nuances I could have easily missed. Additionally, these summaries tend to be very popular with teams because they provide the most critical information and can keep people excited about research throughout a longer generative study.

STEP 4: DEFINE CODES/TAGS

I will use the words codes and tags interchangeably in this section and the remainder of the article. I view them as one in the same.

Now we get to the slightly more difficult and mysterious part of the synthesis process, which is defining codes for your project. Codes are the basis of synthesis, they are the way you decide to organize information for your project. With this definition, they can feel very overwhelming to create.

There are two ways to make codes:

1. Inductive method: With the inductive method, you don't create any codes until you have gone through some data. You then find the codes in your data.
2. Deductive method: You come up with codes before you synthesize your data.

I typically employ a deductive method, and I recommend starting with this. I use global tags in a lot of my research synthesis, even exploratory synthesis. The global tags I use are:

- Goal: What the person is trying to accomplish as an outcome.
- Need: Something a person needs to fulfill a goal.
- Motivation: Why the person is trying to achieve that goal.
- Task: Something a person does to achieve a goal.
- Pain point: A barrier or difficulty toward accomplishing a goal.
- Tools: A tool a person uses to try to accomplish a goal.

I like using global tags because, to be honest, it makes the synthesis process go faster and, usually, I am the only one doing the synthesis. So, I opt for global tags. Additionally, they are typically very relevant for generative, qualitative research because you are trying to discover peoples' goals, needs, and pain points.

If you want to, you can also use your goals to help you define some tags for your project. For example, the original goals from the project were:

- Understand how people make decisions for leisure travel, from inspiration to planning to booking, and their mental models during this process.
- Discover peoples' pain points while planning leisure travel.
- Uncover peoples' needs and goals that emerge when planning leisure travel.
- Identify how people are currently interacting with the fromAtoB website/app based on their last booking experience for leisure travel.
- In addition to my global tags, which would cover pain points, needs, and goals, I could have also used the following tags:
  - Decision-making.
  - Inspiration.
  - Mental model.
  - Interaction.
  - Experience.

The reason I really like using goals to create tags is because the goals are the center of a project—they are literally the information you need to get for your stakeholders to complete the project successfully. So, when you tag using your goals, you make it easier to surface the relevant information for your goals.

As I mentioned, for this particular project, I used the following global tags:

- Pain points.
- Needs.
- Goals.
- Motivations.
- UX/UI.

Again, I did this because I was synthesizing an incredible amount of data alone and the global tags fit what I needed in this situation. Again, if you'd like to use the inductive method, you review your data and then create codes based on the information you are reading. As a quick example, let's say that we heard many times over that people were concerned about price changes when looking to purchase tickets.

For the deductive method, using global tags, I would tag this as a pain point. However, if I was going the inductive route, I could create the tag "price changes."

I recommend, over time, getting comfortable with both approaches.

STEP 5: CODE/TAG THE DATA

In this step, I look through my transcripts I created in Excel and tag the relevant data with the codes I came up with (either deductive or inductive).

Not every line of the transcript will have a tag. Sometimes things people say don't have any relevancy to your codes. But, as you can see below, I go through and tag any relevant data with the corresponding code.

Sometimes a line will have two codes, that is okay. People are layered and complex so we can't expect everything they say to come out and fit neatly into one box. For example, the line:

> For the return, I don't like early morning, it is stressful, went out the previous day, get up, so I booked it based on the fact that I prefer the afternoon, around 1pm, so I prefer that because then you wake up and have some time to walk around the city if you want to.

When I read this, I see both a pain point and a motivation. Early mornings, especially when going out the previous day/night are a pain point to deal with. Additionally, the fact that this person likes to walk around before they leave can lend it to a motivation of why they pick an afternoon departure.

It took me some time to understand what pieces of data corresponded to what codes, and it's okay if you aren't one hundred percent sure all the time if a piece of data is a goal, need, or a motivation.

Tagging takes time and practice. Some of the files from above include tags as well in the transcript. And, if you'd like to practice, you can use my other notes from these sessions to tag them. All you have to do is follow this link and make a copy of the files so you can edit them and practice your tagging.

I wish there was an easier way to explain exactly how to know what each piece of data means and how exactly to tag it, but it really does come with experience and practice. As time goes by, you will feel more comfortable with this part of the process. I recommend starting with and getting confident in global tags and then moving on to creating your own!

STEP 6: COMBINE THE DATA THROUGH AFFINITY DIAGRAMMING

Once you go through all of the individual transcripts and tag the data, it is time for the magic to happen and to bring together the different participants into one view. The entire point of synthesis is to be able to see the patterns across people you spoke to and this step enables you to do just that.

Before Diving into This Step, Let's Define Affinity Diagrams

An affinity diagram is a visual brainstorming tool that allows you to organize large amounts of data into groups or themes based on their relationships. They are perfect for making sense of qualitative data because they are all about bundling and grouping similar information.

Affinity diagrams give you a way to filter through your qualitative data and see what patterns and trends emerge. During this exercise, you use the codes/tags you defined in the previous step. You choose four to six of the tags you defined and split them up into headers. You can do this in Excel or a tool like Miro.

Now, there are two steps within this process, the first one being optional and depending on if you ran a debrief session rather than tagging your transcript. Here are the two steps:

(Optional) Create an affinity diagram for each individual participant. If you held debrief sessions, you will already have an affinity diagram for each participant. In this diagram, you will have filled out the empty board by putting in the data under the relevant code. If you coded your transcript, you can fill out an individual board for each participant or you can skip this step and add each participant into a larger board.

Bring together all the participants' data. Regardless of if you have individual boards or not, this step is all about bringing the data together from each participant into a larger board to see the patterns and trends. If you go straight to a larger board, you fill it out by taking each participant's relevant sticky note and putting it into the board.

Once you start to put the different participant's data points together, you will begin to see similarities across what they have said.

I always recommend putting the participant number on each sticky or choosing different colors for participants so you remember which participant originally said what.

STEP 7: FIND THE PATTERNS

So, you have a large board filled with a bunch of participants data. Now it is time to look at each section and bring the similar pieces of data together across the participants.

That is something I did badly in my above Excel example because, within that example, I don't give any weight to how many people encountered or mentioned a given pain point, need, goal, motivation, or UX/UI issue.

You bring together similar things that different participants mentioned and form clusters of this related information. I tend to go category by category. So, for example, I start with looking at all the data I've collected about needs and form clusters within the needs. Then I move on to goals, then pain points, etc. Let me give a few examples of what that looked like in my project.

Under pain points, we had people talking about:

- Concern about prices raising if they search a destination too many times (about 22/25).
- No alerts when a ticket price drops (13/25 participants).
- No filters or preferences can be set for the search and they reset every time (17/25 participants).

For goals:

- Finding a way to get to a destination both quickly and on a budget (20/25 participants).
- Finding an eco-friendly travel option (14/25 participants).

For needs:

- Being able to compare different days/prices (21/25 participants).
- Confirming a schedule with friends and family (16/25 participants).

For motivations:

- Pushing off planning as much as possible because travel is stressful and they don't want to spend money (17/25 participants).
- Finding a comfortable and budget-friendly way of travel that is still safe (11/25 participants).

Of course, there were a lot more data points, which you can see in the Excel sheet, but I wanted to highlight how many people said each—this is something I should have done on the Excel sheet to indicate the weight of each data point. With a tool like Miro, this is less of a problem because you can see the number of sticky notes per cluster.

In this step, you bring together the similar information across participants within each code/tag and then cluster them. Within this cluster, I always name it something relevant, so, for example:

- Concern about prices raising if they search a destination too many times (about 22/25) → Cluster name: Price changes.
- Being able to compare different days/prices (21/25 participants) → Cluster name: Search comparison.

- Finding a comfortable and budget-friendly way of travel that is still safe (11/25 participants) → Cluster name: Safety.

Your cluster names will make it easier for you to quickly scan the data and find what you need—they don't have to be perfectly encapsulating of everything within the cluster.

The clusters with the most weight (the most participants that mentioned the topic) become your most important patterns and trends. Usually, I define patterns or trends by the sample size. I typically think of a trend if 1/3 (round up) of the total sample size said something similar.

So, for seven participants, if three or more said they had a fear of aging and getting stiff, I would categorize that as a pattern. If I spoke to 15, I would consider a pattern after five people said the same thing.

Now, this isn't an exact science, and there can be exceptions, so you don't need to use this as a hard-and-fast rule. For example, one-off insights can be compelling. As you advance in your process, you will better judge patterns and trends, but the 1/3 rule is a nice place to start.

If you are looking to practice, you can take the sheets from above for tagging practice and use my synthesis board template to move the data over and try clustering.

Additionally, if you are looking for even more advanced practice with a very generative research project, check out my planning to execution course where you get access to real data that you can practice with!

Just like everything else, affinity diagramming takes time and practice until you will feel comfortable and that it comes more naturally. I bumbled around with affinity diagrams until I found what worked best for me, so just be open and practice!

STEP 8: INSIGHTS AND ACTIVATION

The next step is to take the most weighted data points and write insights that you can share with your team. With those, you then pick the most important one to three insights and run an ideation workshop to help the team take the data from a more abstract problem-space to a solution, which you can then test and evaluate, either through concept testing or usability testing.

Writing Insights and Recommendations

23

INSIGHT WRITING

User research is a support system. With that support, we help our teams:

- mitigate risky decisions;
- highlight the most important pain points and unmet needs;
- narrow the scope of possible solutions for a problem or unmet need;
- make more user-centric decisions;
- generate empathy and curiosity toward users.

If you think about your user research as a product, those are the goals you try to achieve with your research studies. You are attempting to help teams make less risky, more user-centric decisions, and also alleviate the pain point of trying to create meaningful products without a user's perspective.

Our research is meant to boost our teams, empower them, and enable them to make the best decisions they can, given the information in front of them. This is the crux of user research and one of the most important parts of our job.

Earlier in my career, I struggled so much with writing insights. I spent more hours Googling what insights were than writing them (and trust me, I spent many, many hours writing insights). They were an enigma, something that was meant to be magical, motivating, realistic, relevant, and concise.

It seemed nothing I wrote could come close to what everyone called an "actionable insight" (I hate the word actionable, by the way, because it is just such a vague word I tripped over for years). Yet, I also couldn't find any concrete examples of insights, seeing as most of them are kept locked away and confidential. The only real examples I found were ones I didn't want to replicate. And while it's helpful to know what not to do, it doesn't fully guide you in best practices.

Similar to my first personas and journey maps, my insights fell flat. They didn't inspire great action and help teams make better decisions. They kind of just relayed the facts of the situation with subjective, vague language. And, repeatedly, I was disappointed in my work. I felt like I wasn't reaching the full potential of my role, and doing what user researchers are meant to. After some time, I decided to dive deeper into user research insights and create something that felt good for me, and that helped my teams in all the ways I strived to.

WHAT IS A USER RESEARCH INSIGHT?

Because it's more interesting and fun, let's start with defining all the things that a user research insight isn't. There are a lot of terms floating out there that seem to get lumped together or used interchangeably with the word insight. Let's take a closer look at these words and what they mean, independent of the word "insight."

1. An observation. An observation, on its own, is not an insight because it cannot tell us why a person is acting in that way. It is simply something you observed happen without additional context surrounding it.
2. Quantitative data trends. Data trends tell you a lot about what actions users are taking on a product, and can also highlight important trends in behaviors, as well as. However, quantitative data doesn't help explain why something is happening.
3. A fact. When we simply state a fact, such as, "Users have a lot to juggle at their jobs" or, "Participant one has poor eyesight," we aren't doing any justice to our projects. Facts are often well-known and lack a high degree of context, and that context is hugely important to insights.
4. A bug. Something being wrong with the product isn't an insight, but rather a bug that needs to be fixed. A bug is very product-centric, which is different from insights.
5. A finding. If you have information that will solve something today, but won't have a significant impact in the future, that is most likely a finding, not an insight. A finding typically doesn't have a big consequence (we will get to define that word later) and is more on the shallow side. You typically have a lot of findings in evaluative research, such as usability tests.
6. A preference or wish. When a participant says, "I would love this feature…" you can't use this as an insight. Dig deeper into why they want the particular feature to understand the outcome they desire. This outcome is the underlying motivation, and is much more valuable (and closer to an insight) than a feature wish.
7. An opinion. Opinions are trickier than the above. When a participant expresses their opinion on something, that isn't necessarily an insight. If a participant says, "Apple products are much better than Microsoft products," that doesn't really tell us much, does it? Similar to preferences and wishes, we need to dig deeper to expose the root of this opinion for it to get into the realm of an insight.

To demonstrate this a bit more clearly, let's take a look at some of the insights I've written in the past that are less than ideal, and break them down into these categories. This was when I was working at a hospitality B2B company, and we were also exploring residential properties as potential customers.

Yes, I titled these as "insights." Feel free to laugh—they make me laugh too. Or, if these look a lot like your insights, know that you aren't alone! Writing insights is super hard work, and it takes a lot of practice. So, let's rip my insights apart.

Example One

"Filtering by type is good (recurring, maintenance, appliances, etc.) because they have a long list of requests."

Now, the team obviously had more context than everyone reading this right now, however, this is distinctly not an insight. Above is an example of an opinion and fact. We have several problems with the above statement:

- It gives absolutely no context surrounding the filtering: when people use it, why they use it, or any problems with the filtering.
- It uses subjective language like "good"—what does "good" mean to our users?
- There is little understanding about what is in that "long list of requests" or what that might mean to users.
- It is extremely product- and feature-centered, rather than user-centered. It talks more about the feature than the people using it.

Example Two

"There is no immediate need for recurrent tasks, but good if allocated as 'future' tasks."

Again, this is not at all an insight, and rather a fact, as it lacks:

- Any sort of context surrounding what a recurrent or future task means to users, and how this kind of task fits into their lives.
- Understanding of why and how people currently use these tasks, and any pain points or unmet needs behind the concepts.
- User-centricity and, again, just a mention of the feature of tasks rather than anything about the user.
- Clarity about the concept or what "good" means.

Example Three

"Quick search is very important for easy access to resident profiles."

Again, this is a fact and a bit of an opinion. For such an important feature for our users, I don't say anything about it in this statement. In fact, I've called out the most subjective and vague information by calling it "important" and using the phrase "easy access." There is absolutely no clarity or context that answers:

- why it is important to users to have easy access to resident profiles;
- what easy access means to them;
- how they currently use it;
- what problems or unmet needs might surround the concept of a quick search;
- what resident profiles are, why they are important.

Let's do what we constantly tell our teams to do and look at our research as a product, and our stakeholders as users of the product.

If my team were looking at these three statements above, what meaningful action would they be able to take? How am I mitigating their risk? How am I narrowing the scope of solutions or helping them make their decisions more user-centric?

How have these "insights" helped them? Spoiler: they haven't.

If I were tasked with improving or creating a product based on this information, I would feel super lost. And believe it or not, my teams still felt lost after my research projects, which made me feel like I wasn't properly doing my job. While user research isn't a magical answer to all our problems, it should still give my teams the support they need to mitigate risk and make more confident decisions.

WHAT MAKES A GOOD USER RESEARCH INSIGHT?

Let's start with a definition of a user research insight:

An insight is a nugget of truth about human behavior that pushes us to challenge our preconceived notions about how people act or perceive the world. It reveals to us the underlying motivations behind behavior, and helps us understand what happened, why it happened, and what the potential consequence is of not addressing the insight.

There are a million different ways we could define this, so please keep in mind that this is my definition, and feel free to tweak and redefine it to your context!

We have a few different components in this definition that we can break down further:

- reveals a truth about human behavior;
- pushes us to challenge our preconceived notions;
- reveals underlying motivations;
- helps us understand what and why it happened;
- highlights potential consequences.

If we revisit any of the examples from above, they are hugely lacking in all of these different components. In fact, I don't think they have any of the above parts of the definition of an insight.

Looking at this list of things included in an insight might seem scary because there's a lot in there. When I first created this definition and included these components, I scared myself. How was I ever going to write something that ticked all these boxes?

Before I go down that rabbit hole of fear and anxiety, let me quickly talk about how I identified these components: user research on my colleagues. I went back to the basics and looked at my insights through the frame of reference of my colleagues, asking them:

- What kind of information would they need to know to make their jobs easier?
- What could I include in my insights that would make them "actionable?"
- What was missing from my current insights?
- What would make my colleagues feel more confident about their decision-making?

I conducted lots of stakeholder interviews on this topic and even went outside my organization to find a more broad understanding. During the interviews, I also had stakeholders share with me what they categorized as helpful versus unhelpful insights, and explain why.

By having these deep conversations with stakeholders that use user research insights (e.g., designers, product managers, developers), I learned so much about what information directly impacts them. Synthesizing the results, I was able to create a definition that included the components the participants most frequently mentioned. Once I had the definition, alongside the examples, I started to write insights much more differently.

HOW TO WRITE AN IMPACTFUL USER RESEARCH INSIGHT

Before we dive into the actual craft of writing user research insights, let's talk through some prework that may be helpful for you to do. Because environments, contexts, and stakeholder needs can vary so much between organizations, I highly recommend doing this prework as it will set you up for success.

Prework

Interviewing your stakeholders

Similarly to what I did above, I would highly recommend interviewing your stakeholders about insights in general, as well as previous insights you've sent to them. I recommend doing this with at least five different stakeholders, or if you can, up to about ten—I found I hit diminishing returns around ten stakeholders.

As I mentioned, during these stakeholder interviews, you can ask them questions on how they think about insights, how they define good insights, and what "actionable" or "empowering" insights mean to them.

I would also encourage you to go through previous reports, and have them highlight insights you've sent that are helpful for them. Ask them to explain why those insights are helpful. Similarly, ask the stakeholders to highlight unhelpful insights, and why they were particularly unhelpful.

To be honest, getting stakeholders' feedback on my insights was sometimes a little tough, and I had to take a huge step back not to take the feedback personally. I recommend getting in a really positive headspace, and remembering that this is about you improving and helping to support your teams even better. Using this information, I'd recommend pulling some themes of what good insights mean to your team and using that to create a definition and model.

Setting up a satisfaction survey

Another really important aspect of getting these insights right is to iterate and improve upon them over time. There's typically not a one-size-fits-all approach to writing insights. Some teams' needs are different. I remember one team where I created a lot of visuals, and they loved all of them, while another team thrived off more story-based information, and another needed clip highlights.

And sometimes those needs change over time. Maybe you get new team members, or priorities shift. Regardless, it is essential to track this information over time, not only to improve but also to have concrete data on how satisfied your stakeholders are with your insights.

For this, I took my user research hat and applied it to my stakeholders. I typically used surveys to track impact over time and to get continuous feedback from users, so why not do that with my stakeholders as well? I set up a satisfaction survey that I sent to each stakeholder after each project, which asked about different aspects of the project and how I could improve.

The survey results were incredibly helpful in understanding what was working, what was lacking, and how I could iterate on my current process. If you are going to dive super deep into your insight-writing craft, I recommend setting up a satisfaction survey based on your insights that you can send after each project. You can include questions like:

- How clear or confusing are the research insights?
  - 5-point scale, 1 = very clear, 5 = very confusing.
- How satisfied or dissatisfied are you with the research insights?
  - 5-point scale, 1 = very satisfied, 5 = very dissatisfied.
- How actionable or unactionable do you find the research insights?
  - 5-point scale, 1 = very actionable, 5 = not at all actionable.
- How do you feel about the insights from the research?
  - Open field.
- What can we improve when it comes to research insights?
  - Open field.

STEP-BY-STEP GUIDE TO WRITING USER RESEARCH INSIGHTS

Now that we've covered the prework let's dive into how to structure and write these beautiful user research insights. Again, this is my process, so always pick and choose the most applicable and helpful parts for you, and tweak anything necessary!

Identifying Insights

First, it's important to identify insights. As we saw above, a lot of things are not insights. So, how do we identify when we have a beautifully rich insight versus something like a finding or a preference?

I generally look at four different aspects of the data to identify insights, and ask questions surrounding those aspects.

1. A discovery about human behavior, and the underlying motivations behind that behavior. Does what you found give you a new understanding of attitudes, pain points, needs, or the context of users (inside and outside your product/service)?
2. Information that challenges what we believe about users and how they exist in the world. Does what you found negate or change the way you have viewed users in the past?
3. Knowledge that reveals fundamental principles that drive us toward seeing users in a new way. Does what you found help you understand the user's mental models on how the world should work?
4. Surprising information that makes you say, "Wow, that is so interesting, I had NO idea!" Does what you found surprise you? Was it unexpected?

When you've ticked one (or multiple) of these boxes, you have uncovered an insight! This data is deep and really helps you uncover something (not necessarily new, but sometimes new) about users that is profound, and can help your team serve your users better.

HOW TO WRITE AN INSIGHT

Now let's dive into actually writing these wonderful nuggets of information. I generally think of insights as including three major components.

1. A key learning. The key learning may be an unexpected attitude, behavior, need, motivation, mental model, or pain point. It's the thing that made you

say, "Wow, that's interesting," and is the major thing you have learned from that piece of data.
2. The why. The why describes the motivation or the "point" behind the attitude, behavior, need, motivation, mental model, or pain point. It's the answer the user gave you when you dug deeper during your interview into why they were feeling a certain way or operating with a particular mental model.
3. The consequence. This is the bit that is left out most frequently from insights and the part that is, to me, the most actionable. What does this particular insight lead to, or what impact does it have on your product/service? Explain what will happen if you don't act on this insight.

If you're having trouble filling out this information, it might indicate to you that you have a finding rather than an insight. By trying to write insights, we can sometimes discover the data is actually too shallow for a full insight, but it can still make for a great finding—remember that findings aren't bad at all.

Since insight writing can feel like some mysterious, veiled process, let's take a look at some concrete examples, to illustrate how to build these from raw data.

Example One

When I was working at a travel company, we were doing some generative research on how people planned their trips, and the concept of purchasing "package trips," where you purchase the transport, hotel, and activities all in one, which we were interested in exploring as a feature.

I saw a major theme come through in the pain points around the concept of "package trips," where participants were hugely concerned about what would happen if something went wrong with these trips. I looked through the data and found various quotes like:

> I'm just not sure what happens if something goes wrong with the package - how do I know who to reach out to and fix it? It's still just as stressful...
>
> (P2)

> Will the company charge a bunch if something goes wrong? And do I even reach out to them? What if they tell me to contact the other company directly?
>
> (P3)

> What if a flight gets canceled? Who is going to figure that out for me, and what will they charge? It makes me want just to plan my own trip.
>
> (P5)

There were quite a few more people who expressed similar concerns. I had assumed people loved package deals because they were cheaper and easier. I hadn't thought much about the consequences or problems associated with them. As I looked through the data, I found it fell into the following categories:

- surprising information;
- knowledge that reveals fundamental principles that drive us toward seeing users in a new way;
- information that challenges what we believe about users and how they exist in the world.

So, I went through my process of building the insight using the three components I mentioned above.

The Key Learning

People are concerned about the policies and consequences of a package deal getting changed or canceled, as they have no idea who would be responsible for helping them and if they'd get charged.

The Why

Many people get stressed about bad things happening to their trip since it is such a painful experience from the past, and with package deals, a lot is out of their control. Many different components are put together in a package with no clear indication of who is responsible.

The Consequence

People might not use a package deal service, because the possibility of something going wrong and not having control over the situation might cause more stress than actually booking their travel.

The insight ended up looking like this:

People are concerned about the policies and consequences of a package deal, as the process is out of their control. Since many different components are put together in a package, there is no clear indication of who is responsible if something goes wrong. This can lead to more stress than booking travel, causing people to choose not to use a travel package service, especially from a third party service. We should consider other avenues, helping users with their additional pain points and unmet needs, rather than a package deal service.

Within this insight, I clearly pointed out what was happening, gave context, then highlighted the consequences if we were to move forward without heeding this insight, and what we should do instead.

Example Two

I'm using the travel company example again because the company went under, so I am able to share much more detail. For this project, we were looking at the process our users went through when booking a ticket on our platform, so that we could make meaningful improvements on the most painful experiences.

Again, while synthesizing my data, I found a major pain point. Prices for travel often change, and people can get quite frustrated feeling the price volatility, and trying to compare prices for travel to get the best deal. Here are some of the quotes from this pain point:

> I have about fifty tabs open from various platforms, comparing all these different prices at once. It's so frustrating, and it feels like if I close one tab by mistake and open it again, the price somehow changes. I just don't get it.–
>
> (P5)

> I noticed the prices for travel change, but I honestly have no idea when they change and why. It makes me not know when to book a ticket, and also I feel like I have to open so many different tabs to make sure I'm getting the best price. It gives me a lack of trust. Like, just tell me the best time to book a ticket and what others are charging.–
>
> (P8)

> The variability in prices is frustrating. I wish there was some sort of alert when prices were going up, or an easy way to compare them without having to go through every website. It makes me trust the platform less, like all you care about is taking my money.–
>
> (P12)

Again, I went through my process of building the insight using the three components.

The Key Learning

Many people experience a high degree of stress when trying to buy a ticket at the best price, and often get frustrated because the prices seem to be extremely volatile, changing in ways they can't understand.

The Why

Because of the constant price changes, people are opening multiple tabs or comparing many different platforms, when looking for the best price. The entire process can be quite time-consuming and frustrating because there is a lack of transparency on when/why the prices for a particular trip will change.

The Consequence

Since our prices constantly change, and we give little indication of this, people might have a hard time trusting our platform, thinking we are trying to charge more than competitors. This could stop them from purchasing from us, and could impact our retention rates and customer lifetime value, if they decide to purchase elsewhere.

The insight ended up looking like this:

Many people experience a high degree of stress when trying to buy a ticket at the best price, and often get frustrated because the prices seem to be extremely volatile, causing them to open multiple tabs or compare many different platforms simultaneously. The entire process and lack of transparency can be quite time-consuming and frustrating. Since our prices constantly change, and we give little indication of this, people might have a hard time trusting our platform, thinking we are trying to charge more than competitors. This could stop them from purchasing from us, impacting our retention rates and customer lifetime value, if they decide to purchase elsewhere.

Example of a Finding versus Insight

Just because it can sometimes be tough to distinguish between insights and findings, I wanted to give a quick example of a finding, and then how it could transform into an insight.

We sent quite a few discount codes to our customers for particular train tickets, and I found that people hugely struggled to find the discount code area. Which meant they were really frustrated when they finally went through the process of finding a trip, and then couldn't use their code.

Here is that information as a finding:

Five out of ten people struggled to find the discount code area in the checkout form when purchasing their train tickets.

Why is this a finding versus an insight? It is much more shallow than an insight, as it doesn't give context, why, or consequence. It states what happened and the frequency of the behavior.

If we wanted to turn it into an insight, we would need deeper information. Now, if you were running a usability test and didn't get that deeper information, it is fine for this to stay as a finding. One change I would make, however, is adding a potential consequence if you can.

If you did have additional information, we could turn this into an insight:

Five out of ten people struggled to find the discount code area when purchasing their train tickets. It was incredibly frustrating for them to get all the way through the process that we triggered through the discount code email, only not to be able to find where to put the code. They spent some time clicking around to find it, but ultimately got annoyed, and since they couldn't apply the code we sent for the sale, they dropped off the website. The average order value during the sale was $50 (with the discount applied). Looking at this population, instead of making $500, we only made $250. We lost 50% of our revenue from this issue.

Within this, we have what happened, the context behind it, and a very solid consequence!

As you can see, building an insight can take some intention, time, and thought, but it is well worth it to find a few of these deep, rich pieces of data, because they can be incredibly helpful to your team.

It's Okay Not to Have a Million Insights

Please keep in mind that not every study will have insights, and that is okay! Insights are rare, and they don't just magically pop up with every study. In fact, I rarely get insights from evaluative research. If I do, it's typically a fluke, where I've gone off track and started straying into more generative questions. My insights tend to come from generative research, and even in those super-deep studies, a handful of them.

I also want to say that findings, observations, facts, and bugs are all fantastic to report on and can be very helpful to the team. I try to have a mix of these outcomes in my report, because although insights are great, they generally need more thought to solve or ideate on, whereas findings or bugs can be quick fixes.

WRITING RECOMMENDATIONS FROM RESEARCH INSIGHTS

Writing recommendations as a user researcher can be a daunting task, and there's no one-size-fits-all formula for it. It's an art that evolves as you gather experience. When I embarked on this journey, I grappled with two fundamental questions.

1. What do recommendations mean to stakeholders?
2. How prescriptive should recommendations be?

Initially, I felt a sense of trepidation, fearing that my recommendations might come across as overconfident or impractical. I didn't want to step on the toes of designers or irk developers with far-fetched suggestions.

Ideally, when writing recommendations, you are sitting with your team and can discuss ideas together. However, sometimes you have to write recommendations on your own. In this situation, clarify with your colleagues that these recommendations might not be completely feasible, but are just some ideas you've brainstormed and want to talk about further. Here are some other tips for writing research recommendations.

1. Flexibility

Recommendations must be flexible. Proposing an initial solution should not lock us into a single path. Instead, it should ignite discussions of alternative ideas and fresh information. It's essential to become comfortable with revising recommendations based on collaborative insights and evolving project dynamics.

2. Detail Orientation

Incorporating photos, videos, or screenshots enriched my recommendations, enhancing clarity and reducing ambiguity. Colleagues appreciated the thoroughness, which reduced the likelihood of misinterpretation and prolonged debates.

3. Justification

The most challenging aspect was justifying recommendations, particularly when my findings clashed with expectations or business objectives. When faced with results indicating we were headed in the wrong direction, I avoided outright condemnation. Instead, I employed the "no, but..." approach. For example, "No, this isn't working, but we found that users value X and Y, which could lead to increased retention." This approach allowed me to offer alternatives constructively, steering discussions toward more productive solutions.

Recommendation Examples

While the list of must-haves proved valuable in shaping my recommendations, I realized that I needed a structured approach to compose them effectively. After some experimentation, I developed a simple formula for crafting recommendations:

> Identify the Observed Problem/Pain Point/Unmet Need
> + Consequence + Suggest a Potential Solution.

Evaluative Research

Let's explore this formula through an example in the context of evaluative research. Imagine we are assessing a travel booking website, and we've observed that users struggle when trying to select the right flight options on the search results page. A poorly framed recommendation might look like this:

- Users find it difficult to choose flights on the search results page.

This recommendation falls short for several reasons.

- Lacks Context and Detail: It fails to provide a clear understanding of the underlying issue.
- No Proposed Solution: It offers no guidance or remedy to address the problem.
- Sounds Judgmental: It emphasizes the problem but doesn't contribute to solving it.
- Lacks Forward Momentum: It doesn't offer actionable steps for improvement.

Now, let's reframe the recommendation using the formula, making it more precise and actionable.

Users experience decision paralysis when selecting flights on the search results page due to an overwhelming number of options. This results in frustration and indecision. To improve the user experience, consider implementing filters, sorting options, and a visual comparison feature, to help users quickly identify and select the most suitable flight based on their needs.

In this revised recommendation, we have:

- Context and Detail: We pinpoint the issue, its cause, and the associated consequence, offering a clear understanding of the problem.
- Proposed Solution: We suggest specific enhancements to address the problem, guiding the team toward potential improvements.
- Constructive Tone: While highlighting the problem, we also present a solution-oriented approach.
- Actionable Steps: The recommendation offers practical steps for implementation, promoting forward progress in resolving the issue.

Another Example

Expanding our understanding of crafting effective recommendations, let's delve into a different scenario. Imagine we've introduced a novel concept for our travel company—a "prime" travel membership. However, our user testing reveals that none of our users perceive sufficient value in this membership model to justify paying for it. They do, however, appreciate specific features, like trip sharing and cost splitting, but remain hesitant about investing in a membership. An underwhelming recommendation might resemble this:

- Users show reluctance to sign up or pay for the prime membership.

This recommendation leaves much to be desired for the following reasons.

- Lack of Context and Detail: It fails to provide a comprehensive picture of the situation.
- No Proposed Solution: It identifies a problem, but offers no actionable guidance.
- Limited Insight: It highlights user resistance but does not explore potential opportunities.

Now, let's refine the recommendation using our formula, addressing these shortcomings, and fostering a solution-focused approach.

Users perceive limited value in the prime membership, resulting in hesitance to sign up. However, they express genuine interest in two specific features: trip sharing with friends and splitting trip costs. Shifting our focus to enhancing these features could attract a broader user base, drive platform engagement, and ultimately boost user retention.

In this revamped recommendation:

- Context and Detail: We articulate the issue, its underlying causes, and the desired features, offering a more nuanced understanding.
- Proposed Solution: We propose a strategic shift toward improving the features that resonate with users, providing a clear path forward.
- Solution-Oriented: While acknowledging the challenge, we steer the recommendation toward potential enhancements and opportunities.

This refined recommendation formula empowers us to not only identify problems, but also outline constructive strategies for addressing them, and for elevating the user experience.

Generative Research Recommendations

Recommendations from generative research studies shift toward identifying broader pain points or unmet needs. Let's delve into this through the lens of a pet adoption example. In our generative research on pet adoption, we uncovered a recurring challenge: many prospective pet owners frequently forget important pet-related tasks and responsibilities, leading to feelings of guilt and rushed decisions.

This discovery, while valuable, encompasses a wide spectrum of potential solutions. We aim to provide recommendations that offer strategic guidance, without constraining our teams to a single path, while avoiding vagueness through detail. To structure generative research recommendations effectively, I employ the "How Might We" approach:

- Finding: People often struggle to remember essential pet-related tasks and responsibilities, leading to last-minute decisions filled with guilt.
- Recommendation: How might we develop tools or reminders that help prospective pet owners manage and remember their pet care responsibilities proactively, fostering a stress-free and guilt-free adoption experience?

I recommend presenting recommendations in a chart format, as it allows for seamless referencing back to the original insight and its prioritization. Here's a typical structure of an insight recommendations chart:

- insight: [relevant insight from research];
- priority: [high/medium/low];
- recommendation: [specific recommendation for action].

By tailoring and refining your recommendations to align with your colleagues' needs, you empower them to make more informed decisions grounded in your research insights.

Additional Insight Techniques

User research is only as valuable as the action it inspires. You might have deep insights and detailed data, but if your stakeholders can't digest or apply them, your hard work goes to waste.

I know because this was my way of life as a user researcher for many years: huge projects with amazing (and admittedly abstract) insights that sat in a folder somewhere.

Then, I reached a point in my career where I couldn't measure my impact because no one was doing anything with these stunning insights that no one could truly understand and act on. So, I stagnated.

And then, when I wanted to go freelance, I realized I had to up the ante. If I wanted good word of mouth and recommendations (read: a steady income), I had to deliver things my clients could actually do stuff with.

So, again, I hit a wall. It was a crappy wall that I didn't enjoy banging my head against for about a year. Until I decided to try something new.

My stakeholders (both in-house and freelance) didn't have time for complexity. They didn't have time to sit and analyze everything that happened in a research study, to digest all the data and then figure out what to do with it.

They needed fast, clear insights they could act on immediately.

Actionability, actionable insights, action, action, action. When I focused on action, my reports changed, and so can yours.

Your insights need to do more than sit in a report. How do you make sure your research delivers impact? By simplifying your reports so that stakeholders can easily digest, understand, and act on your findings.

In this article, I'll cover 15 proven strategies, new techniques, and creative approaches that will transform the way you present your research, ensuring your stakeholders are always clear on what to do next. You don't need to try them all, but pick a few and have fun experimenting with them.

1. *WTF is your goal*

Before I get into the amazing strategies and techniques below, the first thing I need to point out is that is overwhelmingly missing from a report is a goal. What do I mean by this?

Whenever I used to struggle with putting together a report, it usually meant that I didn't know what the point of the report was, which led to confusion on what to include and how to structure it, and typically made it feel disjointed and … useless.

So, every single time I put together a report/presentation/workshop, I ask myself the following questions:

- What is the point of this report?
- What do I want people to do with the information?
- What do I want people to do during and after the presentation?
- What are my expectations of people during the presentation? What do I want them to be thinking, feeling, doing?
- What are the next steps for this report?

- What is my ideal outcome for this report?
- How relevant is this report for my audience? What are they empowered to do with the information?

If I can't answer these, I go back to the drawing board until I can answer them. If I still can't, creating a report probably isn't the right move and I need to think of a different solution or wait until the report becomes more actionable and relevant.

2. Cut the clutter

I'll be blunt because I've done it too: not everything in your research report is equally important. Your stakeholders are busy. They don't need or want to be overwhelmed with every data point you've collected.

To get your insights acted on faster, prioritize only the most impactful findings. Instead of creating a giant list of everything your research uncovered, identify the two to three most important insights that will move the needle. Everything else can go in the appendix or be followed up on once the most important insights are acted on.

Start your report with a clear, bold statement like, "Fixing X will increase conversions by 20%." Then, give them just enough data to support that claim. Everything else is secondary.

For example, imagine you're working on a product with a problematic onboarding process. Rather than providing pages of data showing every issue, highlight the one step that's causing the most friction:

> Step 3 in the onboarding process is confusing 60% of users, leading to a significant drop-off. Simplifying this step could improve conversion rates by 30%.

That's all they need. Prioritizing actionable insights will prevent your report from feeling like a data dump and will instantly get your stakeholders focused on the solution.

3. Structure your deliverables like a news article

People like to skim. Even your most engaged stakeholders are likely skimming through your research deliverables, looking for key points. To accommodate this, structure your insights like a news article—where the headline tells the most important part of the story.

Use bold headlines that clearly state the takeaway, followed by a brief explanation or supporting data. For example:

- Users are abandoning their carts at step 3. Confusion with the payment interface is causing 40% of drop-offs.
- Feature X is overcomplicated. 70% of users avoid it because instructions are unclear.

With this format, even if a stakeholder only reads the headlines, they'll still get the key insights. If they're intrigued, they can dive into the supporting details below.

Keep these headlines under ten words, and avoid jargon. The simpler and clearer, the better. You can also utilize these headlines for your executive summaries.

4. Tell micro-stories

Data doesn't stick with people, but stories do. One powerful way to simplify your research deliverables and make them more engaging is to turn your findings into micro-stories.

Stakeholders love stories because they provide context and relevance. But instead of long, drawn-out narratives, focus on micro-stories—short, impactful anecdotes that highlight user pain points and how your insights solve them.

Make your stakeholders the protagonists. Don't just tell them what users are struggling with—show how it directly impacts the product and their decision-making.

For example, instead of sharing a generic data point like "40% of users abandon their carts at checkout," say:

> Imagine a user named Sarah. She's added products to her cart, but at the final step, she's confused by unclear payment instructions. Frustrated, she leaves without purchasing. This happens 40% of the time. Now imagine we fix this issue. That's a 20% increase in revenue and a potential 25% increase in satisfaction scores.

Micro-stories turn data into a narrative that stakeholders can relate to—and more importantly, act on.

5. Create a risk heatmap

People are visual creatures. Charts, graphs, and infographics are often more effective at communicating complex data than paragraphs of text. However, many researchers are stuck using the same old visuals—bar graphs, pie charts, and basic flowcharts.

I absolutely love using risk heatmaps. In this case, the heatmap is structured around the severity of risk associated with different user touchpoints or features. You'd map each part of the user experience or product based on two factors:

1. Likelihood of the issue occurring, such as how frequently users encounter the problem).
2. Impact on the business, such as how much the issue affects user retention, revenue, or satisfaction).

Here's how you can use this concept:

- High risk (red): Represents areas where user friction is both frequent and has a significant impact on the business (e.g., checkout abandonment rates that are causing revenue loss).
- Moderate risk (orange): Areas where issues are frequent but have a lower impact on business, or where issues are infrequent but severe when they occur (e.g., a niche feature causing confusion among power users).

- Low risk (green): Features or touchpoints with low user friction and minimal business impact (e.g., minor UI inconveniences).

Let's say your research uncovers that:

- 40% of users are dropping off at the payment screen due to confusion (this is a high risk, as it directly impacts revenue).
- 20% of users find the onboarding process overly complicated, but it's not as critical since these users are likely to explore the product more thoroughly (moderate risk).
- 10% of users experience minor frustrations with a search feature, but it doesn't affect their overall engagement with the product (low risk).

It visually shows different areas of risk:

- Red (High Risk): Payment screen with a significant 40% user drop-off, directly impacting revenue.
- Orange (Moderate Risk): Onboarding process, where 20% of users find it too complex.
- Green (Low Risk): Search feature, with minimal user friction and low impact on overall engagement.

This kind of heatmap is a great visual for stakeholders to focus on high-risk areas that need immediate attention.

6. *Start with actions, back up with data*

Most research reports follow the same format: lead with the data, then suggest possible actions. But here's a new approach that will grab your stakeholders' attention faster: flip the script.

Start with the recommended action. Tell them exactly what needs to be done, then back it up with data. This approach frontloads the most important information, making it crystal clear what needs to happen next.

For example, instead of starting with a summary of user behavior, you could start with:

> We need to simplify the onboarding process to stop user churn. Here's the data that supports this.

This immediately tells stakeholders what to do, eliminating the guessing game and making the path forward obvious.

7. *Use of comparative metrics for context*

Sometimes it's not enough to say, "Here's a problem." Stakeholders need to know how big the problem is in relation to competitors or industry standards. This is where comparative metrics can add real value to your deliverables.

Don't just say, "40% of users are abandoning their carts." Put that number in context. For example:

> 40% of users are abandoning their carts at checkout. In comparison, our top competitor sees a 15% drop-off. If we can reduce our rate to match theirs, we stand to gain an additional £X in revenue each quarter.

By showing how your data stacks up against competition, you not only highlight the problem but also create urgency and a clear opportunity for improvement.

8. Try video recaps

If you really want to share your insights with busy stakeholders, create a short video recap instead of sending another slide deck or PDF.

Using tools like Loom or Vidyard, you can record a quick 3–5 minute walkthrough of your findings. Show your screen to highlight key data points and talk stakeholders through your recommendations. The conversational tone and visual element will capture their attention faster than text alone.

Here's how I've used this:

- Start with the key insights: "We found that users are dropping off at Step 3 due to a confusing payment interface. Simplifying this step could increase conversions by 20%."
- Show the data visually: Use a chart or journey map to highlight the pain point.
- End with clear next steps: "Let's redesign the payment interface and A/B test the new version."

Stakeholders can watch it on the go—perfect for executives or remote teams who don't have time to read through a full report.

9. Involve stakeholders in research

We all have heard the advice of inviting stakeholders to participate in the research process and to have them in the sessions whenever possible. But if I have learned anything, sometimes dragging stakeholders to sessions is impossible, especially in the freelance world.

In addition to the invitation and creating clips, I often try to get people talking about the feedback before the report is even out.

For this, you can create highlight reels of user frustrations or successes. Send short clips to stakeholders and ask for their gut reactions: "How would you solve this problem?" Post these reels and questions to Slack to drip-feed insight and already get people thinking about the next steps.

This collaborative approach ensures that your insights don't just sit in a report—they become part of the conversation from the start.

10. Provide activation

Your research is only as good as the actions it inspires. The problem biggest problem I've seen in 90% of research reports is that they stop at insights without giving clear instructions on what to do next.

Your stakeholders are busy and need guidance—not just on what the problem is, but how to solve it. This is called activation, and it is the missed step in most research processes. It is non-negotiable if you want to progress in your career.

For every insight you present, provide a concrete, specific recommendation, along with a clear timeline and responsible parties.

For example, instead of just saying, "Improve user onboarding," give them an action plan:

- Next step: Redesign the onboarding flow to simplify Step 3.
- Timeline: Implement the new design by the end of Q2.
- Team: The design and product teams will own this task, with research providing ongoing usability testing.
- Next meeting: Meet next week for an ideation session on simplifying Step 3.

This level of specificity leaves no room for ambiguity. You're not just presenting data—you're driving decisions and actions.

11. Create an executive summary

Even when you've simplified your findings, some stakeholders just won't have time to dive into the full report. That's where a one-page summary comes in handy. Think of this as the CliffsNotes version of your research. On a single page, include:

- Key insight: What's the most important takeaway?
- Supporting data: One or two data points that back up the insight.
- Actionable recommendation: What needs to happen next?
- Expected outcome: What results can stakeholders expect if they take action?

For example:

- Key insight: Users are dropping off during the checkout process.
- Supporting data: 45% of users abandon their cart at Step 3.
- Recommendation: Simplify the payment process to reduce friction and improve clarity.
- Expected outcome: A 20% increase in conversion rates within the next quarter.

This one-pager is easy to scan, gives stakeholders the key information they need, and ensures that your insights can be quickly referenced and acted upon.

12. Test with non-experts

Test your deliverables with someone outside your team, preferably someone with little or no research background. This is a simple but powerful way to check whether your insights are clear and actionable.

Ask someone from marketing, operations, or customer support to read your report or presentation. If they're confused or need further clarification, that's a red flag that your stakeholders might feel the same.

If a non-expert can understand your report and know exactly what to do next, then your stakeholders will be able to, too.

13. Use decision trees

Another way to simplify decision-making for stakeholders is to include decision trees directly in your deliverables. These trees act as a guide, showing clear paths based on your findings. This way, stakeholders don't just receive insights—they know exactly what actions to take depending on the results.

For example, let's say you found a user friction issue during checkout:

- If 40% of users abandon the cart at Step 3, then simplify the payment process.
- If simplifying the process increases conversions, then implement the change across the platform.

This method simplifies your recommendations and allows stakeholders to act on insights without needing constant back-and-forth conversations. Decision trees are a powerful tool for cutting down complexity and making next steps crystal clear.

14. Use sprints to deliver research in real-time

Instead of waiting until the end of a project to present your full findings, deliver insights in real time—as soon as they become available. This keeps your stakeholders engaged throughout the process and helps them make adjustments along the way, rather than waiting for a big report at the end.

For example:

- Sprint 1: Present early-stage findings after the first round of testing, like identifying a problem in the onboarding flow.
- Sprint 2: Present deeper insights, such as user behavior causing friction during checkout.
- Sprint 3: Offer solutions and recommendations, like testing simplified onboarding steps and updating the flow.

By presenting your insights progressively, you make it easier for stakeholders to act swiftly, and you build momentum for the final deliverable.

This also works beautifully for continuous generative research as you are constantly delivering impact every sprint.

15. Add a sense of urgency

If you want stakeholders to act quickly, you need to create a sense of urgency. Without it, even the most important insights can get pushed to the bottom of their to-do list.

To do this, attach a clear consequence to inaction. Make it obvious what will happen if they delay. Pair it with a clear deadline, and you'll significantly increase the likelihood that your insights lead to immediate action.

For example:

- "If we don't simplify the payment interface by Q3, we risk losing 20% of new customers by year-end."
- "Act now to update the onboarding process and prevent a projected 30% increase in user drop-offs."

Urgency forces decisions. It's not about creating panic, but about showing the real, time-sensitive impact of taking, or not taking, action.

16. Offer a follow-up plan

You've probably delivered countless reports where you never hear what happened afterward. To ensure your stakeholders are acting on your insights, offer a follow-up plan.

In your deliverables, include a "check-in" point for reviewing the progress. For example, suggest a meeting or a sprint review in 30 days to evaluate how well the recommended actions have been implemented and whether they're delivering the expected results.

By scheduling a follow-up, you add a layer of accountability, which encourages stakeholders to act more quickly and makes sure your insights aren't forgotten.

PART SEVEN

Creating Effective and Realistic Deliverables and Outcomes

Writing Reports   24

REPORTS

After years of agonizing over reports, I finally started to find my rhythm. I unlocked the first step in adequately structuring research reports: knowing your audience. Writing hundreds of reports has helped me see the main ways stakeholders like to ingest research information. Now I use three primary templates, which speed up my process and allow the data to shine.

Structure by Research Themes

The most prevalent approach to organizing reports is by themes. In this structure, your report's construction is guided by the insights gleaned from synthesis. But what exactly constitutes a research theme?

Following affinity diagramming, you'll have clusters of data that represent different facets of your research. For instance, suppose I conducted a study on how individuals identify and follow fashion trends online. I might identify the following thematic clusters.

- Inspiration from fashion influencers on social media platforms (e.g., Instagram, fashion blogs).
- Recommendations and tips from friends, family, or online fashion communities.
- Revisiting previously worn outfits that garnered positive attention.
- Utilizing curated fashion deals or promotions.
- Influence from a partner, spouse, or friend's fashion preferences.
- Leveraging fashion trend discovery tools and applications.
- Curating a fashion bucket list of desired styles.
- Serendipitous discovery of intriguing fashion trends online.

Now, each of these themes encompasses a wealth of insights and data points, making it impractical to delve into each one exhaustively. To facilitate comprehension and focus on the most impactful findings, I prioritize the top three to five themes, which typically have the highest participant engagement.

Let's assume I interviewed 20 individuals, and the top three influencers in fashion trend identification were as follows:

1. Inspiration from fashion influencers on social media platforms—17 out of 20 participants.
2. Recommendations and tips from friends, family, or online fashion communities—14 out of 20 participants.
3. Utilizing curated fashion deals or promotions—13 out of 20 participants.

I would leverage these three dominant themes as the foundation for my report structure, starting with the most prevalent theme and concluding with the least. Within the report, I would provide:

a. A Theme Title
b. A Theme Summary, encompassing the primary one to three findings within the theme.
c. A Deep Dive Section, delving into the insights behind the findings, incorporating relevant quotes, videos, or audio clips to amplify the richness of each discovery.

Here's an example of the theme: Inspiration from Fashion Influencers on Social Media.

1. Finding One: Fashion enthusiasts actively follow influencers on social media platforms, such as Instagram and fashion blogs, to stay updated on the latest trends.
2. Finding Two: Many individuals create curated collections or boards to catalog fashion inspirations they encounter on social media, revisiting them when planning their outfits.

Deep Dive into Finding One

Meet Sarah, a fashion-forward individual who often scours Instagram during her breaks at work. She heard colleagues chatting about a recent fashion show and decided to explore the latest trends. Sarah follows various fashion influencers whose posts captivate her. She often compiles intriguing outfits and styling ideas into her saved collections.

However, Sarah doesn't immediately make purchases. Instead, she takes her time researching prices, assessing compatibility with her existing wardrobe, and determining her budget, typically doing so during her leisure time in the evening.

Sarah shares her experience, stating, "When I come across those stunning outfits on Instagram, I feel this urge to explore them further. But buying something isn't a snap decision; it requires careful consideration. I like to investigate the details when I have more time, as fashion is an art, and I want to create my masterpiece."

By adhering to this structural approach, you can effectively present the most crucial research insights, ensuring that stakeholders can swiftly grasp the core findings, while maintaining the flexibility to explore further details as needed.

Research Goals and Questions

Another way to organize findings and insights is through the research goals or questions established at the project's inception. This approach ensures that the report effectively addresses the precise information stakeholders require.

To illustrate this method within the context of the earlier example, let's consider that the research goals were as follows.

- Gain insights into individuals' prevailing mental models regarding the process of identifying and following fashion trends online.
- Uncover the pain points associated with the process of identifying and embracing online fashion trends.
- Identify the tools and platforms individuals currently employ for fashion inspiration and trend identification.

Rather than grouping findings by themes, I structure the report as follows:

Research goal 1: understanding mental models

- Finding Summary: Succinctly outlines one to three key findings directly pertinent to the research goal.
- Finding One: A detailed exploration of a finding intricately linked to Research Goal 1.
  - Evidence of Finding One: Factual data, illustrative quotes, or participant insights, substantiating Finding One.
- Finding Two: Delving into the second finding that directly aligns with Research Goal 1.
  - Evidence of Finding Two: Supporting evidence or participant perspectives, bolstering Finding Two.
- Finding Three: A comprehensive examination of the third finding directly associated with Research Goal 1.
  - Evidence of Finding Three: Tangible proof, participant anecdotes, or relevant observations, fortifying Finding Three.

Let's look at the fashion trend example again.

Research Goal 1: understanding mental models

Finding One: Many participants revealed that their mental model of staying updated with fashion trends online primarily involved following fashion influencers on social media platforms like Instagram and TikTok. These influencers served as their fashion inspiration, and participants actively sought to emulate their styles.

- Evidence of Finding One: A majority of the participants cited specific Instagram and TikTok accounts they follow for fashion inspiration. For instance, Participant A mentioned, "I always check out [Influencer X]'s Instagram because her style is so unique. I love how she combines vintage pieces with modern trends."

Finding Two: Some participants expressed frustration with the overwhelming volume of fashion content online, leading to decision fatigue. They struggled to discern between passing fads and lasting trends, causing anxiety in their fashion choices.

- Evidence of Finding Two: Participant B articulated, "There's just too much out there. One day it's all about oversized blazers, and the next day it's neon colors. It's exhausting trying to keep up."

Finding Three: Participants described using virtual wardrobe management apps and AI-powered fashion trend prediction tools to stay ahead in the fashion game. These tools helped them curate their wardrobes and make informed fashion choices.

- Evidence of Finding Three: Participant C shared, "I use this app that analyzes my clothing preferences and suggests outfits based on current trends. It's like having a personal stylist!"

This structure ensures that the evidence presented in the report aligns directly with the overarching research goals. It equips stakeholders with the precise insights required to make informed decisions.

Usability Testing Reports

The art of composing usability test reports necessitates a distinct template. While I typically begin with a thematic template, I then get into the actual prototype findings through annotations and videos. When it comes to structuring usability test analysis, I recommend two primary approaches.

1. Screen-by-Screen Analysis: This method involves presenting screenshots of each screen alongside annotations summarizing participant feedback on usability issues, providing a granular view of user interactions.
2. Flow Analysis: Alternatively, a flow analysis breaks down the prototype's overall journey into distinct stages, featuring concise bullet points that encapsulate the user feedback pertinent to the flow's efficacy.

For quantitative usability tests, such as evaluating task completion times or success rates, I incorporate a stoplight chart (page X) to offer a quick visual summary of performance outcomes.

The choice between screen-by-screen or flow analysis hinges upon the specific needs of stakeholders and the depth of feedback received from participants. For instance, if extensive feedback is received for each screen, a screen-by-screen analysis proves invaluable.

Conversely, if the team seeks insights into the overall flow of the prototype, I segment the analysis into multiple slides to elucidate feedback concerning the prototype's holistic progression. My usability testing reports are typically structured as follows:

Theme 1: User Onboarding

- Theme Summary: Succinctly outlines one to three main findings within the theme.
- Deep Dive: An immersive exploration of the theme, delving into the insights, supported by relevant quotes, videos, or audio clips from participants.

Examples

- Finding One: Participants encountered difficulties during the initial app setup. Quotes from users like, "I wasn't sure what to do first," emphasize their struggles. Video clips show users attempting to navigate the onboarding process.
- Finding Two: The lack of visual cues caused confusion in creating user profiles. Participants expressed frustration, saying, "I didn't know where to upload my profile picture." Video clips capture users hesitating while trying to add profile details.

Theme 2: Navigation and Search

- Theme Summary: Concisely presents the primary findings within this theme, offering actionable insights.
- Deep Dive: A comprehensive examination of Theme 2, backed by participant quotes, videos, or audio clips that elucidate the findings.

Examples

- Finding One: Users faced challenges while navigating the app's menu. Quotes such as, "I couldn't find the style category," underscored this issue. Video clips showcase users attempting to locate specific fashion categories.
- Finding Two: The search function was less intuitive than expected. Participants remarked, "The search results weren't relevant," reflecting their dissatisfaction. Video clips captured users struggling to find desired fashion items.

Concept/Prototype Analysis: Fashion Trend App

- A Prototype Reminder: A brief refresher on the prototype under scrutiny, setting the stage for the analysis.
- Screen-by-Screen or Flow Analysis: Depending on the depth and nature of feedback received, I employ either screen-by-screen analysis or a flow-based breakdown, offering detailed insights into usability.

- Quantitative Usability Metrics: If applicable, a stoplight chart, highlighting key performance metrics such as task success rates, task completion times, or user satisfaction scores.

These three distinctive structures cater to the most common reports and presentations encountered in the realm of user research. I encourage fellow researchers to explore variations within these frameworks, always bearing their audience's needs in mind, and to actively solicit feedback to continually enhance the effectiveness of their reports.

A Note on Executive Summaries

The enigmatic realm of executive summaries often leaves us searching for clarity amidst buzzwords like "actionable insights." These terms signify their importance, yet their precise definition remains elusive. For years, the significance of including executive summaries in research presentations has been stressed, serving as a quick gateway for readers to grasp the report's essence.

An executive summary serves as a lens through which readers can glean essential findings or insights, if they have the time to peruse a single slide. While we hope that our reports are thoroughly read, the reality is that some stakeholders may opt for brevity. Hence, the executive summary is our conduit to convey the pivotal information succinctly.

This summary empowers teams to extract the most impactful details from a study. Ideally, readers should extract valuable insights that aid in decision-making from a single glance. As user researchers, we must master the art of conciseness, allowing us to surface critical information relevant to project goals within executive summaries.

Structure

While I've come across executive summaries spanning several pages or even multiple slides, the fundamental principle remains concise communication. Typically, the executive summary should encompass one page; in exceptional cases, two. However, the goal is always to strive for brevity.

Within this single page, I structure my executive summaries to highlight the top three to five findings or insights from the study. This structure generally covers:

1. one surprising finding/insight;
2. one to two challenges or negative outcomes;
3. if space permits, an additional insight.

While this structure is pragmatic, it may appear frustratingly vague. How do we discern the most positive insight? Which challenges to spotlight? What information to include and what to defer? To address these questions, let's delve deeper.

QUESTIONS TO ASK YOURSELF

Initially, I approached executive summaries without a clear roadmap, uncertain about how to extract pertinent information. Over time, I developed a set of questions to unearth valuable insights. When crafting an executive summary, the following questions guide me.

Surprising Finding:

- Which assumptions or hypotheses were validated by the research?
- What risks paid off and contributed positively to the study?
- What information has the potential to significantly enhance user experiences?
- What findings reshape our understanding of user behavior?
- What novel insights did we unearth?

Negative Findings:

- What issues or challenges did we unearth?
- Which hypotheses or assumptions were invalidated during the study?
- What information might negatively impact user experiences?
- What insights prompt us to reevaluate our project's direction?

Other Findings:

- What unexpected events or insights emerged during the research?
- What information could help the team make more informed decisions moving forward?

This iterative process yields a list of approximately ten data points. Next, I prioritize these insights based on their potential impact on team decisions and alignment with the study's goals.

FORMAT

Consistency is key when constructing executive summaries. A standardized format streamlines the writing process. My executive summaries follow a consistent structure.

- A concise header (a few words).
- One to two sentences summarizing the insight.
- An illustrative example, such as a user quote.
- The implications or consequences of the insight.
- If applicable, a brief recommendation.

AN EXECUTIVE SUMMARY EXAMPLE

Let's explore an example project related to fashion trend apps:
In this project, our objective was to discern how users, especially young adults, engage with fashion trend apps and what drives their fashion choices.

EXECUTIVE SUMMARY EXAMPLES:

Insight 1: Personal Style Customization

- Header: Tailored Style Preferences
- Summary: Users prioritize customization and personalization when it comes to fashion trends. They seek apps that allow them to curate a unique style, reflecting their individuality.
- Example: "I love apps that let me mix and match outfits virtually. It's like having a personal stylist in my pocket."
- Consequence: Emphasize the importance of robust customization features in our fashion trend app to enhance user engagement and retention.

Insight 2: Social Influence on Fashion Choices

- Header: The Power of Social Approval
- Summary: Social validation significantly impacts fashion choices. Users are more likely to adopt trends that receive positive feedback and endorsements from their social networks.
- Example: "If my friends like a certain fashion trend on social media, I'm more inclined to try it out. It's like a fashion vote of confidence."
- Consequence: Incorporate social features within our app to facilitate trend sharing and peer interaction, leveraging the influence of social validation.

Insight 3: Mobile Shopping Behavior

HEADER: SEAMLESS SHOPPING INTEGRATION

- Summary: Users prefer fashion trend apps that seamlessly integrate shopping functionality, enabling them to purchase trending items effortlessly.
- Example: "I want to buy the clothes I see right away. Apps that make it easy to shop within the platform are the ones I keep."

- Consequence: Prioritize the integration of shopping features to enhance user convenience and drive conversions within the app.

Take the time to practice executive summaries. It took me a while to get to the stage where I could pinpoint the vital information and distill it into one concise slide. Start by asking yourself those questions about your study, do a brain dump, and then work your way down to the top three to five insights. It is well worth it when your research becomes more digestible, and read by people who don't have enough time to take on the full report!

Using the Pyramid Principle 25

The Pyramid Principle, developed by Barbara Minto at McKinsey, is a method for structuring information clearly, logically, and persuasively.

Here's how it works:

1. Start with the answer. (Lead with your main insight—don't bury it at the end.)
2. Support it with key arguments. (Break down why this is true.)
3. Back up those arguments with evidence. (Provide qualitative and quantitative data.)

This flips the usual way research reports are written. Instead of working toward the conclusion, you start with it.

Think of it like a pyramid:

- Conclusion first
- Key arguments
- Supporting evidence

Instead of:

1. Background—Why we did this research
2. Methodology—How we did it
3. Findings—What we discovered
4. Conclusion—What it all means

We flip the structure:

1. Conclusion First—"Users aren't converting because the sign-up process is too complicated."
2. Key Arguments—"We found three primary reasons why: (1) Confusing UI, (2) Lack of trust, (3) Poor onboarding."
3. Supporting Evidence—"40% of users abandon at step 2. Interviews reveal they don't know what happens after sign-up."

This ensures stakeholders get the most critical information first—even if they only read the first page.

This was the hardest shift for me to make. We're trained to present findings the way we uncover them:

- First, we explain the background—Why we did the research
- Then, we talk about the methodology—How we did it
- Finally, we build up to the key insight—What we discovered

But most stakeholders won't make it to the end of your report.

They don't need to know how you got to the answer before hearing what the answer is.

The Pyramid Principle flips this approach by leading with the most important takeaway first, then explaining how you got there.

Why This Matters

Think about it from your stakeholders' perspective:

- A busy product manager opens your report between back-to-back meetings
- A VP of design skims through it while multitasking
- A data analyst checks it while debugging an issue

None of them have time to dig through background information to find the insight. You have to put it right in front of them.

If your key takeaway is buried on page 7, you've already lost them.

START WITH THE ANSWER IN YOUR REPORT

Your first sentence should immediately answer the key question your research set out to explore.

Let's say you conducted a study on why users abandon checkout.

Instead of this typical approach:

> We conducted research to understand why users weren't completing checkout. Our study involved usability testing, surveys, and behavioral analytics. We analyzed the user journey and identified several key pain points. Based on our findings, we believe that the primary issue is a lack of trust in the payment process.

Try this instead:

> Users abandon checkout because they don't trust the payment process.

Right away, your stakeholder knows the most important piece of information. Then, in the next few sentences, you briefly explain why:

> Through usability testing and surveys, we found that 40% of users hesitate at the payment step due to unclear security messaging. Additionally, 60% of users say they don't know what happens after entering payment details. The lack of trust indicators, such as security badges and reassurances, is a major contributor to drop-off.

Now, before they even scroll down, your stakeholder understands the main issue. If they stop reading right here, they've already gotten value.

What If You Have Multiple Findings?

If your research uncovered several important findings, you still need to start with the most critical one.

For example, if your study explored why free trial users don't convert to paying customers, and you found three main reasons, you might structure it like this:

First sentence:

- "Free trial users don't convert because they don't experience value early enough."

Follow-up explanation:

- "We identified three main reasons: (1) Key features are hidden behind complex onboarding, (2) Users struggle to complete setup, and (3) Many users don't realize when their trial is ending."

Now, the reader has the big picture immediately. If they're interested in the details, they can keep reading—but even if they don't, they've already grasped the main insights.

Write a strong first sentence

Here's a simple formula to make this easy:

- [User behavior] happens because [reason].

Or:

- [Key problem] is caused by [main insight].

Some examples:

Instead of this:

- "We conducted research to understand how users interact with the onboarding flow. The goal was to identify pain points that impact activation rates."

Write this:

- "Users drop off during onboarding because they don't understand the product's core value."

Instead of this:

- "Our study analyzed why users are struggling with navigation in the mobile app."

Write this:

- "Users struggle with navigation because key actions are buried in menus, making them hard to find."

The key is to be direct and specific.

Mistakes to Avoid

Burying the insight in background information

- Weak: "Our goal was to evaluate the effectiveness of the sign-up flow. We tested with 15 users and identified key usability issues. One major problem was confusion around account verification."
- Strong: "Users struggle to sign up because the account verification process is unclear."

Being Too Vague

- Weak: "Users find navigation difficult."
- Strong: "Users struggle with navigation because key actions are buried in menus."

Hedging Too Much

- Weak: "Some users may have difficulty understanding the onboarding process."
- Strong: "40% of users don't complete onboarding because they don't see a clear next step."

Focusing on the Process Instead of the Insight

- Weak: "We interviewed 20 users to understand how they perceive the checkout process."
- Strong: "Users don't trust the checkout process, leading to a 40% drop-off rate."

Your first sentence sets the tone for the entire report. Make it clear. Make it specific. Make it impossible to ignore.

Next Steps

If you're new to this approach, start by practicing with a past research report:

1. Take a recent report and find the main insight. What is the single most important thing your stakeholders should know?

2. Rewrite your introduction. Start with that insight instead of background information.
3. Test it out. Share it with a stakeholder and see if they engage faster.

Once you get comfortable, use this method in every research report. It will make your work more readable, more impactful, and more likely to drive action.

Once you've stated your conclusion upfront, the next step is to explain why it's true.

This is where many researchers struggle. They assume that the insight speaks for itself—but for stakeholders to buy into your findings, they need a clear, logical breakdown of the problem.

Think of this step as building the case for your conclusion.

Imagine you're a stakeholder reading a research report that starts with:

- "Users aren't completing checkout because they don't trust the payment process."

If that's all you read, your first question will be:

- "What makes you say that?"

This is where your key arguments come in.

Key arguments are the main reasons your conclusion is true. They provide structure to your report and make your insight hard to ignore.

HOW TO IDENTIFY YOUR KEY ARGUMENTS

Your key arguments should answer this question:

What Are the Two to Four Main Reasons This Problem Exists?

Let's say your research reveals that users aren't completing checkout because they don't trust the payment process. Your key arguments might look like this:

1. Confusing UI—40% of users abandon checkout at Step 2 because they don't know what happens next.
2. Lack of trust indicators—60% of users say they don't feel confident entering their credit card details.
3. Poor error handling—30% of users who encounter an error don't know how to resolve it.

Each of these is a distinct and specific reason that supports the conclusion.

How Many Key Arguments Should You Have?

Two to four.

- If you only have one, it's not enough to build a strong case.
- If you have five or more, you're overwhelming your reader.

Three is usually the sweet spot. It's enough to be persuasive without overloading your audience with too much detail.

HOW TO STRUCTURE YOUR KEY ARGUMENTS

Once you've identified them, structure them in a way that makes sense to your reader.

Option 1: Order by Impact

Start with the most important or surprising reason first. This ensures your strongest argument gets noticed.
Example:

1. Confusing UI—40% of users abandon checkout at Step 2.
2. Lack of trust indicators—60% of users say they don't feel confident entering their payment details.
3. Poor error handling—30% of users who encounter an error don't know how to resolve it.

If you know stakeholders care most about security, you might list "lack of trust indicators" first instead.

Option 2: Order by User Journey

Another approach is to follow the user's experience chronologically.
Example:

1. Users struggle to understand the first step of checkout.
2. They hesitate when they reach the payment page.
3. They abandon when they get an error message.

This approach is useful when your findings relate to a specific flow.
What a weak vs. strong argument looks like
A weak argument is too vague or too broad.
Weak:

- "Users don't like the payment process."
- "Users find the UI confusing."
- "Trust is an issue."

Strong:

- "40% of users abandon checkout at Step 2 because they don't know what happens next."
- "60% of users say they don't feel confident entering their payment details."
- "30% of users who encounter an error don't know how to resolve it."

Specific arguments are easier to understand and act on.

MISTAKES TO AVOID

Blending Multiple Arguments Together

- Weak: "Users don't trust checkout because of poor UI, lack of security messaging, and confusing steps."
- Strong:
    - "40% of users abandon at Step 2 due to unclear steps."
    - "60% don't feel confident entering payment details."

Including Arguments that don't Directly Support the Conclusion

- If your insight is "users don't trust the checkout process," then an argument about high shipping costs doesn't belong here.

Skipping This Step Entirely

- If you only state the conclusion without explaining why, stakeholders won't trust it.

HOW TO APPLY THIS TO YOUR OWN REPORTS

Try this exercise with a past research report:

1. Write down your main insight.
2. List two to four reasons why this is true.
3. Rewrite each argument to be clear, specific, and measurable.

Once you've presented your main insight and broken it down into key arguments, it's time to prove your point.

This is where you back up your claims with clear, compelling evidence that makes your conclusions undeniable.

Even the most well-structured research reports fall apart if they lack strong evidence.

Think about it from your stakeholder's perspective. When you say:

Users don't trust the checkout process.

Their first thought will be:

How do you know that?

Without solid evidence, your insight is just an opinion. But when you back it up with data, patterns, and direct user quotes, it becomes impossible to dismiss.

THE THREE TYPES OF RESEARCH EVIDENCE

There are three main types of evidence you can use in your reports:

1. Qualitative insights (Why is it happening?)
2. User interviews (direct quotes, emotional reactions)
3. Usability tests (observations, confusion points)

This type of evidence is great for showing scale and impact.
Example:

40% of users abandon checkout at Step 2 due to unclear UI labels.

This type of evidence is crucial for understanding the reasons behind the data.

Example:

> When I got to the payment step, I wasn't sure if my credit card info was secure.
>
> (User interview #6)

This type of evidence helps add credibility and context to your findings.
Example:

> Top-performing e-commerce sites display a security badge at checkout, which has been shown to increase conversions by 25%.
>
> (Baymard Institute, 2023)

HOW TO CHOOSE THE RIGHT EVIDENCE

Not all evidence is equally persuasive.
If you want stakeholders to take action, your evidence must be:

- Relevant— It directly supports your key arguments.
- Specific—It uses real numbers, patterns, or quotes.
- Balanced—It combines quantitative and qualitative data.

HOW TO STRUCTURE YOUR EVIDENCE

A strong research report follows a clear hierarchy:

1. Key argument (What's the issue?)
2. Supporting evidence (How do we know this is true?)
3. Implication (Why does this matter?)

Example:
Key argument:

- "Users abandon checkout at Step 2 because they don't trust the security of the payment process."

Supporting evidence:

- 40% of users drop off at Step 2 (Google Analytics data).
- 60% of surveyed users said they were unsure if their payment details were safe.
- Usability testing quote: "I didn't see any security badges, so I wasn't sure if I should enter my credit card details."

Implication:

- "Users need clearer trust signals (security badges, reassurance messaging) to feel confident in completing their purchase."

This structure keeps your findings logical, persuasive, and easy to follow.

MISTAKES TO AVOID

Dumping Too Much Raw Data

- Avoid long lists of stats with no explanation.
- Instead, highlight the most important numbers and explain why they matter.

Using Vague Statements

- Weak: "Users found the checkout process frustrating."
- Strong: "50% of users abandoned checkout, and 70% of them cited security concerns as the reason."

Ignoring Conflicting Data

- If some users had a different experience, acknowledge it. This builds trust and credibility.

HOW TO APPLY THIS IN YOUR REPORTS

Take a past research report and ask yourself:

1. Do I have a mix of quantitative and qualitative evidence?
2. Have I clearly linked each piece of evidence to a key argument?
3. Is my evidence concise and easy to understand?

At this point, you have:

1. Your main insight (the answer upfront).
2. Your key arguments (why the insight is true).
3. Your supporting evidence (proof that backs up each argument).

Now, it's time to bring it all together in a structured report that stakeholders can digest quickly and easily.

This is where the pyramid structure comes in.

Even if your research is airtight, if your report isn't structured properly, it won't get read or acted upon.

Stakeholders don't want to dig through pages of methodology to figure out what's important. They need to be able to find the insights they need in seconds.

A poorly structured report is like an unorganized fridge—everything is in there somewhere, but finding what you need is frustrating and time-consuming.

A well-structured report, on the other hand, makes insights immediately clear.

THE PYRAMID STRUCTURE: HOW TO ORGANIZE YOUR REPORT

The pyramid structure ensures that the most critical information is always at the top, followed by supporting details.

Instead of starting with background information and slowly building up to conclusions, you flip it upside down:

1. Start with the most important insight (the answer).
2. Break it down into key arguments (why this is true).
3. Provide supporting evidence (proof for each argument).
4. Add background information only if needed (research methods, process, additional context).

This means that if a stakeholder stops reading after the first few sentences, they still walk away with the most important insights.

HOW TO APPLY THE PYRAMID STRUCTURE IN YOUR REPORTS

1. Lead with an Executive Summary

The first page of your report should include:

- Main insight: The single most important takeaway.
- Key findings: Two to four bullet points summarizing the most important arguments.
- Actionable recommendations: What should happen next?

Example:
Executive Summary
Main Insight:
Users are abandoning checkout because they don't trust the security of the payment process.
Key Findings:

- 40% of users drop off at Step 2, citing concerns about security
- 60% of surveyed users say they are unsure whether their payment details are safe
- User interviews revealed that most people expect to see a security badge or trust message at checkout

Recommendations:

- Add a security badge and short reassurance text on the payment page
- Provide a clear message explaining how their payment data is protected
- Conduct A/B testing to measure the impact of these changes

This structure immediately delivers value to the reader. If they read nothing else, they still get the key takeaways.

2. Organize the Body of Your Report Using the Pyramid Structure

Once you've provided the high-level summary, the rest of your report should follow a clear hierarchy:

1. Main insight (stated again, with a little more detail).
2. Key arguments (each argument in its own section).
3. Supporting evidence (qualitative + quantitative data for each argument).
4. Additional context (methodology, research process, limitations).

Example:
Finding 1: Users abandon checkout because they don't trust the payment process
Supporting Evidence:

- 40% drop-off rate at Step 2 (Google Analytics).
- 60% of surveyed users said they were hesitant to enter payment details.
- User interview quote: "I didn't see any security messages, so I wasn't sure if my payment was safe."

Implications:

- Users need reassurance that their payment is secure.
- Lack of trust signals is leading to revenue loss.

Recommendation:

- Add a security badge and reassurance message at checkout.
- Test different trust signals to see what resonates most with users.

MISTAKES TO AVOID

Burying Insights under Too Much Background Information

- Avoid starting with a long explanation of research methodology.
- Put findings first, process second.

Not Using Headings and Sections Clearly

- Each key finding should have its own section.
- Make reports scannable so stakeholders can jump to what they need.

Too Much Detail in the Wrong Place

- Avoid dumping all your raw data into the report.
- Instead, summarize the most critical insights and put extra details in an appendix if needed.

HOW TO APPLY THIS TO YOUR OWN REPORTS

1. Try this exercise:
    i. Take a past research report and compare it to the pyramid structure.
    ii. Rearrange it so the key insight is upfront and background details come last.
    iii. Use clear section headings so it's easy to navigate.

You started with the answer—the main insight stakeholders need to know. You broke it down into key arguments that clearly explain why it's true. You provided strong evidence that makes your findings impossible to ignore. You structured your report like a pyramid so that insights are easy to find and digest.

But none of that matters if nothing happens next.
Too many research reports end up sitting in a Google Drive folder, untouched.
Your job isn't just to deliver insights, it's to drive change.
This means you need to make your research actionable.

HOW TO MAKE YOUR FINDINGS ACTIONABLE

A strong research report doesn't stop at describing problems. It provides clear, specific, and realistic recommendations that teams can act on.

Here's how to do it:

1. Translate Every Key Insight into a Clear Recommendation

For each major finding, ask yourself:

- What needs to change because of this insight?
- What should the team do differently?
- How can we test whether the change is effective?

Each insight should have a corresponding action item.
Example:
Finding:
Users don't trust the checkout process, leading to a 40% drop-off rate.
Supporting evidence:

- 60% of surveyed users said they weren't sure if their payment details were safe.
- Multiple users in usability testing hesitated at the payment screen.
- Competitor analysis shows that top-performing checkout flows include visible trust signals.

Actionable recommendation:

- Add a security badge and short reassurance text on the payment page.
- Run an A/B test to measure the impact on conversion rates.
- Include a progress bar so users know what happens next.

This recommendation is clear, specific, and immediately actionable.
Bad recommendation:

- "Improve trust in the checkout process." (Too vague)

Good recommendation:

- "Add a security badge and reassurance text on the payment page, then run an A/B test to measure its impact." (Specific and actionable)

2. Be Specific About What Needs to Be Done

A vague recommendation leads to confusion. A specific recommendation tells the team exactly what to do next.
Example:
Weak recommendation:

- "Make onboarding smoother."

Strong recommendation:

- "Reduce the onboarding process from 5 steps to 3, removing unnecessary fields in the signup form. Test a 'skip for now' option for non-critical setup steps."

If your recommendation is too broad, break it down:

1. What specific change needs to happen?
2. Who needs to take action?
3. What's the first step?

3. Make Recommendations Realistic and Feasible

A great recommendation is useless if it's not practical. Before finalizing your recommendations, ask:

- Does this align with the company's priorities?
- Is this something the team has the capacity to do?
- What's a realistic first step?

If your ideal solution isn't feasible, suggest a smaller, testable version. For example:
Unrealistic:

- "Redesign the entire onboarding flow." (Too big, too vague)

Realistic:

- "Start by testing a new onboarding flow with 10 users before committing to a full redesign."

4. Prioritize Recommendations by Impact and Effort

Not all recommendations are equal. Some will have a big impact with minimal effort, while others require major resources.

Help teams focus on what matters most by ranking recommendations by impact and effort.

Stakeholders are much more likely to act on your insights if they can see which changes are easy wins and which ones require more investment.

5. Assign Ownership and Next Steps

Even the best recommendations can get lost if it's not clear who owns them.

At the end of your report, include a simple action plan:

This eliminates confusion and makes sure someone is accountable for moving the research forward.

Instead of just presenting research findings, your report should end with a concrete action plan. For example:

Executive Summary

Main insight:

Users abandon checkout because they don't trust the security of the payment process.

Key findings:

- 40% of users drop off at Step 2.
- 60% of surveyed users say they are unsure if their payment details are safe.
- Usability testing revealed that users expect visible security badges.

Recommended actions:

1. Add a security badge and reassurance text on the payment page.
2. Run an A/B test to measure the impact on conversion rates.
3. Include a progress bar so users know what happens next.

Action plan:

I wish someone had told me this earlier in my career: no one cares how much effort you put into your research if they don't know what to do with it.

I learned this the hard way.

I used to write research reports like I was submitting a final paper for a university course—methodology first, pages of findings, beautifully detailed charts, and finally, at the very end, my conclusions. I thought I was being thorough. I thought giving stakeholders everything would help them make the best decisions.

It didn't.

Instead, I'd get questions like:

- "Wait, what's the main takeaway?"
- "I don't have time to read all this—can you just tell me the highlights?"
- "So ... what should we do about it?"

I was making a critical mistake: I was writing for other researchers, not for my stakeholders.

Once I started using the Pyramid Principle, everything changed. My research started getting read. More importantly, my research started getting used.

It took me a while to get comfortable with this approach. At first, it felt too direct—almost like I was skipping over the depth of the research. But that's the thing:

Stakeholders don't need every detail. They need clarity.

If they want more depth, they'll ask for it. But if they don't immediately understand the insight and what to do about it, the research won't drive change.

That's the real job of a user researcher—not just to uncover insights, but to make sure those insights lead to better products, smarter decisions, and actual impact.

So the next time you sit down to write a research report, flip it upside down.

- Lead with the answer
- Break it down
- Provide strong evidence
- Structure it clearly
- Make it impossible to ignore

The best research doesn't just sit in a report. It changes what happens next.

Session Summaries 26

User research summaries serve as a pivotal tool in disseminating valuable insights efficiently. They play a crucial role for several reasons.

- Snapshot of Essential Information: Summaries provide stakeholders with a concise overview of critical findings, saving them from sifting through extensive reports.
- Pattern Identification: They enable researchers to spot recurring patterns and themes across various research sessions, helping teams identify the most impactful insights.
- Efficient Digestion: Stakeholders can efficiently digest session details through a combination of textual insights and multimedia elements.
- Actionable Recommendations: Summaries often include actionable next steps and recommendations based on research insights, guiding teams toward informed decisions.
- Customizable for Audience: Summaries are highly customizable to cater to the specific needs and preferences of different audiences.
- Enhanced Findability: Digitized summaries can be easily tagged for improved "findability," ensuring that stakeholders can quickly locate relevant information.

I started writing these research summaries years ago, and have continued with them at every company where I have worked or freelanced. They have provided an easy way for me to communicate findings quickly, and allow for impactful changes within the team mindset and the product.

HOW TO CRAFT A USER RESEARCH SUMMARY

Each research summary comes from a generative research session or a usability test. Through the years, the summaries have evolved, and I have adapted them to different teams. For some organizations, they come in the form of a Google Doc, Google Slides, or a Pages document with more visuals.

Whenever I am summarizing a usability test in this format, I always include screenshots with annotations. I go through the following steps before I begin writing a research summary.

1. Revisit the Research Interview. Listen to the research interview once more to ensure a thorough understanding of the session.
2. Transcribe and Annotate. Transcribe your notes from the entire conversation while listening, using tools like Excel for organization. Tag each relevant data point with a corresponding need, pain point, motivation, or goal.
3. Affinity Diagram. Perform a mini-affinity diagram for the session, grouping related needs, pain points, motivations, and goals.
4. Identify Key Insights. Highlight the most mentioned or repeated information within the session and across previous sessions.
5. Select Relevant Quotes. Choose the most relevant quotes from the session that provide context to the participants' viewpoints.
6. Formulate Recommendations. Consider actionable next steps or recommendations based on the insights gleaned.

While this process may require two to three hours for every one-hour interview, it serves as a valuable time-saving step when preparing for broader synthesis sessions, encompassing multiple research sessions. These screenshots and summaries also allow teams to take place in synthesis sessions more easily. They can scan through these documents and bring ideas to meetings without having to watch every interview. Once I go through the above process, I make a note of what I want to include in the summary.

MY MUST-HAVES CHECKLIST OF A USER RESEARCH SUMMARY

- Participant Description: Briefly describe the individual you spoke to, specifying their segment or persona, and their representation within the customer base.
- Relevant Teams: Indicate which teams, squads, or tribes would benefit most from the summary's insights.
- Project Background: Provide a succinct project background to offer context and clarify the study's goals.
- Notable Quotes: Include verbatim quotes that best represent the user, and can guide teams in making informed decisions.
- Themes and Highlights: Summarize key themes and highlights from the session, drawing connections to previous sessions where applicable.

- Recommendations: If applicable, offer actionable recommendations based on the insights garnered.
- Multimedia: Incorporate multimedia elements, such as video or audio clips, to allow stakeholders to see and hear user insights firsthand. For usability testing, screenshots with annotations are invaluable.
- Links to Resources: Provide links to any additional documentation or research notes that may aid the team in delving deeper into the insights.

User research summaries are structured depending on my audience. They are highly customizable. And you can use these as a way to summarize one particular interview, a series of interviews, or even a monthly summary of the research done for one specific team.

TWO RESEARCH SUMMARY EXAMPLES

Since it may be difficult to imagine what I am describing above, I'll give two examples of how I structure and construct my research summaries. Both of these summaries contain completely falsified data, but reveal the type of information and structure I use.

EXAMPLE ONE

The first example is from a generative research session. For this project, we were looking to understand and report on user's mental models on travel. In this particular research summary, I give an overall impression of the interview and draw parallels from other sessions. I don't provide recommendations because I want the team to digest the information without my bias.

I will send these out before a team synthesis session so colleagues can understand the themes and highlights but come to their conclusions on the next steps.

Date: 10/04/2022
Desktop/App: Desktop
Persona: Moving Mary
Place: Paris
Employment status: Student
Relevant squads mentioned: Booking, Ticketing, and Innovation
Project background

With generative research, we are looking to create a general understanding of how our users think about travel, and how they are interacting, at a high-level, with the TravelBuddy website or app.

NOTABLE QUOTES

I am excited about sustainability, so it would be nice also to include suggestions like, what is the most sustainable way with the least emissions. There are some websites, which let you calculate the impact you have on the environment in terms of CO_2 emissions, but that function would be nice. That way, you can negate the environmental impact (ex: Atmosfair).

I was looking for a trip from Paris to Amsterdam to make a reservation in a special train compartment because I was traveling with a guitar. I know there is a special baby compartment on the trains, but I could not book this on TravelBuddy, so I had to go to the carrier website directly to book. So, sometimes I think, why should I book tickets with you?

If I already searched for a particular trip and didn't finish booking yet, it would say something like "trips in-progress." If you haven't finished booking your trip, you should be able to continue. Or, meanwhile, we found you these other trips we can recommend to you, like the cheapest way. It would be like a travel companion.

THEMES AND HIGHLIGHTS

1. As we've heard before, the number of changeovers are critical in the decision-making process. For this participant, the number of changeovers was paramount, as she was traveling with a guitar and luggage
2. She has been having the same struggles as other participants when trying to edit a trip as everything resets, and she has to start from scratch
   a. "Now I need to try this again and start all over again. I have to organize the search and all the filters again. It is annoying"
   b. "I tried to go back and change a trip to one-way, and there is no way to edit it, which is frustrating. I can't change anything and, if I want to, I have to start from scratch."
3. She is another user who did not know there was an account area, and she recommended we include a travel profile. The travel profile would consist of relevant information, but also stats on CO_2 emissions.
   a. "I would like to see a little more like a log-in function, so you could have a travel profile where I could see my recent trips. If I always go somewhere, based on that, you can make recommendations. It would have easy access to similar trips I've booked before, so then I don't have to re-enter all the stuff."
   b. "If you see I often travel with a certain carrier, you could give me special deals for certain routes. You do email me about some offers, but it would be nice if they were more targeted for me."

OTHER TOOLS SHE USES

- Booking.com for hotels
- Skyscanner
- Google Flights
- Expedia
- Links to resources
- Research notes
- Research session recording
- Participant folder

EXAMPLE TWO

The second research summary I use is much more tangible and consists of direct recommendations or next steps. I do this after a usability test, or when I am synthesizing for a team that needs the next steps. Generally, in this scenario, we might not have time for a group synthesis session, or this could be a summary of the group synthesis session.

Insight One—P1, P4, P5, P6, P8

Insight/problem

We do not provide sufficient engagement analytics for our clients, inhibiting them from making data-driven decisions.

Actions/recommendations

- Visual content analysis metrics (what is in the picture/what performs best).
- Content recommendations based on analysis—Industry/vertical benchmarks.
- Tie revenue back to highest-engaging photos.

QUOTE

"If we knew the most popular photos contained dogs, we could cherry-pick the content that we know would increase engagement and revenue."

Insight Two—P2, P3, P5, P8

Insight/problem

Many clients are asking for manual reports from account managers, as our platform isn't providing sufficient metrics/data.

Actions/recommendations

- Allow users to compare metrics month-over-month or year-or-year.
- Hashtag metrics would allow users to adjust hashtag strategy independently.
- Pull out/recommend content similar to top-performing photos.
- Make note of which photos have been used and in which social channels.

"I need metrics that will help with two things: proving that the platform is worth the price and allowing us to strategize without having to run to our account manager."

These are not the only two ways to provide research summaries to teams. However, these have been incredibly useful in providing an easily digestible snapshot of findings, and for helping the teams synthesize more massive quantities of information into smaller chunks. Doing so increases the likelihood that your research will be taken seriously, and sets the ground for action in the future.

Research Newsletters

27

User research newsletters might not be a groundbreaking concept, but their effectiveness is evident in many organizations. Here we'll explore why they work, what to include, and how to set one up effectively using a template. User research newsletters have proven effective due to several key factors.

- Ease of Saving: People can conveniently save emails to read later, allowing them to consume research insights at their own pace.
- Searchability: In organizations without comprehensive repositories, individuals can store these emails in folders and easily search for specific information when needed.
- Building Connections: Newsletters foster better collaboration and connect different teams by showcasing research findings from various sources.
- Increased Understanding: They enhance the overall organization's understanding of the research team's work, and strengthen the connection with users.

CREATING A USER RESEARCH NEWSLETTER

Step 1: Determine Stakeholder Needs and Pain Points

Before crafting your newsletter, identify the needs and pain points of your colleagues. This ensures that the newsletter addresses specific challenges and provides valuable information.

Step 2: Decide on the Type of Information

Conduct stakeholder interviews and surveys to determine the type of information your colleagues need. Be open to feedback, and adjust the content accordingly. Initially, focus on what is most helpful for your audience.

Step 3: Choose a Cadence

Select a suitable cadence for your newsletter. It could be monthly, bi-weekly, quarterly, or tailored to your organization's research output. Test different frequencies and gather feedback to find the right balance.

Step 4: Conduct a Beta Test

Before sending the newsletter organization-wide, conduct a beta test with a smaller group, such as your product teams. Use this phase to refine the content, format, and structure based on feedback and conversations with the test group.

Step 5: Ask for Feedback and Iterate

Encourage colleagues to provide feedback on the newsletter. Be open to criticism and use this input to make continuous improvements. Engage in conversations and consider incentives, like coffee or lunch, to gather valuable insights.

COMPONENTS OF A USER RESEARCH NEWSLETTER

A well-structured user research newsletter typically includes:

- A Light-hearted Start: Begin with a joke or a light-hearted element, like a meme, to set a positive tone and make readers smile.
- The Month's Theme: Introduce a monthly theme that aligns with product teams' work, business goals, and crucial insights from recent research.
- Top Three Insights: Select and elaborate on the top three insights related to the theme. Include relevant teams, quotes, infographics, links to audio/video clips, and keywords (hashtags) for searchability.
- A Surprising Fact: Share an intriguing fact related to the theme, and provide a link to the relevant presentation or source.
- Last Month's Insight Update: Update readers on any developments or updates regarding insights from the previous month. Highlight the impact of user research and acknowledge teams.
- Upcoming Research-related Events and Information: Inform readers about upcoming ideation workshops, hackathons, or research roadmap updates. Provide links for more information.

- Feedback Survey: Include a link to an anonymous feedback survey (e.g., Google Forms) to gather insights on the newsletter's performance and ways to enhance it.
- Direct Contact: Invite readers to reach out directly with questions or research requests. Include a link to a research intake form to streamline requests.

TEMPLATE FOR A USER RESEARCH NEWSLETTER

Below is a general outline of the sections and content you can include in your user research newsletter.

- Joke or Light-hearted Element
- Monthly Theme
  - Briefly introduce the theme
- Top Three Insights
  - Insight 1
    - Relevant Teams
    - Quotes
    - Multimedia Links
    - Keywords (Hashtags)
  - Insight 2
    - Relevant Teams
    - Quotes
    - Multimedia Links
    - Keywords (Hashtags)
  - Insight 3
    - Relevant Teams
    - Quotes
    - Multimedia Links
    - Keywords (Hashtags)
- A Surprising Fact
- Interesting Fact
- Link to Relevant Presentation
- Last Month's Insight Update
  - Updates on Previous Insights
- Upcoming Research-Related Events and Information
  - Ideation Workshops
  - Hackathons
  - Research Roadmap
  - Information Links

- Feedback Survey
  - Link to Anonymous Feedback Survey
- Direct Contact
  - Contact Information
  - Link to Research Intake Form.

A monthly user research newsletter can be a powerful tool for sharing research insights, and fostering collaboration within your organization. Continuously gather feedback, adapt to your colleagues' needs, and keep refining your newsletter to make it a valuable resource for your team and stakeholders.

Personas 28

I was met with a circumstance, where I had no choice but to face my persona creation skills. It hit a point, where almost once a week, colleagues were asking the question, "Who are our users?" And I continued to fail to answer it.

We didn't know who our main users were, or what they needed from our platform. We didn't understand the goals they were trying to accomplish. We had some idea of the pain points, thanks to account managers and customer support sending over problems they'd heard of repeatedly, and some of the evaluative research we did. However, we really failed to paint a picture of who our users really were.

For a while, I tried to avoid the question, rather than face the facts that I was going to have to do another persona study. I had been burnt in the past by them so many times, I didn't want to have to face the same kind of failure. I was scared about what that would mean for my job and for my credibility within the organization.

But there I was, trying to dance around the question yet again, when I finally gave in. It was time to create personas, but I vowed to do it differently this time.

I went back and did a retrospective on the previous personas I created, and hypothesized all the things that went wrong with them, as to not repeat the same mistakes this time. Thinking back, I listed the following as issues.

1. Held the wrong information. The information on the persona was not particularly relevant to the teams.
2. Did not contain actionable information. Most of the information was so vague that it wasn't actionable by teams due to the lack of context.
3. Poor design. Sliders and poor design choices led to the personas being difficult to use.
4. Lack of activation. I was under the assumption that I just needed to create the persona, and the team would be on their way with the rest. I didn't do a great job activating the personas and helping the teams best use them.
5. Not enough research. My first personas were based on surface-level information and not nearly enough interviews, which led to the vagueness and lack of context. If I didn't feel comfortable properly explaining who this persona was, how could my team feel good making decisions?

With this list, I felt better about my next persona project, but looking it over, I wondered how I was going to accomplish all of this and create personas that were helpful, useful, and actionable to my teams.

A NEW PROCESS

Since I had previously created my personas in such a vacuum (which is how I tend to work when I am nervous or scared of failing), I decided to rip the band aid off and do the exact opposite.

The previous personas had mainly been unactionable and lacking relevant information, so the first thing I did was reverse engineer the process. I wasn't going to lock myself away to create something based on my shoddy Google search queries and horrible templates. Instead, I was going to include the team in every step of the way, starting all the way from the beginning.

1. My new process was to look like:
   1. Information-gathering workshop with the team;
   2. Understanding segmentation;
   3. Building proto-personas through assumptions and current knowledge;
   4. Recruiting and conducting the research;
   5. Analyzing and synthesizing with the team;
   6. Creating the persona;
   7. Activating the persona.

The steps were many more than I initially embarked on for my other persona projects. But this was my big attempt to prove that personas themselves were not useless, and that it was the proper set-up and creation of them that made the difference. I told my team the process we were going to follow, and that it would take some time, around 4 months, to create the first persona or potential personas, depending on the segmentation we decided on.

Usually, since I tend to be a team of one user researcher, when I conduct persona research, I am also still conducting day-to-day research. This means that these bigger projects can take longer than if I were dedicated full-time. The team was okay with the timeline. People had been asking for personas for quite some time, so 4 months seemed like nothing to them.

With this new process and the concept of reverse engineering, it was the first time I built a successful persona. It was extremely gratifying, and I learned so much from the process. Over time, I continued to refine it and create better personas. To showcase this process, I will bring you step-by-step through a project of building a B2C persona for a travel company, so that you can see every step I took.

BUILDING A B2C TRAVEL PERSONA

For some context, I was working at a German travel company called fromAtoB. We hadn't done any research into understanding who our users were, and that was causing a lot of problems in knowing what to work on and prioritizing things.

At this point, I knew immediately that personas would help us in the situation, because without understanding who was using our platform, we would continue to struggle. I wanted to make sure these personas didn't fall into the dark hole of uselessness I'd previously experienced, so I ensured to go through the above process that helped me create them.

INFORMATION-GATHERING WORKSHOP

The first step whenever I consider personas is to have an information-gathering workshop with the team. This workshop has two main goals.

1. To ensure that a persona is the right deliverable for what the team needs by the end of the study and, if not, to determine the correct deliverable for the study.
2. If it is the correct deliverable, then I gather the type of information teams need inside the persona.

With these two goals in mind, my persona immediately becomes more actionable, because I've already started to orient the deliverable around my team's needs, rather than guessing what should be in it. In this particular workshop, I sat down with:

- Three product managers;
- Three designers;
- Three developers.

Within these nine people, we had a product manager, designer, and developer from each of the main squads that would be using the personas. I asked each of the teams before this workshop to also gather information from their respective teams on what they needed to know and the information they were seeking. I set the following agenda for the 60-minute workshop:

1. Introduction to the workshop—5 minutes.
2. Brainstorming and discussing teams' questions—20 minutes.
3. Brainstorming and discussing teams' needs—20 minutes.
4. Discussing initial segmentation—10 minutes.
5. Wrap-up and next steps—5 minutes.

Since we were in the office, I set up the space for post-its in each area. We worked on both divergent and convergent work. For example, during the 20 minutes of brainstorming and discussing teams' questions and needs, I started first with individual work.

Everyone brainstormed all the questions they could think of on their own for the first 5 to 7 minutes (I asked everyone if they needed two more minutes after 5 minutes went by). Then, we brought all the questions together, quickly clustered similar ones, and took the remaining time to discuss them.

Some of my teammates had a hard time coming up with teams' questions and needs, so I helped with prompts.

- What are the gaps in our knowledge?
- What would you need to know about users to make better decisions?
- I need ____(x information needed)____ to make ____(y decision)____ to achieve ____(z goal)____.
- What information would help you make a better decision?
- What information do you wish you knew about users? Why?

In our workshop, we came up with questions.

- Who uses our platform the most often?
- What type of travel are our users doing on our platform?
- Why do people use our platform instead of (or in addition to) others?
- Who should we focus on in terms of upcoming features? Who should we build for?

And the information needed looked like this:

- Top pain points users are experiencing and why;
- What these users are trying to accomplish both inside and outside of our platform when traveling;
- The needs these travelers have while booking travel;
- The values the travelers have.

By the end of the 60-minute workshop, I was sure that a persona would be helpful, and I already started to form the kind of information I would need to put into them to be actionable. Keep in mind that if you find a persona is not the ideal deliverable, that is okay! You just saved yourself a bunch of work and your team a frustrating experience!

UNDERSTANDING SEGMENTATION

Now that I had an idea that a persona would be a helpful deliverable, I had to start thinking about segmentation. For this particular project, we decided to focus on behaviors and usage of the platform. We had some idea that people used our travel platform for three different reasons:

1. Leisure travel (e.g., going on a holiday);
2. Obligatory travel (e.g., going to see family);
3. Work travel (e.g., going on a work trip).

We also saw that people either traveled:

- Completely solo;
- With a partner or a child;
- With family;
- With a group of friends.

I sent out a survey to our audience over the course of two weeks through HotJar to help us understand the breakdown between these different segments. I asked the following questions:

- In the past 6 months, how many times have you traveled for a holiday?
  - I haven't traveled on holiday in the past 6 months.
  - One to three times.
  - Four to six times.
  - Over seven times.

I repeated that for each type of travel. I then asked about who people most usually traveled with by asking:

- In the past 6 months, how many times have you traveled alone?
  - I haven't traveled alone in the past 6 months.
  - One to three times.
  - Four to six times.
  - Over seven times.

I repeated that question for each of the above criteria. This helped us determine the most common type of travel, and how people typically traveled when it came to others. With this, we understood the most common travel that people used our platform for was leisure travel. And most commonly, it was with a partner or a small group of friends (four or fewer people). We decided to focus our efforts on leisure travel for two to four people at once, as that was our biggest revenue driver, which is often who you ended up focusing on first because, well, business.

BUILDING PROTO-PERSONAS

Something that I had skipped in the past was the building of proto-personas, which are essentially personas based on assumptions that can be viewed as prototypes of the personas. There are many things I love about proto-personas, as they really help with:

- Understanding the assumptions and biases the team has about users;
- Getting a base understanding of where our assumed gaps in knowledge are;

- Having a place to start when it comes to understanding (although loosely) who these people are;
- Ensuring the areas we decide to focus on are aligned with what the teams need.

In this workshop, I sat down with:

- Three product managers;
- Three designers;
- Three engineers;
- Head of marketing;
- Head of customer support;
- Head of data analytics.

I set up the meeting to be similar to affinity diagramming, but using our existing knowledge and assumptions, rather than basing it on actual research (yet). I put five categories on the whiteboard, each with its own space:

1. Pain points
2. Needs
3. Goals
4. Motivations
5. Tools

I structured the meeting with both divergent and convergent activities. The schedule looked like this:

1. Brainstorm and post pain points individually—7 minutes.
2. Discuss pain points—15 minutes.
3. Brainstorm and post needs individually—7 minutes.
4. Discuss needs—15 minutes.
5. Brainstorm and post goals individually—7 minutes.
6. Discuss goals—15 minutes.
7. Brainstorm and post motivations individually—7 minutes.
8. Discuss motivations—15 minutes.
9. Brainstorm and post tools individually—5 minutes.
10. Discuss tools—10 minutes.

During the divergent time, each person thought of all the assumptions or previous knowledge they had in each category. I had a few different colors of sticky notes that helped us denote:

- Something based on actual previous research that had been done (green stickies);
- Something based on other data, such as analytics, customer support tickets, etc. (blue stickies);
- Something based on an assumption or bias (yellow stickies).

I encouraged colleagues to brain dump anything and everything during this time, and then, during the convergent work, we discussed what they had put up, grouping similar themes or ideas. During the discussions, we talked about the previous research, why people held certain assumptions (and how risky those assumptions were), and the different data we had.

During the workshop, I really let people talk through their ideas and made sure not to shut down ideas or thoughts because, since these are proto-personas, it wasn't important that everything be based on research. After the workshop, I took photos of the board and digitized the post-its into a spreadsheet to make it easier to share with others and reference during the project.

In the end, it was hugely helpful to use the proto-persona because not only did it give me a jumping-off point for the conversations with users, but it also (eventually) highlighted that everything we assume isn't the truth.

RECRUITING AND CONDUCTING THE PERSONA RESEARCH

Finally, we were at the research stage! I felt like I had done so much planning at this point that I was itching to get to conducting the research. Sometimes it was hard for me to spend so much time in the planning phase, because I was concerned about people seeing it as taking too much time or not seeing progress in the project. Luckily, the team was patient with the process so everyone was excited to get to this stage.

RECRUITMENT

I must admit, to speed up the process, I already started recruiting a bit during the proto-persona workshop, after we had defined our segmentation better. We used a few different ways to recruit.

1. Sending emails to people who had agreed to receive research emails. I had done this earlier by posting in HotJar, asking people who were interested in research participation to sign up.
2. Posting a separate HotJar asking some qualifying questions to get people directly into the study.

I wanted to recruit for the following criteria:

- People who had planned and purchased leisure travel using our platform in the past 3 months;

- People who had travelled with four people and under for leisure travel in the past 3 months;
- People who have also used other platforms to book leisure travel in the past 6 months.

I changed each of these into several recruitment questions:

1. When was the last time you booked leisure travel with up to four people on fromAtoB?
   a. I haven't purchased leisure travel with others on fromAtoB.
   b. 1–3 months ago.
   c. 4–6 months ago.
   d. Over 7 months ago.
   e. Other.
2. How many people did you travel with on that leisure trip (including you)?
   a. Alone.
   b. Me and another person.
   c. Three people.
   d. Four people.
   e. Over four people.
3. Who planned that leisure trip?
   a. I planned the whole thing.
   b. Someone else planned the whole thing.
   c. Me and someone else split the planning.
   d. Other.
4. What other tools have you used in the past 6 months to book leisure travel? (Select all that apply)
   a. Skyscanner
   b. Expedia
   c. Rome2Rio
   d. Flixbus
   e. Deutschebahn
   f. Omio
   g. Kiwi
   h. Other
   i. None of the above.

These screener questions helped us ensure that we got participants who had recently used our platform to book a leisure trip for no more than four people, had participated in the planning of the trip, and had used other platforms. I have made so many mistakes with recruitment in the past by not being thoughtful enough about the recruitment criteria and process, so I was especially careful with this project to ensure we got the right participants. Since we were a B2C platform with a good amount of traffic to our website, I was able to recruit relatively quickly, in about a week.

For persona research, I wanted to talk to 20 people within that segment to reach saturation, so I recruited 25 people to account for attrition. I always over-recruit because, in my mind, the more the merrier. In full transparency, the sessions were 90 minutes each, a mix of remote and in-person. We paid participants €60 for their time. I had tested several different incentive amounts in Berlin, and this was the best one for recruiting quickly, but not completely breaking the bank.

CONDUCTING THE RESEARCH

Recruitment takes a lot of time, I start conducting research as I recruit. In this case, I didn't have to worry about it too much because we had our 25 people in about a week, but I was already scheduling sessions for that very week.

I had a nice combination of in-person and remote interviews. If I recall correctly, about 17 were remote and the remaining 6 were in-person. We ended up with only two no-shows!

Since this was generative research, I structured the sessions as much more of a conversation than any kind of interview. I sat down with my teams to define the overarching goals of the research, which were to:

- Discover and understand how users currently plan and purchase leisure travel, both inside and outside the fromAtoB platform;
- Uncover users' pain points and frustrations when planning and purchasing leisure travel;
- Identify the top needs users have when planning and purchasing leisure travel;
- Identify the tools users engage with when planning and purchasing leisure travel, outside of fromAtoB and how they experience them.

By targeting these goals and getting this information, we would be able to evaluate our proto-personas and build new personas for our leisure travel users. Whenever I structure a generative research session, I always define the overarching goals first, because I use those goals to create my discussion guide. With these goals in mind, I was able to pick the methodology, approach, and write out some guiding questions.

For the method, I chose a combination of a discussion and a walk-the-store interview. The reason I did this was because I wanted to achieve two separate goals. With the up-front discussion, I could:

- Ask questions about leisure travel planning and purchasing outside of the fromAtoB platform;
- Talk through their overarching planning process for leisure without bringing up our platform;
- Hear about additional tools they use for planning and purchasing leisure travel and their experience with them before bringing up our platform.

With the walk-the-store, I could:

- Get a clear play-by-play of how they plan and purchase leisure trips using the fromAtoB platform;
- Observe the pain points they encounter while planning and purchasing leisure trips on fromAtoB;
- Understand their needs when it comes to leisure travel planning and purchasing.

I love using two different approaches during persona work, because it helps ensure I am getting information about the person and not just about the platform.

When building my discussion guide, I looked back at the goals and created guided questions based on each of the goals. I am extremely well-versed and confident in generative research, to the point where I often don't need a script. However, if you are just beginning in generative research, it might be worth having more questions you can fall back on.

This is my guide for the first discussion part that lasted 30 minutes.

Discover and understand how users currently plan and purchase leisure travel, both inside and outside the fromAtoB platform:

- I would love to talk through the last time you planned and purchased a leisure trip. Can you start by telling me the very moment you started planning or thinking about the trip and then walking me through your entire process step-by-step, almost like I am creating a documentary of the process you went through?
- Tell me about why you decided on that particular trip.
- Describe the primary feeling during [identified stage]?
- Explain what you did during [identified stage].
- Talk me through who else was planning with you during [identifying stage]. What was that experience like?
- Describe what was most important to you during [identified stage].

Uncover users' pain points and frustrations when planning and purchasing leisure travel:

- Describe the number one frustration you have during [identified stage]?
  - Explain what happened.
  - Talk me through what you did when you experienced [identified pain point]?
- Walk me through another frustrating experience you had during [identified stage].
  - Explain what happened.
  - Talk me through what you did when you experienced [identified pain point]?
- Talk me through the most frustrating part of the process for you.

Identify the top needs users have when planning and purchasing leisure travel:

- Walk me through what you were trying to accomplish during [identified stage].
- Describe which stage was the most important in the process.
- Talk me through anything that was missing during [identified stage].

Identify the tools users engage with when planning and purchasing leisure travel, outside of fromAtoB and how they experience them:

- Which is the most common website/app you usually use to book leisure travel.
- Describe your last experience with [website/app name].
- Describe what was missing with your experience with [website/app name].
- Talk me through a frustrating experience you've had with [website/app name].

I very much structured my sessions based on the assumption that there would be several stages we would walk through. Because of this assumption, I was prepared to repeat the same questions for each stage. For instance, if participants were talking about the awareness stage (and let's say participants called it "when they became aware of the need"), I would ask:

- Describe the primary feeling when you became aware of the need to travel.
- Explain what you did when you became aware of the need to travel.
- Talk me through who else was planning with you when you became aware of the need to travel. What was that experience like?
- Describe what was most important to you when you became aware of the need to travel.

I then repeated the same for each stage so that I had a clear understanding of the process, and what went on during each part of the process. Looking back, I likely would have expanded the session time to 2 hours, because 90 minutes went by incredibly fast when going to the level of depth I was.

ANALYZING AND SYNTHESIZING WITH THE TEAM

Because we ended up speaking to 23 participants, I knew I had to split up the analysis and synthesis. There was no way we would be able to analyze and synthesize the data from 23 participants all at once—we'd be stuck in a workshop for days.

So, I decided to try something I had experimented with when it came to other research projects, which was a debrief after each interview, and then a mini synthesis session after every seven interviews.

RESEARCH DEBRIEFS

Research debriefs are something that I baked into every session. For the 30 minutes after the interview, I sat with my team and used the same affinity diagram we'd used during our proto-persona building, to put down key findings straight after the interview. This helped a lot with the information being fresh in our mind and also reducing the amount of synthesis I had to do alone. So, after each session, we sat down and listed out all we could remember about the participants' pain points, needs, goals, motivations, and tools.

Because each research debrief was only 30 minutes for a 90-minute interview, I didn't bother with convergent and divergent work. We all worked alone, brainstorming as many categories as we could during the 30 minutes. I cleaned up the board after each session and left the convergent collaboration for the actual synthesis sessions. Some of our findings for each participant included:

> It can be overwhelming to think about how an unfamiliar city works—where to eat, get water, how the public transport works. You get all excited to get there and then you're like, "Uh how do I get around?"

> Having a flexible schedule for holidays is key. I never pick a day before I see and compare all the different prices to understand what is best for us. Even if that means coming back a day or two earlier than we'd like to—it's worth the price sometimes.

> Trying to get everyone to agree on a date, time, and destination can honestly be a nightmare. Sometimes I wish I wasn't the "planner" of the friend group because it can really take a toll. By the time we get to the destination I'm exhausted, and then I'm the one people look to if I forgot to plan a detail, such as knowing every public transport connection.

> It's essential for me to get out of the city to recharge. If I don't have that time away, I will completely lose my sanity. Traveling on holidays away from the city is definitely leisure but also absolutely necessary for me. Without it, I don't know if I would be able to live in Berlin.

MINI SYNTHESIS SESSIONS

I had been burnt previously by waiting until the last minute to do a big synthesis session. Originally, I had learned that you waited to synthesize everything at the end of a research project. That all went to shit for one project, where I was trying to synthesize about thirty interviews at once with a team. To say they resented me after days in a workshop would be kind. I vowed never to do that neither to myself, nor my teams, again.

Instead, if there was a large project with over fifteen participants, I started to have mini-synthesis sessions after every five or seven participants. This reduced the amount of load on my teams and helped us synthesize on the go, which meant that there wasn't as big of a chunk of time between the end of conducting research and the report or deliverable.

For this project, we decided to hold three mini-sessions and one larger synthesis session. I know it might sound like a lot, but it was well worth it. Instead of hours (or days) stuck in one continuous workshop, we broke the synthesis up over a few weeks. Also, the team felt like they were constantly learning through this process.

Each mini-synthesis session was about 90 minutes—I always put 90 minutes, but sometimes, due to lack of complexity or a quieter participant, we were able to finish faster. During the session, we would review the debriefs we had done on those seven participants, and then start to identify themes across the participants.

This is where I reintroduced the divergent and convergent work. We'd bring together the seven participants, add anything that was missing, and then discuss each category. It looked like this:

1. Bring participants 1–7 pain points across to a larger board (keep the participants numbered so you remember the original participant who mentioned the pain point).
2. Cluster similar pain points between participants.
3. Discuss the major clusters (with three or more stickies).

We repeated this for needs, goals, tools, and motivations.

Then, during the last synthesis session, we brought together the three bigger boards, plus the remaining two participants that we hadn't completed yet. We did the same thing where we brought the pain points from the three boards together, clustered similar information, and then discussed the major themes. Some themes included:

- Pain point: Getting everyone to agree upon a destination, budget, and dates for a trip when planning among friends.
- Need: Wanting to be humbled by an experience outside of one's culture.
- Value: Increase understanding of other cultures, lives, and perspectives.

MY SYNTHESIS PROCESS

During this process, I did a bit of my own analysis and synthesis. I often relistened to the recording of the session and added anything we missed into each participant's debrief board. Sometimes, if I had time, I would actually type a transcript of the interview in sheets (hey, low budget!) and tag that as well, then add any missing or additional information to the participant's debrief board. I also reviewed the debrief and mini-synthesis boards after each session to make sure we weren't missing anything or interpreting data incorrectly. Sometimes I wasn't able to include my colleagues in the synthesis process, whether because of timing, devaluing research, or any other reasons.

PRIORITIZING THE CATEGORIES

Once we had our categories and the information for each, I went through the team to prioritize which insights were most important. This was a crucial step because we had way too many insights to fit on to the persona—we had over twenty pain points—and I knew trying to shove them all into the small space of this deliverable would not be helpful.

We decided to prioritize the top four of each category (goals, needs, pain points) based on what was most important to act on ASAP. This prioritization helped the information on the persona to be as relevant as possible and also made it a living, iterative document. We used that to prioritize each of the insights and created a RICE (Reach, Impact, Confidence, Effort) chart for each category.

CREATING THE PERSONAS

If you know anything about me, you know that I am not a designer in the slightest. I can barely even draw a circle. So, when creating a deliverable, I always work with designers to help bring the research to life. For this project, we took the data that we found, and I worked with one of my designers to help me with designing the look of the persona.

And here is our first B2C persona for our organization! I didn't take pictures of subsequent iterations, but here are a few things I wanted to change.

1. Including goals. We missed out on putting goals on this version of the persona, and I felt like that was a huge miss. Goals are super helpful in orienting teams on what users are trying to accomplish as a whole, and can help with innovation or creating experiences that can help users further.
2. Take out the photo and use a gender-neutral name. I didn't like that we had a gendered name and photo, so I removed the photo and created a gender-neutral name. Since gender was of zero importance to this persona, I wanted to take that away.
3. Including more context. I wanted the persona to be easy to read, but I felt some points were way too shallow, especially values. Since we wanted teams to make decisions based on this information, we had to include a lot more context, even if that made it a bit more bulky. So I recommended adding a lot more context to the values section to make it relevant for decisions.

I also created a backlog of remaining needs and pain points that I could use to update the persona, as we fixed different issues or created experiences that met the (unmet) needs of our users.

ACTIVATING THE PERSONA

Finally, the time came to share the persona throughout the organization and not let it get dusty in a Google Drive folder. When it came to activating the persona, I had two separate goals.

1. To help people develop empathy and understanding of our persona.
2. To help teams make better decisions with the information on the persona.

These goals each needed a different way of activation, so I will break down how I approached each goal.

FOSTERING EMPATHY

For the empathy piece, I activated the persona in the following ways.

- I did a few global shareouts of the personas to walk through the process we went through, so that people became familiar with them. I also presented the personas every month at a new joiner meeting.
- I printed out posters of the persona and put them everywhere so people were constantly looking at them. I also put a pen and post-its next to each persona, where people could write feedback or questions—I collected this every week and answered them.
- I had a QR code created so that people could scan the QR code on the poster and be directed to all the materials for that persona, including interviews, the synthesis, quotes, and everything they needed to dive further in.
- I held a gallery night (with wine, beer, and cheese!) where people perused the personas and could ask questions or give feedback.
- I created stories around the personas to help colleagues understand their daily lives and how they operated both inside and outside our platform.
- We started tagging customers as persona names, so that we used them as often as possible.
- We started to tag features or improvements with the persona(s) they would later impact.

It took some time for people to get used to the personas, but I kept on reminding them the personas were there. After a few months, they really took off, and tagging customers as personas or using their names in user stories/roadmap planning became second nature.

MAKING BETTER DECISIONS

Personas are about helping your team make better decisions. I wanted to make sure teams were actually using the persona for that purpose, rather than it just being some vanity metric or checking off a to-do list. So, I went forward with a few different workshops.

1. Ideation workshops are the end-all-be-all of persona activation. In these workshops, you bring one or two of the most critical insights from your persona (based on the prioritization you did earlier) and, together, ideate solutions. In this setting, you're taking your research and making it into something, all while being there to help guide the team and provide context. Then, after the session, you have something to usability test!
2. Internal hackathon is another way to help focus the teams on activating the persona. I took important insights from our persona and broke the organization into several teams, where they each brainstormed solutions (while competing) over two or three days. It's exactly like any other hackathon, but this one is based on your persona insights. For me, it was one of the most fun ways to activate insights.
3. Mini-brainstorm sessions. I left room in my calendar for ad-hoc mini-brainstorming sessions. I invited stakeholders, who had been present in the research sessions. We took some of the quick fixes/low-hanging fruit we'd been hearing about and had a quick brainstorm on how we could solve these issues. Within the session, we either sketched ideas on paper, wireframed potential solutions, or just spoke through potential solutions.
4. Part of planning. I was a part of sprint and roadmap planning, so I made sure to always remind people of our persona and their needs, goals, and pain points. With this, we ensured we could map our projects to certain personas (especially once we created more). This was a huge help in getting colleagues to think about personas while planning work.
5. Persona review. Every quarter, I sat down with my colleagues, and we evaluated the persona on what we had worked on and what we had missed. With this information, I updated the persona, and we discussed how we would tackle the issues we hadn't yet solved and any next steps for the persona.

Not all of these exercises are always hits at different organizations. I've had some teams love internal hackathons while others hate them—same with mini-brainstorms or persona review meetings. The best thing you can do is try different approaches, and always ask your colleagues for feedback.

AWESOME OUTCOMES

After all that work, it was amazing to see the different outcomes from the persona.

1. We were able to narrow our decision-making to better serve our primary customers.
2. Designers felt more comfortable making design decisions, knowing what the user needed, the goals they had, and the pain points they encountered.
3. Designers created a design system based on the personas' needs and goals.
4. Product managers were better able to make feature decisions, and could A/B test two different variations with more confidence.
5. Product roadmaps were centered around our personas and the impact each project had on a given persona.
6. We improved key areas in our product, increasing our SUS score by 15% and increasing overall task success by 25%.
7. The entire organization better understood our primary user, which resulted in more specific marketing campaigns and better copywriting throughout the website.

And many other outcomes came out of that work that I can't even remember off the top of my head. So, if you are thinking about creating personas, but are concerned about their usefulness or effectiveness, I highly recommend trying out this approach (of course, tailor it to your needs!). It's a great learning experience, and I promise you, you will definitely get something for the work you put in!

Ecosystem Maps 29

An ecosystem map was one of the first deliverables I learned about and created. However, since then, they disappeared from my list of deliverables, and I didn't engage with them much. Instead, I was stuck in a world of personas and customer journeys while ecosystem maps took a backseat.

However, a few months ago, I was chatting with one of my mentees about an effective deliverable for a project. We went back and forth about outcomes like journey maps or personas, but none felt quite right for what we were trying to share. And that's when it clicked: an ecosystem map would be the perfect way to convey the information from the study in a digestible format.

Whenever I felt stagnant in my process, I tried to come up with a different technique or way to look at the study/problem. Rediscovering an old (or discovering a new!) approach can be inspiring, especially when repeatedly using the same old deliverables.

WHAT IS AN ECOSYSTEM MAP?

I remember first reading about ecosystem maps and feeling extremely overwhelmed. How was I supposed to map out every interaction between a product and other people in an experience? At first, I closed out the multiple tabs I had opened and walked away from ecosystem maps. I was new to my career and struggled with "the basics" of personas and journey maps. I didn't need a new deliverable to mess up.

But there was something about ecosystem maps that I knew would help us visualize the information we needed. So I went back to investigate these maps and how to use them.

An ecosystem map visualizes all the interactions, dependencies, and people in a given experience. Typically, there is a user, such as a persona, in the middle of this experience, and the ecosystem map shows how other people or products interact with this central person.

Regarding one central user, this mapping allows you to see their different interactions with other people, services, or products. It is especially helpful in giving you a holistic understanding of complex interactions or complicated experiences.

While journey maps are excellent tools, they can fall flat and bring a sense of linearity to an experience far from straightforward. Including an ecosystem map alongside a journey map can help you capture the complex nature of an experience in a non-linear way.

WHEN TO USE AN ECOSYSTEM MAP

More formal definitions like the above can be hard to apply to day-to-day work, so let's go through the situation when I thought an ecosystem map might be a good idea.

I worked on a hospitality platform that helped streamline hotel operations and better manage guest requests. It was a B2B2C platform in that our B2B users were a mix of hotel staff, such as housekeepers, engineers, concierge, and front desk staff, and our B2C users were hotel guests.

Before working at ALICE, I had no idea how complex the hospitality world was. But as I started having interviews with hotel staff, I realized that even the most minor task had a high degree of intricacy due to all the moving parts and interactions.

For example, when you go up to a concierge desk and request a dinner reservation at a recommended restaurant in the area, that sets off a chain of communication events that are in no way linear. I found the same complexity even when you call for an extra set of towels.

- The concierge takes down the request.
- They send the request to the housekeeping team, who logs a ticket.
- Someone from housekeeping has to fulfill the ticket and deliver the towels.
- The task is then marked as complete.
- The concierge gets notified of the towels being delivered and can potentially check in with the guest to make sure everything is fine.

There is a lot of room for error here. Different tasks of varying priority levels can come and require immediate attention. The guest can call again if the towels are taking too long, inadvertently creating a new ticket. Before long, they end up with twenty towels! When understanding these interactions and experiences, a journey map didn't feel like the right approach. I wanted to highlight the back-and-forth and the potential for confusion rather than show a journey of stages.

- Ecosystem maps show the user's experience with your service as a system and how that system and user are connected. With that said, the best time to use an ecosystem map is when you are trying to visualize how a user sits inside your service/product and their interactions during a specific experience. When I chose the ecosystem map for the above project, my goals looked like this:
- Understand the different interactions between the primary user and other people or services.
- Uncover potential pain points or areas where we do not support the user in their different interactions.
- Identify ways of streamlining our product to make interactions between people or services less complex.

HOW TO CREATE AN ECOSYSTEM MAP

I'm not going to lie, I love creating ecosystem maps because I find them really fun to think through, but they can be tricky the first few times you attempt them. But that is why I am here to walk you through the steps I go through when creating an ecosystem map.

1. Determine the Experience/Problem Area. The first step is narrowing the scope of the ecosystem map. While it would be cool to look at comprehensive experiences, the best thing you can do is pick one experience to start with so your map is digestible.
2. Choose the Primary User. As mentioned, the ecosystem map revolves around one particular user. Picking one primary user reduces the complexity of your map and allows you to understand more deeply how the different interactions impact that primary person.
3. List the Services, Products, or Platforms Within the Experience. Within this step, you list out all the touchpoints of the primary user with different apps, websites, platforms, and the main task.
4. List the Other People Involved in the Experience. The last step, before design, is to list the other people involved in the experience and how they relate to or interact with the primary user.

Of course, conducting generative research is necessary if you are unsure about the information for any of these steps. For the project above, I had already done several rounds of 1×1 interviews with concierge staff to understand all the needed information. Now comes the slightly more complicated part: design. There are a few different ways to visualize ecosystem maps. For example, some people use concentric circles, and the further the person/service/product is from the nucleus (the primary user), the less frequently the user has touchpoints with them.

Another approach is to use lines; the longer the lines, the less interaction that person/service/product has with the primary user during this experience. I've used both, and, personally, I like lines, but they can make a complex set of interactions look messy.

BUILDING THE MAP

Once you have all the information above, it's time to start building the map. With the above project, I focused on the experience of the concierge booking a restaurant for a guest. So with that, the concierge staff was my primary user. I then listed the different products and services that the concierge used in this experience:

- Pen and paper to write down the needs of the guest (ex: dietary restrictions, time);
  - TripAdvisor OR a recommendation sheet to look up and choose appropriate restaurants;

- a phone to call the restaurant and make the reservation;
- an email provider to get a confirmation email and send it to the guest;
- our platform to text the guest through our app that the reservation was made and confirmed.

Then we have the people:

- The guests who make the initial request give the necessary information about the booking. The concierge also confirms the reservation with the guest.
- Another concierge that they might ask about a restaurant recommendation if they can't find one.
- The restaurant staff to book the reservation.

Once you have that information, start plotting it out in either circles or lines so you can represent the different services/products, people, and how the primary user interacts with them. Overall, ecosystem maps are a fun and different way to visualize complex interactions between your primary users and other people or products/services. They can give your stakeholders a clear understanding of how a primary user sits inside an experience and can easily highlight opportunities for improvement.

If you want to make this a collaborative effort, you can also have your stakeholders draw the map from their perspective, present it, and create a map based on everyone's input. But, of course, always ensure the information inside is based on concrete research!

UX Scorecard

30

INTRODUCTION

Early in my career, I primarily focused on formative evaluations, often involving usability testing, to identify issues in product design. While this approach was effective for certain aspects of product evaluation, it fell short when addressing broader questions from stakeholders.

1. Comparative analysis: How does our product compare to competitors or similar products in the same industry?
2. Long-term product evolution: How has our product's user experience changed over time?

Usability testing and other formative methods were insufficient for addressing these questions. This dilemma led me to discover the concept of UX scorecards. UX scorecards are valuable tools for summative evaluations, offering insights into overall usability, tracking usability changes over time, and facilitating product comparisons. These scorecards help you achieve the following goals:

- assess the overall usability of a product;
- monitor usability trends over time;
- compare your product with competitors.

UX scorecards can be approached in several ways, but one effective method is heuristic evaluation, where you assess your product against established industry standards. These standards often include usability heuristics, such as Jakob Nielsen's 10 Usability Heuristics for User Interface Design.

However, heuristic evaluations might not always provide the depth of insight required. Some heuristics may be challenging for stakeholders to grasp or difficult for evaluators to assess accurately. In such cases, UX scorecards offer a more comprehensive evaluation method.

HOW TO CREATE A UX SCORECARD

The first time I created a UX scorecard, I wasn't sure exactly which components I should include or how to make it impactful. After some research and practice, I finally created an approach. Here are the exact steps I take to create UX scorecards.

1. Define Your Goals

Start by aligning your project goals with the UX scorecard approach. Common goals for UX scorecards include:

- understand the end-to-end usability of a product when it comes to efficiency, effectiveness, and satisfaction;
- identify the issues and problems across an entire product;
- uncover the differences in usability between our product and the industry benchmarks or competitors;
- track the usability of our product through efficiency, effectiveness, and satisfaction, over time.

2. Select Metrics

The point of a UX scorecard is to evaluate your product, so the next step is to decide which metrics you will use. There are standard metrics for usability, and I have relied heavily on them to create UX scorecards. These are metrics I use to measure usability.

Task-level

- Task success (effectiveness): Whether or not someone can complete a task or struggles on a task.
- Time on task (efficiency): The amount of time it takes for someone to complete, or give up on, a task.
- Single Ease Questionnaire (ease of use): Measures the perceived difficulty or ease of a task.
- Confidence (perception): asks how confident users are that they completed a task successfully.

Product-level

- System Usability Scale (satisfaction): Looks at the overall usability and satisfaction of a product.

- Usability Metric for User Experience (UMUX/UMUX-Lite): This scale is intended to be similar to the SUS but is shorter and targeted toward the ISO 9241 definition of usability (effectiveness, efficiency, and satisfaction).

3. Choose Task Scenarios

Select a set of tasks to evaluate. Focus on critical tasks that align with your project's goals. These tasks should represent actions users must perform to achieve their objectives with the product. For example, if I worked at a travel company that sold tickets to people, the most important tasks would be:

- searching for a destination;
- selecting a ticket;
- filling out any necessary forms (billing, travel information, etc.);
- purchasing the ticket;
- finding/downloading the ticket once purchased.

If you're stuck, ask yourself, "What are the actions people must do to achieve what they want to and what we want them to do?" Then brainstorm all the tasks and ask for feedback from stakeholders.

4. Create Your Grading Rubric

Once you have defined the metrics and tasks, develop your grading rubric. The entire point of a UX scorecard is to grade your product, often against others, so it is essential to understand how you will score the above tasks on the chosen metrics. Here is an example of how you can use these grades.

- A: The task and overall experience are functional, reliable, extremely easy to use, and delightful for the customer.
- B: The user can complete tasks and use the product without a problem. The product is functional, reliable, usable, and generally satisfactory.
- C: The user can complete tasks and use the product but might have a light cognitive load, including some hesitation, struggle, or confusing steps. The product is functional and somewhat reliable and relatively usable.
- D: It is difficult for the user to complete tasks and use the product. The user sometimes fails at certain tasks. The product is somewhat functional and reliable.
- E: Users cannot complete the tasks or use the product, and the experience is viewed as very poor. The product might be functional but is not considered reliable, usable, or satisfactory.

5. Identify Competitors

Determine which competitors or similar products you will assess. This step is crucial for benchmarking your product against others in your industry. Seek input from colleagues and senior leadership to select relevant competitors.

6. Decide on a Testing Method

Determine whether you will conduct internal evaluations, external evaluations, or a combination of both. Internal evaluations may be a practical starting point but should not replace user testing entirely.

7. Conduct the Study

Conducting a UX scorecard study is similar to benchmarking or usability testing. Check out my usability test checklist and how to tackle a benchmarking study for more details.

8. Create Your Scorecard

After completing the study, generate UX scorecards. These may include a general scorecard for overall comparisons and specific scorecards for each task. Use letter grades, colors, and clear metrics to facilitate straightforward comparisons between tasks and products.

UX scorecards provide a comprehensive and structured approach to evaluating product usability and benchmarking against competitors. They offer valuable insights for making informed decisions about product improvements and enhancements.

PART EIGHT

Activating Your User Research

Bring Your Insights to Life 31

HOW MIGHT WE STATEMENTS

I hope I am not the only one who has felt the sting after spending hours and hours on a research report and crafting insights only to have it either ignored or pushed over to the side. It is a horrible feeling, especially when you know the insights could help improve the product/service so much.

But, it can be really difficult to get colleagues to listen to insights or to get them to rearrange their work to include your findings on a roadmap or in the next sprint. Even if it seemed obvious to me, it wasn't always the case with others.

For a long time, I just kept repeating the same cycle of creating reports and watching most of the work go unused. Sometimes people listened, sometimes they didn't. The inconsistency really confused me and I figured it was because some of my work was just better or more appealing.

But I knew that it wasn't realistic for my career. I couldn't just leave it up to chance whether or not people would listen to my work. I had to find a better way to ensure my insights were recognized and utilized.

This meant, at first, I held a lot of meetings in which I read and reread reports, presented findings, had follow-ups, and supplied plenty of colleagues with lots of coffee. However, I kept coming back to the same issue.

My colleagues understood the insights and they found (most of) them interesting and important, but we kept getting caught at the same crossroads:

"So, what do we do next?"

To be honest, I wasn't entirely sure how to answer this question. I figured, as a researcher, I had done what I had to do and it was up to my team to figure out the next steps.

However, I came to realize this wasn't the best way to collaborate with teams and I was missing a huge part of what I came to later learn was the activation portion of my role. In this part of the process, I would work together with teams to bring the insights from the problem space to solution land. Without this guidance, teams often felt unsure how to move forward from insights, especially if they were on the more abstract side of things.

Over time, I picked up several ways to activate user research insights, but one of the first and one of my favorite ways to collaborate with teams when it comes to this part of the process is How Might We Statements.

WHAT ARE HOW MIGHT WE STATEMENTS?

How Might We statements are small but mighty questions that help us with bringing insights that are currently in the problem space to a place where teams can start thinking of solutions.

HWM statements are originally part of the Design Thinking approach. This method of questioning allows for the teams to take the research into the ideation phase.

As I mentioned above, it can be really difficult to go from presenting your insights to helping the team to create something from those insights, especially if the insights feel more abstract and are large, generative-based findings. Often, teams can feel overwhelmed trying to navigate this situation and can feel stuck bringing insights to life.

How Might We statements are a fantastic way to frame the problem/insight in a way that spurs creativity and solution-based thinking, all with a user-centric focus.

WHY ARE THEY CALLED "HOW MIGHT WE'S?"

There is a reason why these three special words were chosen for this approach. Each of these words holds a key to the innovative and collaborative nature of How Might We statements:

- "How" suggests that we do not yet have the answer. It allows us to consider multiple avenues for innovation and reinforces that we are still exploring the problem and solution space.
- "Might" emphasizes that there are many different paths we can go down when thinking about solutions. This allows for open-minded creativity and brainstorming and thinking about the problem from multiple perspectives. This "might" is where innovation becomes part of the process!
- "We" immediately brings in the idea of teamwork. "We" should all work collaboratively to come up with a joint understanding of the problem and put our heads together to come up with a joint solution.

Using these three words can help open your team up to innovation, creativity, and, most importantly, using your insights to create user-centric solutions.

THE BENEFITS OF USING HOW MIGHT WE STATEMENTS

It might already be obvious how beneficial How Might We statements can be, but just in case you might meet resistance with stakeholders, it's important to really understand what using these statements can truly achieve.

These statements help to stimulate creative thinking and collaboration in a team by framing insights or user-centered problems as open-ended questions. They encourage teams to think beyond conventional solutions while still focusing on users. Instead of picking a problem from scratch or using an idea that came to someone in the shower, How Might We's empower you to take direct insights and problems from reach and turn them into questions the team can answer with creative solutions.

How Might We's not only inspire creativity and help ensure research is properly used, but they also give so many other benefits, such as:

ENCOURAGES POSITIVITY AND MOTIVATION

- Shifts Perspective: HMW statements reframe challenges as opportunities, encouraging teams to view obstacles not as insurmountable problems but as chances to innovate and improve. This shift in perspective can transform the team's approach to challenges, leading to more positive and productive outcomes.
- Maintains Morale: By focusing on possibilities rather than limitations, HMW statements help maintain a high level of morale among team members, even when tackling difficult issues. This optimistic outlook is contagious and can uplift the entire team's spirit.

FOSTERS COLLABORATIVE INCLUSIVITY

- Democratizes the Ideation Process: HMW statements invite input from all members of a team, regardless of their role or level of experience. This inclusivity ensures that a diverse range of perspectives is considered, enriching the ideation process.
- Levels the Playing Field: By framing challenges as open-ended questions, HMW statements create a neutral space where all ideas are valued equally. This can empower quieter team members or those who might typically feel marginalized, encouraging them to share their insights and contribute more actively.

- Encourages Co-creation: HMW statements naturally facilitate collaborative brainstorming sessions, where team members build on each other's ideas. This co-creation process not only generates more innovative solutions but also fosters a sense of ownership and commitment among team members.
- Breaks Down Silos: By bringing together diverse groups within an organization to answer a common question, HMW statements can help break down silos. They encourage cross-functional collaboration, leading to more holistic and well-rounded solutions.

ENHANCES FLEXIBILITY

- Adaptable to Various Contexts: The versatility of HMW statements means they can be applied across different stages of product development, organizational change, service design, and more. This flexibility allows teams to use them as a tool for a wide array of challenges.
- Promotes Agile Thinking: In today's fast-paced work environments, the ability to quickly pivot and adapt is crucial. HMW statements support agile thinking by keeping the problem space open and fluid, enabling teams to explore multiple solutions and adapt their strategies as needed.

STIMULATES CREATIVITY

- Invites Diverse Solutions: The open-ended nature of HMW statements encourages creative thinking and invites a wide range of solutions. This openness can lead to innovative ideas that might not emerge through more conventional problem-solving methods.
- Prevents Premature Convergence: Often, teams rush to converge on a solution too quickly, which can stifle creativity. HMW statements keep the exploration space wide open, preventing premature convergence and encouraging a thorough exploration of possibilities.

BUILDS A RESEARCH CULTURE

- Encourages Experimentation: HMW statements promote a culture where experimentation is valued as part of the learning process. They support the idea that not every attempt has to be successful as long as it provides insights and learning that can lead to better solutions.

- Facilitates Reflective Practice: The process of working with HMW statements encourages teams to reflect on their assumptions, question established norms, and continuously seek improvements. This reflective practice is a cornerstone of a learning culture, driving ongoing innovation and growth.

PUTS RESEARCH AT THE FOREFRONT

- Uses User-Centric Ideas. Instead of the common "what should we do next" question or "I had an idea in the shower" statement, How Might We's encourage teams to build on findings and insights from user research. This means the work is based on the users' needs and pain points and will have a powerful impact.
- Brings Teams from Problems to Solutions. If you have ever struggled with activating insights, How Might We's give you the chance to help teams go from problems to solutions while still maintaining creativity and the user at the center of the idea.
- As I said, How Might We statements are powerful little questions! They not only help us with bringing creativity to our work, but they can also empower cross-departmental collaboration, innovation and help us work toward building a solid research culture at an organization.

Now let's dive into how you can craft these statements and integrate them into your process in an efficient way!

CRAFTING EFFECTIVE HOW MIGHT WE STATEMENTS

Characteristics of How Might We Statements

Although How Might We's are small questions, they do need to be written in a way that strikes a delicate balance between breadth and focus, inviting a wide range of creative solutions while being specific enough to direct efforts toward actionable outcomes. That's a lot to think about at once and, trust me, I made a lot of mistakes in my earlier How Might We statements. After many years of using these statements, here are the best practices I use whenever I am formulating my How Might We statements:

1. User-centric

Focuses on User Needs: A well-crafted HMW statement always centers around the needs, pain points, or desires of the target user group. It's grounded in empathy and a deep understanding of the user experience, ensuring that the solutions developed are genuinely useful and relevant.

Example: "How might we help new parents easily track their baby's sleep patterns?"

2. Broad yet specific

Invites Creativity: The statement is open-ended enough to encourage a broad exploration of ideas, avoiding premature limitation on the types of solutions that can be considered. It welcomes innovation from any direction.

Retains a Clear Focus: While being open, HMW statements must have a clear focus area or challenge that guides ideation towards relevant and actionable solutions. It needs to be specific enough to prevent aimless wandering during brainstorming sessions.

Example: "How might we make our public transportation system more accessible to people with disabilities?"

3. Action-oriented

Implies Action: The point of HMW statements is to encourage action and suggest that there is a solution to be found. It needs to be formulated in a way that gets the team thinking about the steps they can take to address the challenge.

Example: "How might we reduce the time customers spend waiting in line at our stores?"

4. Inspiring and engaging

Sparks Interest: An effective HMW statement is inspiring; it should energize the team and provoke curiosity. It's crafted in a way that makes people excited to start exploring solutions.

Example: "How might we transform our workspace to boost creativity and collaboration?"

5. Addresses a real challenge

Based on Insight: The statement should stem from real user insights or identified business challenges. It's not based on assumptions but on verified needs, ensuring that the solutions developed are grounded in reality.

Example: "How might we integrate sustainable practices into our product lifecycle to meet our environmental goals?"

6. Ambiguous enough to explore

Allows for Exploration: While being focused, the statement should also leave room for interpretation, allowing the team to explore different angles and perspectives. This ambiguity encourages a deeper dive into the problem, often leading to more innovative solutions.

Example: "How might we reimagine online education to better engage students?"

It took a lot of practice to feel comfortable writing How Might We's that encapsulated all of these different characteristics. It was a lot of trial and error, and I recommend giving yourself the space to try and experiment with your statements. Trying to balance all these points at once can feel overwhelming, but, with practice, it becomes more natural and intuitive.

The key is to craft a question that is sufficiently broad to open the door to innovative, unexpected solutions, yet sufficiently focused to ensure that the solutions are relevant and actionable. This allows the question to guide the ideation process in a productive direction but without being too blue-sky.

Let's now dive into how we can write these statements effectively.

WRITING HOW MIGHT WE STATEMENTS

One of the biggest mistakes I made with How Might We statements was either going way too broad or too narrow—it felt like it took me forever to write an HMW that was right in the middle and struck that amazing balance I'd been searching for. Once I felt more confident and comfortable with creating How Might We statements, I moved over to teaching others how to write them.

I had no idea how difficult it was going to be to explain something that seemed so small and simple. But, over time, I created a step-by-step process I use and teach to others who are looking to write impactful How Might We statements:

Step 1: Gather Insights and Identify Problems

Start with user research, customer feedback, and team insights to identify the pain points or needs that have come from recent research. This step is absolutely critical to creating effective How Might We's as the entire point of them is to base them on user-centric data. Without this step, the team is just creating ideas from nothing.

This step comes after you've done the research and prioritized the most important and unaddressed pain points and needs from the research. You can do this through affinity diagrams.

Step 2: Define the Core Problem or Opportunity

Once you identify the most important and unaddressed needs and pain points, it's time to choose some to turn into problem statements. A point-of-view (POV)/problem statement allows you to focus on your users and their needs. You can create a problem statement by combining three elements: user, need, and insight into a fill-in-the-blank.

- A model to use for this is: user (fill in user) needs to (fill in need) because/to (fill in insight/consequence)
- Example Problem Statement: "Users need a simpler way to understand and manage their finances to reduce anxiety."

Step 3: Use the HMW Formula

Once you have a problem statement, you can then create an HMW question. I always use the two following formulas:

- Basic Formula: How might we [verb] [outcome] for [user]?
  - Example: "How might we increase engagement for teenage users?"
- With Specific Action: How might we [verb] [outcome] for [user] by [action]?
  - Example: "How might we improve learning outcomes for high school students by integrating interactive technologies?"

You might not always need the "by [action/means]" part, as it can sometimes limit the scope of ideation. Use it when you want to guide the brainstorming process in a specific direction.

- Example (basic) HMW Statement: "How might we simplify financial management for users to reduce anxiety?"

Step 4: Refine for Broadness and Specificity

Ensure your HMW statement is broad enough to allow for creative exploration but specific enough to be actionable. It should invite a wide range of solutions but be directed towards a clear outcome.

TACKLING BROAD HMWs

Here are some examples of HMW statements that are too broad and vague:

- How might we redesign our website to make it better?
- How might we make our app more usable?
- How might we innovate on weather apps?

These statements give minimal direction or inspiration and can actually feel overwhelming to try to answer. Imagine trying to think of all the potential ways to make an app more usable. What does usable even mean? There are way too many solutions and not nearly enough focus, meaning your HWM participants will be confused at where to even begin to define a solution.

Signs that your HMW statement is too broad include:

- It could apply to almost any organization or situation.
- It invites a vast range of solutions, making it hard to know where to start.
- It doesn't clearly relate to your specific user needs or business goals.

You can fix broad HMW statements by adding specificity through introducing specific user groups, contexts, or outcomes to focus your statement. Consider who you're designing for or the particular aspect of the problem you want to tackle.

Example Broad Statement: "How might we improve education?"

Fixed Statement: "How might we enhance online learning for rural high school students with limited internet access?"

Example Broad Statement: "How might we make workplaces better?"

Fixed Statement: "How might we create more collaborative workspaces for remote teams to enhance productivity and connection?"

Tackling Narrow HMWs

HMW statements can also be too narrow:

- How might we change the CTA button on the Add to Cart to a different color to make it more engaging?
- How might we make the perfect weather app by telling people the weather before they wake up?
- How might we make children less hyper during school by extending recess for 20 minutes?

When HMW statements are too narrow, we lose all the incredible, innovative ideas that can come from them. With too much focus, we are stuck on one particular solution already. We want several different ideas to test at the end, so focusing too much on one solution will limit creativity and innovation.

Signs Your HMW Statement Is Too Narrow:

- It suggests a specific solution or technology.
- It focuses on minor issues, missing the bigger picture.
- It doesn't leave much room for exploration or alternative approaches.

You can fix narrow HMW statements by broadening the scope through removing constraints and opening up the statement to a wider range of possibilities. Avoid mentioning specific solutions or technologies.

- Example Narrow Statement: "How might we develop a mobile app to improve English vocabulary for eighth graders?"
- Fixed Statement: "How might we make learning English vocabulary more engaging for eighth graders?"
- Example Narrow Statement: "How might we add a chat feature to our project management tool?"
- Fixed Statement: "How might we facilitate better communication among project team members in a remote work environment?"

Example (specific) HMW Statement: "How might we make financial management feel more accessible and less intimidating for young adults?"

Step 5: Test and Iterate

For a while, I went into sessions without first sharing or getting feedback on my How Might We statements, only to be met with blank stares or confused faces. By sharing your How Might We's ahead of time with a few colleagues, you can get feedback on how they feel about them ahead of any ideation workshops. Are they inspired? Do the statements generate a wide range of ideas? Do they force them down a certain solution path? Or do they feel overwhelmed hearing the question?

Once I started getting feedback on my HMW statements beforehand, my ideation sessions became much more productive and I started to refine the craft of writing these statements. I iterated and learned so much by gauging people's reactions to statements—this is where most of my learning came from, tweaking these statements based on colleagues' feedback.

Step 6: Finalize Your HMW Statement

Refine your statement based on feedback and your own insights. The final version should be inspiring, clear, and focused, ready to guide your team's ideation process.

Example Final HMW Statement: "How might we design an intuitive financial management tool that empowers young adults, including those less tech-savvy, to overcome their anxiety about finances?"

Examples of Effective vs. Ineffective How Might We Statements

It takes some practice to get used to writing these statements in the most effective way possible. Below are some examples of effective vs. ineffective HMW statements you can use as inspiration when creating your own:

Example One

- Ineffective: How might we design a new app?
- Why Ineffective: It's too broad and lacks focus on the user's needs or the problem being solved.
- Effective: How might we make it easier for busy parents to track their children's after-school schedules?
- Why Effective: This statement clearly identifies the target audience (busy parents) and the specific challenge (tracking after-school schedules), inviting targeted and meaningful solutions.

Example Two

- Ineffective: "How might we reduce customer service calls?"
- Why Ineffective: It suggests a goal (reducing calls) that might lead to solutions focused only on deflecting customer interactions rather than improving service quality or addressing underlying issues.
- Effective: "How might we enhance our customer service experience to increase satisfaction?"

- Why Effective: This opens up a broader range of solutions focused on improving the overall customer experience, addressing the root causes of dissatisfaction that may lead to calls, and not just the symptom of high call volume.

Example Three

- Ineffective: How might we use AI in our products?
- Why Ineffective: It focuses on a solution (using AI) rather than the problem or opportunity, which can limit creative thinking.
- Effective: How might we personalize our customers' experience to better meet their needs?
- Why Effective: This statement is open to a wide range of solutions, including but not limited to AI, and is centered around improving the customer experience, encouraging innovation in service of the user.

Example Four

- Ineffective: "How might we drive more traffic to our website?"
- Why Ineffective: While increasing traffic is one way to boost sales, focusing solely on traffic doesn't address the quality of the visitor experience or conversion rate optimization. It could lead to solutions that increase numbers without necessarily increasing sales.
- Effective: "How might we improve the online shopping experience to convert more visitors into customers?"
- Why Effective: This statement focuses on the quality of the visitor experience and conversion, encouraging solutions that are likely to have a direct impact on sales. It invites a wide range of creative approaches to enhance the shopping experience.

Example Five

- Ineffective: "How might we use less paper in our office?"
- Why Ineffective: It's narrowly focused on paper usage, which is just one aspect of sustainability. This narrow focus might limit the scope of solutions to those that only address paper consumption.
- Effective: "How might we foster a culture of sustainability in our workplace?"
- Why Effective: It broadens the scope to include all aspects of sustainability, not just paper usage. This encourages a comprehensive approach to promoting sustainable practices across the organization.

Example Six

- Ineffective: "How might we comply with accessibility guidelines?"
- Why Ineffective: While compliance is important, focusing solely on meeting guidelines may not fully address the needs of users with disabilities. This statement frames accessibility as a checkbox task rather than an opportunity to genuinely improve user experience.

- Effective: "How might we make our product more accessible and user-friendly for people with visual impairments?"
- Why Effective: This statement is specific about the user group (people with visual impairments) but open in terms of potential solutions, encouraging innovation beyond mere compliance. It focuses on improving the user experience, which is a more inspiring and user-centered approach.

INTEGRATING HOW MIGHT WE STATEMENTS INTO YOUR RESEARCH PROCESS

One of the amazing things I learned about How Might We statements was how I could use them throughout my research process to help define, refine and solutionize. Originally, I only used them as a way to frame my insights after I completed a project, but then I saw how they could be hugely helpful in so many different parts of the process that I started using them in many different situations.

I highly recommend using these statements throughout your process, as they can help you so much at each different stage. Here is when and how I use HMW statements at different parts of the research process.

INITIAL PROBLEM IDENTIFICATION

One of the most powerful ways I learned to use How Might We's was at the beginning of my research process to help set the direction and focus of a project.

How to incorporate them at this stage:

Gather Preliminary Insights: Start with user interviews, observations, and data analysis to understand your users' needs, frustrations, and desires.

Draft HMW Statements: Based on these insights, formulate HMW statements that capture the core challenges or opportunities you've identified. These statements should inspire you toward a future research project that strikes the balance between openness to explore and focus.

Example HMW for problem identification:

Scenario: Users find it challenging to maintain a healthy diet due to a busy lifestyle.

HMW Statement: "How might we help busy individuals easily integrate healthy eating habits into their daily routines?"

Usage: This HMW statement sets the stage for understanding the broader challenge of maintaining a healthy diet amidst a hectic schedule. It guides initial research efforts, encouraging the team to explore users' daily routines, their understanding of healthy eating, and the barriers they face.

Another great way to incorporate HMW statements is during ideation sessions after you have a solid understanding of your users and their needs. This stage is about generating solutions, and HMW statements help ensure that your ideas are aligned with user needs and open to innovative approaches.

How to incorporate them at this stage:

Facilitate Brainstorming: Use the HMW statements as prompts in brainstorming sessions to generate a wide range of ideas. Encourage participants to think freely and build on each other's ideas.

Diversify Thinking: Rotate through multiple HMW statements to explore different aspects of the problem or to challenge the team to think from various perspectives.

Example HMW for ideation sessions:

Scenario: During research, you find that users often resort to fast food because they lack time to prepare healthy meals.

HMW Statement: "How might we make healthy meal preparation quick and appealing for people with little spare time?"

Usage: This HMW statement can spark creativity in brainstorming sessions by focusing on the specific challenge of time constraint in meal preparation. It encourages the team to think of innovative solutions that reduce preparation time, enhance the appeal of healthy meals, or both.

SOLUTION DEVELOPMENT

HMW statements should guide the selection of ideas for development and be a reference point throughout the prototyping and testing phases. They can help keep the team aligned on the project's goals and ensure that the solutions developed are meaningful and user-centered.

How to incorporate them at this stage:

Narrow Down Ideas: Use HMW statements to revisit the core challenges and opportunities as you begin to narrow down your list of potential solutions. They can help ensure that the ideas you choose to develop further are both innovative and directly address the user needs identified.

Prototype and Test: As you develop prototypes, refer back to your HMW statements to guide your design decisions and ensure that your solutions remain focused on addressing the specific challenges or opportunities you've identified.

Example HMW for solution development:

Scenario: Ideation generates ideas around meal kits, quick recipes, and educational content on healthy eating.
HMW Statement: "How might we design a meal kit service that caters to the needs of the time-strapped yet health-conscious user?"
Usage: As the team moves into developing solutions, this HMW statement helps to focus on creating a meal kit service that addresses users' time constraints while supporting their desire to eat healthily. It guides the prototyping of meal kits, selection of recipes, and the development of complementary digital content.

REFINEMENT AND ITERATION

You can also use HMW statements throughout the refinement and iteration stage as you refine your solutions based on feedback. HMW statements can help ensure that your iterations are focused and purposeful, continually aiming to better meet user needs.

How to incorporate them at this stage:

Iterative Feedback: Use HMW statements to frame questions and discussions during user testing and feedback sessions. They can help elicit insights on whether the solution effectively addresses the problem and inspire ways to improve it.
Iterate on Solutions: Based on feedback, revisit your HMW statements to refine your solutions or to ideate new approaches that better meet user needs.

Example HMW for refinement and iteration:

Scenario: Testing reveals that while users find the meal kit useful, they struggle with meal variety and staying motivated.
HMW Statement: "How might we continuously engage users with our meal kit service, encouraging variety and sustained healthy eating habits?"
Usage: This statement prompts the team to consider ways to enhance the meal kit service, possibly by introducing new recipes regularly, incorporating feedback mechanisms, or developing community support features. It ensures that iterations on the product directly address user feedback and enhance engagement and satisfaction.

See? Powerful and mighty little statements! They can really keep you on track to ensure you are focused on the user at all times while also inviting collaborative creativity on solutions. By incorporating HMW statements at each stage of your user research process, you can help the team maintain a clear focus on user needs and innovative problem-solving, ensuring that the solutions developed are both creative and deeply rooted in addressing real user challenges.

USING HOW MIGHT WE STATEMENTS IN IDEATION SESSIONS

Although HMW statements can be used in a variety of ways, one of the most common and powerful ways to incorporate How Might We's is through ideation sessions. These sessions are one of the best ways to get your insights in front of people and have your colleagues act on your research. An ideation session can solve the original problem of colleagues ignoring insights or not knowing what to do with them.

Here's how to effectively incorporate HMW statements into brainstorming sessions and workshops, encourage diverse perspectives, and prioritize ideas for further development.

FACILITATING BRAINSTORMING SESSIONS WITH HMW STATEMENTS

Prepare Your HMW Statements. Before the session, select or develop HMW statements based on prior research insights. Ensure these statements are broad enough to encourage creative thinking but focused enough to be relevant to your users' needs.

ENCOURAGE DIVERSE PERSPECTIVES

- Diverse Participation: Include participants from different roles, backgrounds, and departments. Diversity in the room brings diverse ways of thinking, leading to a richer set of ideas. Consider inviting users or external stakeholders to participate or provide input ahead of the brainstorming session.
- Create a Safe Space: Establish ground rules that support a judgment-free environment. Emphasize that all ideas are welcome and that critique is reserved for later stages. Use facilitation techniques like round-robin (everyone takes turns sharing ideas) or anonymous idea submission (using post-its or digital tools) to ensure quieter voices are heard.
- Foster an Inclusive Environment: Actively encourage participants to build on each other's ideas, which can lead to even more innovative solutions. Be mindful of dynamics in the room to ensure that dominant voices don't overshadow others. Facilitators can redirect the conversation to include more participants.

HOW TO PRIORITIZE AND SELECT IDEAS

Group and Theme Ideas: After generating a wide range of ideas, group them into themes or categories. This helps identify patterns or areas of interest that emerged during the session. Look for clusters of ideas that address the HMW statement in unique or particularly promising ways.

Criteria for Selection: Establish criteria for prioritizing ideas, which might include feasibility, potential impact, alignment with user needs, or innovativeness. Consider using voting methods (dot voting, for example) to allow participants to express which ideas they find most compelling based on the criteria.

Narrow Down and Plan Next Steps: Select a handful of ideas to explore further. This selection can be based on the outcomes of the voting, facilitator insight, and discussion among participants. Outline next steps for each selected idea, which may include more detailed research, prototyping, or incorporating the idea into a larger project plan.

Document and Share Outcomes: Ensure that all ideas, not just the selected few, are documented and shared with participants and other stakeholders. This can foster a sense of ownership and appreciation for the collaborative effort. Highlight how the HMW statements guided the ideation process and how the selected ideas will be explored further.

To make this more concrete, I've included a sample agenda I've used that incorporates an HMW ideation session while using the Crazy 8's technique:

SAMPLE AGENDA FOR AN HMW IDEATION SESSION USING CRAZY 8's

Goal:
To generate a diverse set of solutions to improve the user experience on a mobile banking app, guided by HMW statements.
Duration: 1.5 Hours

1. Welcome and Ice Breaker (5 minutes)
    A quick welcome with an icebreaker activity to get everyone comfortable. I particularly love either:
    The Aliens Have Invaded, in which you ask everyone to explain a concept to aliens who can only speak via emojis.
    Paperclip Uses, in which people take a few minutes to brainstorm all the things they could use a paper clip for—it's hilarious!

2. Session Overview and Goal (5 minutes)
   Explain the session's goal: To ideate solutions for improving the mobile banking app experience for users.
   Introduce the concept of HMW statements and the Crazy 8's method.
3. Introduction to the HMW Statement (5 minutes)
   Present the chosen HMW statement: "How might we make the mobile banking app more intuitive and secure for first-time users?"
   Briefly discuss the background and user research that led to this HMW statement.
4. Explanation of Crazy 8's Method (5 minutes)
   Explain the Crazy 8's method: Each participant will fold a sheet of paper into eight sections and then, given 8 minutes, sketch or write down an idea in each section, moving quickly from one to the next.
5. Round 1 of Crazy 8's (8 minutes)
   Participants work individually on their Crazy 8's, focusing on the presented HMW statement.
6. Share and Discuss Ideas (10 minutes)
   Participants briefly share their ideas with the group, explaining their sketches or concepts.
   Facilitate a quick discussion to highlight interesting or recurring themes.
7. Refine HMW Statement (Optional) (2 minutes)
   Based on the discussion, slightly refine or introduce a new HMW statement for the next round to explore different aspects of the problem, e.g., "How might we personalize the mobile banking experience to build trust with first-time users?"
8. Round 2 of Crazy 8's (8 minutes)
   Repeat the Crazy 8's process with the new or refined HMW statement, encouraging participants to build on ideas from the first round or explore new directions.
9. Share and Discuss Ideas (10 minutes)
   Another round of sharing and discussion, focusing on the new ideas generated.
10. Idea Grouping and Voting (10 minutes)
    Group similar ideas together on a wall or digital board.
    Use dot voting to identify the most promising ideas, allowing each participant a limited number (usually two or three) of votes.
11. Discuss and Select Ideas to Develop (10 minutes)
    Discuss the top-voted ideas in more detail, considering feasibility, impact, and alignment with user needs.
    Select a subset of ideas for further exploration.
12. Define Next Steps (5 minutes)
    Outline the process for further researching, prototyping, and testing the selected ideas.
    Assign responsibilities or create small teams for each idea if applicable.
13. Closing Remarks and Feedback (5 minutes)
    Thank participants for their energy and creativity.

Briefly gather feedback on the session to improve future workshops. You can also send out a post-workshop survey to gather even more feedback (highly recommend this!).

IDEATION SESSIONS

After successfully completing the phases of research, synthesis, and gaining valuable insights, you've reached a critical juncture in your role as a user researcher. You now possess a treasure trove of insights that have the potential to drive positive change within your team and organization. The challenge now is how to ensure these insights are not just collected and documented but actively utilized to spark innovation and foster positive change. One powerful strategy to breathe life into your insights and inspire your team is by facilitating an ideation workshop.

An ideation workshop is a safe space to trigger creativity, where the team proposes solutions to the problems identified through research. The primary objective of an ideation workshop is to ignite innovation and tap into the creative potential of your team. During these sessions, participants come together to openly discuss and share ideas, fostering a culture of collaboration and creative thinking.

In this environment, all team members are encouraged to contribute freely, without worrying about the feasibility or practicality of their suggestions. The magic of an ideation workshop is that ideas are explored, celebrated, and documented, with evaluations postponed until later stages.

In this workshop, you aim to brainstorm as many ideas as possible, focusing on quantity rather than quality. The topic for ideation is carefully chosen based on the problem statements derived from your user research, ensuring a clear and relevant focus.

Ideation workshops play a pivotal role in the research process for several compelling reasons.

1. Guiding Teams: Ideation workshops provide clear direction to your teams. If you've uncovered valuable insights but aren't sure about the next steps, these workshops can serve as a wellspring of ideas, charting a course for usability testing and further development.
2. Diverse Perspectives: By bringing together individuals with diverse backgrounds and perspectives, ideation workshops enable your team to break free from the constraints of traditional thinking. The collective brainstorming fuels innovation by encouraging participants to build upon each other's ideas.
3. Fostering Creativity: Ideation workshops create a safe and judgment-free space for creativity. In these workshops, the word "No" is often banned, allowing participants to explore even the most unconventional ideas. This environment encourages adventurous thinking, leading to innovation.
4. User-Centric Focus: Since ideation workshops are based on user research, the ideas generated are inherently focused on addressing real customer problems.

This contrasts with solutions rooted in gut feelings or business priorities, ensuring that the user remains at the center of the innovation process.
5. Engaging and Exciting: These workshops are designed to be fun and exciting. Participants who might initially be hesitant often find themselves eagerly awaiting the next session. People who were previously quiet often become enthusiastic contributors by the end of the workshop. The majority of participants genuinely enjoy ideation workshops and recognize their value.
6. Closer to Solutions: With the multitude of ideas generated during ideation, your team takes a significant step towards finding a viable, user-centric solution. By carefully selecting the best ideas, you can move forward with prototyping, aligning your efforts with user needs, goals, and expectations.

Ideation workshops serve as a dynamic forum for stimulating creativity within your team. Not only do they energize participants, but they also yield a concrete set of ideas ready for testing and refinement.

How to Run a Successful Ideation Workshop?

Running a successful ideation workshop involves following best practices to maximize its impact.

Begin with User Research

Ensure that your workshop is grounded in user research. Without this foundation, you risk exploring irrelevant topics that don't align with user needs, motivations, or pain points. Start with a clear problem statement derived from user insights.

Define Expected Outcomes

Set clear expectations for what you aim to achieve by the end of the workshop. These outcomes typically include gaining a deep understanding of the problem, generating a multitude of ideas, selecting the top ideas for testing, and determining the next steps for testing those ideas.

Craft a Problem Statement

A well-defined problem statement is crucial. It should outline a current user problem, their goal, and the challenges they face. Problem statements must be broad enough to generate diverse ideas but focused on addressing specific user needs.

Select Ideation Techniques

Choose ideation techniques that suit your workshop's objectives. Here are some favorite ideation techniques.

- Flip the Problem: Invert the original problem statement and brainstorm ideas around the reversed question. Then, take some of these negative ideas and invert them back to solve the original problem.
- How Would [Company] Do It?: Explore the problem space as if you were a CEO of a completely different company (e.g., Google, Amazon). This exercise encourages thinking outside your industry's norms.
- Crazy 8's: A sketching technique where participants create eight different ideas in 8 minutes. This approach is inclusive and suitable for designers and non-designers alike.
- Method 6-3-5: Six people write down three ideas in 5 minutes, passing their sheets to others to build on the concepts. This collaborative approach sparks creativity and innovation.
- Worst Possible Idea: Encourage participants to generate terrible, absurd, or even illegal ideas. Then challenge them to transform these terrible ideas into good ones by considering their opposites or extracting valuable aspects.

Follow-Up

After the ideation workshop, ensure that the generated ideas don't languish. Collaborate with designers and product managers to plan usability testing for the selected ideas. The ideation workshop is just the beginning; follow-through is essential to turn ideas into tangible solutions.

Ideation workshops are a dynamic means of harnessing your team's collective creativity and converting your research insights into actionable ideas. When executed effectively, they can serve as a springboard for innovation and user-centered product development. For further inspiration and ideation techniques, explore these resources:

- Gamestorming
- Innovation Cards
- Trigger Cards
- Board of Innovation
- HI Toolbox.

USABILITY BINGO

Let's dive into the concept of Usability Bingo, a creative approach to making user research more engaging. Imagine a 5×5 bingo board with randomly allocated phrases, quotes, pain points, needs, goals, and bugs from your usability tests instead of numbers. Much like traditional bingo, someone calls out these phrases, and participants cross out spaces on their boards in the hopes of getting five in a row—horizontally, vertically, or diagonally.

It's an effective way to keep teams engaged and focused on research findings. So, what's the connection to usability? Usability Bingo replaces bingo numbers with:

- notable phrases/quotes from usability tests (e.g., "I couldn't figure out how to apply the discount code");
- pain points or user struggles (e.g., "User can't fill out the form")
- user needs or goals (e.g., "I need to be able to search for multi-city destinations");
- bugs.

Rather than calling out numbers, you compile video clips from your usability tests that feature these phrases and issues. As your team watches these clips, they mark off corresponding spaces on their bingo boards, aiming to be the first to achieve five in a row and win a prize. Trust me, it's a fun and effective way to make research findings come to life!

Setting Up Usability Bingo

Now, let's explore how to set up Usability Bingo at your organization. While it may seem a bit daunting at first, with practice, it becomes easier and more efficient. Here are the steps to create a successful Usability Bingo session.

1. Determine the right test

Usability Bingo is most effective after a usability test. It's ideal for identifying usability issues and bugs, making it less suitable for generative research. Here's how to decide if it's the right study for Usability Bingo:

- The usability test isn't overly complex or lengthy, and the tasks and issues are relatively straightforward.
- There aren't too many severe findings; Usability Bingo is best for highlighting problems, not addressing urgent issues.
- You have enough unique usability issues, phrases, and quotes (about 30–50).
- Your team is interested and willing to participate.

2. Identify Bingo spaces

Identify phrases, needs, goals, pain points, or issues from your usability tests that can serve as Bingo spaces. You'll need around 30–50 of these. While synthesizing, highlight potential Bingo spaces with a specific color or use colored sticky notes to make them stand out.

Alternatively, you can identify video clips that contain potential Bingo spaces during the synthesis process. Choose spaces based on:

- surprising findings;
- critical information you want the team to pay attention to;
- issues that can be fixed easily.

3. Pull together the evidence

Create video clips that showcase the identified Bingo spaces on the board. These clips are equivalent to calling the Bingo numbers. Review your usability test recordings and extract clips that match your chosen spaces. The entire set of clips should be no more than 10 minutes, with each clip lasting about 2 minutes for better focus.

4. Create Bingo boards

You can manually create Bingo boards for participants if you have a small group (under 10). This approach gives you control over the design. Alternatively, use a Bingo board generator if you have a larger group or limited time. Some generators offer various designs, so choose one that suits your preferences.

5. Consider snacks and prizes

To make the session more enticing, consider providing snacks and prizes. Hosting the session on a Thursday or Friday afternoon is often a good idea. Offer beverages like beer, wine, and non-alcoholic options. You can order pizza or burgers or prepare snacks like chips, dips, popcorn, and candy. Award prizes for first, second, and third place, such as:

- coffee shop vouchers
- dinner vouchers
- Spotify vouchers
- fun office items.

Tailor the prizes to your participants' preferences.

6. Present your work

Once your video clips and Bingo boards are ready, it's time to present your findings. Explain the concept of Usability Bingo, and provide an example if needed. Play the video clips, and let participants cross off their Bingo spaces. The first person to achieve Bingo wins, but don't forget to acknowledge runner-ups.

7. Ask for feedback

After the session, collect feedback to improve future Usability Bingo sessions. Inquire about the effectiveness of this approach, what participants learned, whether certain clips were too long or too short, and what improvements they suggest. Use this feedback to refine your sessions and keep your team engaged.

Incorporate creativity and fun into your user research practice with Usability Bingo—it's an enjoyable way to share insights and boost team engagement.

UX RESEARCH HACKATHON

A few years back, I worked at a company with a strong user research culture. My colleagues were actively engaged with research findings, translating them into actionable roadmap items and leveraging my deliverables for informed decision-making. It was a researcher's dream come true.

However, amidst this dream scenario, I grappled with recurring insights that didn't seem to align with any specific team or project. They weren't substantial enough to cause chaos, yet they nagged at me during research sessions. These issues demanded resolution, but their lack of clear ownership presented a challenge.

One weekend, while participating in a hackathon, I had an epiphany. Why not apply this innovative format within the organization to tackle these persistent, unclaimed insights? And that's when the idea of a User Research Insight Hackathon was born.

The User Research Insight Hackathon is a unique approach to address those vexing, unassigned insights. It's a creative way to engage the entire organization in solving persistent research findings that might not fit neatly into any team's roadmap.

Here's how I set up and run a successful User Research Insight Hackathon.

1. Create a Hackathon Document

Start by creating a comprehensive document outlining the hackathon's purpose, goals, expected time commitment, guidelines, and any potential legal considerations. Ensure that your organization permits such events, especially if they involve late working hours.

2. Gauge Interest via Email

Before investing too much time, send out an initial email to gauge interest among your colleagues. Share the hackathon document to explain the concept and the time commitment involved. This step helps ensure that there's sufficient interest before proceeding.

3. Choose Your Insights

Once you know you have participants, revisit your persistent insights from the last few quarters. Focus on issues that reoccur and lack a clear place in the roadmap. Prioritize them based on criteria like reach (how many users are affected), impact (severity), and complexity (ease of implementation). Create a table to help rank these insights.

4. Pick Suitable Dates

Select dates for the hackathon sessions based on participants' availability. Form teams, aiming for around five members each, including a mix of roles. If you don't have enough participants for all insights, prioritize the top ones or let participants choose their preferred projects.

5. Prepare for the Hackathon

Block out calendars for the hackathon days, both for teamwork and presentations. Automate reminder emails to participants to ensure they don't miss the sessions. Collect necessary materials, including paper, pens, markers, glue, sticky notes, highlighters, and portable whiteboards. Don't forget to arrange snacks and refreshments.

6. Set Up a Presentation Day

Before the hackathon, organize a presentation session to introduce the hackathon's purpose, expectations, guidelines, and goals. Provide participants with access to research materials related to their assigned insights. Use this time to address any questions or concerns.

7. Launch the Hackathon

Let the hackathon begin! Participants work in their respective teams to tackle their assigned insights. Be available for questions and support throughout the process.

8. Host the Presentations and Voting

On the final day of the hackathon, each team presents their findings and solutions to the entire company. Allocate 10 minutes per team for presentations. After all teams have presented, hold a company-wide vote to determine the most innovative and creative solution. Award prizes to the winning teams.

9. Prepare for Research

Following the hackathon, you'll have multiple prototypes to test. Set up user testing for each prototype to gain valuable insights. Move forward with the most promising solutions and track their progress with the respective teams.

Incorporating a User Research Insight Hackathon into your organization's culture can not only address lingering issues but also foster innovation and collaboration. In my experience, these hackathons became a quarterly tradition, driving positive change and resolving those pesky, recurrent research insights.

HOW TO TRACK THE IMPACT OF YOUR RESEARCH

User researchers love uncovering insights, but let's be honest, tracking the impact of our work? That's a different beast. If you've ever felt like your research disappears into a black hole after presenting it, you're not alone. But if you want a seat at the strategic table, you need to show your value in ways that are undeniable.

This isn't about vanity metrics or feel-good storytelling. It's about hard data, real influence, and making sure your work leads to tangible product decisions. Here's how to track impact like a pro, using a structured framework that aligns with your UXR Impact Tracker.

Step 1: Set Up Your Impact Tracker from the Start

Most user researchers make the mistake of thinking about impact tracking after the research is complete; by then, it's too late. The key to ensuring your work drives real change is planning for impact before you even start.

If you don't define success from the beginning, you'll have nothing concrete to measure later, and your research could be dismissed as "interesting but not actionable." Let's fix that.

Define What Success Looks Like

Before launching into research, pause and answer these critical questions:

- What is the problem this research is solving? (Be specific, don't just say "improve usability" or "increase engagement.")
- Who are the key stakeholders, and what decisions will they make based on this research?
- What specific metric, KPI, or business outcome will this research impact?
- How will we measure whether the research was successful in 3–6 months?

Without clear answers, your research may be valuable in theory but won't drive real product changes.

Example: Good vs. Bad Goal-Setting

Bad Research Goal: "Improve the onboarding experience." (Too vague!)

Good Research Goal: "Identify usability barriers in onboarding that prevent users from completing the setup process. Success will be measured by an increase in onboarding completion from 60% to 75% within 3 months of implementation." (Clear and measurable!)

Log Your Research in an Impact Tracker

Once you've defined the goal, immediately document it in your UXR Impact Tracker. This ensures the research is tied to a tangible outcome from the start.

Set up a new entry in your tracker with these fields:

- Project Name ensures clarity about what the research is for.
- Impact Statement defines what success looks like in measurable terms.
- Research Type specifies the type of study (usability test, survey, etc.).
- Stakeholders identifies who will use this research to make decisions.
- ROI Type connects research to business impact (retention, cost savings).

Align with Stakeholders

To ensure research is used, you must get stakeholder buy-in before starting. This means having direct conversations with the people who will act on your findings.

Steps to take:

Schedule a 15-minute alignment meeting with key stakeholders (PMs, designers, leadership, engineers). Ask them directly:

- "What decisions do you need to make, and how will this research inform them?"
- "What's the biggest risk if we don't solve this problem?"
- "What kind of insights will be most useful for your team?"

Example:

PM: "We need to know why 40% of users abandon onboarding after step 3. If we don't fix this, we risk losing potential customers."

Designer: "We need usability feedback on the new dashboard layout before launching it."

If stakeholders don't feel personally invested in the research, they won't use the results.

End every meeting with: "What would make this research a success for you?"
Their answer will help you tailor insights to drive action.

Define What Type of Impact You're Measuring

Not all research influences product changes immediately. Some research influences strategy, while other studies drive immediate fixes.

The 3 Main Types of Research Impact:

1. Direct Product Impact: Research findings result in product changes, UI updates, or feature adjustments.
   a. Example: "Our study on checkout friction led to a redesigned payment flow, decreasing drop-off by 12%."
2. Strategic Influence: Research shifts company priorities, informs a roadmap, or changes a long-term strategy.
   a. Example: "Our research showed that users prioritize speed over new features, leading leadership to invest in performance improvements."
3. Operational/Process Impact: Research improves internal workflows, saves time, or enhances research efficiency.
   a. Example: "We streamlined participant recruitment, reducing turnaround time from 10 days to 4 days."

Log the expected impact type in your tracker. This will help when measuring long-term results.

Establish How You Will Measure Impact

Once research is complete, how will you know if it worked?

Every research project should have at least one measurable impact metric that is reviewed at 1, 3, and 6 months. Possible metrics to track:

- If you're researching a pricing page redesign, track conversion rates before and after implementation.
- If you're testing a new signup flow, measure if more users complete registration after the update.

Set a reminder to check these metrics at 1, 3, and 6 months. If impact isn't visible, follow up with stakeholders to investigate why.

Next Steps

By now, you should have:

- Defined what success looks like before starting research
- Logged the project in an Impact Tracker
- Aligned with stakeholders on expected decisions and impact
- Identified the type of impact (product, strategy, or process)
- Defined how you will measure success and set check-in reminders

Go document your next research study in an Impact Tracker and align with a stakeholder.

Step 2: Ensuring Research Gets Seen and Used

You've done the research. You've gathered valuable insights. Now, the real challenge begins: making sure people actually use it.

One of the biggest reasons research fails to drive impact is because stakeholders don't engage with it or don't know how to act on it.

This step ensures your findings are not just read but discussed, referenced, and used in decision-making.

Choose the Right Format for Sharing Findings

Different stakeholders consume information in different ways. If you want your research to be actionable, present it in a format they will actually engage with. Match the format to the audience. Before creating a report, ask stakeholders:

- "What's the most useful way for you to consume these insights?"
- "Would a summary, a deep dive, or a quick walkthrough be best?"

Structure insights in a way that answers their key questions:

- What's the main problem?
- Why does it matter?
- What should we do about it?

Use clear, concise, and scannable formats:

- Avoid long paragraphs.
- Use bullet points and data highlights.
- If possible, create an "Actionable Insights" section at the top.

Example:
Bad:
"We conducted a usability test with 10 participants to understand how they interact with the onboarding flow. Several issues were identified, including confusion around step two, lack of guidance, and unclear terminology."

Good:
"Users drop off at step two of onboarding due to confusion. 70% of participants didn't understand the next action. To fix this, add a progress indicator and clarify step two's instructions. If addressed, this could increase onboarding completion by 15%."

Present Findings in a Discussion, Not Just a Document

If you only send a research report via email or Slack, there's a good chance it will be skimmed or ignored. Instead, schedule a research readout or discussion session where you can walk stakeholders through the insights and ensure they understand them. How to run a research readout session:

- Keep it short (15–30 minutes).
  - Stakeholders have limited time. Focus on the most critical insights.
- Start with the conclusion.
  - Lead with the main takeaway, not the background.
- Make it interactive. Ask stakeholders:
  - "Does this align with what you expected?"
  - "What questions does this raise for you?"
  - "How can we apply this immediately?"
- Have clear next steps at the end.
  - Assign owners to actions.
  - Get verbal commitments from PMs or designers on what they'll do next.

A discussion ensures engagement. A report alone can be ignored, but a conversation forces action.

Track Stakeholder Engagement and Reactions

Once research has been shared, it's important to track who engaged with it and how they responded. If no one asks follow-up questions or discusses the findings, that's a warning sign that the research is not being absorbed.

If you share findings and receive silence, take action:

- Send a follow-up message:
  - "I wanted to check in; do you see any immediate next steps based on these findings?"
- Tie it back to roadmap goals:
  - "Since this aligns with the Q2 roadmap, I want to make sure we discuss implementation."
- Set up a quick 10-minute sync:
  - "Would a quick discussion help clarify anything? Happy to jump on a call."

Research that isn't engaged with won't be acted on. Ensuring discussion and action is critical to making research impactful. Even if stakeholders love the insights, research won't drive impact unless someone is responsible for acting on it.

1. At the end of your readout, assign clear action items:
   a. "PM to update the roadmap to include X change."
   b. "Designer to update UI elements based on findings."
   c. "Engineer to investigate feasibility of the recommendation."
2. Log these next steps in the Impact Tracker.
3. Follow up within 2–4 weeks.
4. If no action has been taken, check in with assigned owners.

Without clear ownership, research can sit idle. Assigning responsibility ensures it turns into real changes.

By now, you should have:

- Shared findings in the right format for your audience.
- Presented research in a discussion, not just a document.
- Tracked who engaged, what was said, and what actions were taken.
- Assigned clear owners for next steps.

Go back to your last research project and check:

- Was it shared in the most effective way?
- Did stakeholders engage with it?
- Are there clear next steps documented?
- If not, adjust how you share research going forward.

Step 3: Measuring Impact Over Time

You've shared the research. You've got stakeholder engagement. But how do you prove the research actually made a difference? This step is about tracking what happens after research is delivered, following up to ensure action is taken, and measuring long-term impact.

Most research impact doesn't happen overnight. Stakeholders may agree with your findings, but implementation takes time. Without a structured follow-up process, research can get lost in the shuffle.

This step ensures that your insights turn into real changes and that you can quantify their impact.

Establish a Follow-Up Timeline

Measuring research impact is not a one-time event. It requires scheduled follow-ups at key intervals. The first follow-up should happen within a week after you've shared your research. This is when you check if any initial actions have been taken.

What to check:

- Were any Jira tickets or roadmap changes created based on the research?
- Did a PM reference the findings in a planning meeting?
- Did a designer start making UI updates?
- Did leadership discuss the research in strategic planning?

If no action has been taken within a week:

- Follow up with stakeholders via Slack or email:
  - "Hey [PM/Designer], just checking in on whether we're moving forward with [research recommendation]. Let me know if you need anything from me to help."

- Ask directly in the next planning meeting:
  - "Are there any blockers preventing us from implementing these research findings?"
- Offer to present again if needed:
  - "Would it be helpful to walk through the key findings again in our next sync?"

The first week is critical. If research isn't acted on quickly, there's a higher chance it will be forgotten.

At the 1-month mark, check whether changes are in progress. What to check:

- Have designs been finalized based on research?
- Are engineering teams working on the recommended updates?
- Are stakeholders referencing research in decision-making?
- Is there any resistance or pushback to implementing the findings?

One-month follow-up questions to ask PMs and Designers

- "I saw the new onboarding flow in Figma; was that based on our research?"
- "Are there any challenges in implementing the research recommendations?"
- "Are we testing this with users before launch?"

If implementation hasn't started after a month:

- Ask what's blocking it:
  - "Is there something preventing us from moving forward with this?"
- Tie it back to business goals:
  - "This change could improve onboarding completion by 15%; do we still consider that a priority?"
- Provide alternative solutions:
  - "If full implementation isn't possible right now, is there a smaller test we can run?"

Once the research-driven changes have been implemented, it's time to measure actual impact. This is where research becomes indisputable proof of value. After the 3–6-month mark, you can measure:

- User behavior changes (did more users complete onboarding?)
- Business metrics (did checkout conversion rates improve?)
- Operational efficiency (did the research save time or reduce support tickets?)

How to track this data:

- Request pre/post data from analytics teams
- Use A/B testing results to compare old vs. new versions
- Check customer support tickets to see if reported issues decreased

Communicate Impact Back to the Organization

- Quarterly Impact Reports: Summarize key research-driven changes and their results.
- Slack/Email Updates: Send a message highlighting how research influenced a decision.
- Internal Presentations: Share research impact in all-hands meetings.

If leadership regularly sees research impact, it becomes easier to secure buy-in for future projects.

Understanding Leading vs. Lagging Indicators for Measuring Research Impact

Tracking research impact requires more than just checking business metrics after changes have been made. You need to monitor both leading and lagging indicators to understand how and when research is influencing outcomes. Many researchers only focus on lagging indicators (revenue, retention), but these take time to show up. Leading indicators help track progress before major business changes occur.

Establish a Research Impact Reporting System

To make research impact visible, you need a structured way to track and share it consistently. This means creating a quarterly or monthly Research Impact Report that summarizes:

- What research was conducted?
- How it influenced decisions?
- What measurable impact it had?

What to include in a research impact report?

- What was the research question?
- What insights were uncovered?
- Actions taken based on research
- What product changes were implemented?
- What strategic decisions were influenced?
- Measurable business impact
- What leading and lagging indicators improved?
- How did the research contribute to company goals?

Example research impact report: Q2 Research Impact Summary

Research conducted:

- Checkout Usability Study
- Customer Retention Interviews
- Feature Prioritization Survey

Key insights:

- Users abandoned checkout at Step 3 due to unclear payment options
- High-retention customers rely heavily on automated reminders
- Users ranked "one-click save" as a top feature request

Actions taken:

- Checkout flow redesigned for better clarity
- Automated reminders built into product
- Prioritized "one-click save" for Q3 roadmap

Measurable impact:

- Checkout completion increased from 55% to 68%
- Retention among new users improved by 12%
- 40% of users adopted "one-click save" within 1 month of launch

How to share the research impact report

- Post a short update after major research-driven changes
  - Example: "The onboarding research we conducted led to a new flow that increased completion rates by 20%. Great collaboration between research, design, and product!"
- Roadmap & planning meetings. Reference past research findings when discussing new features.
  - Example: "Our retention study showed that users engage more when they receive automated reminders. Should we consider applying this insight to another feature?"
- Company all-hands & leadership updates. Ensure research is included in high-level discussions.
  - Example: Present a slide during an all-hands meeting showing how research influenced business KPIs
- Design & engineering syncs. Embed research insights directly into Figma, Jira, and Notion.
  - Example: Attach usability testing findings to a Figma file so designers see them in context

Research is only as valuable as the decisions it influences. And making that influence clear isn't someone else's job, it's yours.

As a user researcher or someone doing research at your organization, there is a lot to consider and handle. From intake documents to prepping the right recruitment to prioritizing the most impactful projects and making sure everything gets done on time, it can feel like a juggling act. Often, researchers or those doing research in their organization can feel this pressure, which leads to some negative consequences.

In this part, we will talk through the all-famous concept of democratization, as this is always something that comes into play, especially if you are a solo user researcher or the only person doing research in your company.

Then, we will talk through the really important aspects of time management and burnout, which can be really difficult for all of us.

Let's dive in!

PART NINE

Juggling It All

Using AI as a Thought Partner 32

A few years ago, I walked out of a research presentation feeling frustrated. I had spent weeks conducting in-depth interviews, analyzing insights, and crafting a compelling story. The findings were solid, the recommendations were clear, and I had data to back them up.

Yet, as I wrapped up my presentation, I could feel the hesitation in the room. The product team nodded politely but quickly shifted the conversation to engineering constraints. The leadership team asked if the findings were "statistically significant." The marketing director questioned whether the research really applied to their audience segment.

Instead of sparking action, my research findings were met with skepticism and roadblocks.

At first, I chalked it up to stakeholder resistance—maybe they just didn't want to hear the results. But as I reflected, I realized something deeper: I had failed to anticipate their concerns before I stepped into the room.

I had been so focused on conducting the research that I hadn't fully thought through how the research would land with different stakeholders. I hadn't preemptively addressed objections, framed the insights in a way that tied to business goals, or challenged my own assumptions along the way.

That was the moment I realized that being a great researcher isn't just about gathering insights. It's about sharpening the way we think, anticipate reactions, and frame our work to drive action.

Fast forward to today, and I approach research differently. Before I finalize my study design, I pressure-test my assumptions. Before I present findings, I practice responding to stakeholder pushback. Before I lead a brainstorming session, I generate alternative ways to frame the discussion.

I still do all the heavy lifting—conducting interviews, synthesizing findings, and crafting compelling narratives. But I use AI as a thought partner to help me:

- Challenge my own biases so I don't get stuck in my own thinking.
- Anticipate objections before they come up in meetings.
- Generate alternative study designs when I feel like I'm relying on familiar methods.
- Help stakeholders brainstorm research ideas so they feel ownership over the process.
- Frame research insights in ways that connect to business goals so they have real impact.

AI isn't doing the research for me, but it's making me a better researcher.

USING AI TO CHALLENGE MY ASSUMPTIONS

One of the biggest risks in user research is confirmation bias—our tendency to seek out and prioritize information that supports what we already believe. This bias isn't just a personal flaw; it's a fundamental part of how human cognition works. We naturally build mental models based on our experiences, expertise, and the patterns we've observed over time. While these models help us navigate complexity, they can also create blind spots.

This is especially problematic in user research, where the goal is to uncover truths that may be counterintuitive, uncomfortable, or disruptive to existing business assumptions. If we approach research with a fixed idea of what we expect to find, we may subconsciously steer interviews, usability tests, or analyses toward confirming our expectations.

AI can act as a neutral third party, helping us check our biases, challenge our assumptions, and think more expansively about our research. Instead of being limited by our personal experiences or professional background, we can use AI to pressure-test our thinking in ways that might not come naturally.

HOW I USE AI TO CHALLENGE ASSUMPTIONS

"What am I missing?"

One of the simplest yet most effective ways I use AI is by feeding it my research question, assumptions, or early insights and asking:

- What counterarguments exist?
- What potential flaws are in this reasoning?
- What alternative explanations should I consider?

For example, if I'm conducting a study on why users are dropping off during onboarding, I might assume that complexity is the main issue—perhaps too many steps, too much cognitive load, or unclear instructions. But before diving into a study design that focuses on usability, I might ask AI:

"What are other possible explanations for onboarding drop-off that I might not be considering?"

In response, AI might surface alternative hypotheses that shift my perspective:

- Users could be experiencing technical issues that aren't about complexity but about system errors or browser incompatibility.
- The drop-off could be tied to perceived value misalignment—users don't see a compelling reason to complete onboarding.
- It could be a matter of timing—users sign up when they have a moment of interest, but by the time they reach onboarding, they've lost motivation.

None of these are groundbreaking, but they force me to pause and expand my lens before committing to a single research direction.

Role-playing Different Perspectives

Stakeholder buy-in is a major factor in the success of user research. Even if your insights are sound, they need to resonate with the right people in the right way.

To anticipate the reactions of different stakeholders, I prompt AI to act as key decision-makers and critique my conclusions from their perspective. For example, I might ask AI to respond as:

- A skeptical executive who prioritizes revenue impact
- A product manager who is concerned about feature deadlines
- A designer who has already spent months crafting a solution

A typical prompt I might use:
"Pretend you're a VP of Product. Based on these research insights, what concerns or objections might you have?"

AI might generate responses like:

- "How does this finding directly translate to revenue impact?"
- "Are we sure this isn't just a vocal minority of users?"
- "This problem seems important, but do we have data on whether fixing it will move the needle?"

These are exactly the kinds of questions I might get in a stakeholder meeting. By engaging with them upfront, I can strengthen my case before presenting findings.

I can also do the reverse—if I anticipate a particular stakeholder being too eager to jump on a single insight, I can ask AI to challenge their assumptions so I'm prepared to offer a balanced perspective.

HOW YOU CAN TRY THIS?

Next time you're preparing a research report or hypothesis, ask AI:

- What might someone who disagrees with this argue?
- What are three alternative explanations for this finding?
- If I had to argue the opposite of my conclusion, how would I do it?

By making AI a challenger to our thinking, we can become more rigorous, thoughtful, and persuasive as researchers.

BRAINSTORMING RESEARCH QUESTIONS AND STUDY DESIGNS

A research project is only as strong as the questions it asks. The right research questions help uncover meaningful insights, while poorly framed questions lead to vague, inconclusive, or even misleading results.

Even experienced researchers can fall into predictable patterns when structuring a study. We default to the same types of questions we've asked in the past. We rely on familiar methodologies. And sometimes, we frame our questions in a way that unintentionally limits the scope of discovery rather than expanding it.

AI can help break these patterns. By serving as a brainstorming partner, it can generate alternative ways of framing research questions, suggest new study designs, and push us to think beyond our usual approaches.

HOW I USE AI TO BRAINSTORM RESEARCH QUESTIONS AND STUDY DESIGNS?

Expanding how I frame research questions

Writing good research questions is both an art and a science. A slight rewording can dramatically shift the kind of insight you get.

For example, let's say I'm conducting research on why users aren't engaging with a new feature in an app. My initial research question might be:

"Why aren't users engaging with Feature X?"

This is a valid starting point, but it's quite broad and could lead to vague insights. To refine it, I might ask AI:

"What are alternative ways to frame this research question?"

AI might generate variations like:

- What are the main barriers preventing users from engaging with Feature X? → This version shifts the focus to obstacles.
- What types of users engage most and least with Feature X, and why? → This prompts segmentation analysis.
- What expectations did users have before trying Feature X, and how did reality compare? → This brings in expectation vs. experience mismatch.
- What problem do users expect Feature X to solve, and does it align with how they actually use it? → This checks whether the feature addresses a real need.

Each variation subtly shifts the lens of the research, which can lead to richer insights.

Avoiding Leading or Biased Questions

One of the biggest risks in research is accidentally leading participants toward a specific response. It's easy to write a question that subtly implies a preferred answer. For example, let's say I'm preparing interview questions and one of them is:
"How frustrating was your experience using Feature X?"
This assumes the experience was frustrating. A more neutral way to phrase it might be:
"Can you describe your experience using Feature X?"
To check my biases, I sometimes copy-paste my research questions into AI and ask: "Do any of these questions contain leading language? How can I make them more neutral?"
AI will often highlight subtle biases I didn't notice and suggest ways to rephrase the questions. This is particularly useful when designing surveys or structured interviews where wording precision is critical.

Generating Unexpected Research Angles

Sometimes I'll ask AI for completely fresh research angles to ensure I'm not missing opportunities.
For example, if I'm researching why customers cancel their subscriptions, I might expect responses about pricing, lack of value, or competition. But I can ask AI: "What are some unexpected reasons users might cancel a subscription?"
AI might surface ideas I hadn't considered, like:

- Emotional reasons—Users might associate the product with a past project or job they no longer need.
- Identity misalignment—Users may not feel like the product "fits" their self-image anymore.
- Subscription fatigue—Not just a pricing issue, but an overall feeling of being oversubscribed.

These suggestions prompt me to explore new angles in my research—maybe by including questions that dig into the emotional side of cancellation, rather than just focusing on price and value.

Exploring Creative Methodologies

Once I have a clear research question, I need to decide on the best method to investigate it. But as researchers, we tend to rely on our go-to methodologies—interviews, usability tests, surveys, etc.
AI can suggest alternative study designs that might not be my first instinct. For example, let's say I need to understand how people use a fitness app over time. My first

instinct might be to conduct interviews or look at usage data. But if I ask AI: "What are creative ways to study long-term app usage?"

It might suggest:

- Diary studies—Having users document their app experience over weeks instead of relying on one-time interviews.
- Mobile screen recordings—Observing how users naturally navigate the app over time.
- Cognitive walkthroughs—Asking users to articulate their thoughts aloud while using the app in real-time.
- Co-creation workshops—Having users redesign parts of the app that feel frustrating to them.

By surfacing alternative methodologies, AI pushes me beyond my default approaches and helps me design richer studies.

Next time you're structuring a research study, ask AI:

- What are five alternative ways to frame this research question?
- Do any of my questions contain leading or biased language?
- What are unconventional ways I could study this problem?

By using AI as a brainstorming partner, we can expand our research thinking, explore new methodologies, and ultimately, design better studies.

Conducting user research is only half the battle. The other half—arguably the more difficult half—is getting stakeholders to act on the findings.

Even when we uncover compelling insights, they can be met with skepticism, resistance, or outright dismissal. This isn't necessarily because stakeholders don't value research, but because they have their own priorities, constraints, and biases that shape how they interpret findings.

AI can help us anticipate pushback before it happens, allowing us to refine our recommendations and craft stronger, more persuasive arguments. Instead of walking into a stakeholder meeting and getting caught off guard by objections, I use AI to role-play these conversations in advance, pressure-test my insights, and ensure I'm presenting my findings in a way that aligns with business goals.

HOW I USE AI TO ANTICIPATE STAKEHOLDER PUSHBACK?

Testing How My Arguments Land

When I prepare a research presentation or report, I don't just focus on what I want to say—I focus on how it will be received.

One of my favorite ways to use AI is to feed it my research summary and ask it to respond as a skeptical stakeholder.

For example, if my research shows that a new onboarding process is confusing to users, and I recommend simplifying the flow, I might ask AI: "Act as a product manager who is skeptical of these findings. What concerns or objections might they raise?"

AI might generate responses like:

- "Do we have quantitative data to back this up, or is this just from a few interviews?"
- "We already simplified onboarding last quarter—why would another round of changes help?"
- "What evidence do we have that a simpler flow will actually improve retention?"

These are exactly the kinds of questions I might face in a real meeting. By seeing them ahead of time, I can prepare evidence-backed responses rather than scrambling for answers in the moment.

Identifying Gaps in My Reasoning

AI is also useful for spotting weak points in my arguments before stakeholders do. If I'm presenting findings that suggest users struggle with a certain feature, but I haven't explored whether it's an onboarding issue, a UI problem, or a gap in user expectations, AI might point out that my conclusion is too broad.

A typical prompt I use: "Challenge my research findings. What potential weaknesses exist in my conclusions?"

AI might respond with:

- "You're assuming the problem is usability, but could it be an issue of user motivation instead?"
- "How do you know this is a widespread problem and not just an issue for certain user segments?"
- "What trade-offs exist? If we fix this issue, what might we break or deprioritize?"

These questions force me to tighten my logic and make sure my recommendations are well-supported before presenting them.

Framing Insights to Align with Business Goals

One of the most common reasons research gets ignored is that it's presented in a way that doesn't resonate with business stakeholders. For example, a researcher might say: "Users are frustrated with our checkout process because they have to enter their credit card details manually."

A stakeholder might think: Okay... but how big of a problem is this really? Instead, AI can help me reframe the same finding in a way that aligns with business priorities.

If I ask AI: "How can I make this research insight more compelling to an executive audience?"

It might suggest a version like: "Our data shows that 60% of users abandon checkout when they reach the payment screen. Based on our qualitative research, many cite frustration with manual credit card entry. If we implement an autofill feature, we could reduce drop-off and increase revenue."

This version:

- Quantifies the problem (60% drop-off)
- Ties it to business impact (lost revenue)
- Links it to a concrete solution (autofill)

By proactively reframing insights in this way, I make it much harder for stakeholders to dismiss the findings as "just another research report."

Before presenting your research, ask AI:

1. What are the top three reasons someone might push back on this insight?
2. What potential weaknesses exist in my conclusions?
3. How can I frame this finding in a way that aligns with business goals?

By using AI as a stakeholder simulator, we can anticipate resistance, refine our arguments, and make a stronger case for the impact of our research.

User researchers often act as facilitators, whether we're leading research planning discussions, running ideation workshops, or helping stakeholders refine their own thinking. These sessions can be incredibly valuable—but they can also be frustrating.

Stakeholders sometimes come in with preconceived notions about what the research should reveal. Teams may struggle to think beyond their own assumptions. And without a structured approach, brainstorming can feel like an unfocused conversation rather than a productive session.

AI can act as a silent co-facilitator, helping to structure discussions, surface unexpected ideas, and encourage teams to think more expansively. It's not about AI replacing human creativity—it's about using it to remove friction, introduce fresh perspectives, and make brainstorming more effective.

HOW I USE AI TO FACILITATE BRAINSTORMING?

Creating Structured Brainstorming Prompts

Brainstorming is often most productive when it's framed in the right way. A poorly worded prompt can lead to generic ideas, while a well-crafted one can push participants to think in new directions. For example, if I'm leading a brainstorming session on why user engagement is declining, I might start with a basic question like: "Why do we think engagement is dropping?"

This might generate predictable answers—too many notifications, a clunky UI, or a lack of compelling features. But if I ask AI to suggest more thought-provoking prompts, I might get:

- "If we assumed engagement would drop again next quarter, what would be the most likely reasons?" → Forces the team to think proactively.
- "If we had no access to analytics, how would we figure out why engagement is declining?" → Encourages creative problem-solving.
- "What are the most counterintuitive reasons engagement might be dropping?" → Pushes beyond obvious explanations.

By varying the way I frame the discussion, I can get more diverse, creative ideas from the group.

Generating Unexpected Connections

One of the biggest challenges in brainstorming is that teams tend to stay within their comfort zones. They focus on what they already know rather than considering new, unfamiliar angles.

AI can help by drawing unexpected connections between ideas. For example, if I'm helping a product team brainstorm ways to improve feature adoption, I might ask AI: "What are lessons from completely different industries that could apply here?"
AI might respond with:

- Retail: Grocery stores use end caps (highly visible displays at the end of aisles) to promote new products. Could we apply a similar strategy to highlight new features in our UI?
- Education: Language learning apps use streaks and gamification to keep users engaged. Could we apply these mechanics to our onboarding process?
- Fitness: Many workout apps use accountability partners to drive engagement. Could we explore social features that encourage users to adopt new features together?

These types of cross-industry insights often spark fresh thinking that wouldn't have come up in a typical product meeting.

Acting as a "Third Mind" in Workshops

Workshops can be unpredictable. Some participants dominate the conversation, while others hesitate to share their thoughts. AI can help by acting as an impartial third voice that introduces ideas without being influenced by group dynamics.

If a session is feeling stagnant, I might use AI to generate:

- Alternative viewpoints → "If we were forced to argue against this idea, what would be the best counterarguments?"
- Wild card ideas → "What's an extreme or 'out-there' solution we haven't considered?"
- Common failure patterns → "What are common ways this type of initiative has failed in other companies?"

By injecting unexpected perspectives, AI keeps the discussion dynamic and ensures we're exploring a wide range of possibilities.

Before your next brainstorming session, ask AI:

1. What are five unexpected questions I could ask to get people thinking differently?
2. What are lessons from other industries that could apply to this challenge?
3. How might someone completely unfamiliar with this problem approach it?

By using AI as a co-facilitator, you can structure more engaging sessions, unlock fresh ideas, and drive deeper discussions.

One of the biggest challenges in user research is ensuring our work drives real change. It's not enough to uncover meaningful insights—we have to make sure those insights resonate with stakeholders, align with company objectives, and influence decision-making. Yet, many researchers struggle with this. It's common to hear:

- "Leadership isn't acting on our findings."
- "Stakeholders don't see the value of research."
- "Our work feels disconnected from business goals."

The reality is that research doesn't exist in a vacuum. If we want our insights to have impact, we need to bridge the gap between user needs and business priorities. AI can help by reframing research insights in ways that speak the language of decision-makers, identifying connections to key business metrics, and making research findings more actionable.

HOW I USE AI TO CONNECT RESEARCH TO BUSINESS IMPACT

Translating Research Insights into Business Terms

Stakeholders—especially executives—aren't always interested in raw user research insights. They care about how those insights affect business outcomes. For example, if I conduct a study and find that users are frustrated with the checkout process, I could present that insight as: "Users find the checkout experience frustrating and cumbersome."

While true, this doesn't tell stakeholders why it matters. Instead, I can ask AI: "How can I frame this research finding in a way that aligns with business goals?"

AI might suggest: "Our research shows that friction in the checkout process is leading to a 20% increase in abandoned carts. Simplifying this flow could result in an estimated X% revenue uplift."

Now, the insight is tied to a tangible business impact: cart abandonment and revenue loss. This makes it significantly harder to ignore.

Crafting Executive-Friendly Summaries

Executives don't have time to read a 20-page research report. They need insights that are concise, high-impact, and actionable. When I finish a study, I'll sometimes ask AI: "Summarize these research findings for an executive audience. Focus on business impact and next steps."

A detailed research report might say:

> Users struggle with Feature X because the interface is unintuitive, leading to increased frustration and drop-off at the second step of the flow. Many users report not understanding the purpose of the feature, leading to low adoption rates.

An AI-generated executive summary might reframe this as:

> Low adoption of Feature X is costing us potential engagement. 60% of users drop off at Step 2 due to confusion. Simplifying this flow and clarifying the feature's purpose could improve retention.

By making insights clear, concise, and outcome-driven, I increase the chances of leadership actually acting on them.

Mapping Research to Strategic Goals

User research is often seen as separate from business strategy. But the most impactful researchers actively connect their work to broader company goals—whether it's increasing revenue, improving retention, or reducing churn. To ensure my research aligns with business priorities, I'll sometimes ask AI: "How does this research connect to our company's strategic goals?"

For example, if my company's goal is to increase customer lifetime value (CLV), AI might suggest ways my research findings tie into that goal:

- If users find onboarding confusing, they may churn early, lowering CLV.
- If they struggle to discover valuable features, they may not see long-term product value, impacting retention.
- If checkout is frustrating, they may not convert to paying customers at all, reducing revenue.

By explicitly linking research to key business objectives, I make it easier for stakeholders to see why research matters—not just for users, but for the company's success.

After completing a research project, ask AI:

1. How does this insight connect to key business objectives like revenue, retention, or engagement?
2. Can you summarize this finding for an executive audience in two sentences?
3. What are three ways to make this insight more actionable for stakeholders?

By using AI as a business translation tool, we can make research more influential, more actionable, and more valuable to the organizations we work with.

AI has become an unexpected ally. It doesn't do the research for me, but it helps me think better, challenge my assumptions, and communicate more effectively. It's like having a sounding board that never gets tired, a debate partner that always pushes back, and a brainstorming collaborator that constantly expands the way I approach research problems.

If you're a researcher who's ever felt stuck, faced resistance from stakeholders, or wanted to make your insights more impactful, I encourage you to experiment with AI—not as a shortcut, but as a tool for deeper thinking. Next time you're prepping for a big research project or stakeholder meeting, try asking:

- What might I be missing in my research approach?
- What's the strongest counterargument to my findings?
- How can I frame this insight in a way that connects to business priorities?

You might be surprised at how much sharper, more strategic, and more persuasive your research becomes.

Democratizing User Research

33

THE COMPLEX LANDSCAPE OF RESEARCH DEMOCRATIZATION

User research is at an inflection point. Demand for research insights is growing exponentially, but research teams remain small. This imbalance forces organizations to explore democratization—enabling non-researchers to conduct research.

At its best, democratization scales insights, increases research buy-in, and enhances customer centricity across an organization. At its worst, it leads to poor-quality research, biased data, and diluted research rigor. For researchers, democratization can feel like a double-edged sword: it helps meet demand, but it can also erode the depth and expertise of the field if done poorly.

This chapter explores how organizations can approach research democratization intentionally and responsibly, ensuring that research maintains its impact, quality, and integrity while also being more accessible.

THE GROWING DEMAND FOR RESEARCH ACROSS ORGANIZATIONS

User research has expanded beyond the traditional UX and product development lifecycle. Today, research is needed for:

- Product strategy—Understanding user needs before features are even conceptualized.
- Marketing validation—Ensuring messaging aligns with real customer pain points.

- Customer support optimization—Identifying friction points that lead to high support ticket volumes.
- Business decision-making—Using research to inform investment, expansion, and prioritization.

As research extends into these diverse functions, the traditional researcher-to-team ratio has become unsustainable. Many researchers find themselves spread too thin, juggling too many projects with too few resources. In some cases, researchers must reject critical research requests simply because they don't have the bandwidth. This leads to frustration among stakeholders who feel they lack access to the insights they need.

Enter democratization—a means to scale research beyond the core research team by enabling others to participate in the research process.

THE GROWING DESIRE FROM NON-RESEARCHERS TO ENGAGE IN RESEARCH

It's not just research teams feeling the pressure; stakeholders themselves are becoming more eager to engage with user insights. Product managers, designers, and even marketing teams want direct access to users. They see the value in speaking with customers, testing hypotheses, and gathering feedback.

This shift is largely positive. When more people across an organization have a user-centric mindset, better decisions are made. However, without structure, this enthusiasm can lead to problems:

- Biased research—Without training, non-researchers may unconsciously lead participants toward desired answers.
- Unethical practices—Mishandling of participant consent, privacy, and data security.
- Poor research methodologies—Relying on convenience sampling, asking leading questions, or misinterpreting results.

Despite these risks, the demand from non-researchers will not go away. Instead of resisting it, researchers must proactively shape democratization in a way that enhances, rather than diminishes, research integrity.

THE RISKS AND REWARDS OF DEMOCRATIZING RESEARCH

Like many trends in UX and product development, democratization is neither inherently good nor bad; it depends entirely on how it is implemented.

Potential Benefits of Democratization:

1. Scalability—More research gets done without overburdening researchers.
2. Stakeholder Buy-in—Teams feel more ownership of insights, increasing the likelihood of acting on findings.
3. Faster Decision-Making—Teams don't have to wait weeks or months for research results.
4. User-Centric Culture—More teams engaging with research can help embed user thinking into company culture.

Potential Risks of Democratization:

1. Compromised Research Quality—Without structure, teams may conduct poorly designed studies, leading to misleading conclusions.
2. Research Fragmentation—Multiple teams running isolated studies without alignment, leading to duplicated work and inconsistent data.
3. Undermining the Value of Research—If anyone can "do research," the expertise of trained researchers may be devalued.
4. Ethical Concerns—Improper consent collection, storing sensitive data insecurely, or asking questions that could cause harm.

The key to democratization is finding the right balance by enabling access to research while ensuring rigor and ethical responsibility.

A PERSONAL REFLECTION

I'll never forget the first time I experienced the impact of ungoverned research democratization. At one company, a well-intentioned product manager decided to run their own customer interviews. They were frustrated that the research team couldn't prioritize their request, so they took matters into their own hands.

On the surface, it seemed great; my stakeholders were taking initiative. But when they presented their findings, I quickly realized the data was riddled with issues:

- They had only interviewed three participants, all of whom were personal contacts.
- The questions were leading, designed to confirm the PM's assumptions rather than uncover real insights.
- They had misinterpreted responses, turning neutral feedback into positive validation.

As a result, they advocated for a product change that was completely misaligned with actual user needs. It wasn't until months later, after the launch failure, that the team realized their mistake.

This experience solidified my belief that democratization without structure is dangerous. However, the opposite extreme—gatekeeping research—also isn't the answer. If research teams hoard insights, they risk becoming bottlenecks and alienating stakeholders.

This chapter is not about whether research democratization should happen because in most organizations, it already is. Instead, this chapter will focus on:

- How to structure democratization responsibly.
- How to ensure research quality while increasing accessibility.
- How to empower non-researchers without devaluing the research discipline.

By the end of this chapter, you'll have a clear framework for implementing research democratization in a way that benefits both researchers and stakeholders.

WHAT IS USER RESEARCH DEMOCRATIZATION?

User research democratization is one of the most polarizing topics in the research community. Some see it as a practical solution to the growing demand for insights, a way to embed research into every aspect of an organization. Others view it as a risky dilution of expertise, leading to flawed insights and misguided decisions.

In reality, democratization isn't inherently good or bad. It's a tool. Whether it helps or harms an organization depends entirely on how it's structured and executed. When done right, democratization scales research in a way that preserves quality and rigor while enabling teams to make faster, more informed decisions. When done poorly, it can lead to shallow, biased research, misinterpretation of findings, and, ultimately, decisions that steer a product in the wrong direction.

Defining Democratization in a Research Context

At its simplest, research democratization is the process of making research more accessible beyond the UX research team. It allows product managers, designers, marketers, customer support teams, and even engineers to engage with research, conduct studies, and apply insights. But accessibility doesn't mean a free-for-all; it requires structure, training, and well-defined boundaries.

For democratization to work, it must be intentional. It's not about handing research tools to anyone who wants them. It's about equipping the right people with the right skills to conduct the right kinds of research under the right conditions.

What Democratization Looks Like in Practice

A well-structured approach to research democratization includes:

- Training and education—Non-researchers need to be taught not just how to conduct research but how to recognize its limitations, avoid bias, and synthesize insights properly.
- Clear guidelines on who can conduct what research—Not all research should be democratized. Simple usability tests? Yes. Complex generative studies? No.
- Templates and frameworks—Providing standardized interview guides, usability testing scripts, and survey templates reduces the likelihood of poorly designed studies.
- A review and oversight process—Researchers should act as coaches and advisors, ensuring studies are structured correctly and that findings are interpreted responsibly.
- A centralized research repository—Without a system for documenting and sharing insights, research efforts become fragmented, leading to duplication and inconsistencies.

At one company, we introduced a tiered democratization system to balance access with quality control:

- Product managers and designers were trained to run usability tests using a structured process. They had to submit a research plan before running any sessions, and a researcher reviewed their findings before they were shared.
- Marketing and customer success teams were given access to pre-approved survey templates but needed a researcher's sign-off before launching a survey.
- All generative and exploratory research remained the responsibility of trained researchers, ensuring foundational insights were handled by those with the expertise to do them properly.

This system allowed the research team to focus on high-impact projects while enabling stakeholders to conduct low-risk research on their own. It wasn't about giving away research; it was about scaling it responsibly.

Common Misconceptions about Democratization

Much of the resistance to research democratization comes from misunderstanding what it actually entails. Let's break down the biggest misconceptions.

Misconception #1: "Democratization Means Replacing Researchers"

One of the most common fears among researchers is that democratization is a thinly veiled cost-cutting measure, a way for companies to avoid hiring or retaining research talent. The reality is, if democratization is implemented as a replacement for researchers, it will fail. Research quality will drop, teams will make decisions based on incomplete or biased findings, and the organization will ultimately feel the consequences in lost revenue, increased churn, or misguided product investments.

Democratization should extend the impact of research, not eliminate the need for researchers. When stakeholders conduct basic research, it frees up researchers to focus on deeper, more complex studies—the kind that require a trained researcher's skill set.

A responsible approach to democratization: A product team struggling with usability issues trained designers to run usability tests using a pre-approved script. However, researchers still guided the study setup, reviewed findings, and ensured insights were properly synthesized. This allowed research to happen faster while maintaining quality.

A dangerous approach to democratization: An organization decided researchers weren't needed because product managers could "just talk to users." Without training or structure, these conversations were riddled with leading questions, incorrect assumptions, and cherry-picked data that confirmed pre-existing biases. The result? A product launch based on faulty insights, leading to poor adoption and wasted development time.

Misconception #2: "Anyone Can Do Research Well"

It's tempting to think that research is just about asking people questions. After all, everyone talks to users in some capacity; doesn't that mean anyone can conduct research? Not exactly. Good research requires more than just talking to customers. It involves:

- Knowing how to frame a study to uncover real insights, not just confirm assumptions.
- Asking the right kinds of questions—ones that don't lead or bias participants.
- Understanding how to analyze responses in a way that reflects true patterns, not just individual anecdotes.
- Recognizing the limits of what a given method can tell you.

I once worked with a marketing team that wanted to "validate" a new pricing strategy by running a customer survey. When I reviewed their draft, I found that nearly every question was leading: "Would you be excited to see this new lower price?" "How much better is this compared to what we had before?" The survey was structured in a way that guaranteed positive responses, and they nearly made a major pricing change based on biased data.

The solution isn't to ban stakeholders from doing research, it's to train them on how to do it properly and put safeguards in place.

A balanced approach: Educate non-researchers about common biases, provide pre-approved templates, and have researchers review research plans before launch.

A risky approach: Assume that because someone understands their product, they automatically understand how to conduct valid research.

The Spectrum of Research Democratization

Not all organizations take the same approach to democratization. There's a spectrum, ranging from tightly controlled research to fully open, self-directed studies.

1. No Democratization:
   a. Research is conducted solely by dedicated UX researchers.
   b. Insights are centralized but often bottlenecked by research bandwidth.
   c. Teams rely entirely on the research team for user insights.
2. Partial Democratization:
   a. Non-researchers conduct some research but within a structured framework.
   b. Usability tests, surveys, and small-scale studies can be run by trained stakeholders.
   c. Researchers maintain oversight and provide guidance.
3. Full Democratization:
   a. Research is open to everyone with minimal oversight.
   b. Teams run studies independently, without researcher involvement.
   c. Insights are often fragmented, with no centralized knowledge base.
   d. Without strong governance, this approach usually leads to unreliable data and misalignment across teams.

Most organizations benefit from structured, partial democratization. It allows research to scale while maintaining rigor.

The Case for Democratizing Research

Democratizing research isn't just about efficiency, it's about survival. The landscape of product development moves at an unforgiving pace. Decisions are being made constantly, whether research has informed them or not. Research teams, however, rarely scale at the same speed as their organizations. While demand for research has skyrocketed, the number of dedicated researchers often remains stagnant.

This gap has forced research leaders to rethink traditional models. If a research team can't directly support every initiative, how can research still be embedded in decision-making across an organization? The answer, for many, has been some form of research democratization—empowering non-researchers with the tools, training, and guardrails to conduct research on their own.

Done correctly, this creates a system where research isn't just something that happens within the confines of a UX research team. It becomes part of how the organization operates. It allows for more user-centered decisions at scale, better alignment across teams, and an overall stronger connection to customer needs.

But before getting into how to democratize research effectively, it's important to understand why this shift is happening and what's at stake.

The Need for Scale

Most research teams face an impossible task: meeting an increasing demand for research with limited resources.

- A single researcher might be responsible for supporting five to ten product teams, each with multiple ongoing projects.
- Companies are making huge strategic bets on product roadmaps, go-to-market strategies, and design decisions, but often without the research capacity to inform them properly.
- Many research teams spend their time prioritizing projects rather than conducting research, meaning valuable but lower-priority questions go unanswered.

I've seen this firsthand. In one company, I was the only researcher supporting seven product teams. There were simply not enough hours in the day to conduct research on every feature, design iteration, or customer pain point that needed attention. No matter how well we prioritized, important questions were left unanswered.

At the same time, my colleagues—product managers, designers, and marketers—were desperate for insights. They wanted to understand users, but without access to a researcher, they were forced to rely on assumptions or whatever anecdotal evidence they could gather on their own.

This is the core problem democratization attempts to solve. If every research question has to go through an overburdened research team, insights become a bottleneck. But if teams are enabled to conduct certain types of research themselves, more questions get answered, and research scales alongside the company.

The key is to ensure this doesn't lead to a free-for-all where bad research does more harm than good.

The Benefit of Increased Empathy

One of the most overlooked benefits of democratization is how it transforms the way teams think about users.

Research isn't just about gathering insights; it's about changing perspectives. When product managers, designers, or marketers engage directly with users, it fundamentally shifts how they approach their work. They start making decisions based on what they've heard and seen, not just what they assume.

- A designer who watches users struggle through an onboarding flow will never unsee those frustrations. Instead of relying on second-hand reports, they will instinctively advocate for a better experience.

- A product manager who sits in on user interviews stops thinking about features in isolation and starts seeing the bigger picture—the messy, real-world contexts in which customers actually interact with their product.
- A marketing team that tests messaging directly with users will refine their approach based on evidence, not just gut feeling.

I once worked with a product manager who, before engaging in research, had a firm belief that customers wanted more customization options. He pushed hard for this, confident that flexibility was the key to retention. But after sitting in on just three customer interviews, he completely changed his mind. Customers didn't want more customization; they were overwhelmed by the complexity of the product and wanted simpler, more guided experiences.

That shift in thinking didn't come from a research report; it came from direct engagement with users. That's the power of democratization.

When more people in an organization interact with customers, it builds a culture of customer empathy, where decisions are made with a deeper understanding of real user needs.

However, this benefit only materializes when teams are engaging with research in the right way. Without structure, direct engagement can just as easily reinforce biases rather than challenge them. That's why a thoughtful approach to democratization is critical.

Faster Decision-Making

Speed matters. In fast-moving companies, decisions are made quickly, often without research, simply because waiting weeks for insights isn't an option.

- Product teams are pressured to ship. They can't always afford to wait for a dedicated researcher to become available.
- Executives expect quick answers. Delays in research can sometimes mean the difference between launching a feature and missing a market opportunity.
- Customer expectations are evolving constantly. The faster a company can learn, the faster it can adapt.

Democratization, when done well, allows teams to validate assumptions quickly, reducing the risk of making costly missteps. For example:

- A design team that has been trained to conduct usability testing can validate whether a new checkout flow is intuitive in days, not weeks.
- A product team with access to survey tools can gather user sentiment data before launching a feature, ensuring they're not blindsided by poor reception.
- A marketing team can test messaging with real users before committing to a campaign, avoiding misalignment with customer expectations.

By giving teams the ability to get user feedback quickly, democratization reduces reliance on guesswork. However, the key here is ensuring that teams know when to move fast and when to slow down. Not all research can or should be done quickly. Usability tests and surveys? These can often be done efficiently. Generative research or behavioral studies? These require more time and expertise.

Without a clear framework for what research should be democratized and what should remain within a dedicated research team, organizations risk prioritizing speed over accuracy, which can lead to even bigger problems down the road.

THE RISKS AND CHALLENGES OF RESEARCH DEMOCRATIZATION

Research democratization, if structured well, can expand an organization's ability to incorporate user insights into decision-making. But when done poorly—or without enough oversight—it can introduce serious risks that undermine the credibility of research altogether.

Scaling research across non-researchers means reducing barriers to participation, but without guardrails, it also increases the likelihood of biased findings, ethical missteps, and fragmented efforts that don't drive meaningful change.

Quality Control Issues

One of the most immediate risks of democratization is a decline in research quality. When individuals without formal training in research conduct studies, common methodological mistakes can creep in, sometimes with significant consequences for product and business decisions.

1. Risks of biased research, leading questions, and poor methodology

Non-researchers often approach research with the best of intentions, but without training, they can unintentionally introduce bias at every stage of the process:

- Confirmation bias—Asking questions designed to validate existing assumptions rather than uncovering new insights.
- Leading questions—Steering users toward certain responses rather than letting them express their true thoughts.
- Poor sampling—Interviewing a narrow or unrepresentative set of users, leading to skewed conclusions.
- Flawed synthesis—Cherry-picking insights that align with stakeholder preferences rather than accurately reflecting patterns in the data.

At one company, a product team wanted to "validate" a new feature idea. Since the research team was at capacity, a product manager ran a quick round of interviews. But instead of an open-ended discovery study, they asked leading questions like, "Wouldn't you find this feature helpful?" Predictably, most users responded positively.

The team took this as a green light to move forward, investing months of development resources. After launch, usage was almost nonexistent—because while users agreed in interviews, their actual behavior told a different story. The issue wasn't the idea itself, but the flawed research approach that had given them false confidence.

2. The danger of superficial or cherry-picked insights

Without proper synthesis, research findings can become oversimplified, misinterpreted, or cherry-picked to support pre-existing ideas. Teams conducting their own research may:

- Over-rely on a few strong opinions, mistaking them for broad trends.
- Ignore conflicting feedback that doesn't align with their preferred narrative.
- Mistake usability issues for lack of user interest, discarding features too quickly.

A marketing team wanted to refine its messaging and conducted a quick user survey. Most responses were positive, leading them to assume their messaging was strong. But when a researcher later reviewed the data, they found that negative feedback had been dismissed as "outliers."

In reality, those "outliers" represented a critical segment of potential customers who found the messaging unclear. Because this nuance had been ignored, the company missed an opportunity to improve conversion rates.

Ethical Concerns

User research involves handling people's personal data, stories, and behaviors. When research is democratized, it's critical to ensure that ethical best practices aren't compromised.

1. Consent, privacy, and proper handling of sensitive data

When non-researchers conduct studies, they may not fully understand data protection laws or consent protocols. Common mistakes include:

- Failing to obtain proper consent before recording or storing user data.
- Not anonymizing sensitive information, increasing the risk of privacy violations.
- Misusing user data beyond the scope of consent, which can lead to legal repercussions.

A designer I worked with ran an unmoderated usability test using a third-party tool but forgot to include a consent disclaimer. Participants were unaware their sessions were being recorded, violating privacy policies. This led to a compliance issue that required removing all collected data, wasting weeks of work.

2. The risk of manipulating research to confirm pre-existing biases

Research can be weaponized. When stakeholders conduct their own studies, there's a risk that they will design the research to confirm what they already want to believe. This can lead to:

- Over-reliance on supportive data while ignoring conflicting insights.
- Framing research questions in ways that guarantee a preferred outcome.
- Misrepresenting insights to push a particular agenda.

An executive wanted to push a new subscription model and asked for research to support the decision. Instead of conducting an unbiased study, they only surveyed customers who had previously expressed interest in subscriptions. The results? A misleadingly high approval rate that didn't reflect the broader customer base.

When the new model launched, churn increased dramatically because the real majority of customers had never been considered in the research.

Undermining the Value of Professional Research

One of the most contentious risks of research democratization is the fear that it diminishes the role and expertise of trained researchers. As more non-researchers take on research tasks, there's a real concern that leadership will begin to deprioritize the need for dedicated research professionals altogether.

When organizations assume that "anyone can do research," they often fail to recognize the depth of expertise required to conduct meaningful, unbiased, and methodologically sound studies. This can lead to fewer dedicated research hires, underfunded research teams, and a loss of credibility for research as a discipline.

But this problem doesn't emerge overnight. It often starts subtly by shifting responsibilities away from researchers and making research a distributed, secondary task rather than a core business function. If this shift goes unchallenged, researchers can quickly find themselves fighting for relevance rather than driving strategic impact.

How Democratization Can Devalue Research Roles

Democratization, when unchecked, can lead to a misunderstanding of research as a profession. Instead of being seen as a specialized discipline requiring training, rigor, and experience, research is sometimes reduced to a simple task that anyone with access to a survey tool or a scheduling link can handle. There are a few ways this devaluation takes shape:

1. The erosion of research credibility

When non-researchers conduct studies without proper training, they often produce flawed, biased, or misleading insights. These insights, if used to inform decisions, can lead to failed product launches, wasted development resources, or misaligned marketing strategies.

However, when these failures happen, the blame doesn't always fall where it should. Instead of acknowledging that the methodology was flawed, teams may conclude that research itself isn't valuable or that it doesn't lead to actionable insights.

Over time, this weakens the perception of research within an organization. Instead of being seen as a critical function, research becomes an optional, nice-to-have activity that doesn't always justify investment.

At one company, product managers were given the freedom to conduct their own research. Over time, they ran dozens of studies, but because they lacked training, their insights were inconsistent, biased, and often contradicted each other.

Executives began questioning the value of research altogether. "Why are we spending time on this if every study seems to say something different?" they asked. Instead of realizing that the issue was the lack of research rigor, they assumed that research itself wasn't producing useful outcomes.

2. The shift from research as a discipline to research as an admin task

When democratization isn't structured properly, research risks being reduced to a tactical, administrative function rather than a strategic discipline.

Instead of being valued for their critical thinking, synthesis, and ability to uncover deep insights, researchers may find themselves relegated to checking survey drafts, reviewing discussion guides, or approving stakeholder-run studies. This shift has serious long-term consequences:

- Researchers lose their influence in shaping business and product strategy.
- The organization stops seeing research as a driver of innovation and only values it for usability testing and validation.
- Research teams become service providers rather than thought leaders.

A UX research team at a large company started a democratization initiative that allowed product managers and designers to run usability tests. Over time, stakeholders became accustomed to doing their own research and started relying less on the research team.

Eventually, leadership began questioning the need for a dedicated research function at all. "If product teams can do their own research, why do we need a full research team?"

Instead of scaling research, democratization led to the gradual defunding of the research department, reducing it to a small oversight function rather than a core driver of decision-making.

3. The budget and hiring freeze effect

When leadership perceives that research is happening without dedicated researchers, they may start questioning the need to invest in research at all. This can result in:

- Reduced budgets for research tools, participant recruitment, and training.
- Hiring freezes for research roles, even when the demand for insights remains high.
- Reallocation of research responsibilities to non-researchers, leading to burnout and ineffective studies.

This often happens gradually. At first, democratization is seen as a way to scale research—but without careful structuring, it can quickly lead to justification for cost-cutting.

At one startup, researchers trained designers to conduct usability tests. Initially, this helped the research team focus on generative studies. However, when budget season rolled around, leadership pointed to the success of democratization as a reason not to hire additional researchers.

Within a year, the research team was stretched even thinner, and designers—who were supposed to be running only tactical usability tests—were now expected to handle all product research. The result? A research culture built on speed, not depth, with major gaps in insight quality.

How to Protect the Value of Research While Scaling Access

If democratization is necessary, researchers must take an active role in shaping its implementation rather than passively accepting it. Here's how to do that:

1. Define the boundaries of democratized research
    a. Be clear about what types of research can and cannot be democratized.
    b. Ensure that high-risk, high-impact research remains with trained researchers.
2. Establish research standards and oversight
    a. Create a research framework with clear guidelines for methodology, synthesis, and reporting.
    b. Require peer reviews and quality checks before insights are shared.
3. Position research as a strategic partner, not just a service
    a. Proactively contribute to decision-making conversations, not just research execution.
    b. Show how research can drive innovation, reduce business risk, and uncover opportunities that teams hadn't considered.
4. Continuously advocate for research expertise
    a. Educate leadership on the depth and complexity of research.
    b. Track and report the impact of research on business outcomes, so it's clear why dedicated researchers are still essential.

WHEN AND HOW TO DEMOCRATIZE RESEARCH RESPONSIBLY

Democratizing research isn't an all-or-nothing decision. Done well, it can scale research efforts, integrate user insights across an organization, and build a stronger culture of customer empathy. Done poorly, it can introduce bias, lead to poor decision-making, and undermine the credibility of research as a function.

The key to responsible democratization isn't just who conducts research, but how, when, and under what conditions. This section breaks down the circumstances in which democratization makes sense, when it doesn't, and how to ensure that research remains rigorous even as it becomes more widely distributed.

When Should Research Be Democratized?

Democratization works best when it's filling a gap, not replacing expertise. In the right contexts, it can help teams make better, faster, and more user-centered decisions while allowing researchers to focus on high-value work. Here are the conditions that make democratization beneficial:

1. When research demand exceeds researcher capacity

Research teams—especially in growing organizations—are often stretched thin. The number of product teams, marketing initiatives, and business strategies that could benefit from research far outweighs the available researcher capacity. In these situations, democratization allows research to scale beyond the limitations of a small team.

However, this does not mean handing over all research responsibilities to non-researchers. Instead, it means creating a system where smaller, tactical studies can be owned by trained stakeholders, freeing researchers to focus on more complex, high-impact work. Without this structure, research functions become bottlenecks, delaying projects and forcing teams to make decisions based on assumptions rather than data.

To manage this well, researchers should define the types of studies stakeholders can conduct and establish guidelines for when their involvement is required. This ensures that research demand is met without compromising quality or overwhelming the research team.

2. When teams need quick, low-risk insights

There are times when teams need immediate feedback on relatively small decisions—such as refining copy on a landing page, testing a minor UI change, or gauging user reactions to a new feature layout. These types of research questions are not deeply exploratory and do not require advanced methodologies, making them ideal for democratization.

But even these quick-turnaround studies need guardrails to ensure findings are still meaningful. Without structure, teams may conduct rushed, poorly designed research that introduces more noise than clarity. For democratization to work in these cases, organizations need:

- Pre-approved templates and research guides to ensure consistency.
- Baseline training on research bias and question framing to avoid leading questions or faulty assumptions.
- Access to a repository of past research so that teams don't conduct unnecessary studies when existing data already holds the answer.

By putting these supports in place, teams can run research without reinventing the wheel or making common mistakes that undermine their findings.

3. When non-researchers are trained and supported

One of the biggest mistakes organizations make with democratization is assuming that anyone can do research effectively without training. In reality, even seemingly simple methods—such as usability testing or surveys—can introduce bias or misinterpretation when not handled correctly.

For democratization to succeed, non-researchers must be properly trained in research fundamentals. This doesn't mean turning them into full-fledged researchers, but rather ensuring they have enough knowledge to avoid common mistakes and recognize when they need additional support. Training should include:

- How to ask unbiased questions and avoid leading participants.
- How to recruit representative samples rather than relying on convenience sampling.
- How to synthesize findings in a way that reflects patterns rather than isolated opinions.
- How to understand ethical considerations, such as participant consent and data handling.

Beyond training, ongoing support is necessary. Research should not be a one-time training session that leaves stakeholders on their own. Researchers should act as mentors, reviewing research plans, helping synthesize findings, and ensuring that non-researchers have the support they need to conduct meaningful studies.

4. When research rigor is maintained through structured oversight

Democratization should never mean unstructured or uncontrolled research. While it allows for more people to participate in research, it should still operate within a defined system that ensures research quality remains high. This requires clear oversight mechanisms, including:

- A standardized research review process where trained researchers sign off on study designs before they are executed.
- A centralized research repository where all findings are logged and cross-referenced to prevent duplication and inconsistencies.
- Regular research audits to evaluate the quality of democratized studies and refine processes over time.

Without these structures, research can become fragmented, inconsistent, and difficult to trust—leading to decisions being made based on unreliable data.

When Should Research NOT Be Democratized?

Just as there are times when democratization is beneficial, there are also clear situations where research should remain exclusively within the domain of trained researchers. These tend to be higher-risk studies where poor execution can have serious consequences.

1. When the study requires advanced methodologies

Some research methods are simply too complex to be handled by non-researchers. These include:

- Generative research that explores unmet needs and uncovers new opportunities.
- Behavioral research that requires deep observation over time.
- Mixed-method studies that involve advanced synthesis across qualitative and quantitative data.

These methods require expertise in study design, recruitment, analysis, and synthesis to ensure findings are valid, reliable, and actionable. Handing them over to non-researchers can lead to inaccurate conclusions that derail business strategies.

2. When biases could significantly distort findings

All research contains some level of bias, but certain situations make it especially difficult to remove. If the person conducting the research has a vested interest in the outcome, there is a high risk of unintentional—or even deliberate—bias shaping the results.

For example, if a product manager is testing their own feature, they may subconsciously lead users toward positive feedback or ignore negative comments that challenge their assumptions.

In cases like these, research should be handled by an independent researcher who can approach the study with neutrality and objectivity.

3. When ethical or privacy concerns exist

Studies that involve sensitive topics, vulnerable populations, or legally protected data require a high level of ethical oversight. If non-researchers are not trained in research ethics, they may unknowingly:

- Fail to obtain proper consent before recording user data.
- Collect and store sensitive data in ways that violate privacy regulations.
- Ask questions that unintentionally cause harm or distress to participants.

For any study that involves healthcare, finance, children, or legally protected information, research should be conducted only by trained professionals who understand compliance, consent, and ethical risk mitigation.

THE FRAMEWORK FOR RESPONSIBLE RESEARCH DEMOCRATIZATION

Scaling research while maintaining rigor is not a simple process. Without structure, democratization can result in misleading insights, ethical missteps, and wasted effort. However, when implemented correctly, it empowers teams to make user-centered decisions while ensuring that research retains its credibility and influence.

This framework is designed to help research leaders establish a structured, effective, and scalable democratization model, one that enables non-researchers to contribute to research without compromising quality.

Step 1: Define What Can and Cannot Be Democratized

One of the biggest mistakes in research democratization is assuming that all research methods can (or should) be conducted by non-researchers. That is not the case.

A successful framework begins with clear definitions of what research activities can be democratized and what must remain with trained researchers. This prevents low-quality research from being used in high-stakes decision-making and ensures that non-researchers are only conducting studies that fit their skill set.

Create a categorization system for research methods

Break research activities into four tiers:

1. Fully Democratized—Can be run by non-researchers with minimal oversight.
2. Democratized with Oversight—Can be conducted by non-researchers, but requires a trained researcher's review.

3. Guided Research—Non-researchers can be involved, but a trained researcher must lead the study.
4. Restricted to Researchers—Must be conducted exclusively by trained researchers.

Create a decision framework for stakeholders

Once research categories are defined, build a decision tree that helps stakeholders determine:

- When they can conduct research independently.
- When they need to partner with a researcher.
- When they need to escalate to a research team.

For example:

- Does this research involve sensitive user data or compliance risks? → If yes, it must be conducted by a trained researcher.
- Is this a usability test for a minor UI update? → If yes, a trained non-researcher can conduct it following a structured template.
- Is this a strategic or generative study exploring unmet needs? → If yes, it must be conducted by a research professional.

Having a clear framework removes ambiguity and prevents research from being misused or diluted.

Step 2: Create Clear Guidelines and Guardrails

Without clear guidelines, research democratization can quickly spiral into inconsistent methods, poor-quality data, and confusion across teams.

1. Develop standardized research protocols

To ensure consistency, create a set of research protocols that all teams must follow. These should include:

1. Usability Testing Guides—Pre-written usability testing scripts, rubrics for evaluating responses, and success metrics.
2. Survey Templates—Guidelines on how to write unbiased survey questions and analyze responses correctly.
3. Participant Recruitment Best Practices—Prevents teams from relying on biased, unrepresentative samples (only interviewing internal employees).
4. Data Storage and Handling Policies—Ensures that participant privacy and legal compliance are followed.

2. Implement pre-approved research templates

Rather than letting teams design research studies from scratch, provide pre-approved templates that ensure structured, repeatable processes. For example, a usability test template might include:

- Scripted introduction to ensure consistency in test facilitation.
- Pre-written, unbiased tasks for participants.
- A standardized results sheet to ensure that findings are logged consistently.

Templates help prevent ad hoc, low-quality research from creeping into the organization.

3. Build research governance into the process

- Require all studies to be logged in a central repository before they are conducted.
- Assign a researcher to review methodologies for any study run by non-researchers.
- Create a decision tree for ethical considerations, ensuring that sensitive studies are escalated appropriately.

By creating strong governance from the start, research democratization remains structured, not chaotic.

Step 3: Provide Training and Ongoing Support

Training is not optional in research democratization. It is the foundation that determines whether non-researchers will conduct studies that actually improve decision-making or introduce flawed, misleading insights into the organization.

Without training, democratization does not scale research, it scales bad research. Untrained stakeholders may run usability tests with leading questions, interpret survey data incorrectly, or unknowingly introduce bias into their studies. Worse, they may present their findings with false confidence, leading to major business or product decisions being made on inaccurate or incomplete data.

Many organizations make the mistake of treating research training as a one-time event—a workshop, a few documentation pages, or an online course. But research is a skill that requires reinforcement, practice, and feedback. Even experienced researchers continually refine their craft.

For democratization to be effective, organizations need to establish an ongoing, structured training system that aligns with the level of research responsibilities stakeholders will have.

1. Build a tiered training program

Not every stakeholder needs the same level of research expertise. The goal of training is not to turn product managers or designers into full-fledged researchers; it's to ensure that they have enough knowledge to conduct certain types of research effectively while knowing when to escalate more complex studies. A tiered approach ensures that training is scalable, relevant, and structured.

Level 1: Research Awareness (Mandatory for All Stakeholders Involved in Research)

This is the foundational level for anyone conducting or relying on research insights. It is designed to ensure that all stakeholders understand the purpose of research, when it is appropriate for them to conduct studies, and when they need to escalate to a trained researcher. Topics covered:

- Bias Awareness and Mitigation—How to recognize and reduce bias in research questions, participant selection, and interpretation of results.
- When to Conduct Research vs. When to Escalate—A clear decision framework for determining whether a study should be owned by a researcher or if it can be conducted by a non-researcher.
- Ethical Considerations in Research—Understanding participant consent, privacy requirements, and ethical issues related to data collection and storage.
- How Research Fits Into the Organization—The role of research in decision-making and how democratized research should feed into the broader research ecosystem.

This training should be a required baseline for anyone involved in research—no exceptions.

Level 2: Basic Research Training (for Those Conducting Tactical Studies)

This level is for stakeholders who will be running their own research studies, such as product managers, designers, or marketers conducting usability tests or small-scale surveys. Topics covered:

- How to Conduct Usability Testing—Structuring usability tests, avoiding leading questions, and synthesizing findings.
- Survey Design Best Practices—Writing unbiased questions, selecting appropriate response formats, and analyzing survey data responsibly.
- Basic Interviewing Skills—When and how to ask open-ended vs. closed-ended questions, active listening techniques, and how to probe deeper without leading.
- How to Synthesize Findings Responsibly—Avoiding cherry-picking data, recognizing patterns, and presenting insights objectively.

At this level, stakeholders should still have oversight from researchers, but they can conduct certain studies independently with structured templates and review processes in place.

Level 3: Advanced Research Training (Optional for Stakeholders Seeking Deeper Expertise)

This level is not required for most democratized research participants but can be beneficial for stakeholders who want to develop more advanced research skills and greater autonomy. Examples of who might pursue this level:

- Senior designers who frequently run complex usability studies.
- Product leaders who want to deeply integrate research into their strategy.
- Marketers conducting ongoing customer insights research.

Topics covered:

- Advanced Interviewing Techniques—Learning how to facilitate in-depth qualitative research, including Jobs-to-Be-Done (JTBD) interviews.
- Behavioral Data Analysis—How to connect qualitative insights with analytics data for a more comprehensive understanding of user behavior.
- Longitudinal and Diary Studies—How to structure longer-term research that tracks user behavior over time.
- How to Lead Research Synthesis and Workshops—Training on how to facilitate research readouts and stakeholder engagement sessions.

Stakeholders at this level may require less oversight for certain research types, but they should still have their work peer-reviewed by professional researchers.

2. Set up ongoing research mentorship and coaching

Training is only effective if it is reinforced through practice, feedback, and ongoing support. Organizations that simply provide training sessions but fail to offer continuous coaching often find that:

- Stakeholders forget key research principles over time.
- Poor research practices start creeping back in.
- Teams still struggle with synthesizing and interpreting insights correctly.

A structured mentorship and support system ensures that research remains high quality over time and that non-researchers have access to expert guidance when needed.

1. Office hours with researchers

Setting up weekly or bi-weekly office hours allows non-researchers to:

- Get feedback on their research plans before launching a study.
- Ask questions about synthesis and reporting.
- Discuss challenges or uncertainties they're facing in their research.

This system creates a structured yet flexible way for researchers to provide ongoing guidance without needing to hand-hold every study.

2. Research coaching programs

Some organizations may benefit from a formal coaching program, where trained researchers mentor non-researchers through their first few studies. A structured coaching model might look like this:

1. Observation Phase—The non-researcher shadows a researcher conducting a study, taking notes on best practices.
2. Co-Facilitation Phase—The non-researcher conducts part of a study under the guidance of a researcher.
3. Supervised Execution—The non-researcher conducts a full study independently, with a researcher reviewing their work and providing feedback.
4. Independent Research with Oversight—The non-researcher is approved to conduct select studies on their own but still submits research plans and synthesis for review.

This gradual introduction to conducting research ensures that stakeholders build real skills rather than diving in with little preparation.

3. Quality review check-ins

To maintain consistency, all democratized research should be subject to regular quality reviews. This includes:

- Pre-study reviews—A researcher approves study designs before they begin.
- Post-study reviews—Researchers check that findings are synthesized correctly and insights are actionable.
- Quarterly audits—Reviewing all democratized research to identify trends, common mistakes, and areas for additional training.

These regular check-ins act as a safety net, ensuring that non-researchers remain aligned with best practices and that the research function maintains credibility.

Step 4: Establish a Centralized Research Repository

One of the biggest risks in democratizing research is fragmentation. When multiple teams conduct research independently, findings often remain siloed, trapped in Notion docs, personal Google Drive folders, Slack threads, or scattered across different tools. This leads to duplication of effort, wasted resources, and inconsistencies in decision-making.

A centralized research repository solves this problem by ensuring that all research findings—whether conducted by trained researchers or non-researchers—are collected, organized, and accessible in a single location.

A well-structured repository prevents knowledge loss, enhances collaboration, and strengthens the credibility of research across the organization. But building an effective system requires clear processes, defined ownership, and strategic oversight.

Without a central repository, research efforts become disorganized and inefficient. Here's what typically happens in organizations that lack one:

- Duplicate studies are conducted because teams aren't aware that similar research has already been done.
- Insights are lost over time as documents get buried in forgotten folders, Slack messages, or email chains.
- Decision-making becomes inconsistent because different teams rely on fragmented, disconnected findings.
- Research credibility suffers when there's no single source of truth, leading stakeholders to cherry-pick data that supports their existing beliefs.

A proper research repository ensures that research democratization leads to more knowledge-sharing, not more knowledge silos.

Key Components of a Centralized Research Repository

To be truly effective, a research repository must be more than just a place to dump reports. It should be a dynamic, structured system that:

1. Houses all research findings in an organized, searchable format.
2. Provides visibility into past and ongoing research efforts.
3. Encourages synthesis across multiple studies, making it easy to identify patterns and insights.

1. A database where all research findings are logged and categorized

At the core of a repository is a structured, easily searchable database that acts as the organization's single source of truth for all research insights. What you can include in this database:

- Study Metadata—Information about each research study, including the research question, methodology, date, and responsible team.
- Findings and Key Insights—A structured summary of the study's most important learnings.
- Raw Data or Reports—If applicable, links to full reports, interview transcripts, usability test recordings, or survey results.
- Tagging System for Easy Searchability—Studies should be tagged by topic, product area, research method, and audience segment so they can be easily retrieved later.

Choosing the Right Tool for the Repository

The repository should be built in a tool that is intuitive, accessible, and scalable. Some organizations use dedicated research repository tools like Dovetail or Airtable, while others adapt existing internal tools like Notion, Confluence, or Google Drive. The best choice depends on:

- Scalability—Can it handle an increasing volume of research?
- Searchability—Can stakeholders easily find relevant insights?
- Accessibility—Can all relevant teams contribute and retrieve findings easily?

A repository that is difficult to use or lacks strong search functionality will not be adopted, leading to the same fragmentation issues that existed before. I recommend doing a lot of research into the tool that would best fit you and your stakeholders' needs.

2. A research request system to avoid duplication

A common problem in democratized research is different teams unknowingly conducting similar studies, wasting time and resources. A research request system prevents this by allowing teams to:

- Check whether a similar study has already been conducted.
- See ongoing research efforts before launching a new study.
- Submit a request for new research if no relevant findings exist.

How to Structure the Research Request System

1. Create a research intake form. Before running a study, teams must submit a research request form that:
   a. Outlines the research question.
   b. Defines the scope and intended impact of the research.
   c. Specifies the method they intend to use.
   d. Checks for overlap with existing studies.
2. Assign review and approval steps. If the study is being conducted by a non-researcher, the research team should:
   a. Review the request to confirm it's necessary.
   b. Provide recommendations on research methods.
   c. Assign a research mentor for oversight.
3. Build transparency around research in progress. A public research roadmap should exist where teams can see all ongoing and completed studies, preventing redundant efforts.

With this system in place, research becomes more coordinated, reducing inefficiencies and reinforcing a culture of shared knowledge.

3. A synthesis framework to ensure consistent structuring of insights

Research democratization does not work if insights are presented inconsistently or in ways that make synthesis difficult. A standardized synthesis framework ensures that findings across different studies are comparable, actionable, and trustworthy. The problems with unstructured insights include:

- Some teams produce long, dense reports, making it difficult for others to extract key takeaways.
- Others share only raw quotes without synthesis, leaving room for misinterpretation.
- Some insights are framed in overly tactical ways rather than being tied to broader business or user needs.

How to structure research synthesis for maximum impact:

1. Standardize research reports. Every research study should follow a consistent report structure, including:
   a. Research Question—Clearly states what the study aimed to uncover.
   b. Methodology—How the research was conducted, including participant details.
   c. Key Findings—The top 3-5 insights in clear, actionable language.
   d. Supporting Evidence—Direct quotes, usability testing results, or data points.
   e. Implications & Next Steps—What actions the team should take based on these insights.
2. Develop a research summary format for easy sharing. Not every stakeholder will read a full research report. Create 1-page research briefs with key takeaways and next steps for quick consumption.
3. Ensure that research feeds into larger synthesis efforts. Findings from multiple studies should be synthesized into broader themes and trends. Researchers should conduct quarterly research synthesis sessions where they:
   a. Identify common patterns across different studies.
   b. Connect findings to business goals and product strategies.
   c. Share updated research-backed recommendations with leadership.

By following this structure, research democratization leads to a well-organized body of insights that teams can confidently use to inform decisions.

Step 5: Set Up a Research Review Process

Even with strong training programs, standardized templates, and clear research guidelines, research conducted by non-researchers must undergo quality control. Without a structured review process, democratization can quickly erode research credibility, introduce bias, and result in poor decision-making based on flawed insights.

A research review process ensures that all research, regardless of who conducts it, meets a baseline standard of rigor, accuracy, and ethical responsibility. It acts as a safeguard against misinterpretation, biases, and poor methodologies slipping through and influencing product, business, or design decisions.

1. Require researcher review before insights are used

One of the biggest risks in democratized research is stakeholders making decisions based on flawed data before a researcher has had a chance to review it. Non-researchers may unintentionally misinterpret findings, overstate conclusions, or overlook nuances that a trained researcher would immediately catch.

To prevent this, all research studies conducted by non-researchers must be reviewed by a trained researcher before being used in decision-making.

What Should Be Reviewed?

The research review process should focus on critical points where errors are most likely to occur:

- Before launching a survey: A researcher must review the survey design, question phrasing, and sampling approach to ensure that it does not include leading questions, ambiguous wording, or flawed logic.
- Before usability test results are presented: A researcher should check for misinterpretation of observations, ensuring that usability issues are correctly identified and that insights are not overstated or misrepresented.
- Before any research insights are shared company-wide: A researcher should validate the synthesis, ensuring that key takeaways are accurate and that findings are not cherry-picked or used selectively to push an agenda.

By implementing this review requirement, organizations prevent poor research from influencing business-critical decisions.

How to Make This Process Efficient?

1. It is important that this review process does not become a bottleneck. To streamline it:
    1. Set clear turnaround times for research reviews—Researchers should commit to reviewing non-researcher studies within a defined time frame (2–3 business days).
    2. Use a structured research review form—Create a checklist for researchers to quickly assess:
        a. Does the study follow the correct methodology?
        b. Are the questions free of bias?

    c. Is the sample size appropriate?
    d. Are the insights being interpreted correctly?
 3. Leverage a peer-review system—If the research team is small, trained peer reviewers within product or design teams can conduct an initial review before escalating to a researcher.

This system ensures that research quality is controlled without slowing teams down unnecessarily.

2. Implement regular research audits

Beyond reviewing individual studies, organizations should conduct regular audits of all democratized research efforts to identify trends, gaps, and areas for improvement.

Even with training and oversight, patterns of common mistakes will emerge. Conducting audits allows research teams to:

- Identify recurring errors in methodology, synthesis, or interpretation.
- Spot knowledge gaps where additional training is needed.
- Evaluate the overall effectiveness of research democratization.
- Ensure research findings are actually being used in decision-making.

A quarterly audit is recommended for most organizations, though companies scaling research rapidly may benefit from bi-monthly reviews.

A research audit should assess the entire system of democratized research and how well it is functioning. The audit should examine:

1. The quality of democratized studies
    a. Are non-researchers following standardized research protocols?
    b. Are usability tests, surveys, and interviews producing valid, reliable insights?
    c. Are synthesis documents structured correctly?
2. Common mistakes or gaps in execution
    a. Are there patterns of bias creeping into surveys or usability tests?
    b. Are non-researchers struggling with participant recruitment, synthesis, or question framing?
    c. Are some teams conducting research effectively, while others struggle?
3. The overall impact of democratization
    a. Has democratized research improved decision-making?
    b. Are teams using research findings, or are studies being ignored?
    c. Have research findings led to measurable improvements in product, marketing, or business outcomes?

Audit Process

1. Select a sample of democratized studies for review
    a. Choose studies from different teams and research methods (usability tests, surveys, interviews).

    b. Ensure representation across product, design, and marketing teams to identify patterns.
 2. Assess studies using a research quality checklist
    a. Check for bias in question phrasing and study design.
    b. Evaluate how insights were synthesized—were they clear, actionable, and well-supported?
    c. Determine whether findings influenced actual decision-making.
 3. Hold a research audit review meeting
    a. Share key findings with researchers and democratized research participants.
    b. Discuss trends, challenges, and areas where support or training needs to be improved.
 4. Refine training and oversight based on audit findings
    a. If audits reveal widespread issues with survey design, schedule a refresher training session.
    b. If audits show research findings are not being used, adjust the way insights are shared with teams.
    c. If some teams consistently struggle with research execution, provide additional mentorship or pair them with experienced researchers.

By treating audits as an opportunity for continuous improvement, organizations ensure that research democratization remains high-quality, reliable, and strategically impactful.

Refining the Democratization Process Over Time

Research democratization is a continuous process that requires refinement as an organization scales and evolves. To ensure that democratization continues to be effective, organizations should:

 1. Regularly update training materials and guidelines
    a. If research audits identify new common mistakes, update training sessions accordingly.
    b. Keep best practices up-to-date as new research tools or methods emerge.
 2. Monitor the adoption and use of research insights
    a. If research findings are not being applied, investigate why stakeholders are not using the insights.
    b. Adjust how research is shared—perhaps a 1-page insight summary is more useful than a 20-page report.
 3. Foster a culture of research accountability
    a. Encourage teams to own the accuracy of their research and be transparent about what they don't know.
    b. Create a feedback loop where researchers can regularly discuss how democratized research is being used.

By continuously refining the democratization process, organizations can scale research in a way that remains credible, high-quality, and strategically influential.

Scaling Research without Sacrificing Rigor

Research democratization is not a one-size-fits-all solution. What works for one company might fail in another due to differences in team size, research maturity, leadership buy-in, and decision-making culture. Instead of adopting a democratization model blindly, your first step should be research on your own organization.

This chapter has outlined multiple approaches to research democratization, from fully decentralized models to research-led approaches with controlled access. But choosing the right approach requires an honest evaluation of your company's unique needs, challenges, and research maturity.

This is where your own research skills come into play. Before deciding how to scale research within your organization, take time to assess your current environment, define your goals, and determine the level of structure and oversight required to ensure success.

Assess the current state of research in your organization

To scale research without sacrificing rigor, you first need a comprehensive understanding of how research currently functions within your organization. Without a clear baseline, democratization efforts risk becoming chaotic, misaligned, or ineffective. Don't skip this step! We do this:

- To identify exactly who is conducting research.
- To understand the types of research being performed.
- To find bottlenecks preventing effective research.
- To gauge how leadership values research.
- To document how research insights are shared and consumed.

Let's dive into how to assess the current state.

1. Map out current research roles and responsibilities

Objective: Clarify exactly who is conducting research, formally or informally.
Steps:
1. List all individuals conducting research regularly, including:
    a. Trained researchers (User Researchers, UX Researchers, etc.)
    b. Designers
    c. Product Managers
    d. Marketers
    e. Engineers
    f. Customer Support or Success Teams
2. Determine the frequency with which each role performs research:
    a. Is research part of their job description, or are they doing it informally?
    b. How frequently do non-researchers independently initiate studies?

2. Inventory types of research currently conducted

Objective: Understand what research methods are being used and by whom.
Steps:
1. Catalog recent research projects over the last 3–6 months.
2. Categorize these by research type:
   a. Usability testing (quick tests, prototype evaluations)
   b. Surveys (customer satisfaction, feedback)
   c. Interviews (generative or evaluative)
   d. Analytics reviews (product usage analysis)
   e. Generative or strategic studies (exploratory, opportunity-focused research)
3. Highlight gaps between desired and actual types of research performed.

3. Identify research bottlenecks and pain points

Objective: Determine the obstacles preventing effective and timely research.
Steps:
1. Conduct stakeholder interviews or surveys asking:
   a. "How often are you delayed by waiting for research results?"
   b. "Have you ever skipped research due to lack of availability?"
   c. "How often do you have to conduct research on your own without support?"
   d. Quantify these pain points if possible ("70% of Product Managers skip research due to long wait times").

Example survey question (with rating scale):
"On a scale of 1–5, how often do you find research availability a blocker for timely decisions?"
(1 = Never, 5 = Always)
Example finding:
"80% of Product Managers rated research availability as 4 or higher, indicating significant delays."

4. Evaluate leadership's attitude toward research

Objective: Assess how research is valued by leaders and decision-makers.
Steps:
1. Conduct targeted leadership interviews or distribute a leadership-focused survey. Ask clear, pointed questions such as:
   a. "Do you consider research essential, helpful, or optional for decision-making?"
   b. "Can you provide examples of recent decisions influenced by research?"
   c. "How much are you willing to invest in research resources and training?"
2. Analyze responses to determine if leadership views research as:
   a. A critical component
   b. An occasional input
   c. A luxury or nice-to-have

Example question:
"Describe a recent instance where research directly impacted your decision-making."
Example finding:
"We delayed launching the new pricing model until the UX team conducted surveys—research is crucial for big decisions like pricing."

5. Assess how research insights are currently shared and stored

Objective: Understand how research insights are documented and made accessible.

Steps:
1. Identify all locations where research insights currently live:
    a. Centralized (Dovetail, Airtable, Confluence)
    b. Decentralized (Google Drive folders, Slack, emails)
2. Check how consistently insights are documented:
    a. Do insights consistently include the research question, methods, results, and actionable recommendations?
3. Evaluate accessibility and discoverability:
    a. Are insights easy to find by people across the organization?
    b. How often do stakeholders complain about not finding past research?

6. Summarize your findings into a clear research landscape report

Objective: Create a succinct, actionable summary highlighting gaps, strengths, and weaknesses.

Suggested structure:
- Current research roles:
    - Who's conducting research (trained vs. informal)?
- Research types in use:
    - Methods commonly and rarely used.
- Identified bottlenecks:
    - Delays in conducting or accessing research.
- Leadership alignment:
    - How critical is research viewed by leadership?
- Research documentation & sharing:
    - Current status of knowledge management and accessibility.

Example:
"Research is primarily done by one full-time UX researcher, supported informally by designers and PMs. Usability testing is frequent, but generative research is nonexistent. Teams often skip research due to delays, and leadership sees it as important but secondary. Documentation is decentralized, causing frequent duplication and wasted efforts."

Define Your Organization's Research Needs and Risks

Not all organizations require the same level of research rigor, nor can they accept the same level of risk. Clearly understanding your organization's specific needs and risk tolerance is essential to creating a democratization model that is both effective and safe. This step is necessary to:

- Ensure the democratization model aligns with your organization's specific risk and rigor requirements.
- Prevent costly errors resulting from inappropriate levels of oversight.
- Leverage existing skills within your organization efficiently.

1. Determine the level of research rigor required

Research rigor refers to the quality standards and methodological thoroughness expected within your organization.
Steps:

1. Classify decision types and their consequences. List recent or upcoming decisions influenced by research. Categorize these by the impact and risks involved.
2. Categorize the decisions into tiers of required rigor:
   a. High Rigor: Decisions have significant financial, legal, or safety implications.
   b. Medium Rigor: Decisions impact user satisfaction, retention, or moderate financial outcomes.
   c. Low Rigor: Decisions are incremental, reversible, or experimental.

Prompting questions:

- What kinds of decisions does your organization regularly face?
- What is the worst-case scenario if research for these decisions is inaccurate or incomplete?
- Can you group your decisions into categories based on the potential risk or consequence?

2. Clarify your organization's risk tolerance

Risk tolerance defines how much uncertainty or potential harm your organization is willing to accept as it expands research responsibilities.
Steps:

1. Conduct internal interviews or workshops to gauge comfort with risk:
   a. Ask stakeholders to rate their tolerance for potential research errors (low, medium, and high).
   b. Discuss potential consequences openly and document responses.
2. Create a risk assessment matrix to visualize tolerance clearly.

Prompting questions:

- How comfortable is leadership with research findings from non-researchers driving key decisions?
- What types of errors or biases can your organization afford, and what is completely unacceptable?
- Which areas (finance, regulatory, health) require the strictest oversight, and which can afford some flexibility?

3. Evaluate existing research skills in your organization

Understanding the research skills and experience within your organization is essential for deciding how much oversight or training you'll need to implement.
Steps:

1. Create an inventory of current research skills among non-research stakeholders.
2. Use surveys or interviews to capture their research experience.
3. Categorize teams by experience (high, medium, and low).
4. Assess the gap between current skills and desired research rigor levels.

Prompting questions:

- Do your product or design teams have formal research training?
- Are there team members regularly conducting interviews, usability tests, or surveys without oversight?
- Which teams consistently produce reliable insights, and which require significant researcher intervention?

Identify the Right Democratization Model for Your Context

Selecting the appropriate democratization model is critical. The right model enables your organization to effectively scale research without sacrificing quality, credibility, or reliability. Using insights gathered from assessing your current state (Step 1) and defining your organization's research needs and risks (Step 2), follow the guide below to pinpoint exactly which model aligns best with your organization's unique circumstances.

You May Need a Hybrid Model

This approach empowers non-researchers to run tactical studies like usability tests and surveys, provided there's clear oversight and structured guidelines.

- Define which types of research non-researchers can conduct (usability tests, surveys).

- Develop standardized templates and checklists for non-researchers.
- Create a structured review process where trained researchers review study plans and syntheses regularly.

Example:
At Shopify, designers and product managers regularly run usability tests independently. However, all tests follow standardized scripts and must pass researcher approval before sharing insights broadly. Researchers remain responsible for generative or strategic research.

If your organization has fast-moving teams who need quick access to user insights:

You may need a decentralized model (with required training and quality controls).

Non-researchers gain autonomy to quickly validate smaller decisions while maintaining quality through mandatory training and periodic audits.

- Conduct mandatory, regular training for everyone who will run research.
- Clearly document acceptable research types (low-risk studies like usability tests, rapid surveys).
- Implement quarterly quality audits to ensure ongoing rigor and minimize bias or misuse.

Example:
Atlassian encourages a decentralized approach where product teams rapidly conduct small usability tests and user validation. However, every team member must complete basic user research training, and research outputs are periodically reviewed for quality by dedicated UXRs.

You May Need a Research-Led Model

All research remains under the control of trained researchers due to the significant risks associated with regulatory and legal compliance.

- Clearly define policies stating only trained researchers conduct all research.
- Establish clear processes for non-researchers to submit research requests formally.
- Researchers regularly share insights proactively to ensure teams have necessary data without conducting research independently.

Example:
Fidelity Investments uses a research-led model. Due to regulatory compliance, financial risk, and ethical considerations, only professional UX researchers conduct studies. Stakeholders access insights via a controlled central repository and structured insight-sharing sessions.

You May Need a Centralized Repository Model

Establish a single, accessible, and organized repository for research documentation and insights, ensuring consistent storage and preventing duplication of work.

- Choose and implement a dedicated research repository tool (Dovetail, Airtable, Notion).
- Establish standards for documentation, tagging, and summarizing insights.
- Train stakeholders to use, contribute to, and search within the repository.

Example:
At HubSpot, a centralized research repository allows stakeholders company-wide to search, discover, and use insights, significantly reducing duplicated studies and enabling faster decision-making.

If your organization already has non-researchers conducting research informally:
You may need a Hybrid model with governance to standardize and improve quality
Leverage existing informal research practices, but introduce standardized methods and clear governance to ensure consistency, reliability, and ethical standards.

- Document current informal practices across teams.
- Introduce clear governance (templates, research plans, and mandatory review points).
- Provide training to standardize methodologies and ensure consistent research quality.
- Regularly audit informal research practices to identify and close quality gaps.

Example:
Airbnb initially found many teams informally conducting user research. They established clear, standardized research frameworks and mandatory review checkpoints. Now, informal research follows consistent standards, significantly enhancing overall research quality and reliability.

Questions to Help You Choose

Use these guiding questions to clarify your context, highlight the strengths and challenges of your current setup, and confidently choose the right democratization approach.

Understanding Your Organization's Research Environment

- How many dedicated researchers do you currently have?
  - Could you list their primary responsibilities?
  - Are these researchers overloaded or struggling to keep up?

- How frequently do teams request research support?
  - Do you find your team turning away important research requests?
  - Are stakeholders conducting their own informal studies without oversight?

Clarifying the Importance of Research Rigor in Your Context

- What is the consequence of a research mistake in your industry?
  - Could it lead to financial loss, regulatory fines, legal action, or reputational damage?
  - Or would the consequences be minor and quickly reversible (quick product fixes)?
- What level of evidence or rigor do executives or leadership expect from research insights?
  - Do executives require detailed, formal research reports?
  - Are informal, rapid insights acceptable for decision-making?
- Evaluating stakeholder skills and experience
- Do stakeholders already conduct informal research?
  - What kinds of research do they currently run (surveys, usability testing, informal interviews)?
  - Have you reviewed the quality of their work? What have you found?
- Have stakeholders received formal training or support previously?
  - If yes, was it effective or insufficient?
  - If not, how confident are you in their ability to learn quickly?

Examining Your Organization's Pace and Decision-Making Culture

- How quickly does your organization move?
  - Do product and design teams regularly release new features or products weekly, monthly, quarterly, or annually?
  - Is research a bottleneck or a helpful part of the process?
- Do teams often bypass research due to speed pressures?
  - If yes, what kinds of research do they skip most often (generative research, usability tests)?

Considering Your Organization's Documentation and Sharing Practices

- How are research insights currently documented and shared?
  - Are insights scattered across different teams, Slack channels, or Notion pages?
  - Or is there a reliable, centralized source of truth accessible to all?

- Do teams often duplicate research because insights are not easily discoverable?
  - Can you provide examples of recent duplicated studies or lost insights?

Reflecting on Your Desired Future State

- What would successful democratization look like in your ideal scenario?
  - Would it involve more teams confidently running their own studies?
  - Or would it mean researchers have more bandwidth to focus on strategic research, with stakeholders handling only tactical tests?
- How will you know democratization is successful in your organization?
  - What metrics or signs would indicate successful scaling of research?
  - What signs would indicate that democratization isn't working?

Considering the Trade-Offs

- What risks are you most concerned about with democratizing research?
  - Poor research quality?
  - Ethical concerns or privacy risks?
  - Losing research credibility internally?
- What benefits do you think democratization could bring your organization?
  - Increased speed of decision-making?
  - More teams using research to inform decisions?
  - Better stakeholder empathy with customers?

Organizational Readiness

- Do you have leadership buy-in for increased democratization?
  - If no, what would you need to demonstrate to build leadership support?
- Are you prepared to allocate resources (time, people, budget) toward training and oversight?
  - If resources are limited, can you realistically implement a robust oversight or training program?

Future Scalability and Evolution

- As your organization grows, how sustainable will each democratization model be?
  - Can your chosen model scale effectively if your teams double or triple in size?
  - Will more centralized oversight become impossible if research requests grow significantly?

Based on your reflections:

- Which model seems most aligned with your current resources, goals, and constraints?
- If you're still uncertain, what's one small step or experiment you could run to test this model before fully committing?

Document Your Chosen Democratization Model Clearly

Clear documentation ensures everyone understands exactly what your democratization model involves, how it functions, and the responsibilities of all stakeholders.

Your documentation should clearly outline:

- What: Explicitly state the chosen democratization model (e.g., Hybrid, Decentralized with oversight).
- Why: Explain your rationale and how it aligns with organizational goals.
- Who: Define clearly who can and can't conduct research, including oversight roles.
- How: Describe precisely how research should be conducted within this model (protocols, approvals, and roles).

Steps:

1. Summarize Your Model
   a. "We've chosen a Hybrid Democratization Model, allowing non-researchers to conduct usability tests and small surveys after receiving standardized training and templates, with oversight from trained researchers."
2. Create clear role descriptions
   a. Non-researchers: Who qualifies, what they can do (e.g., usability tests).
   b. Researchers: Their oversight responsibilities (reviewing research plans and findings).
3. Define limits and boundaries
   a. Clearly state what research methods (generative studies, complex behavioral analyses) are exclusively reserved for trained researchers.
4. Document governance structure
   a. The governance structure clarifies who approves, reviews, and ensures the quality of democratized research. This prevents confusion, maintains rigor, and safeguards research integrity. Your documentation should explicitly define three things:
      i. Approval workflows—Clearly defined steps for research approval.
      ii. Quality checkpoints—Specific points when research quality is assessed.
      iii. Escalation paths—Clear instructions on when and how to escalate research concerns.

Approval Workflows

Purpose: Ensures all research conducted by non-researchers adheres to your organization's standards.

Steps:
1. Identify who must approve each type of study:
    a. Who reviews usability tests, surveys, and interviews?
    b. Differentiate between trained researchers and peer reviewers (trained non-researchers).
2. Define the exact approval steps clearly:
    a. Initial submission:
        i. What documents or plans must stakeholders submit?
        ii. Where do they submit these documents (e.g., centralized Notion, Google form)?
        iii. Who receives submissions?
    b. Review and feedback:
        i. Who is responsible for initial reviews (a researcher, senior stakeholder)?
        ii. What criteria are used to review (methodology, ethics, clarity)?
        iii. How quickly will reviews be conducted (e.g., 1–2 business days)?
    c. Approval or revision:
        i. Clearly state how approvals or requested revisions are communicated back (e.g., via Slack, email, Notion comments).
        ii. What happens if research is not initially approved (guidance for revision)?

Quality Checkpoints

Purpose: Ensure research quality remains high throughout the process.
Define exactly when research quality is evaluated:
Before launch:

- Has the researcher approved the study plan?
- Are participant recruitment criteria met?

Mid-research (optional but valuable for complex studies):

- Is the method working as planned?
- Are participants responding well (no unforeseen issues)?

Post-research (before insights are shared):

- Are insights accurate, actionable, and unbiased?
- Did stakeholders correctly interpret participant feedback?

Escalation Paths

Purpose: Provides clarity on how to handle problems and issues efficiently.
Clearly define scenarios that require escalation:

- When stakeholders disagree with reviewer feedback.
- When ethical or compliance concerns arise (privacy/data issues).
- When research methodology requires significant changes.
- When timelines are consistently not met or quality repeatedly falls below standards.

Sample Governance Structure Document

Below is an example format you can use directly or adapt:

Governance Structure for Democratized Research

Approval workflows:

- Simple studies (usability tests, small surveys): Submit the research plan via [Notion link]. Approval within 2 business days by designated researcher or peer reviewer.
- Complex studies (interviews, behavioral studies): Submit via [Research Intake Form]; expect review within 3–5 business days by Senior Researcher.

Quality checkpoints:

- Pre-launch: Approval required (check methodology, recruitment plan, ethics).
- Mid-study check (optional): Scheduled for longer or complex studies.
- Post-study review: Mandatory before insights are shared broadly.

Escalation paths:

- Stakeholders should escalate directly via Slack or email, clearly stating the issue, research type, and reason for escalation.
- First point of contact: Assigned researcher
- Second escalation: Senior Researcher
- Final escalation: Head of Research

Communicate Your Choice Broadly across the Organization

Communication ensures alignment, buy-in, and clarity. Everyone should understand the democratization model you've chosen, how it benefits them, and their specific roles.

Your communication should include:

- The reason for democratizing research.
- How it impacts stakeholders (clarifying roles, responsibilities, and benefits).
- Clear guidelines for getting involved or escalating research needs.
- Opportunities for training, questions, and clarification.

Steps:

1. Craft a clear announcement. Write a concise, compelling explanation of why this model is beneficial.
2. Host a kick-off meeting or town hall. Present the model, answer questions, and provide clarity.
3. Provide continuous updates. Use newsletters, Slack channels, or monthly updates to reinforce the democratization model and any adjustments.

Example:
Slack announcement example:

Launching Our New Research Democratization Model!

To scale our research impact, we're adopting a Hybrid model. Product Managers and UX Designers can now conduct usability tests and small surveys independently, provided they complete mandatory training and follow clear templates.

Benefits for you: Faster insights, more direct user feedback, and increased ownership over your research questions.

Next Steps: Join our kick-off session this Thursday at 3 pm for detailed Q&A and access training links here [link]."

Creating a Detailed Implementation Plan

An implementation plan translates your democratization model into tangible, structured steps your teams can follow. This prevents ambiguity, ensures alignment, and increases adoption.

Below is a step-by-step approach, complete with concrete examples, prompts, and checkpoints:

Step 1: Define Clear Objectives and Success Criteria

Clarify what success looks like so you can measure progress and effectiveness later.
Prompts:

- What are the top three goals of democratizing research at your organization?
  - Example: Improve decision-making speed, reduce researcher bottleneck, and increase user-centered decisions.

- How will you measure success? Define metrics such as:
  - Research turnaround time reduction
  - Number of teams using research insights regularly
  - Stakeholder satisfaction (surveys)
  - Reduction of research bottlenecks

Step 2: Assign Roles and Responsibilities

Clearly define who is accountable for each component of the implementation.
Prompts:

- Who will lead and oversee the democratization initiative?
- Who is responsible for developing and maintaining documentation?
- Who will deliver training and ongoing support?
- Who manages the centralized research repository?

Step 3: Create and Organize Core Documentation

Ensure everyone has easy access to standardized information.
Essential documentation:

- Governance and approval workflows (approval process, checkpoints, and escalation paths)
- Research protocols and templates (usability scripts, survey templates, and interview guides)
- Ethics and compliance guidelines (consent forms, data handling procedures)
- Training materials (slides, video recordings, and FAQs)

Step 4: Develop and Schedule Training Programs

Equip non-researchers with skills necessary to conduct quality research.
Training levels:

- Awareness training (Level 1): Bias awareness, when to escalate, ethics overview
- Basic research training (Level 2): Usability testing, basic surveys, interviewing techniques
- Advanced training (Level 3): Advanced interviewing, complex study designs, advanced analysis

Step 5: Launch and Communicate Broadly

Ensure organization-wide awareness and adoption.

Launch & communication steps:

- Schedule organization-wide launch event (virtual webinar or town hall)
- Announce via internal communication channels (Slack, Teams, newsletters)
- Provide simple, one-page "quick-start guides" tailored to stakeholders (product managers, designers, marketers)
- Hold dedicated Q&A sessions post-launch to address concerns and clarify processes

Setting Checkpoints to Periodically Review and Adjust

Regular checkpoints are critical to ensure your democratization framework remains effective, responsive, and aligned with your organization's evolving needs. Without structured reviews, research quality and effectiveness can degrade over time.

Step 1: Define Clear Objectives for Checkpoints

To maintain clear focus and ensure each review meaningfully assesses key areas of your democratization model.

For checkpoints:

- Evaluate adherence to established protocols and governance.
- Assess overall quality of research conducted by non-researchers.
- Monitor the impact and effectiveness of research democratization on decision-making.
- Identify any new or emerging issues related to democratization (skills gaps, misalignment, repository challenges, etc.).
- Review and revise your training and support strategies.

Prompts:

- "What specific outcomes do we hope to achieve at each review?"
- "What would trigger us to change or update our current model?"

Step 2: Schedule Regular Review Cadence

Establish a consistent schedule so teams can prepare, and adjustments become part of your organization's operating rhythm.

Recommended review cadence:

1. Monthly check-in: Brief meetings (~30 minutes) to discuss ongoing democratization progress, surface emerging issues, and address quick concerns.

2. Quarterly audits: Structured audits reviewing samples of research projects, assessing research quality, documentation compliance, and repository use.
3. Bi-annual stakeholder surveys: Send out surveys to assess stakeholder satisfaction, ease of access, perceived quality of democratized research, and additional support needs.
4. Annual strategic review: Dedicated strategic session to review long-term impact, align on adjustments to the democratization approach, and reset objectives for the following year.

Step 3: Design a Standardized Review Template

Streamline the review process and ensure consistency each time you conduct a checkpoint.

Template for quarterly audits:

Review period: [Q1 YYYY]
Conducted by: [Name/Title]
Date of audit: [Date]

Overall findings:

- [Summary of key strengths]
- [Summary of areas for improvement]
- [Recommendations for actions to take before next audit]

Step 4: Communicate Results and Action Items

Ensure transparency and accountability by communicating results to stakeholders clearly, and ensure action items are addressed promptly.

Steps:

1. Host a brief stakeholder meeting or webinar after each formal review to present findings and outline next steps.
2. Distribute a concise summary of audit results via internal channels (e.g., Slack, Teams, email newsletters).
3. Clearly assign responsibilities for each action item, with specific due dates.

Example:

"Our quarterly review highlighted strong adherence to protocols (96%) and high-quality insights (92%). However, we've identified gaps in repository documentation. The UX Research Ops team will lead an improvement plan and provide additional training by the next audit (date). We'll share an update on progress monthly."

Step 5: Take Action and Adjust the Model Accordingly

Use your review findings to make targeted, informed adjustments to your democratization model.

Prompts

- "Are there recurring issues that suggest we need to revise our training program?"
- "Are stakeholders consistently facing the same challenges, suggesting a need for new resources or support?"
- "Is our current repository setup working effectively, or do we need adjustments in how research is documented or accessed?"

Start Small, Test, and Iterate

Once you have identified a starting model, don't roll it out across the entire company at once. Instead, start small and iterate, just as you would with a research-driven product change.

Test Your Democratization Approach in a Low-Risk Way

1. Start with a pilot team.
2. Choose one product or design team to test research democratization.
3. Provide training, mentorship, and oversight to guide their first few studies.
4. Measure the impact.
5. Track whether the team's research efforts led to better, faster decisions.
6. Assess whether research quality remained high or if biases/errors crept in.
7. Identify areas for improvement.
8. Were non-researchers able to apply their training effectively?
    a. Did studies get logged in a centralized repository, or were insights lost?
    b. Refine the process before scaling.
9. Based on feedback, adjust training, review processes, and access levels.
10. Slowly expand the model to additional teams, ensuring quality control at each step.

By treating democratization as an iterative process, you reduce risk while ensuring that your model is optimized for your organization's needs.

Maintain Research Integrity over Time

Democratization requires continuous refinement to ensure research remains high-quality and impactful. To maintain integrity:

- Conduct regular research audits.
- Review a sample of studies every quarter to ensure they meet research standards.
- Identify gaps in training or oversight and adjust accordingly.
- Keep the training program updated.
- As the organization evolves, new research needs will emerge; ensure training materials stay relevant.
- Ensure that research findings continue to drive decisions.
- If democratized research is not being used effectively, investigate whether the issue is quality, visibility, or stakeholder engagement.

By continuously evaluating and improving the democratization model, organizations can ensure that research remains an embedded, high-value function rather than becoming a diluted or ineffective process.

Done right, democratization strengthens the research function, rather than diluting it. It allows organizations to move faster while still making decisions grounded in strong, reliable user insights.

The future of research is about scaling insights responsibly. By balancing access, training, and governance, your organization can create a research culture that is not just functional, but foundational.

Time Management 34

User researchers often find themselves immersed in a whirlwind of meetings and responsibilities. But balancing these demands with research can be a formidable task. Here are some strategies and recommendations to help user researchers manage their time effectively.

PRIORITIZE YOUR INVOLVEMENT

While it's empowering to participate in various meetings across the organization, over-committing can lead to research neglect. Be selective about the meetings you attend, focusing on those directly aligned with your research goals.

ESTABLISH WEEKLY OBJECTIVES

At the end of each week, set a clear goal for the upcoming week. Identify the most critical work you need to accomplish and make it your weekly objective. This provides a clear direction for your research efforts.

CREATE A WEEKLY TASK LIST

Break down your weekly objective into manageable tasks for each day. Organize your week by assigning themes to different days. For example, allocate specific days for deep work on your report, coding research, creating content, or designing the report.

SCHEDULE MINDFUL WORK BLOCKS

Align your work with your natural rhythm. If you're a morning person, tackle deep work in the morning, have lunch, attend meetings in the afternoon, and reserve the evening for administrative tasks. Adjust your schedule to suit your energy levels and focus.

DISABLE NOTIFICATIONS DURING DEEP WORK

Maximize productivity by turning off all notifications, including work chat and personal messaging, during deep work sessions. Close unnecessary windows and minimize distractions to maintain your focus.

HOST OPEN OFFICE HOURS

To consolidate meetings and avoid scheduling conflicts throughout the week, designate specific open office hours for colleagues seeking research-related guidance or clarification.

CARVING OUT PERSONAL TIME

Balancing your time effectively also involves preserving personal time for your well-being and professional growth. Here are additional recommendations.

Book Mental Breaks

Schedule short breaks, even just 15 minutes, away from your computer to refresh your mind. Use this time to meditate, take a walk, do breathing exercises, or engage in a brief physical activity.

Screen-Free Lunch Breaks

Whenever possible, have a proper lunch away from screens. Disconnecting during lunch allows your brain to reset and re-energize for tasks in the afternoon.

Advocate for No Meeting Days

Discuss the possibility of implementing shared heads-down or no-meeting days with your team or manager. These designated periods can help safeguard your focused work time.

Prioritize Personal Development

Dedicate two to three hours each week to personal development. This could include reading articles and books, attending conferences, or indulging in creative activities related to your craft.

Take Time Off

Regularly schedule time off to recharge. Extended breaks outside of weekends can significantly boost your productivity and overall happiness.

Establish a Clear End to Your Workday

In remote work environments, it can be challenging to disconnect. Develop a ritual to signify the end of your workday, such as shutting down your work computer, lighting a candle, or meditating for a few minutes.

Calendar Auto-Decline

Consider using calendar features like auto-decline for your time blocks. Configure your calendar to automatically decline any meeting requests during your dedicated heads-down time, lunch, or mental breaks.

Juggling multiple priorities can be counterproductive. Focus on a single priority each week, breaking it down into smaller tasks. This approach ensures that you can efficiently select a task when you have short windows of time between meetings. By implementing these time management strategies and prioritizing your objectives, you can maintain a productive balance between attending meetings, conducting research, and preserving personal time for growth and well-being. Remember, effective time management is key to thriving in a demanding research role.

Navigating Burnout 35

In the tech and product industry, burnout is a common and real issue. I've been there, and I want to share my experience and offer some advice on how to handle it. Burnout crept into my life gradually, and its signs became all too familiar.

- Unending Fatigue: I found myself constantly tired, eagerly awaiting the weekend to recharge. Yet, even after a weekend break, I still felt drained.
- Wavering Passions: My once-steadfast passion for user research started to waver. Some days, I woke up wanting to escape to the woods, write novels, or run a doggy daycare. User research, my lifelong love, no longer held the same appeal.
- Overwhelming Tasks: Every task, no matter how trivial, felt like an insurmountable mountain. My to-do list kept growing, and I struggled to keep my head above water.

I've experienced bits and pieces of these feelings at various points in life, but burnout brought them all together in a relentless storm. It's not a situation anyone should endure alone.

RECOGNIZING BURNOUT: SYMPTOMS TO WATCH FOR

Burnout manifests differently for everyone, but here are some common signs to watch for:

- Inability to Focus: Difficulty concentrating on tasks, often leading to scattered work and unfinished projects.
- Desire to Avoid: Overwhelming responsibilities make you want to hide away and avoid tasks. The mounting to-do list becomes paralyzing.
- Feeling Unappreciated: You may start to believe that your efforts go unnoticed and unappreciated, even though these tasks are part of your job.
- Consistent Demotivation: Tasks that were once fulfilling become unimportant. Even simple tasks feel daunting, and work loses its luster.

- Reduced Performance: A drop in performance, missed deadlines, and decreased engagement in your role become more apparent. It feels like every day is a struggle.
- Overwhelming Exhaustion: A unique kind of fatigue takes over, sapping your energy and leaving you unable to tackle even simple tasks.
- Difficulty Sleeping: Despite exhaustion, you may find it challenging to get restful sleep, often staying awake at night or waking up frequently.

SUPPORTING EACH OTHER IN TIMES OF BURNOUT

Burnout affects many of us, and it's crucial that we shift our mindset collectively to support one another. Even if you're not personally experiencing burnout, your colleagues, managers, or peers might be. Here are some ways we can create a more supportive environment.

- Non-Work Check-Ins: Most of our interactions revolve around work. Take time for casual conversations. Schedule a quick coffee catch-up with a colleague to talk about life beyond work.
- Respect Lunch and Thinking Time: Avoid scheduling meetings during lunch breaks or designated thinking time. These moments are essential for mental breaks and recharging.
- Open Conversations: Create a culture where it's okay to express how you're feeling. Speak to your colleagues, managers, or anyone who will listen. Sharing your feelings can help, and you might encourage someone else to open up.
- Seek Help: Many companies offer programs to help employees deal with work-related stress. Explore these resources, and if they don't suffice, reach out to your support network. There are always people willing to listen.
- Delegate and Prioritize Tasks: If possible, delegate tasks or seek help with your workload. Prioritize essential tasks and let go of less important ones. Learning to say no when necessary is crucial for preventing future burnout.

COPING AS A USER RESEARCHER

As user researchers, our role can be emotionally taxing, and burnout can intensify these challenges. Here's how to navigate burnout as a user researcher.

- Avoid Back-to-Back Sessions: Whenever possible, schedule breaks between research sessions. It allows you to reset emotionally and mentally, ensuring you're fully present for each session.

- Set Realistic Goals: Set achievable goals and expectations for yourself. Don't strive for perfection; instead, focus on doing your best within reasonable limits. You don't need to conquer everything in a single day or week.
- Allocate Thinking Time: As researchers, we need time for creative thinking. Allocate this time in your schedule. Research is a creative process, and thinking is an essential part of it.
- Honesty About Workload: Don't hesitate to discuss your workload with your manager or peers. It's okay to admit when things become unmanageable. Encourage your reports to overestimate their project timelines to reduce stress.
- Set Boundaries: Establish clear boundaries between work and personal life. Avoid checking work emails or taking work-related calls during your personal time. Create a dedicated workspace at home to separate work from relaxation.
- Take Time Off: If it helps, take a vacation or mental health days. Stepping away can provide the mental clarity you need.
- Practice Stress-Reduction Techniques: Incorporate stress-reduction techniques into your daily routine. This can include deep breathing exercises, progressive muscle relaxation, or yoga. Regular practice can help manage stress levels.

Remember: it's okay to face burnout, and it's essential to prioritize your mental and physical health. Find what works for you, whether it's opening up to someone, scheduling breaks, or reevaluating your workload. Together, we can overcome burnout and foster a supportive environment in our industry. Be kind to yourself—you deserve it.

PART TEN

Test and Iterate

Feedback and Iteration 36

Feedback and iteration are as crucial for self-development as they are for product development. As researchers, getting feedback is essential, but it can be challenging for your work to be assessed regularly. There may be limited time and capacity to gather feedback, especially if your manager is not a user researcher or is unfamiliar with user research.

There are a handful of ways to get frequent feedback from stakeholders. This feedback is essential for your development and allows you to understand your blind spots.

ASK FOR FEEDBACK AND SHARE EARLY

Although it might sound obvious, you need to make it clear that you want feedback from your colleagues. It can be terrifying to get comments or questions from stakeholders about your research plan or report.

Sending over any documents as soon as possible and asking for people's feedback is a great way to show initiative. If colleagues know you are open to feedback, they will give it to you!

SEND A STAKEHOLDER SATISFACTION SURVEY

While typically used for customer feedback, anonymous surveys are a great way to get authentic feedback from anyone. Try using an anonymous satisfaction survey with colleagues to gather input about a project.

Even if you do ask for it, it can be difficult to keep track of the feedback and stakeholders' satisfaction. A great way to do this is by using a stakeholder satisfaction survey to anonymously track how stakeholders feel about your research over time. This survey includes questions like:

- "How easy or difficult was it to work with the research team?"
- "Overall, how satisfied or dissatisfied are you with the research process?"

- "How satisfied or dissatisfied are you with the outcome of the research?"
- "How do you feel about the insights from the research?"
- "What can be improved about the process?" and/or "What can we improve about the outcome of the research?"

Send this survey at the end of every project to each stakeholder involved, and ask them to fill it out. This information can help you understand the kinks in your process and where things can be improved.

HOLD A RETROSPECTIVE

If you are looking for direct feedback from team members, the best thing you can do is hold (or be a part of) a retrospective. Many teams have retrospectives at the end of projects, and you can either hold your own or join a pre-planned retrospective. I generally structure my retrospectives with three discussion questions.

1. Stop: What needs to be changed or improved about the current process?
2. Start: What new processes or steps can we introduce to try improving the current process?
3. Continue: What went well and should continue happening?

Similar to the survey, this will give you great feedback on your processes and how you work with stakeholders.

SELF-ASSESS

The tips above can help you get critical feedback on your processes, communication, and overall framework, but you might not always get the granular comments. Instead, you can conduct some self-assessment.

- This template gives you an easy way to grade your interviews. I used this after every interview I conducted, and it helped me understand where I needed to improve. I also wrote a 10-principal framework with more information on this.
- Failure is the best tool for learning and improving. This template allows you to track what went well and what needs to improve. Over time, this should give you an understanding of your most significant opportunity areas (e.g., stakeholder management) and where you have improved most.
- Taking inventory of your skills each quarter can give you a great idea of what you still need to learn to level up in your career.

USER RESEARCH REVIEWS

If you have a team of researchers or colleagues with research experience, setting up a user research review might be a great place to get feedback on your work. You can structure your user research reviews as weekly recurring meetings on your calendars, usually about one hour long (so people are more likely to come). Within this format, typically, one or two researchers can present their work, with each researcher having about thirty minutes to present and then get feedback.

This meeting is an excellent opportunity to get more granular feedback on documents, reports, or processes.

TALK TO YOUR MANAGER

Even if your manager isn't super comfortable with user research, you can still use this relationship to your advantage. When I've worked with managers outside of user research, I made sure to:

- Create weekly 1x1s. During this time, share with your manager where you are blocked or struggling. Having this visibility helps your manager become aware of the issues you're encountering, so you both can strategize on how to solve them.
- Share your work. Even if your manager isn't a user researcher, share your work and ask for feedback. Chances are, your manager is in a position to help give you helpful feedback on areas such as communication, storytelling, or stakeholder management. This information can be beneficial when going into meetings or presenting your work to others.
- Speak about development goals. Every quarter, make sure to share your goals with your manager and talk about acting on them. Even if your manager isn't super clear about your career progression, you can still align on expectations and needs.
- Ask for a budget. For funding, I recommend first asking for books, training courses, and tools. If you share your struggles during the weekly 1x1s, you can make a case for tools to help your processes, like recruitment agencies, transcription services, or a research repository tool.
- Ask for a headcount. Listing out everything you're contributing to and what else you need allows you to approach your manager about headcount and propose both a lean scenario and an ideal scenario. For example, a lean strategy would be hiring an intern or freelancer for a few months to help during a busy time, whereas hiring one or two full-time employees would be ideal.

SEEK MENTORSHIP INSIDE AND OUTSIDE OF YOUR ORGANIZATION

There are many ways to learn both inside and outside of your organization. If there is another user researcher on the team that you look up to, ask them if they would be willing to help you with your specific goals. Also, many people in an organization, outside of user research, can help you. For example, you can work closely with product analysts to understand quantitative data or with the marketing team to learn about content testing.

There are also many opportunities for mentorship and learning outside of your organization. I always recommend reaching out to the UXR community and looking for events or programs. Many companies will offer to pay for these learning instances, either fully or partially.

A FINAL GRAIN OF SALT

Just as an aside, take the feedback you receive with a grain of salt, especially if it is from people unfamiliar with user research. While new perspectives can give you a fresh outlook, they may not always guide you in the right direction.

Whenever you receive feedback, always look at the whole picture of who you received it from, how they gave it, and how many times you've received similar information from others.

Feedback can unlock areas of opportunity that you weren't even aware of and enable you to climb in your career. It can sometimes be hard to receive criticism, but opening yourself up to feedback loops is one of the best ways to learn. So start small and keep your head up!

Index

A

A/B testing/tests, 181, 241, 244
    labels, 256
accessibility testing, 147
acquisition, 34–36, 138
actionable insights, 147
activation, 36–37, 160
    business metrics, 36–37
    maintain and iterate phase, 182
    problem definition, 167
    problem discovery, 160
    solution design and refinement phase, 172
    testing and execution phase, 177
active listening, 200–201, 334
adaptive pairwise comparison, 302–303
admin task, research, 505
affinity diagramming, 341–343
    create categories or clusters, 342
    gather and review qualitative data, 342
    generative research, 353
    identifying common themes, 342
    identify patterns and insights, 343
    stakeholders and, 343
    subgroups, refining, 342
    visual representation, 343
After Scenario Questionnaire (ASQ), 290
AI, thought partner, 481–492
    acting as "third mind," workshops, 489–490
    avoiding leading or biased questions, 485
    brainstorming research questions and study designs, 484–486
    challenge assumptions, 482–483
    connect research to business impact, 490–492
    creating structured brainstorming prompts, 488–489
    creative methodologies, exploring, 485–486
    executive-friendly summaries, crafting, 491
    facilitate brainstorming, 488–490
    framing insights, align with business goals, 487–488
    generating unexpected connections, 489
    generating unexpected research angles, 485
    identifying gaps, reasoning, 487
    mapping research to strategic goals, 491–492
    research report or hypothesis, preparing, 483
    role-playing different perspectives, 483
    stakeholder pushback, 486–488
    testing my arguments, 486–487
    translating research insights, business terms, 490–491
alpha testing, 274
    shaping the initial vision, 275

B

B2B research OKRs
    example, 27
    how to approach, 26
    how to create, 27
    key focus areas, 26–27
    research challenges, 26
B2C research OKRs
    example, 28–29
    how to approach, 27–28
    how to create, 28
    key focus areas, 28
    research challenges, 28
benchmarking, 277–289
Benedek, 243
beta testing, 274
    continuous user research, 276
    engaging your user community, 275–276
bonus uncommon methods, 327–330
    FIDO (freehand interactive design online), 327–328
    Run of Post study, 328–329
    true intent study, 329–330
brainstorming, 7
    research questions and study designs, 484
budget, 506
burnout
    coping as user researcher, 544–545
    navigating, 543–545
    recognizing, 543–544
    supporting each other, 544
    symptoms to watch for, 543–544
business metrics
    acquisition, 34–36
    activation, 36–37
    formulating a plan, 33
    impact of research to, 6
    pirate metrics, uncovering, 34
    referrals, 39–40
    research outcomes, mapping, 32–40
    retention, 37–38

retention research, 38–39
revenue, 40
stakeholder interviews, 33–34
tying user research to, 34
business objective, 88

C

card sorting, 246–254
  analyzing, 252–253
  closed *versus* open *versus* mixed, 248
  creating cards, 249–250
  example, 248
  header and primary navigation, 250–251
  highlight and sort, cards, 253
  identify patterns, 252–253
  make decisions, 254
  moderated *versus* unmoderated, 248
  moderating, 252
  online *versus* in-person, 249
  rainbow chart, 253
  setting up, 251–252
  smaller numbers, delete, 253
  spreadsheet matrix, 253
  techniques, choosing, 247
  unmoderated *versus* moderated, 249
centralized research repository, 515–518
  choosing the right tool for, 517
  components of, 516
  research request system, structure, 517–518
closed-card sorting, 247
codes/tags, demystifying, 334–336
cohesive process, 3
collaboration, 147
communication skills, 148
comparative testing, 241
complete pairwise comparison, 301
concept testing, 40, 234–246
  affinity diagramming, 245–246
  analyzing the data, 245
  coding and, 245
  comparative testing, 241
  definition, 235
  fidelity, concept, 242
  generative research and, 237–238
  goals, 239
  how to conduct, 236
  Lego, example, 239–240
  moderated *versus* unmoderated, 244–245
  monadic testing, 240
  outcomes, 246
  preamble, 237
  problem, 236
  problem space, 243–244
  protomonadic testing, 241
  qualitative usability testing *versus,* 259–260

sample size, 244
sequential monadic testing, 240–241
setting up, 238–239
writing questions, 242–243
confidence, 278, 314
content testing, 270–274
  cloze tests, 270–271
  highlighter tests, 272–274
  recall-based tests, 271–272
contextual inquiry, 207–209
  conducting, 208
  introduction and explanation, 208
  observation, 209
continuous benchmarking, 289
continuous learning, 147
core research operations, 67–141
  approximate timelines, 75, 80, 84
  deliverables/outcomes and next steps, 75, 80, 84
  discussion guide/task script, 76, 80–81
  effect size, 109–110
  evaluative research, B2C context, 126
  evaluative research plan, 81–82
  examples, 129–131
  future-based questions, 122
  general timelines, setting, 125
  generative research, B2B setting, 125
  generative research plan example, 77
  hybrid research, B2B2C scenario, 126–127
  hypotheses and assumptions, 71–72, 78, 82
  include stakeholders, research plan, 76–77
  intake document, 112–114
  intake process, creating, 111
  internal stakeholders, 77
  internal stakeholders involved, 71
  interview guide, 87–90, 96
  jobs to be done (JTBD) research plan and interview guide, 85–86
  key stakeholders, 89
  leading questions, 122–123
  methodologies, 73–74, 79, 83
  outcome-based research roadmap, 128, 131, 133
  outcomes, 128–129
  personas, 86
  positive questions, 123–124
  practice makes perfect, 85
  prioritizing research projects, 116–117
  product/tech jargon, questions, 121
  project background, 70–71
  prototype guide, 90–94
  put together a research plan, 76
  recruitment and participants, 74–75, 79, 83, 105–107
  research plans, 67–70
  research question prioritization, 119–120, 124
  research roadmap and backlog, design, 127–128
  research statement and goals, 72–73, 78, 82

resources, project, 76, 81, 85
roadmap components, 131–133
screener surveys, 101–104
session logistics, 79, 83
shallow questions, 120–121
simple project prioritization process, 117–119
stakeholders, questions, 110
statistical significance, 107–108, 110–111
success criteria, 73, 78–79, 83
survey research, B2B setting, 127
user research plan, 68–69
UX metrics, 74
customer acquisition cost (CAC), 34
customer satisfaction practice, 291

D

data triangulation, 39, 187, 192
design refinement, 153
diary studies, 218–229
    activities/prompts, writing, 225
    compensation, 221–222
    deadline for this particular study, 226
    the device(s), 225
    goals, use for, 218–219
    length of, 222–223
    logging protocol, 223–224
    logistics, 222
    overview of, 225–226
    productivity tool study, 228
    prompts, writing, 227
    prompt using formula, example, 227–229
    recruitment, 220–221
    research plan, writing, 220
    sample size, 221
    set up, 219
    social media usage, 228–229
    tools, 224–225
    travel experience, 228
digital-card sorting, 249
disconfirmation scales, 293–294
    choose appropriate metrics, 293
    data collection methods, 293
    feedback tracking system, 294
    iteratively improve, 294
    measure progress and showcase impact, 294
    qualitative and quantitative data, combining, 293–294
    segment and group users, 293
dual-budget approach, 148

E

ecosystem maps, 434–437
    building, 436–437
    how to create, 436
    when to use, 435

effectiveness, 4
efficiency, 4
empathy, 147
empirical evidence, 147
ethical conduct, 147
evaluative research goals, 72
evaluative research plan, 81–82
    internal stakeholders, 82
    research project, background, 81–82
    usability task script, 84–85
event-based logging, 223
executive summaries, 386, 387, 389
    examples, 388

F

feedback and iteration, 549–552
    ask and share early, 549
    hold a retrospective, 550
    new perspectives, 552
    seek mentorship, organization, 552
    self-assess, 550
    stakeholder satisfaction survey, 549–550
    talk to your manager, 551
    unlock areas of opportunity, 552
    user research reviews, 551
FIDO (freehand interactive design online), 327–328
    example, 328
flexibility, 148
forced pairwise comparison, 302
formalized practice, user research, 5
future-based questions, 122

G

generative interview script, 195–196
generative research
    affinity diagramming, 353
    analysis and synthesis process, 346–355
    background, 347
    codes/tags, defining, 350–352
    code/tag the data, 352
    find the patterns, 353–355
    goals, 347
    highlight important notes or quotes, 349
    insights and activation, 355
    methodology, 347
    record the session, 347
    research summary, creating, 349–350
    resources, 348
    review each interview, 348–349
generative research discussion guides
    examples, 204–207
    practice makes progress, 207
generative research goals, 72
GenZ, 101

556 Index

good objective
    actionable, 11
    impact-driven, 11
    specific but not restrictive, 11

H

highlighter tests, 272–274
    conducting, 273–274
    follow-up questions, 274
    highlighter colors, defining, 273
    present the content, 273
    score and analyze, 274
    select your content, 273
hiring freeze effect, 506
How Might We (HMW) statements, 445–462
    action-oriented, 450
    addresses a real challenge, 450
    ambiguous enough to explore, 450–451
    benefits of using, 447
    broadness and specificity, refining, 452
    broad yet specific, 450
    characteristics of, 449–451
    core problem or opportunity, defining, 451
    crafting effective, 449–451
    encourage diverse perspectives, 459
    encourages positivity and motivation, 447
    enhances flexibility, 448
    facilitating brainstorming sessions with, 459
    finalize, 454–456
    formulas, using, 452
    fosters collaborative inclusivity, 447–448
    gather insights and identify problems, 451
    in ideation sessions, 459, 460–462
    initial problem identification, 456–457
    innovative and collaborative nature, 446
    inspiring and engaging, 450
    integrating into your research process, 456
    prioritize and select ideas, 460
    refinement and iteration, 458
    research at forefront, 449
    research culture, building, 448–449
    sample agenda, 460–462
    solution development, 457–458
    stimulates creativity, 448
    tackling broad, 452–456
    test and iterate, 454
    user-centric, 449–450
    writing, 451–452

I

ideation sessions, 459–464
    begin with user research, 463
    expected outcomes, defining, 463
    follow-up, 464
    ideation techniques, 464
    problem statement, crafting, 463
    successful ideation workshop, running, 463
image pairwise comparison, 302
impact orientation, 147
inclusivity, 147
insights, 445–478
insight writing
    are rare, 367
    the consequence, 364, 366
    example, 363–365
    finding *versus* insight, example, 366–367
    how to write an insight, 362–367
    key learning, 364, 365
    and recommendations, 356–378
    the why, 364, 365
intake document, 112–114
    questions and expected time, 112–114
internal stakeholders, 77
internal testing, stakeholders, 232–257
    employee user testing, benefits, 233
    employee user testing, challenges, 232–233
    internal user testing, setting up, 234
    internal user testing, when to use, 233
interview guide
    Alert Screen, 91, 93
    Edit Menu screen, 90–92
    My Menu screen, 90–94
    Pop-up screen, 91, 93
    Success Bar screen, 91–94
interviews, 40
interviews, stakeholders, 53–55
    analyze, 55
    conduct, 54–55
    goals, 53
    goals, needs, and pain point questions, 54
    outcomes, 53
    UX research questions, previous experience, 54–55
investigator triangulation, 192
iterative approach, 147

J

Jarret, Caroline, 328

K

key stakeholders, 89

L

leading questions, 122–123
lean budget, 148

Index   557

lightning synthesis, 343–345
  approach, 344–345
  streamlines synthesis process, 344
literature reviews, 185–192
  conducting, 188–189
  example of, 190–192
  importance, 186–188
locations, 101
logging protocol, 223–224

M

"Mad Libs" game, 270
maintain and iterate phase, 179–182
  activation, 182
  approximate timeline, 180
  follow-up research, 181
  goal, 179
  outcomes/deliverables, 181–182
  potential methodologies, 180
  pre-research activities, 179–180
  visual testing, 181
McClure, Dave, 34
measuring and iterating stage, 153
methodological triangulation, 192
Miner, 243
minimal in-session notes, 334
Minto, Barbara, 390
mirroring, 200–201
mixed (or hybrid) card sorting, 247
monadic testing, 240
monitor and iterate methods, 277–326
  benchmarking, 277–289
  continuous benchmarking, impact, 289
  guide to writing surveys, 305–326
  pairwise comparison, 299–305
  quantitative usability tests, 277–289
  UX surveys, 290–294
  visual testing, 294–299

N

narrative literature reviews, 186
non-product teams, 29–32
  challenges of conducting research, 29

O

objectives and key results (OKRs), 6, 145
  align with available resources, 20
  align with team-level priorities, 23
  ambition and reality, balance, 20
  B2B *versus* B2C research, 26–29
  brainstorming goals, 8–10
  broad goal into clear objective, 11–13
  broad goal into objective, refining, 12
  broad goals, prioritizing, 10–11
  business fundamentals, example, 22
  business fundamentals, focus, 22
  clarity with peers, test, 19
  common scenarios, 21–32
  company, aligning UXR goals, 6–7
  company goals are unclear, 22–26
  create strong objective, formula, 12
  customer support teams, 30–32
  evaluating and refining, 17–21
  example, based on past research, 24
  gathering input, research goals, 8
  identify broad goal, 7–11
  identify team-level priorities, 23
  key focus areas, 7–8
  key principles of evaluating, 18
  marketing teams, 29–30
  mistakes to avoid, 13, 21
  non-product teams, 29–32
  operational improvements, example, 25
  operational OKRs, key areas, 24
  past research insights, leverage, 24
  personal development, example, 25–26
  personal growth, key areas, 25
  questions to ask, uncover team priorities, 23
  refining broad goal, example, 12–13
  research operational improvements, work, 24
  score, confidence scale, 20–21
  SMART criteria, apply, 19
  stakeholder review, 19
  strong objective, characteristics, 11
  team-level alignment, example, 23
  tracking plan, creating, 20
  understanding, 6–7
  ways to leverage past insights, 24
  writing, step-by-step process, 7–13
one-on-one interview, 6
open-card sorting, 247
operational efficiency goals, 10
operational hurdles, 62
opportunity gap survey, 158, 165, 209–217
  analyze, 214–216
  creating, 211
  example, 216–217
  Jobs to be Done framework, 210
  minimize time inputting expenses, 213
  sending the survey, 214
  setting up study, 211–212
  survey questions, creating, 212
organizational hurdles, 62
outcome-based research roadmap, 128, 131, 133
  example of building, 137
  gather research projects/requests, 135–136, 138–139

get familiar with team goals, 134–135, 138
highest-impact projects, prioritize roadmap, 137, 140–141
iterate and improve, 141
no product vision or goals, 134
organizational vision and goals, 133–134, 137–138
projects/requests to outcomes, map, 136, 139–140
teams don't have clear goals, 135

P

pain point mapping, 9
pairwise comparison, 299–305
　adaptive pairwise comparison, 302–303
　complete pairwise comparison, 301
　food for party, 300–301
　forced pairwise comparison, 302
　image pairwise comparison, 302
　motivation, 303
　pain point, 304
　partial pairwise comparison, 302
　risk, 304
　unmet need, 304
　value, 303
　ways to analyze, 304–305
paper-card sorting, 249
partial pairwise comparison, 302
perceived satisfaction metrics, 292
performance satisfaction metrics, 290–291
personal development goals, 10–11
personal growth, 8
personas, 86, 101, 417–433
　activating, 431
　analyzing and synthesizing, team, 427
　awesome outcomes, 433
　B2C travel persona, building, 418–419
　conducting research, 425–427
　fostering empathy, 431–432
　information-gathering workshop, 419–420
　making better decisions, 432–433
　mini synthesis sessions, 428–429
　my synthesis process, 429–430
　new process, 418
　prioritizing categories, 430–431
　proto-personas, building, 421–423
　recruitment, 423–425
　research, recruiting and conducting, 423
　research debriefs, 428
　segmentation, understanding, 420–421
post-session transcription, 334
problem definition, 153, 162–167
　activation, 167
　analysis (page X), 165

　approximate timeline, 163
　boundaries, examples, 167
　follow-up research, 165
　goal, 162
　lean out the stage, 167
　potential methodologies, 164
　　primary research, 164–165
　　secondary research, 164
　pre-research activities, 162–163
　sample sizes, 163–164
　synthesis (page X), 166
problem definition methods, 218–231
　diary studies, 218–229
　walk the store interviews, 229–231
problem discovery, 153, 155–161
　activation, 160
　analysis (page X), 158–159
　approximate timeline, 156
　boundaries, examples, 161
　follow-up research, 158
　goal, 155
　lean out the stage, 160–161
　outcomes/deliverables, 159–160
　potential methodologies, 157–158
　　primary research, 157
　　secondary research, 158
　pre-research activities, 155–156
　sample sizes, 156–157
　synthesis (page X), 159
problem discovery methods, 185–217
　active listening and mirroring, 200–201
　components, discussion guides, 200
　contextual inquiry, 207–209
　enhance validity, 193
　generative interview script, writing, 195–196
　generative research, 194–195
　generative research discussion guides, 195–196, 204–207
　get into mindset, 203–204
　give insights more credibility, 194
　interview questions, 196–197
　literature reviews, 185–192
　one-on-one generative research interviews, 194
　opportunity gap survey, 209–217
　"probe"/conduct improv research, 200
　question-writing framework, 197–198
　reliable follow-up phrases, 202–203
　to see complete picture, 193
　subjective or vague words and phrases, probe, 201–202
　TEDW versions, 197–199
　triangulating data, 192–193
process improvement, 8
product development process, 3, 153, 279
product-focused goals, 10

product-focused OKRs, 21
product impact, 7
product metrics
    brainstorming session, 46
    collect baseline data, 42
    financial or business impact, 44
    gather baseline data, 42
    hypothesis, crafting, 42–43
    hypothesis, evaluating, 44–45
    IDEO's design research process, 47
    impact estimation template, 45–46
    potential impact, model, 43–44
    potential improvements, estimating, 41–47
    quantify the results, 44
    research process, creating, 46
    target metric, defining, 41–42
product/tech jargon, questions, 121
protomonadic testing, 241
p-value, 107, 108
Pyramid Principle, 390–406
    apply this in your reports, 397, 399–400, 402–403
    assign ownership and next steps, 405–406
    being too vague, 393
    choose right evidence, 398
    focusing on the process, 393
    hedging too much, 393
    identify your key arguments, 394–395
    ignoring conflicting data, 399
    make recommendations realistic and feasible, 404
    make your findings actionable, 403–406
    mistakes to avoid, 393, 396, 399
    multiple arguments, 396
    multiple findings, 392–393
    next steps, 393–394
    order by impact, 395
    order by user journey, 395–396
    prioritize recommendations, impact and effort, 405
    raw data, dumping, 399
    research evidence, types, 397–398
    specific about what needs to be done, 404
    start with answer in your report, 391–394
    structure your evidence, 398–399
    structure your key arguments, 395–396
    translate every key insight, clear recommendation, 403–404
    vague statements, 399
pyramid structure, 400
    apply in reports, 400–402
    burying insights, background information, 402
    lead with executive summary, 400–401
    mistakes to avoid, 402
    organize body of your report, 401–402
    organize your report, 400
    too much detail in wrong place, 402

Q

qualitative feedback session, 260
qualitative research, 108
    uses non-statistical methods, 108–109
qualitative usability testing/tests, 258, 259; *see also* Usability testing
    coding and, 266
    versus concept testing, 259–260
    goals, 260–261
    quantitative usability testing/tests *versus*, 259, 279
    questions, creating, 261–263
qualitative user research, 236
quantitative research, 108
quantitative usability testing/tests, 258, 277–289; *see also* Usability testing
    analyze the results, 287–289
    assign task completion colors, 288
    big impact, 278
    categorize issues, 288–289
    choose your metrics, 281
    create a plan, 280
    create stoplight chart, 288
    describe each issue, 289
    effectiveness, 278
    efficiency, 278–279
    fidelity, 280
    follow-up questions, 287
    how to run, 280
    identify tasks, 281–282
    populate the chart, 288
    prioritize and plan action, 289
    versus qualitative usability tests, 279
    run a dry run, 285
    running, study, 285–286
    satisfaction, 279
    tasks and surveys, 286–287
    task scenario, writing, 283–285
    usability test results, preparing, 288
    warm-up questions, 286
    when to run, 279
    wrap-up, 287
    write tasks, 282–283
question-gathering workshop, 114
    after the workshop, 116
    brainstorm questions, 115
    do an icebreaker, 115
    introducing workshop goals and outcomes, 115
    next steps and wrap up, 116
    plan the workshop, 115
    prioritizing questions, 116

R

RACI (Responsible, Accountable, Consulted and Informed) model, 71
rapid literature reviews, 186
recruitment, 74–75, 79, 83, 97–98, 105–107
   common recruitment methods, 105–106
   incentives, budget, 106–107
referrals, 39–40
reports, 381
   concept/prototype analysis, 385–386
   executive summaries, note, 386
   fashion influencers on social media, 382
   Fashion Trend App, 385–386
   format, 387
   questions to ask yourself, 387
   research goals and questions, 383–384
   research themes, structure, 381–382
   seamless shopping integration, header, 388–389
   structure, executive summaries, 386
   understanding mental models, 383–384
   usability testing, 384–385
   writing, 381–389
research, tracking the impact, 469–478
   align with stakeholders, 470
   establish how you will measure impact, 471
   follow-up timeline, establish, 474–476
   leading *vs.* lagging indicators, research impact, 476
   log your research, impact tracker, 470
   measuring impact over time, 474
   next steps, 471
   present findings in discussion, 472–473
   research gets seen and used, ensuring, 472
   research impact reporting system, 476–478
   right format for sharing findings, 472
   set up your impact tracker, 469
   track stakeholder engagement and reactions, 473–474
   type of impact you're measuring, defining, 470–471
   what success looks like, defining, 469
research credibility, 505
research debriefs, 337–338
   collaborative board, 340
   discussion points, 339
   example, 339
   explain each section/point, 340
   invite the right participants, 339
   running, 338–339
   sessions, 337
   timeboxing, 340
   time management, 340–341
   utilize the calendar trick, 340

research framework, creating, 142–150
   components, 143–144
   conducting research, 149
   hiring, 150
   importance, 142–143
   tooling, 150
research goals, 89
research newsletters, 413–416
research opportunities, 8
research plan, benchmarking, 94–95
   anticipated timeline, 95
   background, 94
   business objectives, 94
   hypotheses, 94
   methodology, 95
   metrics, 95
   participants, 95
   research goals, 94
   top user goals, 95
research plans, 67–70; *see also* User research plan
   components, 70
   for usability testing, 88–89
   using, 69–70
research question prioritization, 119–120
research statement, 72–73, 78, 82
retention, 37–38, 138
   research, 38–39
revenue, 40
reverse engineering success, 9
rigorous methodology, 147
roadmap components, 131–133
   approximate timeline, 133
   current status, project, 133
   incentive amount, 133
   need/problem, 131
   outcomes, 132
   priority level, 132
   project goals, 131
   project name, 131
   project type, 132
   resources, 133
   support level, 132
   team/stakeholders, 132
Run of Post study, 328–329
   example, 329

S

satisfaction, 4
scoping literature reviews, 186
screener surveys, 101–104
   craft well-written questions, 102–103
   dry run, conducting, 104
   example, 104–105
   formulate questions, 102
   ideal participant criteria, define, 102

Index   561

open text field and N/A (not applicable) options, 103
organize questions, logical order, 103
question types, diversifying, 103
strategic use, advantages, 101–102
segmentation, 98
    behaviors/usage, 98–99
    environmental context, 99–100
    feelings, 99
    interaction, 99
    primary demographics, 98
    profit, 100
    study goals, 100–101
    timing, 100–101
SEQ (Single Ease Questionnaire), 74
sequential monadic testing, 240–241
session logistics, 79, 83
session summaries, 407–412
setting up, user research practice, 5
shallow questions, 120–121
simple project prioritization process, 117–119
Single Ease Question (SEQ), 278, 290, 314
social desirability bias, 122
solution design and refinement methods, 232–257
    card sorting, 246–254
    concept testing, 234–246
    internal testing, stakeholders, 232–257
    tree testing, 254–257
solution design and refinement phase, 168–172
    activation, 172
    analysis (page X), 171
    approximate timeline, 169
    boundaries, examples, 172
    follow-up research, 170
    goal, 168
    lean out the stage, 172
    outcomes/deliverables, 171–172
    potential methodologies, 170
        primary research, 170
        secondary research, 170
    pre-research activities, 168–169
    sample sizes, 169–170
    synthesis (page X), 171
stakeholder conversations, 8
stakeholder engagement, 8
    goals, 10
    OKRs, 21
stakeholder management, 51
stakeholders, users, 51–59
    current process, ways to improve, 57–58
    empathize with, 52–53
    interviews, 53–55
    needs and goals, align your work, 55
    overarching needs and learning style, choose a deliverable, 56–57
    pain points or anxieties, ways to address, 56
    potential research ideas, affinity diagram, 55–56
    shifting your mindset, 52–59
    working with, 58–59
standardized practice, 5
standardized user research practice, 3, 5
statistical significance, 107–108, 110–111
    getting comfortable with, 107–108
    and qualitative data, relationship, 108
    question, ideas on what to say, 110–111
    sample size and, 107
stoplight chart, 287, 289
strategic budget, 148, 149
strategic hurdles, 62
Subjective Mental Effort Question (SMEQ), 279, 314
success criteria, 73, 78–79, 83
synthesis process, user research
    demystifying, 333–336
    good notes, taking, 334
synthesis sessions, running, 337–345
systematic literature reviews, 186
System Usability Scale (SUS), 193, 279, 292, 314

T

TEDW framework, 242
testing and execution methods, 258–276
    comparative usability testing, 268–269
    content testing, 270–274
    usability testing, 258–268
testing and execution phase, 153, 173–178
    activation, 177
    analysis (page X), 176
    approximate timeline, 174
    boundaries, examples, 178
    follow-up research, 176
    goal, 173
    lean out the stage, 177
    outcomes/deliverables, 177
    potential methodologies, 175
        primary research, 175–176
        secondary research, 175
    pre-research activities, 173–174
    sample sizes, 175
    synthesis (page X), 176–177
theory triangulation, 192
time-based logging, 223
time management, 540–542
    book mental breaks, 541
    calendar auto-decline, 542
    clear end to your workday, establish, 542
    create weekly task list, 540
    disable notifications, deep work, 541
    establish weekly objectives, 540
    host open office hours, 541

no meeting days, advocate for, 542
prioritize personal development, 542
prioritize your involvement, 540
schedule mindful work blocks, 541
screen-free lunch breaks, 541
take time off, 542
top-of-funnel (TOFU) metrics, 35
train, case study, 96–97
transparency, 147
tree testing, 254–257
    A/B testing labels, 256
    analyze, 257
    defining, 255
    map, creating, 255
    task phrasing, 256–257
    tasks, writing, 256
    when to use, 254–255
trigger-based logging, 223
true intent study, 329–330
    example, 330

U

UMUX (Usability Metric for User Experience), 74
usability, 4
Usability Bingo, 464–466
    collect feedback, 466
    consider snacks and prizes, 466
    create Bingo boards, 466
    determine the right test, 465
    identify Bingo spaces, 465
    present your work, 466
    pull together the evidence, 466
    setting up, 465–466
Usability Metric for User Experience (UMUX and UMUX-Lite), 279, 292–293, 314
usability testing, 38, 40, 88–89, 147, 258–268
    affinity diagramming, 266–267
    analyzing the data, 266
    formative *versus* summative testing, 109
    go screen by screen, 264–265
    logistics, 267
    moderated *versus* unmoderated, 267
    outcomes, 268
    overall setup, 263–264
    overarching scenario, 264
    reports, 289, 384–385
    session length, 267
    wrap-up, 265
user advocacy, 147
user-centeredness, 147
user-centricity, 274
User Experience Maturity, 60
user research buy-in, 61
user research democratization, 493–539

advanced research training, 514
approval workflows, 532
assess current state of research, organization, 522
assign roles and responsibilities, 535
basic research training, 513
biases could significantly distort findings, 509
build research governance, 512
case for, 499–500
categorization system, research methods, 510–511
centralized repository model, need, 528
centralized research repository, 515–518
clear objectives and success criteria, 534–535
clear objectives for checkpoints, 536
common misconceptions, 497–499
communicate results and action items, 537
communicate your choice, organization, 533–534
complex landscape of, 493
core documentation, 535
critical points, errors, 519
current research roles and responsibilities, 522
decision framework, stakeholders, 511
defining in research context, 496
democratized research, governance structure, 533
desired future state, 530
detailed implementation plan, creating, 534–536
devalue research roles, 504–506
document your chosen democratization model, 531
escalation paths, 533
ethical concerns, 503–504
ethical or privacy concerns exist, 510
faster decision-making, 501–502
framework for responsible, 510
future scalability and evolution, 530–531
hybrid model, need, 526–527
implement regular research audits, 520–521
importance of research rigor, 529
increased empathy, benefit, 500–501
inventory types of research, 523
launch and communicate broadly, 535–536
launching new research democratization model, 534
leadership's attitude toward research, 523–524
maintain research integrity, 539
making this process efficient, 519–521
need for scale, 500
non-researchers are trained and supported, 508
non-researchers to engage in research, growing desire, 494
office hours with researchers, 514–515
ongoing research mentorship and coaching, 514
organizational readiness, 530

Index 563

organization's documentation and sharing practices, 529–530
organization's pace and decision-making culture, 529
organization's research environment, 528–529
organization's research needs and risks, 525–526
personal reflection, 495–496
pre-approved research templates, 512
protect value of research, scaling access, 506
quality checkpoints, 532
quality control issues, 502–503
quality review check-ins, 515
questions to help you choose, 528
refining process, 521
research across organizations, growing demand, 493–494
research awareness, 513
research bottlenecks and pain points, 523
research coaching programs, 515
research demand exceeds researcher capacity, 507
research insights, shared and stored, 524
research landscape report, 524
research-led model, need, 527
research review process, 518–519
research rigor, structured oversight, 508–509
right democratization model, 526
risks and challenges, 502–506
risks and rewards, 494–495
sample governance structure document, 533
scaling research without sacrificing rigor, 522–524
schedule regular review cadence, 536–537
spectrum of, 499
standardized research protocols, 511
standardized review template, design, 537
study requires advanced methodologies, 509
take action and adjust the model, 538–539
teams need quick, low-risk insights, 507–508
test your democratization approach, 538
tiered training program, 512–513
trade-offs, 530
training programs, 535
value of professional research, undermining, 504
well-structured approach, 497
user research framework, creating, 144; *see also* research framework, creating
break down goals, 145–146
budget, 148–149
mission, defining, 144
principles, defining, 146–148
roadmap and prioritization process, 146
track impact of research over time, 146
vision, creating, 145

user research insight, 357–359
actions and back up with data, 374
additional insight techniques, 371–378
add sense of urgency, 378
comparative metrics for context, 374–375
create a risk heatmap, 373–374
cut the clutter, 372
detail orientation, 368
evaluative research, 368–369
example, 358–359, 369–370
executive summary, creating, 376
flexibility, 367
generative research recommendations, 370
good, 359–360
identifying insights, 362
interviewing your stakeholders, 360–361
involve stakeholders in research, 375
justification, 368
offer follow-up plan, 378
provide activation, 376
recommendation examples, 368
satisfaction survey, setting up, 361
step-by-step guide to writing, 362
structure your deliverables, news article, 372–373
tell micro-stories, 373
test with non-experts, 377
try video recaps, 375
use decision trees, 377
use sprints to deliver research, 377–378
write an impactful, 360–361
writing recommendations, 367–378
WTF is your goal, 371–372
user research maturity, current, 60–63
assess, 60–63
model at from AtoB, 62–63
user research mindset, 4
user research newsletter, 413
choose cadence, 414
components, 414–415
conduct beta test, 414
decide on type of information, 413
feedback and iterate, 414
stakeholder needs and pain points, 413
template, 415–416
user research plan, 68–69
importance, 68–69
user research summary
actions/recommendations, 411, 412
crafting, 407–408
examples, 409, 411
must-haves checklist, 408–409
notable quotes, 410
other tools, 411
quote, 411–412
themes and highlights, 410

user research surveys, 305–306
　analyze individual questions, 322–324
　analyzing the survey, 321–324
　ask about past behavior, 309–310
　best practices, 309
　clean your data, 321
　closed question types, 312–313
　compile your data, 321
　confidence intervals/margin of error, 317
　confidence level, 317
　data points, combining, 324
　descriptive statistics, 321
　different surveys, 306
　double-barreled questions, avoiding, 311
　dreaded sample size, 317
　effective survey questions, formulating, 309
　engagement and responses, 318–319
　ethical considerations and accessibility, 325–326
　explore changes over time, 325
　failure, 306–307
　first-person questions, 310
　follow-up questions, 316–317
　gathering feelings/perceptions, questions, 315–316
　goal of understanding/identifying behavior, questions, 314–315
　goal of usability, questions, 314
　goals, defining and setting, 307–309
　ideal survey length, 319
　keep it simple, 309
　loaded questions, leave out, 311
　look for correlations, 324–325
　mix of questions, 311
　open-ended survey questions, 313
　personalization, 319
　pilot testing, 320–321
　population size, 317
　prioritizing qualitative data, questions, 316
　quantitative usability test surveys, 318
　question types, 311–312
　segment your data, 324
　standard deviation, 317–318
　starting with understanding, 307
　survey length and complexity, balancing, 319–320
　survey length and fatigue, 319
　turning goals into questions, 313
UX metrics, 74
UX research hackathon, 467–468
　choose your insights, 467
　gauge interest via email, 467
　hackathon document, creating, 467
　launch hackathon, 468
　pick suitable dates, 468
　prepare for hackathon, 468
　prepare for research, 468
　presentation day, set up, 468
　presentations and voting, host, 468

UX scorecard, 438–441
　choose task scenarios, 440
　conduct the study, 441
　create your scorecard, 441
　define your goals, 439
　grading rubric, creating, 440
　how to create, 439–441
　identify competitors, 441
　product-level metrics, 439–440
　select metrics, 439–440
　task-level metrics, 439
　testing method, 441
UX surveys, 290–294
　customer satisfaction practice, 291
　disconfirmation scales, 293–294
　perceived satisfaction metrics, 292
　performance satisfaction metrics, 290–291
　understand user journeys, 291
　Usability Metric for User Experience (UMUX and UMUX-Lite), 292–293

V

visual testing, 294–299
　methods, 296–299
　suitable for objectives, 295
　usability testing, precedence, 295–296

W

walk the store interviews, 229–231
　clear research goals, defining, 229–230
　conducting, 229
　customized discussion guide, 230
　expected deliverables, 230
　participant recruitment, 230
　sample interview questions, 231
　starting interview, 230
well-defined goals, 10
well-written objectives, 13
　alignment with stakeholders, 16
　effective key results, characteristics, 14
　identify relevant metrics, 15
　impactful key results, prioritize, 16–17
　key results formula, 14–15
　measurable key results, defining, 14–17
　operational efficiency key results, 17
　operational efficiency objectives, 13
　outputs *versus* outcomes, 16
　personal development key results, 17
　personal development objectives, 14
　product-focused key results, 17
　product-focused objectives, 13
　set ambitious and realistic targets, 16
　stakeholder engagement key results, 17
　stakeholder engagement objectives, 13